IBERIAN JEWRY
FROM TWILIGHT TO DAWN

BRILL'S SERIES IN JEWISH STUDIES

GENERAL EDITOR

DAVID S. KATZ (Tel Aviv)

ADVISORY EDITORS
STUART COHEN (Bar-Ilan)
ANTHONY T. GRAFTON (Princeton)
YOSEF KAPLAN (Jerusalem)
FERGUS MILLAR (Oxford)

VOL. X

IBERIAN JEWRY FROM TWILIGHT TO DAWN

The World of Rabbi Abraham Saba

BY

ABRAHAM GROSS

E.J. BRILL
LEIDEN · NEW YORK · KÖLN
1995

The paper in this book meets the guidelines for permanence and durability of the Committee on Production Guidelines for Book Longevity of the Council on Library Resources.

ISSN 0926-2261
ISBN 90 04 10053 9

PRINTED IN THE NETHERLANDS

לזכר אבי ז״ל

״איש ישר שנהנה מיגיע כפיו״

CONTENTS

PREFACE

In January 1980, at the very beginning of this study, I had the chance to discuss its relative merits with two visiting scholars at Harvard University - one a philosopher, the other an historian. Stated the philosopher: "There seems to be nothing important in *Ẓeror ha-Mor*...unless, of course, you will find an esoteric level in it," while the historian admitted: "Some time ago, I tried to follow the weekly Torah Portion along with *Ẓeror ha-Mor* but soon gave it up because it was so dull." Despite their warnings I persisted. I sincerely hope that the results of my efforts will renew interest in Saba's writings.

I would like to express my gratitude to Professor I. Twersky and Professor Y.H. Yerushalmi, my teachers at Harvard University, from whose guidance I have benefitted during my years there and ever since. Professor B. Septimus added another measure of incisive criticism and the value of his comments for the final version of my study were invaluable. Dr. H. Fedaya remarked on various Qabbalistic aspects of it.

The final stage of a work which started at Harvard and continued in Toronto and Be'er-Sheva took place during my sabbatical at the Institute for Jewish Studies in University College London. I would like to take this opportunity and thank its director, Professor Mark Geller, for his hospitality and friendship.

At the early stages I was aided financially by a generous grant from the Social Sciences and Humanities Research Council of Canada. The Faculty of Arts and Social Sciences of the Ben-Gurion University of the Negev also contributed towards the publication of this volume.

The professionalism of the people at E.J. Brill deserves special mention. The care with which they handled the manuscript and the patience and courteous manner with which they treated its author are profoundly appreciated.

Finally, I would like to acknowledge the great continuous contribution of my wife, Yehudit, who has been supportive in more than one way. Our children, Dubi, Yael, Ariel, Amit, and Yoav, who occasionally drew me away from my historical studies, helped me maintain a balanced perspective on the importance of present, future, and past.

London
3rd Tamuz 5754

INTRODUCTION

The historical study of the last generation of Spanish Jewry on Spanish soil is of great importance. The Expulsion from Castile-Aragon in 1492 has been considered a watershed from several perspectives of Jewish history, and rightfully so. Its repercussions were felt far and wide, profoundly, and through many decades thereafter. Due to the great demographical shift and the cultural weight of the Sefardim they became a dominant force in many of the communities that absorbed the refugees, and hence the additional importance of understanding the various aspects of its historical reality and thought in that crucial generation.

The problem of the Sefardic heritage in different areas of intellectual history has been treated only partially thus far, though the 500th anniversary of the Expulsion had scholars produce a flurry of articles, many of them of a popular nature.

Some of the important studies can be termed as thematic.[1] While this method which attempts to generalize and present a final overview might be a higher stage on the historiographic ladder, we feel that the prior step, namely, detailed and careful monographic studies of individuals is, to an extent, still a *desideratum*, thus making some of the thematic presentations and generalizations premature.[2] One cannot simply detach a detail and use it indiscriminately without first examining the picture as a whole. We can safely use details from one's writing only after knowing his biographical background, his thought, and the literary nature of his writings.

It seems that scholars who in recent years concentrated their efforts in illuminating the history of the Sefardic diaspora in North Africa and in the East in the 16th century, are beginning to realize that such studies are often very shallow and lack historical basis when detached from the centuries that precede it. There is no area of cultural creativity in the Sefardic centers that can be understood in and of itself without reaching back at least to the 15th century. This renders studies such as the present one essential.[3]

Rabbi Abraham Saba, whose literary works belong to the last decade of the 15th century, was discussed more than four decades ago by N.S. Libowitz in a biographical sketch which focuses on the chronographical and autobiographical material found in the printed editions of Saba's works.[4] Libowitz also tried to depict Saba's writings by quoting from his sayings, rhymes, anecdotes etc. Though this slim volume apparently attempts to present the man and his commentaries on a popular level, the work is sensitive and perceptive.

The recent interest in the period and its thought on the thematic level also bore monographic fruit. G. Nigal attempted an overview of Saba's thought on several important issues in a very short essay, considering the topic.[5] Needless to say, in such an essay not only is there no possibility of properly analyzing the topics under discussion, but it is difficult to exhaust the material even on the descriptive and informative levels, and so we get a fragmentary presentation.[6]

In the same year, an M.A. dissertation was completed at the Hebrew University in Jerusalem by D. Manor.[7] The latter was the first to check most of the extant manuscripts. The autobiographical passages he discovered are of great importance.[8]

The contribution of this study lies mainly in the additional biographical data, and in the analysis of the theme of "Exile and Redemption," where technical terms such as "the Days of the Messiah," "the World to Come," resurrection etc. are discussed. However, at least one central question was not asked. How important was the definition of these technical terms to Saba himself? Moreover, if this theme is to be put in the historical context as well as in the broader context of Saba's thought, then one must review the issue of despair, which cannot be simply by-passed, and one must also discuss fully the structure of human history according to Saba.

Finally, one more study merits special mention. We refer to I. Tishbi's series of articles, concerning an anonymous author of a unique messianic tract.[9] That author went through the same major experiences as Saba, and a comparison between them only sharpens the focus on Saba's different attitude to Messianism.

Rabbi Abraham Saba lived in the second half of the 15th century in Castile. In 1492, when the Jews were expelled from Spain, he settled in Guimarães (northern Portugal). There he composed most of his writings - commentaries on the Pentateuch, on the Five Scrolls, and on the Mishnaic tractate, Avot. After five years, Saba and the rest of the Jews of Portugal were forced to go to Lisbon, from where their Expulsion was to take place. However, in Lisbon the Jews were converted to Christianity by force. In the course of events Saba lost the manuscripts of his works as well as his two sons who were baptized like the majority of the Jews. Saba himself was arrested with a group of about forty Jews and put in jail for refusing to covert willingly. After six months this group was expelled to North Africa. There, despite his poor physical health, Saba rewrote some of his lost works.

In this study we have tried to reconstruct Saba's intellectual and spiritual world. He was an exegete, a preacher, and a Qabbalist. These three elements dominated Saba's world and therefore provide the *foci* for our study.

The first chapter constitutes a biographical description and analysis followed by an analysis of Saba's commentary on the Book of Esther, where we attempted to show the impact of historical and biographical events on Saba's exegesis.

The following section deals with *Ẓeror ha-Mor* (Ẓ.M.), his main work. It focuses on its main characteristics as an exegetical work including such topics as the influence of Saba's preaching career on the style and content of the book, midrashic hermeneutical methods employed by him, and the influence of Qabbalah on his non-mystical exegesis.

In the section devoted to Qabbalah we tried to confront two main issues: a) the role of Qabbalah in a basically non-mystical commentary. b) Qabbalah in Saba's thought. The first issue was treated through a discussion of the problem of popularizing the esoteric, and the second through investigating the author's view of Qabbalah in its relation to Halakhah.

The historical section includes three chapters. The first concerns itself with Saba's social and religious criticism of the Jewish community, as well as of those who abandoned it - the Marranos. The following chapter examines Saba's view of Israel among the nations, and his particular understanding of Christianity. This leads to the final chapter that attempts to demonstrate the centrality of the historical problem of despair in Saba's writings and the ways in which he deals with it. This includes a treatment of such issues as theodicy and redemption. Throughout this section we have tried to show the steady influence of the homiletical and Qabbalistic elements.

Many topics or points that merit lengthier or even full separate discussions, but did not fit into the overall scheme or into the natural flow of things, were limited to short (or long) remarks in the footnotes.

The quotations from Ẓ.M. are generally based on and paginated according to the Warsaw edition of 1879 due to it availability. When there is a significant change in other versions, and another edition of manuscript was preferred, the specific reference was noted. This is also valid for references to *Éshkol ha-Kofer* (É.K.) on the books of Ruth and Esther.

NOTES

[1] Among the better ones that serve as historiographic milestones are the two articles by H.H. Ben-Sasson; "The Generation of the Spanish Exiles on Its Fate," *Ẓion* 26, 1961, pp. 23-64; and, "Exile and Redemption Through the Eyes of the Spanish Exiles," *Y. Baer Jubilee Volume*, Jerusalem (1960), pp. 216-27.

[2] One such study is B. Netanyahu's, *Don Isaac Abravanel*, Philadelphia, 1972. Some themes of Abravanel's literary creation which are essential for the understanding of this towering figure still await examination in depth. The study by S. Heller-Willensky (*Rabbi Isaac Aramah*, Jerusalem, 1956), is philosophically inclined and does not cover some areas of interest for the understanding of the man in the broad historical context. Rather it examines merely his thought against the background of the medieval philosophical tradition. More recently some important studies on figures such as R. Abraham ben Eliezer Halevi and R. Joseph Garson, were written.

[3] This understanding recently found fine expression in most lectures published in *Peàmim* 26, 1986.

[4] N.S. Libowitz, *Rabbi Abraham Saba and His Books Ẓeror ha-Mor and Éshkol ha-Kofer*, New York, 1936. A. Marx added some notes at the end of the book.

[5] G. Nigal, "A Chapter in the Thought of the Generation of the Expulsion from Spain," *Sinai* 74, 1974, pp. 67-80.

[6] The author recognized these limitations (ibid., p. 68).

[7] D. Manor, *Exile and Redemption in the Thought of R. Abraham Saba in Light of His Biography and Historical Background.*

[8] Manor published them in an article, "Abraham Saba: His Life and Works," *Jerusalem Studies in Jewish Thought* 2, 1982-3, pp. 208-31. They were republished, A. Gross, "Rabbi Abraham Saba: 'Expelled in two Expulsions,'" *Studies in Memory of the Rishon le-Ẓion Rabbi* Y. *Nissim* vol. 4, Jerusalem, 1985, pp. 205-24. Manor also published a bibliography of Saba's works in *Sefunot* [n.s.] 3 (18), Jerusalem, 1985, pp. 317-38.

[9] Initially published in *Ẓion* 48, 1983, pp. 55-102, 347-85, and ibid. 49, 1984, pp. 26-60. They later appeared as a book: *Messianism in the Time of the Expulsion from Spain and Portugal*, Jerusalem, 1985.

CHAPTER ONE

BIOGRAPHY; EXPULSION, WANDERING, AND LITERARY ACTIVITY

The tribulations of Spanish Jewry in its last century in Spain reached their climax with the final Expulsion in 1492. In its long history, that Jewry achieved an excellence in virtually every Jewish and universal intellectual area of activity, as well as in the political realm as manifested in the long list of important personae in the service of Moslem and Christian kings in the Iberian Peninsula, and in the far-reaching privileges accorded to its communities and individuals. The Jews of Spain took pride in the courtiers who, for them, represented Jewish royal power and glory; considered themselves the pre-eminent Jewry of the Diaspora;[1] and were also recognized by many as such.[2] Their tradition that saw themselves as a remnant of the most distinguished families of Jerusalem only enhanced that special pride.[3]

The surprise blow of losing their homeland - which Spain was for them, as probably no foreign country had been for any other Jewry before modern times; the short time between the publication of the edict and the Expulsion itself; plus the sufferings and torture at the hands of nature and of man, which the refugees endured on the roads and at sea, contributed to the initial depression, disorientation and confusion which seized the refugees in the tumultuous years that followed.[4] The majority that chose the short-cut of crossing the border to neighboring Portugal, were soon to realize that a very long road of suffering lay ahead.[5]

These events were to have profound repercussions on the religious and literary creativity of the Jews who survived them. Messianic literature in the shape of treatises and epistles, historiographical works, and the transformation of Qabbalah from an esoteric into a popular doctrine, are of the phenomena that might be attributed in some measure to the aftermaths of the Expulsion.[6]

1. Itinerary

One of the most intriguing products of these turbulent times was Rabbi Abraham Saba, who had to endure two expulsions: the first, from Spain with the multitude of his coreligionists; the second, his almost personal expulsion from Portugal less than six years later.

We do not know when and where he was born. He describes his father Jacob as "the pious" [*he-ḥasid*], which does not necessarily mean that he was a

Qabbalist but, considering Abraham's spiritual tendencies, it is probable that he was not an adherent of philosophy.[7] Unless we are dealing with a scribal error, it would seem that his grandfather, Isaac, wrote a commentary on Tractate Avot.[8] Abraham himself lived in Zamora at least during the last eight years prior to the Expulsion.[9]

1.1. In Zamora; "The uttermost parts of the North"

Zamora, was a city in northern Castile not far from the border with Portugal. In the 15th century the Jews lived there in two districts.[10] The population in the *aljama* was small and numbered only a few hundreds. Nevertheless, it was larger than the surrounding communities and is mentioned among the major ones in the tax-collection for the war against Granada.[11]

Lacking in quantity, this vibrant Jewish community more than made up for it in quality. It became famous as one of the foremost centers of Talmud study in fifteenth-century Castile. There the great Rabbi Isaac Qanpanton headed his *yeshivah* which was to become the source of a unique analytic method of Talmudic study.[12] That method was spread by his disciples throughout Castile and on to the East after the Expulsion.[13] After Qanpanton's death (1463), Zamora shared its fame with other centers, notably Toledo and Guadalajara. Rabbi Samuel Valenci, one of Qanpanton's foremost disciples, was his master's successor in Zamora and produced such scholars as Rabbi Moses Al'ashqar and Rabbi Jacob Ibn Ḥabib. We know also that the great philosophical preacher, Rabbi Isaac Arama, lived there before accepting a position elsewhere. Arama's praise for Zamora is unequivocal. When he tells about his intellectual life there he describes its location and his feelings toward it in phrases such as "Fair in situation, the uttermost parts of the North," appropriated from the Psalmist, who used these expressions to describe Jerusalem - "the joy of the whole earth..." (Psalms 48,3).[14]

Zamora also produced one of the earliest Hebrew printing-houses (1484). Generally, this was a sign of the cultural centrality of a community, as evident from the fact that the other printing-houses were established in Toledo and Guadalajara, in those years the other major Talmudic centers in Spain.[15] This holds also for Lisbon, which was the major center of Portuguese Jewry,[16] and for the printing-houses in Italy and Turkey in the 16th century. It was in such a Torah center that Saba lived.[17] It was also there that he wrote the first part of his commentary *Ẓeror ha-Mor* on most or all of Genesis.[18]

Although he seems to have had a secular occupation, we do not know what it was.[19] We do know that in the religious sphere he was active as a preacher.[20] As such, he was important enough to speak at the "gathering of the scholars in Castile" [*qibbuẓ ha-ḥakhamim*], probably held outside of Zamora[21] and was praised for it.[22]

Aside from the documents concerning Abraham's brother, Saul,[23] there is a reference to "Jacob Cava" who owned property in Zamora.[24] Jacob was the name of Abraham Saba's father. But the more interesting document for us, is from the years immediately prior to the Expulsion. "Rabi Abraham Cava" was charged ten *Reales* by a municipal official for expelling from the aljama *unas judias malas mugeres*. In all probability those women were Jewish prostitutes.[25] The document does not tell us whether Saba acted on his own initiative or as a representative of the community. Nonetheless, the fact remains that Saba not only preached but also acted accordingly.[26]

Unfortunately, medieval autobiographical descriptions are usually produced as the result of a disturbance in one's normal routine. At any rate, this is the case with Saba, and the information he supplies is mainly from the tragic period of his life - the final eight years of the 15th century.

1.2. Writing in Guimarães

Contemporary sources tell us that in the early summer of 1492 Portugal was flooded with 90,000-120,000 Castilian Jews. The admission of such an influx of refugees was contrary to reason. This country, whose population numbered barely one million, could not afford such a move that would create chaos from socio-economic, health, and religious perspectives. Nevertheless, João II, who needed money to finance Portugal's North African campaign, decided against the opinion of most of his advisors. He accepted most of the Jews for a limited period of eight months for a payment of eight *Cruẓados*. Only a few hundred important families were admitted on a permanent basis, after prior negotiations and a special fee.

Expelled from Spain with the rest of the Jews that chose to remain loyal to the religion of their forefathers, Saba left Castile, moving westward to Portugal. Zamora was the northern center through which the refugees, who intended to cross over to Portugal, went. Andrés Bernaldes, the Spanish historian, talks about 30,000 Jews who departed from Zamora and crossed the border, passing through the Portuguese town of Miranda do Douro.[27] Saba, we assume, was one of them. He settled in Guimarães, a small town with a small Jewish community.[28] It seems clear that the choice of place was due to its proximity to the border about 35km. away. At this stage, Saba was not looking for a large Jewish center such as Lisbon and preferred a small quiet community where he could concentrate on writing. There he completed most of his commentaries[29] under the ideal or idealized conditions of relative peace and an outstanding midrashic and Qabbalistic library.[30]

Taking into account the size of other personal libraries of Iberian Jewish scholars at this period, we can estimate Saba's. Judah Ḥayyat, a Castilian rabbi and Qabbalist, went to Portugal and in the winter of 1493 left by ship reaching North Africa after much travail. Ḥayyat, who had been held in prison there, was finally rescued by the Jews who paid a handsome ransom for his release. The thankful rabbi left them his library of two hundred books.[31] Rabbi David ben Joseph Ibn Yaḥya of Lisbon, who brought upon himself the wrath of the Portuguese king by helping the refugees and the Marranos who wanted to "Judaize," had to escape for his life. He tells in a letter that when he became ill he had to sell over three hundred out of a library of more than four hundred books in order to provide himself with the cash needed to survive.[32] Saba, who writes about the "unbelievable" amount of books he possessed, must have had a few hundred, most of them collections of the classical Midrash, Qabbalah, and medieval exegetical and ethical literature. This is evident from his own writings. One must assume that he also owned a large number of volumes of medieval works dealing with the Talmud and Halakhah, though these did not leave any major mark upon his writings which, after all, belong to the genre of biblical exegesis.

He tells us that he did not rush his work,[33] which seems to have been the result of many years of study and preaching. Since what we have before us today is an abridgement of Saba's original writings, we can only imagine the size of the first version of the commentaries he produced and had to leave behind in Portugal.[34]

In Guimarães, he lived with his wife and two sons who were already married but by 1497, but had no children.[35] It is likely that Saba was not a poor man. We can deduce this not only from his rich library but from the fact that he was not harassed by the Portuguese authorities when the original eight months stay, granted to most of the Castilian refugees, was over. His apparent 'retirement" for the purpose of writing also indicates that his financial state was sound. Saba himself alludes to it only once. In North Africa he bemoans the loss of "house, property, and every precious thing" he owned.[36]

1.3. "Expulsion" in Lisbon - the Final Solution

The last year of the Jews in Portugal is characterized by a series of persecutions perpetrated by the Crown, the climax of which was the well-planned kidnapping of Jewish teenagers during Passover. This was designed in order to pressure their parents to convert to Christianity. As it turned out this was a prelude to the mass forced conversion that was going to befall upon the Jews in Lisbon instead of the expulsion. This event left its traces both in Hebrew and Portuguese literature. The criticism of this of extreme cruel act was voiced clearly by a high ranking clergyman:

> The time now approached when the Jews, who would not become Christians, were to leave the kingdom and all of them were busy to prepare for their departure. It gave Emmanuel great uneasiness to think that

> so many thousand men should be driven into banishment, and he was desirous at least to bring over their sons. For this purpose he devised a scheme, which in fact was contrary to justice and equity.... He ordered all the sons of the Jews under fourteen years of age to be forcibly taken from their parents, that they might be instructed and educated in the Christian faith. This could not be put in execution without producing some affecting circumstances. It was indeed a moving spectacle to behold children torn from the embraces of their mothers, fathers dragged from the necks of their sons, and used with violence; cries and lamentations from all quarters, and every place filled with female shriekings. Some were moved with so much indignation that they destroyed their sons by throwing them into wells; others were distracted to such a degree that they laid violent hands upon themselves.[37]

We have almost no information about Saba and his family during that year. He did not lose his sons in this decree. The loss of his property occurred in Lisbon, for we can assume that he had sold his house, though at a considerable loss, in the year between the announcement of the edict (December 5 1496) and the "Expulsion" itself, 10-11 months later.[38] His library was lost during that year as well. At a certain stage during their final year in Portugal, the Jews were ordered to turn all their Hebrew books over to the authorities. This measure - among others taken by the Crown, like the closing of the synagogues, the confiscation of the valuables held therein, and the prohibition on praying - was designed to harass mentally and religiously the Jews and pressure them into converting to Christianity. It is also possible that King Manuel already had their mass forced-conversion in mind and decided to confiscate their books at this early stage as a preliminary step to ease their future assimilation.[39] As far as Saba was concerned, the decree concerning the books meant carrying them a distance of about 10km. south-west of Guimarães, to Porto, which seems to have served as a collection spot for that northern region of Portugal. So Saba brought his library there,[40] except for his own writings with which he could not part.

Saba and his family made their way to Lisbon, for the Jews had been promised ships to carry them out of the country. Despite the persecutions they endured during their stay in Portugal, and especially in the months prior to the Expulsion date, they did not know what was going to take place there. Some of the Jews, who had come in their thousands, apparently camped just outside the city. In any event, that is what Saba himself did.[41] But the hope of getting out of Portugal vanished soon with the persisting order commanding the Jews to bring all their books to the "great synagogue of Lisbon" under penalty of death.[42] Dear as his writings were to him, Saba decided to hide them to prevent them from falling into impure hands and leave a ray of hope of retrieving the treasure one day.[43] He and another Jew[44] dug into a big root of an olive tree[45] where he hid his writings, which he claimed were even more precious to him than his children.[46] The event that took place soon thereafter was to leave a profound imprint on his life, thought, and writings. Saba summarized it in a few sentences:

> Afterwards they put them all in one yard, about ten thousand Jews and they forced (Ms. Oxford: and tempted) them to convert, and after four days there were left less than forty men and women. In short, they stripped me, and took away my sons and daughters,[47] and all that I had remained there,[48] and I was left with nothing. And I and the (Ms. Parma: forty) others were imprisoned and chained (Ms. Parma: so that we would convert), and after six months (Ms. Parma: When the king realized that he did not succeed),[49] the king ordered to give us one broken ship to take us to Arzila, and I remained here, in El Qsar el Kebir, and this holy community clothed my nakedness and supplied me with all my needs...and I was here for a long while sick with heavy head and eyes, for I remembered my sons and books that I had left behind, especially, those books that I had composed.[50]

We know about the mass forced conversion in Lisbon from many sources, both Hebrew and Portuguese. The Jews were put in the palace of Os Estãos, a complex which consisted of a large building and a big yard behind it.[51] The Jews who were crammed in there numbered between 10,000-20,000.[52]

Saba tells us that they were in jail for six months, which is only a round figure. One of the group tells us the exact date on which they were released from jail and sent to North Africa. It was on February 1. 1498.[53]

While Saba does not tell us any details about the voyage, we can surmise from some comments of his that it was not a pleasure cruise. He alludes to it, saying: "As a result of the abundance of troubles that came upon me at sea as well as on land, I forgot..."[54] In an interesting comment on Psalms 107, Saba says, "... since one who travels by sea is likened to someone who is lost in the desert, and like a prisoner, and like the sick who vomits everything he ate and even what he did not eat, and he cannot eat, turning from his food with loathing."[55]

1.4. North Africa; El Qsar el Kebir - Fez - Tlemcen

Saba and his friends were let off the boat at Portuguese-controlled Arzila on the shore of the Atlantic,[56] from which he proceeded to his first station on African soil - El Qsar el Kebir. We do not know much about that Jewish community which came to his aid in the warmest manner. From the fact that there Saba reconstructed his lost Ẓ.M. from memory, with the help of no books but a *Ḥumash* alone, we can surmise that the cultural situation of the community was nothing to be proud of.

Another mention of this community by a refugee we read in an extant fragment of the introduction to the book *Keter Shem Tov* by Rabbi Shem Tov Ibn Gamil, who writes about his tragic post-Expulsion experiences. This man, from Navarre, tried to cross Spain from north to south in an attempt to reach Almeria and, from there, to embark on a boat to Oran in North Africa. He spent about a year in jails in Andalusia. Finally he was brought to Safi, but his sons remained in Spain and had been given as slaves to noblemen. He tells us that he spent nine months in El Qsar el Kebir, hoping to hear some news about his sons' fate. When he found out how much money he would need in order to gain their freedom, he left that community for Fez.[57] For Ibn Gamil as well as for other refugees, El Qsar was a way-station. In all probability it was a small community that, beyond good will and first aid, could not be of great help. It was not a choice place to settle.

Saba spent between 14-16 months there.[58] He completed the second edition of his Ẓ.M. on most of the Pentateuch there,[59] and then decided to move south-east to Fez.

This city, founded in the end of the 8th century, slowly evolved into the most important Moslem center in the Maghrib. Although it was influenced by the Andalusian culture during the Ommayyad period, it is assumed that until mid 13th century it was Marracech that served during the Almoravide and Almohade periods not only as the seat of temporal power but also of Moslem culture.[60] The Marinide dynasty, moved the capital to Fez after overthrowing the Almohades in 1276. They expended much attention, energy, and funds on creating the "University of Fez" with its cluster of *madrasas*.[61] The ever-growing power and threat of the Christians in the Iberian Peninsula brought about a migration of scholars from Andalusia, many of whom reached Fez. Thus it became a cultural center that attracted many students from all over Morocco.[62]

The Jews prospered under the Marinides, who employed many of them as government officials. This, in turn, enraged Moslem religious leaders who tried to incite the crowd against the Jews. In 1437, pogroms broke out and the King transferred the Jews, for their own protection, to Fez Djedid (New Fez), which the Marinides had built, into a quarter that was called Mellaḥ due to the salty nature of the area. This did not save the Jews from partial destruction in 1465, when a revolt against the powerful Jewish courtier Saul Ibn Batas ended up in the killing of the King himself.[63]

This happened less than thirty years before the Expulsion from Spain. But Banu Wattas, who took over from the Marinides, were liberal toward the Jews, and the king Mulai a-Sheikh (1472-1505) is described as "the great king, one of the pious of the Gentiles [*me-ḥasidei úmot ha-òlam*]... who accepted the Spanish Jews in all his kingdom and received them with great favor."[64] The fact that many of the refugees chose to go to Fez shows that the community had to a large extent recovered from the pogrom of 1465.

The first year of the refugees in Fez was disastrous. An eye witness tells about the fire that broke out in the Jewish quarter, was followed by "starvation and great plague and more than twenty thousands people died."[65]

But the resilience of the refugees, a characteristic they showed in those harsh times in many other locations where they settled, helped them overcome all hardships, and it did not take long before their tenacity changed things in their favor. The recovery was swift:[66]

> And after that time, God in his mercy pitied them. From the year 258 (1498) God blessed us and we built spacious and artistically decorated houses with attics, and God, may He be blessed, blessed us with yeshivot and students, and beautifully built synagogues...until the fame of the Mellaḥ is spread nowadays all over the land of Ismael.[67]

Thus the community in El Qsar el Kebir could not offer him what Fez could. The latter, which was already a vibrant Jewish center on an upward swing after recovering from the immediate problems resulting from the influx of the refugees in 1492, had more of the books which Saba missed so badly.[68] Fez' scholarly circles included many of Spanish origin who formed a prominent group. One must also consider the special desire and need of an active preacher for a public to whom he would be able to transmit his message, and it is clear that Saba felt a sense of a special mission as a survivor of the tragic Portuguese "Expulsion."[69]

Thus, sometime between May 2 - June 30 1499 he left for Fez, where he took ill almost immediately upon arrival. He had just started his commentary on Deuteronomy.[70] He lay in bed for five months until Hanukkah 5260 (October 28 - December 3 1499).[71] This was the reason for not completing Ẓ.M. before the first of Nissan of that year (March 2. 1500).[72] It took him another two months to rewrite his commentary on Tractate Avot.[73] In another very short time, probably 3-4 months, he wrote the commentaries on the books of Ruth and Esther.

In other words, in about a year and a half[74] he wrote about 600 folios under tremendous mental strain.[75] Several reasons may be offered for this outburst of literary activity. We must imagine a man who had to reconstruct and rewrite so much because the first version was extant only in an autograph and only in the possession of its author. He must have learned his lesson and wanted to write and "publish" it as soon as possible. In addition, Saba was determined to bequeath something valuable to future generations since he had lost his sons to Christianity. His spiritual creation was the only thing left for him to leave behind for posterity.[76] He was a man who saw death in Lisbon, at sea, and on his sick-bed, having, for a while at least, head and eye problems and then serious intestinal disorders. He was not young anymore[77] and there was no time to waste. Another factor which determined the hasty manner of his writing was the message he wished to communicate to the remnants of the quickly "shrinking" nation.[78]

We have almost no certain information about his activities in the following years, but we do know that he left Fez and reached Tlemcen. A copy of the famous Qabbalistic book *Livnat ha-Sappir* completed in Tlemcen on the 4th of Kislev, 5268, was copied by Abraham Saba.[79] A short Qabbalistic treatise on the *Ten Sephirot* was written by our Abraham Saba as a responsum to the request of Alal ben Alḥaikh of Tlemcen. In it he writes: "And I have already discovered to you this secret mouth to mouth on the holy Sabbath."[80] and this proves that he was physically in Tlemcen. Saba also wrote a Qabbalistic commentary on the prayers for him.[81] All this indicates that he was considered an authority on Qabbalah there.

To this point in the itinerary, Saba represents a relatively large number of refugees. Many of them came directly from Spain to Tlemcen. Rabbi Abraham Baqrat talks about 12,000, of whom many died in a plague.[82] Others arrived at Fez and only later moved to Tlemcen. Such was the case of the famous Rabbi Jacob Berav who, right after the Expulsion, came to Fez and served as a rabbi there. Then he moved to Tlemcen, from which he eventually proceeded to the East.[83]

Rabbi Abraham Zacut, a resident of Salamanca (not far from Zamora), went to Portugal and was apparently in Saba's group in the Lisbon jail.[84] He is known to have spent some time in Fez and then in Tlemcen. Eventually, he continued to Damascus and ended his itinerary in Jerusalem.[85]

Tlemcen served as a refugee haven. Alongside Fez, it was the most important Jewish center in North Africa. Leo Africanus describes the greatness of Tlemcen.[86] He says that the Jews live in the southern part of the city, where one could find the lawyers, notaries, students, and professors of the five colleges. He adds, though, that while in the past a large part of the city was inhabited by the Jews and they were rich, today (mid 16th-century) they are poor due to the looting that took place in 1516 when the mob took advantage of a political *interregnum*.[87]

Thus in Tlemcen, which was a political and economic center, a large and rich Jewish community developed. It was here that the above-mentioned Shem Tov Ibn Gamil was sent by the leaders of the Jews in Fez to seek financial help.[88]

Now since most references to this community in this period make mention of Abraham Saàdon, the local leader and Nagid of the Jews, we must assume that he was the main attraction for the Spanish exiles.

He is described as a generous person who did all within his power to help his brethren at that time of crisis. Moreover, he was interested in the intellectual contribution he could elicit from the Spanish rabbis. It was at his request that Zacut wrote an astro-eschatological treatise, Zacut's area of expertise.[89] It was at the request of his brother in-law, Alal, that the Spanish rabbi, Judah Khalaẓ, settled in Tlemcen just before the Expulsion, and it was for him that Khalaẓ wrote a supercommentary on Rashi's commentary on the Pentateuch.[90] It was apparently the same Alal for whom Saba wrote the two Qabbalistic works. From the literary point of view, Tlemcen seems to have been the most important center in North Africa in the turn of the century, even more so than Fez.

But while some might have remained there, others used Tlemcen merely as a station on their route elsewhere. With the exception of Khalaẓ, whose arrival was pre-Expulsion, all the others mentioned above continued their wanderings.

1.5. Turkey or Italy?

The conjecture that Saba ended up in Turkey is plausible, though not conclusive, and merits some attention. The literary evidence pointed out by scholars is found in Rabbi Elijah Mizraḥi's *Responsa*. There we find two letters sent by Rabbi Abraham Ẓaba and one responsum by Mizraḥi.[91] The second letter is of importance to us. Ẓaba seems to be a student of Mizraḥi's. He tells about an intestinal illness from which he suffered for ten days, and from which he clearly recovered. He signs off: "And I am kissing your feet and the holy hands of the holy company of the Yeshivah. From your most insignificant disciple, Abraham Ẓaba".[92]

The responsum starts with praise for "the excellent medical doctor Abraham Ẓaba," who is described as a sharp witted and erudite scholar. This document has already been discussed at length.[93] However, the only conclusion it allows is that we have no information that stands conflicts with our knowledge of Saba. One interesting parallel that might connect the two personalities is the intestinal illness. If, indeed, there is an identity between Saba and Ẓaba, then we will have to assume that he joined Mizraḥi's scholarly close circle at an old age.

One more responsum might have bearing on our subject. It concerns the problem of what custom must the Sefardic Jews follow when theirs does not agree with the local one.[94] It is written to Rabbi Jacob of Adrianople. We learn from it that the scholar [*he-ḥakham*] Rabbi Abraham Saba had a certain opinion concerning the matter under discussion.[95] This Saba was obviously from Spain. I tend to think that he and Ẓaba are the same person. This would strengthen the conjecture that our Saba and the one mentioned in Mizraḥi's Responsa are identical.

The date of his death is unknown. From Ibn Ḥaviv's responsum written in 1509,[96] we might learn that Saba was still alive then. From the opening page of the first printed edition of Ẓ.M. (Venice, 1523) we learn that Saba was already dead.[97]

The unique story about its circumstances is worth quoting in full, not in order to derive from it any empirical biographical information, but to learn about the image Saba apparently had acquired for himself as a holy man of miracles.[98]

> Rabbi Abraham Sabaḥ, the author of the *Ẓerorot*[99] hurried to go to the cities of Franqia.[100] And it happened at sea that he was fallen sick of his sickness whereof he was to die, and between him and the city of Verona there was a three days' journey. And the Lord hurled a stormy wind into the sea so that the ship was like to be broken, and the men rowed hard to bring it to land but could not for the sea grew more and more tempestuous against them. Wherefore they cried every man unto his God, and they said to the rabbi: "Behold we know that thou art a man of God and that the word of the Lord in thy mouth is truth. Please pray for us unto the Lord your God so that we shalt not die, and see our toil and our oppression." And the rabbi told them: "Behold I am dying. And now mark, I pray you, and see and prove me in this, and you will be saved from stormy wind and tempest. Accept upon yourselves that at the time of my death you shall not cast me forth into the sea in order to lighten it unto you. Behold now, this city is near, talk to the Jews that they might take me from the ship and bury me in the sepulchres of my fathers.[101] Thus thou shalt make your ways prosperous and the waters shall no more destroy all flesh." And so it indeed happened. And the sea ceased from its raging, and the above-mentioned rabbi passed to eternal life on the eve of Yom Kippur. And it came to pass on the morrow that the captain and some of his men went to the synagogue of the holy community of Verona, and he asked them for their welfare.[102] And he told them: "You should know, Jews, that in my ship died a pure man, and he commanded me so and so at the time of his death, and I have done all that he ordered me to do. You too, the house of Israel, do what is imposed upon you." And all Israel buried him and they eulogized him in the evening after Yom Kippur in the city of Verona. May his soul be bound in the bond of life![103]

In the following century we find people who claimed to be his descendants. It would seem - if the claims were authentic - that they were the offspring of Abraham Saba's son (or sons) who must have escaped from Portugal.[104]

2. *History and Biography Reflected in Biblical Exegesis*

Commenting on the duration of Noah's stay in his ark, Saba says:

> ...and this is the meaning of "six months with the oil of myrrh", which is cold and therefore gives off its fragrance only when it is heated. As the Sages said: "My beloved is unto me as a bundle of myrrh [*ẓeror ha-mor*]" - this is Abraham our Patriarch. Similar to myrrh, which is the head of the spices, Abraham is the head of the righteous, and similar to the myrrh which gives off its fragrance as the result of fire, Abraham's deeds did not become known until he was thrown into the furnace of fire..."And the ark rested in the seventh month" - for the wicked waters [*ha-mayyim ha-zedonim*] calmed down.[105]

Whether in the last sentence Saba also alludes to his six months in the Lisbon jail or not, it is clear that the events around the Expulsion from Portugal were a decisive factor which left its profound impression on him in more ways than one. Let us simply list all that he had prior to his personal disaster and that was lost to him within a very brief period. He had a wife and two very beloved, married sons. He owned a big library, which was a rare and precious property in those days. From the fluency of his quotations from memory, it is obvious that he made good use of it, and consequently was sentimentally attached to it. He had autographs of his commentaries on ten biblical books (Pentateuch and Five Scrolls), on one tractate (Avot), and a code of Qabbalistic laws and customs,[106] which represented several years of labor. Besides this, he must have had material possessions the value of which is unknown to us but seems to have been considerable. All that was close and dear to him vanished, swallowed by cruel Catholic fanaticism. Moreover, his enduring troubles weakened his eyesight and seriously damaged his digestive system. He was also a man who faced physical death more than once: in prison in Lisbon, (probably) at sea and on his sick-bed in Fez. In addition, he saw a mass "spiritual death" - the loss of the great Jewry of Portugal, including the refugees from Spain, after the various stages of persecutions - previously unheard of and conducted by the Crown itself.[107]

Saba himself tells us several times that the man rewriting his lost books is but a shadow of the man who not so long ago in terms of time, but so far in the past in terms of nostalgia, lived peacefully in such an ideal Jewish center as Zamora. He complains repeatedly about his loss of memory, his inability to recreate his books in their old image, and the loss of all that was precious to him, including his physical health.

The Expulsion from Spain, which might have had an impact on the man and his original commentaries, was superseded by the persecutions in Portugal and his Expulsion from there, because of their more brutal and cruel nature, both on the personal as well as on the national level.[108] We also have to consider the fact that Saba's most satisfying period of literary creativity occurred after 1492 and, while the Expulsion probably served as a catalyst for that creativity, the latter served in turn as a personal tranquilizer for the author.

Saba was a survivor of a catastrophe. As a preacher who felt that he was charged with a holy mission, he responded to the new reality of the almost total collapse and disappearance of the distinguished Jewry of the Iberian Peninsula in an energetic fashion, both orally and in writing.[109] While the introductions to all his works bear the imprint of his personal tragedy,[110] his writings are permeated with deep feelings for the tragedy which befell his people. It expresses itself in discussions of such motifs as despair, exile, and redemption. In terms of isolated comments, there are numerous passages that are clearly a dircet consequence of his experiences. Let us demonstrate both the personal and the national historical experiences as reflected in the following passages.

When Ben-Hadad, the king of Aram, sent his messengers to Ahab, the king of Israel, a second time, telling him "whatsoever is pleasant in your eyes, they (Ben-Hadad's servants) shall put in their hands and take away" (I Kings, 20,6) Saba says:

> ...it was generally understood that he demanded the precious gems and the hidden treasures. But that was not true, for what he really meant was the [books of the] Torah that he wanted to take, and to convert them so that they would worship idols.[111]

We have here an original interpretation based on two points: a. A demand to take the Jews' holy books (an idea that already appears in the Midrash). b. The wish to convert them. The former is the means to the latter. One cannot fully understand how this idea came into Saba's mind without being aware of the decree of the Portuguese king to surrender all the Hebrew religious books in an effort to prevent their study and teaching, especially to children, as Saba mentions elsewhere: "... and they took all the books and synagogues so that they would not be able to pray and study Torah, to the point that Torah was almost forgotten..."[112]

Saba several times, in a very emotional way, shows his identification with parents who were about to lose a son.[113] He describes their feelings, using rhymes and biblical poetic expressions, One such incident is that of Jacob and Joseph, his supposedly dead son. After a psychological interpretation, saying that the brothers "dipped the tunic in blood and tore it in half to take revenge on the striped tunic, since they could not do it to Joseph himself," Saba goes on to describe Jacob's guilt feelings as the reason for his excessive mourning.

> And perhaps he did that because he believed himself guilty of his death, since he sent him alone... and he said: I shall lament and wail. I shall go naked, dressed (only) in a sack of cloth, and I shall take no consolation all my life, and I shall go down to my son, mourning, to the grave, for I killed him.[114]

Saba here uses two elements that betray his own emotions: a. poetic language. b. dramatization of Jacob's reaction that does not appear in the biblical narative. We are not suggesting that this is an expression of Saba's own guilt feelings - which indeed he might have had.[115] However, we believe that having seen Jewish parents' emotional state after the loss of their children in Portugal, increased Saba's sensitivity to biblical stories which present a similar situation. A few lines later, at the verse "And the Midianites sold him to Egypt" (Gen. 37, 36), Saba comments "to teach us that the gates of tears have not been locked, and Jacob's weeping helped that they did not take him to a far away island". This seems to be borrowed directly from the cruel decree that ordered the sending of Jewish children to São Tomé in 1493.

Similarly, the reader who is immersed in Saba's writings, biography, and way of thinking, can guess that the verse from the Reproof Section in Deuteronomy, "Your sons and daughters will be given to another nation" (28, 32), would be taken as having contemporary significance, and sure enough we read:

> ...this is another curse that happened to us because of our sins in Portugal, when the king took the little sons and daughters and sent them on ships to the Snakes Islands[116] in order to establish a settlement there.[117]

These examples of the isolated instances where historical and biographical incidents permeated Saba's understanding of parts of the biblical text.[118] But these factors find their full expression in Saba's commentary on the book of Esther.

2.1. The Expulsions and the Scroll of Esther

As we have already indicated, we cannot doubt that Saba went through a series of shocking experiences both as an individual and as a member of a nation. He himself does not fail to tell us this in almost every introduction and colophon.[119] It is only natural that a commentary on Esther would serve as a mirror, reflecting the two major events of his life and, more importantly, of that generation of Iberian Jews. It is almost inconceivable that his understanding of this book - its characters and its plot - would not be affected by the experiences of the two Expulsions.

As a methodological introduction let us begin by comparing biblical exegesis to another literary genre. With fiction, it has been widely claimed that much of the novel's appeal lies in the fact that it deals with concrete problems of our lives. Thus, through the characters and the story one finds a sense of identification which compensates for personal frustration. The author's biographical factor often reveals itself in the words he uses, his choice of phrases and emotional tone.

It is obvious, however, that one must recognize the necessity for a balance between the biographical and literary elements, since the novel as a genre has rules and dynamics of its own, and therefore one should not ignore the impact of the intrinsic characteristics of the work as a literary creation.[120]

All this has been said about fiction. But it is possible and even logical to extend these guidelines to exegesis, which can be defined as an autonomous creation limited by an already existing text. This autonomous element in the creative process of the commentary is personal and draws from the same sources as fiction does. Hence, writing an exegetical work under historical conditions which in their general outline, fit the narrative commented on, will, in the psychological function it fulfills for the exegete, parallel the novel and its author, with the limitation mentioned above, namely, the already existing text.

This can be hidden even in comments regarded as *peshat*, or in use of certain interpretations drawn from the midrashic or post-midrashic traditions, but it would manifest itself in interpretations detached from the text, in raising new questions, in emotional outbursts at points of the narrative which have contact with contemporary reality, and in inner conflicts expressed in contradictions. It is all the more so when we deal with a preacher who, by the nature of his occupation, looks for the actual relevance of the biblical text to the present. For him, the temporal gap between himself and the Bible can be closed very easily when this parallelism is manifested, since his exegetical mind works this way. In other words, the projection of the text on reality creates a contact between the two which makes it easy to project back from reality to the text as a two-way process and to assimilate elements of the former in the latter.

We are not claiming that Saba's experiences prompted him to write his commentary on Esther, nor are we trying to interpret it necessarily on the subconscious level. What does seem clear is that the Expulsions served as conscious and possibly subconscious models for Saba's conception of the Esther narrative and, on a subconscious level, the writing of the commentary might have served to compensate for the ordeals of the two Expulsions.[121]

We do not know how long the impact of his tragic experiences lasted. Generally, we believe that most of the forceful reactions to the Expulsions were written close to the events, as was the case with Rabbi Joseph Yaàveẓ, or soon after the return to Judaism of people from Portugal, like Rabbi Joseph Garson. Yaàveẓ' references to the Expulsion from Spain are strong in his Ór *ha-Ḥayyim* and *Ḥasdei ha-Shem*, which were written almost immediately àfter 1492, when he finally settled in Mantua. This theme fades away in his later writings. Garson's emotional sermon concerning the events he experienced, including forced baptism and crypto-Jewish life in Portugal, was given after his escape and wanderings, upon arrival at Salonika.[122] But Saba wrote this commentary in the first year after his release from jail and his subsequent arrival in Fez, so that the events were still fresh and he was definitely preoccupied with them.

The association between Haman's edict and that of the Expulsion from Spain is not rare. Rabbi Elijah Qapsali uses the biblical style of the book of Esther in recounting the story of the Expulsion in a most interesting way, and he is not the only one.[123] The main characters - the king, the anti-Jewish advisor, and the Jewish courtier trying to step into the breach in order to save his people - simply invite the comparison.[124] Let us start with the image of Ahasuerus as drawn and painted by a post-Expulsion artist - Rabbi Abraham Saba.[125]

Ahasuerus was "a great king... and great among the giants, who knows courtly tactics [*takhsisei melukhah*] ...experienced in wars."[126] He was good to his people and "moreover he appointed a Jew as the viceroy, over the rest of the courtiers. This is indeed a great thing."[127] All whose names are doubled in the Bible were, according to the Midrash, righteous enough to merit this world and the world to come, so was he. Then, asks Saba, since "from all this it seems that Ahasuerus was an honest person in all his actions, how could it come to pass that during his life, and from him, such evil emerged, to agree with Haman."[128] His answer is that "even though he was from the (dynasty of) good Persian kings and himself was a good man, he was, however, a fool who believed everything, and was tempted very easily by Haman's advice."[129]

As the plot develops, Saba changes his tone somewhat: "... for although Ahasuerus was wicked [*rasha*], his wickedness was not like that of Haman, but he was a fool who believes everything, and was confused [*mevulbal*] and an inconsistent person [*metoraf hafakhpakh*], who did not have the wisdom to differentiate between good and evil, between truth and falsehood."[130]

Thus, the same king who was described as good to his people, knowledgeable in the tactics of diplomacy and politics, smart enough to use the good services of an outstanding Jew in his court, is also described as a "fool" and as a "confused, and inconsistent person", a man who could not make the correct decision. Moreover, he was "ignorant [*nivàr mi-daàt*] and could not respond logically [*lo yada le-áhadorei sevara*], but responded to Haman simply by the bad act of removing his ring, for he hated Israel."[131]

Saba attempts, however, to compromise between the two extremes, saying, "So that it seems from all this that all Ahasuerus' matters were done by him honestly, only he had bad advisors and was tempted by their advice to good or bad, and since Israel sinned, God swayed Ahasuerus' heart to (agree to) Haman's advice ..."[132] Finally, then, we get a combination of three factors: Haman, a descendant of Amaleq, was the obvious villain and the direct natural cause. Ahasuerus was a minor anti-Semite who, in addition, was also a fool. The unholy trinity is completed by the sins of the Jews, without which God would not have allowed the king to agree to Haman's plan, despite his foolishness.

The solution offered here does not seem to resolve the obvious contradictions between the passages quoted above. It seems to us that the ambivalence with which Saba treats Ahasuerus is paralleled by his view of Ferdinand, the monarch of Spain, and of Manuel, King of Portugal.[133]

Saba is the only medieval exegete for whom Ahasuerus' image remains, so to speak, in *limbo*. The Midrashic tradition sees the king in a negative light, while medieval exegesis in Spain - where the king was generally considered as an ally of the Jewish minority - looked upon him favourably.[134] Saba mentions Ferdinand while recounting his life story. "And then God's anger rose against His people and He cast them out of their land, and the King, Ferdinand, expelled all the Jews of his kingdom."[135] He does not say anything negative about him. The king only carries out the sentence decreed by God, the Cause of all causes.[136] In comparison, he adds after King Manuel's name, "May his name and memory be blotted out."[137] Obviously, the latter's wickedness was much clearer, crueler through his brutal series of decrees in the year before the "Expulsion," topping it all with forced conversion that did not exist during the Expulsion from Spain.

Haman, the descendant of Edom, the eternal enemy of Israel, is described as a very cruel in the religious sphere as well. Although this is not entirely novel, Saba's specific description creates a very contemporary picture when he says that Haman wore on his chest an image which was "like the Edomite kings who have their officials come in, carrying on their clothes a cross which is their abomination, so that everyone who sees them would kneel or bow down."[138]

Haman's power lies in his sophistication of expression and "grandiloquence." The Edomites are, in general, people "of wisdom and knowledge... for they know every wisdom", and so Haman was

> a man of slander, and knew how to arrange his words properly [*ve-yodeà le-sader devarav àl nakhon*], shrewdly, and with grandiloquence [*lashon medaberet gedolot*], and smooth words for his evil intentions...[139]

At present, Saba tells us, the main Christian threat is not in physical agression, the way the Moslems treat the Jews, but in their ability to influence by their smooth talk:

> ...for this alludes to Edom who has that power in his tongue to lower and degrade every being by arranging his words properly [*mi-ẓad siddur leshono*], by his smooth lips [*ḥalaqlaqot sefatav*] and his grandiloquence, so that by their wisdom they do much evil to Israel...You should know that it is easier to recover from a blow of a sword, then from that of the tongue.[140]

The description of Haman's tactics is also suggestive. It is impossible, says Saba, that a king will agree to the genocide of a people that "take refuge under his shade," for two reasons: a. international political, because of the reputation that his rule will acquire;[141] b. moral, "for how is it possible that he would agree to slaughter a whole nation living securely under his shade, which would be treachery and great cruelty",[142] since they came to settle "by the command of the ancient king."[143] Haman was aware of the objective loss to the king if they would be killed. He concluded, therefore, "that the king would not agree with him immediately to annihilate all the Jews, a wise and understanding people at whose head stands Mordecai the Jew, a distinguished person, who was an appointee of the king... and his intention was during that year to divert the king more and more by denouncing them to him for many evils and faults they possess."[144]

Another reason for the postponement of the implementation of the edict for a whole year after its initial announcement lay in Haman's religious intentions. He hoped that during that long period the Jews, fearing for their lives, would have time to consider the option of conversion.[145] In addition, "the common people [*àmei ha-árez̧*] will have killed some of them before the implementation of the edict, so that even if the latter were not be carried out, the dead would not revived..."[146] Saba also explains how the psychological pressure would drive the Jews towards conversion, "...and perhaps if there would be a long interim period some of them would rationalize [*yitḥakmu*] and others would despair."[147] Some would find a rationalization to leave their faith, while others, without any subtle theological or philosophical excuses but simply out of despair, would convert. This was the reason that Mordecai insisted on acting quickly, in order not to lose Jewish souls.[148] This danger was the consideration behind Esther's tactics in trying to fight the edict.[149]

And if one still doubts the historical background of these comments, Saba tells us explicitly:

> And there is no better proof than our own experience that we saw with our own eyes, that the Edomites do all sorts of tricks to Israel to frighten and cause them to panic, so that they will pity their children and convert. And this was Haman's intention.[150]

We can well imagine the confusion before the Expulsion from Spain. We have also some sources from both sides confirming it.[151] Saba's description, however, fits the Expulsion from Portugal much better, for between the announcement of the edict and its supposed implementation 10-11 months elapsed (while the respective period in Spain was only three months), and also the persecutions during these months were much more intense.[152] In general, Saba's final and crucial year in Portugal had a much more profound effect on his writings. In his commentary on Esther he alludes to it in the passage where he says that a king cannot agree to a genocide, "...and it is well known that even the kings who oppress Israel [*ha-z̧orerim ét yisraél*] and decree their conversion [*shemad me-haàvarat ha-torah*][153] or taking away their sons and daughters etc., they all agree not to kill the Jews in their kingdoms, so that people will not say that theirs is a barbarous kingdom [*malkhuta qetià*]"[154]

Esther, on the other hand, tried to show the utility of the Jews, and that their loss would become "a damage to the king."[155] Indeed, when the king realized what Haman had attempted to accomplish, he was furious, since such a decree against the Jews is in the final analysis a "great treachery" against the king himself.[156] This was also the only way that Spanish Jewry could try to fight against pressure by the Church, namely, showing the king their usefulness to him in terms of services and wealth, and this seems to have been the main tactic they employed in their attempt to have the Crown rescind the edict.[157]

A personal side of the writer is revealed in the following passage where he discusses the question of how Mordecai allowed Esther to be taken to the king:

> And now that he heard the king's announcement ordering each one who had a daughter or sister to bring them to the king to have sexual intercourse with an uncircumcized idol worshipper, why didn't he put himself in danger to lead her to a land which is cut off (in order) to hide in rocky caves or in the clefts of the rocks..., or to lead her to another country? And if he could do neither of these, behold we have seen with our own eyes in the kingdom of Portugal at that time of the Expulsion... that they strangled and slaughtered themselves and their wives... they took their sons and daughters and threw them into wells in order to kill them in their (i.e. the parents') lifetimes...And why didn't Mordecai do any of these things, which were done by the common people of Israel [*qetanei yisraél*] in Portugal. It was fitting for Mordecai to kill himself for such a thing rather than see with his own eyes... and why did he wait until they took her... Why didn't he protect Esther, the righteous, from idolatry, and why wasn't he careful?... and where was his righteousness, his piety, his courage, a man whose heart was like that of a lion, and now he gave over all his delight.[158]

Through his outstanding, lengthy presentation of the problem, his excessive use of question marks, and his use of poetical expressions, we can feel Saba's emotions pouring out. He does not tell us that the question could be self-motivated, since his own two sons were taken in Lisbon and forced to convert. But he does tell us of this fact in his introduction to the commentary[159] so that the reader knows about it. Moreover, while describing the relations between Mordecai and Esther, his charge, Saba describes the tragedy using the verse "Those that I have dandled and brought up, my enemy consumed (Lam. 2, 22)." He uses the same verse in describing the loss of his own children.[160]

Saba's answer is that the circumstances were such that Mordecai didn't have the time to do anything about it, for she was taken right away. This was the result of the fact that Mordecai lived close to the court, and here, clearly in retrospect, Saba interprets the words "... lived in Shushan the capital," as intended to explain why Mordecai could not prevent her from being taken to the king. Perhaps, in a similar way, Saba tried to excuse himself for failing as the head of the family to somehow prevent his sons' conversion.

At this point we can conclude that the Expulsion from Spain, and especially the so-called "Expulsion" from Portugal, had a direct influence on Saba's understanding of the biblical story. This comes across clearly and forcefully through the motif of conversion which is central in his writings, as well as through the characters and the different stages of the narrative.

But the happy ending of the biblical drama was not to repeat itself two thousand years later. Haman and his followers were not killed and Mordecai did not succeed in his diplomatic efforts to prevent the tragedy. Instead of "The Jews had light and joy...and honour,"[161] the Jews' lot was "great mourning...weeping and wailing,"[162] and rather than "and many of the people of the land became Jews,"[163] we read "in those depressing days thousands and myriads of Jews converted."[164]

This might have served as a catalyst for Saba's over indulgence in idealization at the end of the Book of Esther. The relationship between the Jews and the king reach an unprecedented peak,[165] and the Jews themselves had the pleasure of executing Haman and his followers, who plotted against the king and his most loyal citizen, the Jews.[166] Mordecai, the courtier, who becomes the viceroy, exempts the Jews from paying even the regular taxes imposed on the population.[167] Instead, the king imposes on those that had any connection with Haman an extra heavy load of taxes, to teach them a lesson and break their spirits.[168] And as for the king, he became even more successful and prosperous than before. Of course, there is no trace of the king's hatred of the bad old days. Mordecai entered the official chronicles of the Persian kings as "A Jew wrapped with a prayer-shawl and phylacteries, who became the viceroy...and beloved by all the courtiers...."[169] He also led the Jews in the ideal path, thus creating external and internal peace. This is a perfect idyll, a medieval exilic Utopia!

The idealization of the past is a process triggered by some immediate dissatisfaction with present reality. While in our case we have an already existing text which paints the end of the drama in idyllic colours (and the discussed idea might reflect the state of affairs at the time of its composition), one cannot but be impressed with the excessive indulgence and tone of satisfaction in Saba's comments on the final chapter of the book, which are rooted in the frustrations of the present. This commentary gave Saba the opportunity to relive the tragedy of the Spanish and Portuguese Jewries, only with a different and happy ending.

In conclusion, the similarities between the Expulsions and the story of Esther were recognized by Saba. Several times he makes explicit comparisons, and it seems to us that the projection of the Expulsions onto the biblical narrative was also implicitly done in many details. All this opens a peephole for us into the sensitive soul of the exegete who was profoundly influenced by his tragic experiences, a fact that found its expression in his literary creation. Curiously enough, Saba's commentary also helps us better to understand the tense atmosphere of the "Portuguese experience" in the final year of the Jews there.[170]

3. *The Portuguese Experience in Contemporary Eyes*

While Jewish historiography deals primarily with the Expulsion from Spain, we have seen that for Saba it was overshadowed by the tragic affairs in Portugal. A survey of the literature of that generation referring to those events shows that he was not an exception.

Saba himself sees the affair in Portugal as a continuation of the 1492 Expulsion. In his long autobiography of suffering he starts: "And then the Lord's anger was kindled against His people," briefly describing the Expulsion from Spain, and later continues: "And again the anger of the Lord was kindled against His people and King Manuel expelled (i.e. decreed to expell) all the Jews from the kingdom of Portugal."[171] The description of what happened there occupies the bulk of the story.

We have shown elsewhere that the same phenomenon is also true for Rabbi Abraham ben Eliezer Halevi, whose itinerary was apparently quite similar to that of Saba. Halevi's references to Portugal and the events there show unmistakably deeper traces in his consciousness than the Expulsion from Spain. Halevi refers to the tragedy in a very touching passage which he wrote many years later, and most of his hatred is reserved for the Portuguese, whom he calls "butchers." Yet the beginning of the Divine move that culminated in the forced conversion in Lisbon was in 1492.[172]

Rabbi Joseph Garson, who converted to Christianity in Lisbon, escaped and reached Salonica in 1500. Upon arrival, he gave a public sermon. Garson refers to the conversions and to the converts and their post-conversion Jewish life and hopes. He uses the term *gerush sefarad* and *ba-shemad ha-gadol bi-sefarad* to describe the Portuguese ordeal.[173]

Some of the extant elegies written in commemoration of the Expulsion from Spain, prove the point conclusively. These were written as lamentation, with the intention of integrating them into the *qinot* of the Ninth of Av. Consequently, they were not written as personal poetry, but as an attempt to reflect the prevailing national mood and the religious comprehension of the tragedies.

About midway in the dirge entitled *Qinah al Shemad Castilla* the poet writes: "We went to Portugal..." and goes on to lament the events in Portugal at relative length.[174]

The elegy that starts with the refrain "On the day when my light was darkened with the Expulsion from Castile," after only two lines, swiftly moves away from the 1492 Expulsion, and the last seven out of the eight stanzas of lamentation are devoted to the national disaster in Portugal. Yet the refrain remains with the reminder of the "Expulsion from Castile."[175]

Quite clearly, the poet saw the events as a continuation of a divinely planned retribution against the Jews of Spain. The tribulations endured by the Jews of Portugal cannot be understood without obvious connection to the extra-ordinary influx of the refugee Jews from Spain to that small kingdom. Thus in terms of socio-economic cause and effect it was correct to see the Portuguese experience in the 1492-97 years as part of the initial Expulsion from Castile-Aragon. This is apart from the fact that for many Jews Portugal was a part of Sefarad by being a geographical part of Iberia. It was also quite natural that the cruel events in 1497, leading to what was believed by the Portuguese king to be the "final solution" of Judaism in Portugal, would be viewed by the refugees as the culmination of the series of divine measures against the Jews of *Sefarad*.

NOTES

1 See Ben-Sasson, Generation, pp. 23-25. H.J. Zimmels, *Ashkenazim and Sephardim*, London (1958), pp. 61ff. So we read: קהלות קשטילה וקטלוניא אשר היתה מדרגתם באומה מדרגת האברים הראשיים לשאר הגוף. (P. Duran in *Qinah ve-Hesped*, appended to Maàseh Éfod, Vienna (1865), p. 191).

2 See, for example, the responsum sent to the Jews of Rome and Lombardy published by F. Baer, *Die Juden im Christlichen Spanien* vol. II, Berlin (1936), no. 360.

3 Ben-Sasson, Generation, p. 23 n. 2. See especially: *Shevet Yehudah* [A. Shoḥat ed.], Jerusalem (1947), pp. 33-4.

4 For an additional factor see Y.H. Yerushalmi, "Clio and the Jews: Reflections on Jewish Historiography in the Sixteenth Century," *PAAJR Jubilee Volume*, Jerusalem (1980), p. 621.

5 For a detailed description of their *via dolorosa* until their final...forced baptism, see H. Graetz, *The History of the Jews* [Hebrew tran. by S.P. Rabinovitz] vol. 6, Warsaw (1898), vol. 6 pp. 378-93. S.W. Baron, *Social and Religious History of the Jews* vol. 11 (2nd ed.), Philadelphia (1967), pp. 245-48, and the recent and updated summary by Tishbi, Messianism, pp. 24ff.

6 See G. Scholem, *Major Trends in Jewish Mysticism*, New York (1961), pp. 244ff., and Y.H. Yerushalmi, Clio, pp. 607-38. For the the possibility of an indirect connection to Luria's Qabbalistic doctrine see below p. 153.

7 E.K. Ruth, p. 10b. About the term *hasid* see Y. Tishbi's, *Mishnat ha-Zohar* vol. II, Jerusalem (1961), pp. 655-63. (Rabbi Judah Ḥayyat calls his father *he-ḥasid* in his introduction to his *Minḥat Yehudah*, and Ibn Verga uses it to describe Rabbi Shem Tov ben Shem Tov (*Shevet Yehudah*, p. 119). Abraham Saba's father was still alive in 1485, as attested by a Spanish document (See below note 9).

8 In *Ẓeror ha-Ḥayyim*, fol. 38r, we read: וכתב זקני הרי יצחק ז"ל, נראה לי...עכ"ל But then he continues: שהרי יצחק הזקן רצה לכלול... This is an unusual way to refer to a grandfather. In addition, five lines earlier he quotes פיי הפרקים של הרי יצחק ישי ז"ל so that a scribal error is a possibility here. Nevertheless, the name Isaac fits "symetrically" into a family which had names such as Abraham and Jacob and two possible Isaacs (see below n. 103). It seems probable that Abraham Saba came from a distinguished family, considering the repeated emphasis on *yiḥus*, which, according to him, determines to a large extent one's personality and character through genetics and upbringing, (Ẓ.M. Lev, p. 29b. Num. p. 40b. Deut. p. 50a. É.K. Ruth pp. 6a, 39b. É.K. Esther, pp. 33, 36, 37, 43).

9 Four documents revolving around a death sentence to Rabbi Saul (Abraham's brother) by the municipal court of Zamora in 1485, were published by Baer (Die Juden vol. II, no. 351). Abraham registers a complaint to the Crown concerning his and his

father's arrest, maltreatment in jail and threats, since it was claimed that they had not confessed to all they knew about Saul's property (which was to be confiscated). Abraham also appealed the sentence (perhaps in order to reclaim the confiscated property, since Saul himself had evidently already been killed). He gathered evidence which, he claimed, would change the verdict. Finally, after being released, he asks for a *carta de seguro* to protect him against possible corporeal attack or property damage that he might suffer. From one document it seems that Abraham had more brothers (About Rabbi Samuel Valenci's testimony against Rabbi Saul in the trial see also Baer, History, p. 342, and A. Gross, "Rabbi Abraham Saba; 'Expelled in two Expulsions'," *Memorial Volume of Rabbi Yiẓhak Nissim, the Rishon le-Ẓion* vol. 4, Jerusalem, 1985, p. 206). We do not know whether Abraham's efforts were successful. However in Ẓ.M. we read: ומדרך המלך לשמוע ולתת אוזן למדברים לפניו אחר ששואלים משפט (Gen. p. 113a)

10 M.F. Ladero Quesada, "Apuntes para la historia de los Judios y conversos de Zamora en la edad media (siglos XIII-XV)," *Sefarad* 48 (1988), p. 56.

11 Luis S. Fernandes, *Documentos acerca de la Expulsion de los Judios*, Valladolid, 1964, pp. 65-72.

12 For a reference to the *yeshivah* in a Spanish source see ibid., p. 37 n. 34. Qanpanton's greatness and centrality as the man responsible for the flowering of the Castilian *yeshivot* in the 15th century, are recognized by all 16th century historiographers. He was responsible also for the new expanding rabbinic genre of *kelalim*. (He apparently did not write any halakhic works save, perhaps, the thin volume of *Darkei ha-Talmud* and it would seem to us that his gigantic stature also stood partially behind the fact that, contrary to the practice in the 13th and 14th centuries, most of the great scholars of that century did not write many commentaries on Talmudic tractates or codes, with the obvious exception of Rabbi Isaac Aboab). For a study of Qanpanton and the *yeshivot* see, A. Gross, "Rabbinic Academies in Castile in the 15th century," *Peàmim* 31 (1987) , pp. 3-21.

13 His greatest disciples were considered Rabbi Isaac de Leon, Rabbi Isaac Aboab and Rabbi Samuel Valenci. Rabbi Shimon Meme from Segovia and Rabbi Joseph Ḥayyun who was active in Lisbon, were apparently his disciples also (E. Qapsali, *Seder Éliyyahu Zuta*, Jerusalem, 1976, vol. I, chapter 55, p. 179. Ḥayyun's biblical commentaries show clear traces of Qanpanton's method). About the spread of Qanpanton's method of learning see H.Z. Dimitrovsky, "Rabbi Jacob Berav's Academy," *Sefunot*, 7 (1963), pp. 43-102. H. Bentov, "Methods of Study of Talmud in the Yeshivot of Salonica and Turkey After the Expulsion from Spain," *Sefunot* 13 (1971-78), pp. 5-102. On its influence on Ashkenazic methods see H.Z. Dimitrovsky, "About the Way of Pilpul," in *S.W. Baron Jubilee Volume* [Hebrew Section], Jerusalem (1975), pp. 111-181. A short analysis of the method was published by D. Boyaren, "On the Talmudic Method of the Exiles from Spain," *Peàmim* 2 (1979), pp. 73-82. See now Boyaren's book, *The Sefardi Ìyyun*, Jerusalem, (1989).

14 ז"ל המה הגיבורים אשר בדורנו... המעמיקים שקלא וטריא בהוויות דאביי ורבא עד היסוד בה... ונרוץ הגלגל ונהפכה מסבה ורוח ה׳ נשאתני ממקום חפצי ומקום רבצי סמורה יפה נוף ירכתי צפון. (Introduction to his Àqedat *Yiẓḥaq*, Presburg, 1849).

15 H. D. Friedberg, *The History of Hebrew Typography in Italy, Spain, Portugal etc.*, Tel-Aviv, 1956, pp. 91-7.

16 See the first chapter of our monograph: *Rabbi Joseph Ḥayyun: Leader of the Lisbon Jewish Community and His Works*, Ramat Gan, 1993.

17 He quotes a single comment of Qanpanton (Ẓ.M. Gen. p. 38b). We possibly find a trace of Qanpanton's method as elaborated in *Darkei ha-Talmud*, when Saba in one of his reference to Rashi says: ...ואי"כ איך היה יעקב רוצה להנות ממנו ולקבל ברכתו ומזה נשמר רש"י ואמר תודה לי על הברכות. (Ẓ.M. Gen. p. 92a). The method of studying Rashi in the method of "guarding" [*shemirah*], namely, looking for the problems and faulty alternative interpretations that Rashi avoided by his choice of interpretation and its precise wording, is prescribed originally in *Darkei ha-Talmud* (Vienna, 1878, p. 16). Rabbi Judah Khalaẓ and Rabbi Abraham Baqrat, as well as other contemporaries of Saba, applied this method in their supercommentaries on Rashi. See our study in *AJS Review* 18, 1993,

pp. 1-20). Saba, who describes the study of Torah as "the true happiness...the true ever-lasting reward...the true everlasting pleasure" (Ẓ.M. Gen. p. 82a, b), seems to speak enthusiastically about the method of *pilpul*: ן החכם בפלפולו משבר הרים הקשים ומחליקן בדברי פיו ולכן קראו שם החכמים סיני ועוקר הרים לפי שהם שוחקים ופוצצים הסלעים וההלכות הקשים והעמוקים... שידע בחכמתו להפשיט ולהחליק הדברים הקשים כאבן... החכם בחכמתו משנה פני אותו דבר העז והקשה, וכל זה בעיון נמרץ והשקפה נפלאה ובטורח גדול עד שמתישים כוחם. (ibid.. Cf. Rabbi Moses Al'ashqar in his *Responsa*, Jerusalem, 1959, no. 23).

He does have one reservation however, saying that it can lead to laxity in practical religious observance: לפי שידוע שיושבי הפרזים אין בינהם כ״כ תורה כמו בכרכים...ואע״פ שאין בהם תורה כ״כ הם שומרים המצוות ומדקדקים בהם יותר מהעוסקים בתורה, וזה לפי שהם הולכים בתמימות בדרכי התורה. אבל הלומדים מרוב חריפותם וחידודם הם מראים צדדים להיתר... וזה מצד הקושיות וההויות בענין שהבעל תורה הוא מורה היתר לעצמו ומראה פנים להיתר מתוך פלפולו. אבל מי שאינו חריף הוא תם וישר והולך בתמימות ושומר המצוה בלי פקפוק וגמגום. (E.K. Esther p. 92. Saba quotes *SeMaG*, positive no. 12). This is different of course from Yaàvez' criticism that blames the *pilpul* method for diverting students from what he terms as "piety." (*Ór ha-Ḥayyim*, Lublin (1912), introduction p. 2c). Compare also the positive assessment of *pilpul* by RaMA, according to whom the *heterim* it allows balance the built-in tendency of the Halakhah towards excessive stringency, (H.H. Ben-Sasson, *Haggut ve-Hanhagah*, Jerusalem, 1959, pp. 24-25), and that of Rabbi Efrayim Luntshitz, who is for the *pilpul* method despite the danger of the excessive laxity it might create (ibid pp. 28-9). For an interesting Qabbalistic positive interpretation of *pilpul* see *Kaf ha-Qetoret*, ms. Paris 845, fol. 131r.

18 Gross, Saba, p. 220.

19 The opinion that Saba was a medical doctor (Libowitz, p. 36, Manor, pp. 222-23) has no real basis in his own writings. On the other hand, one is impressed with his knowledge and understanding of royal customs [*nimusei malkhut*], court politics, and diplomatic tactics [*takhsisei malkhut*], which manifest themselves in Z.M. (Gen. pp. 33a-b, 50b ff, 58a, 90b, 106b, 111a, 112b ff. Ex. pp. 3b, 22b, 31a-b, 34a) and in E.K. Esther, (pp. 26,32, 60, 83, 94ff).

20 "I have preached this many a time before the Expulsion." (Ẓ.M. Ex. p.57b)

21 In a well-known and most interesting conclusion to a sermon of his he says: וזה היה כתוב בספר ארוכה (באריכות בספר צרור המור הראשון) ודרשתי אותו בקשטילייא בקיבוץ החכמים ושבחוהו. וחכם אחד מהמקובלים בזוהר היה מגמגם ואומר שנראה שהוא מהזוהר, ואמרתי לו *שאם ישלחהו אלי* עבידנא יומא טבא לרבנן, ולא ראיתיו עד הנה. ופשפשתי בספרי הזוהר ולא מצאתיו. (Ẓ.M. Gen. p. 99a, and below Appendix C). It seems from this that "the gathering of the scholars" was away from Saba's permanent home and thus away from Zamora (if he lived there then). As to the location, it is difficult to determine, but there is a description of Aboab's *yeshivah* in Guadalajara that might fit the "the gathering of scholars": ומצאתי שכתב הרב המובהק מהרר״י פאסי ז״ל שגדולי ספרד היו אומרים שטעות הוא שנפל בספרים בסוף לשוננו (של הרמב״ם)... והעיד ז״ל (ר״י פאסי) שלשון אברבאנל ז״ל בהיותו לומד בישיבת מהרר״י אבוהב, ושהרב מהרר״י פאסי ז״ל הגיד לפניהם יישוב זה ויכשר בעינהם מכל אשר הוגד שם. (*Kesef Mishneh*, Berakhot 3,8). A second possibility is a special gathering place. Here is a description of such a gathering by Rabbi Jacob Ibn Ḥabib: בימי חרפי זה מ״ה שנים או יותר היה ראש ישיבה בעיר שלמנק״ה ומורה הוראות בישראל החכם המופלא... יצחק דילאו״ן ז״ל. ויקר מקרה שם בעירו בחור ששידך ושלח סבלונות. אח״כ התבלבל הזיווג ורצה הרב הנזכר להחמיר ולהצריך גט, ולא הסכימו לסברתו חכמים זקנים אשר בדור ההוא... ולהסיר ספק צוו לש״ץ אשר בבה״כ הגדולה *באותו יריד* יכריז ויודיע לכל יושבי המלכות אשר ביריד הוא שכבר נמנו וגמרו שלא לחוש לסבלונות. (*Responsa Zera Ánashim*, Husiatin, 1902, no. 46, p. 36b). The fair in Medina del Campo where that legal decision was taken was the most important one in Spain in this period (J. Vicens Vives, "The Economies of Catalonia and Castile," *Spain in the Fifteenth Century 1369-1516* [R. Highfield ed.], New York, Evanston, San Francisco, London, 1972, p. 43). About the participation of Jews in that fair see now M. Fuencisla Garcia Casar, "Jewish Participation in Castilian Fairs: The Example of Medina del Campo in the Fifteenth Century," *Mediterrenean Historical Review* 6 no. 2 (1991), pp. 12-24.

If the term *qibbuẓ ha-ḥakhmim* was coined by Saba, then there is a passage that can throw some light on it: וזהו הקבצו ושמעו בני יעקב, לשמוע דברי חכמה ומוסר... ולכן אמר שם ויחן שם ישראל, כאיש אחד בקיבוץ אחד כמו שאמר כאן הקבצו ושמעו. (Ẓ.M. Gen. 123a).

As to Saba's story itself, our friend Professor Harry Fox has brought to our attention that it includes motifs that exist in midrashic sources. The story that most resembles it is to be found in *Megillat Taànit* [Z. Lichtenstein ed.], *HUCA* 8/9 (1932), p. 24. At any rate, all this does not discredit the reliability of Saba's story, though it is in his own praise.

22 Above n. 21.

23 Above n. 9.

24 Ladero Quesada, p. 53.

25 Ladero Quesada, p. 37 n. 34.

26 On the religious responsibility of the communal leaders to enforce the obedience of the commandments see Ẓ.M. Numbers, p. 43b. See also Saba's colorful description of the contemporary prostitute (ibid., Deut., p. 32b. Our edition talks about an "Ismaelite" or "Arab" prostitute, but mss. and earlier printed editions have "Gentile.") This reported act by Saba should be connected historically to a statement of his contemporary preacher, Rabbi Isaac Arama, a former resident of Zamora: וכמה פעמים נתחבטתי על זה על אודות הנשים הקדשות שהיה אסורן רופף בידי שופטי ישראל אשר בדורנו ולא עוד אלא שיאותו בקצת הקהלות ליתן להם חנינה (חניה?) ביניהם, גם יש שמספיקין להם פרס מהקהל כי אמרו כיון שמצילות את הרווקים או הסכלים מחטא אסור אשת איש החמור או מסכנת הגויות מוטב שיעברו על לאו זה משיבאו לידי אסור סקילה או סכנת שריפה. ואני דנתי על זה פעמים רבות לפניהם ולפני גדוליהם והסברתי להם שהחטא הגדול אשר יעבור עליו איש איש מבית למחות בו הנה הוא זמה ועון ישראל...אמנם החטא הקטן כשיסכימו עליו דעת הרבים והדת נתנה בבתי דיניהם שלא פלילי וחטאת הקהל כלו. (*Àqedat Yiẓḥaq*, Genesis, no. 20, p. 162a [The pagination is faulty]).

27 M. Kayserling, *Geschichte der Juden in Portugal*, Leipzig (1867), p. 112. There was a more northern crossing-point between Benavente and Braganza, but for only relatively few Jews. It is interesting to note that in the Spanish Crown's letter of October 10 1492, calling Jews to return from Portugal to Spain and convert to Christianity, Zamora was mentioned together with Badajoz in the south as one of the two locations designated for entry to the country and baptism (Fernandes, Documentos, pp. 487-9). Jewish communal property was seized in Zamora by the Crown immediately after the Expusion, and the synagogue became the Church of San Sebastian (Jose L. Lacave, "The Final Disposition of the Synagogues and Other Jewish Communal Property After the Expulsion," *Judaism* 43 (1992), pp. 244, 246.)

28 Gross, Saba, p. 220. On the importance of Guimarães in the Middle Ages see A.H. de Oliveira Marques, *History of Portugal* (2nd ed.) New York (1976), pp. 47, 89, 166. A Jewish community existed there at least from the fourteenth century (M.J. Pimenta Ferro, *Os Judeus em Portugal no Século XIV*, Lisboa (1970), pp. 38, 264). On the exact location of the community see: Idem, *Os Judeus em Portugal no Século XV* vol. I, Lisboa (1982), p. 103 n. 305. For a list of Jewish inhabitants of that community who are mentioned in 15th century Portuguese records, see: Idem, *Os Judeus em Portugal no Século XV* vol. 2, Lisboa (1984), pp. 155-61. It is difficult to determine the size of the community based on that data. In the 16th and 17th centuries we learn occasionally, mainly from Inquisitorial documents, of New Christians who came from there. Rachel Abravanel, Menasseh ben Israel's wife, was from Guimarães. (*Nishmat Ḥayyim*, Leipzig (1862), 3, 27, p. 86b).

29 He tells us that he composed his *Ẓeror ha-Kesef* in his youth (E.K. Esther p. 22, Ruth p. 10b). The first part of Ẓ.M. on Genesis was written just before the Expulsion from Spain when he lived "in Zamora at ease and settled on his lees" (Gross, Saba, p. 220. See Jer. 48,11. It might indicate that he grew up there). Thus, one cannot suggest that his entire literary work was the result of the Expulsion. (Concerning É.K. he says, however: והנה בהיותי בפורטוגאל...עלה בדעתי לפרש חמש מגילות ופרשתי אותם. (Esther, p. 22).

30 He tells us in rhymed prose about his healthy eyesight and unique library: לפי שהיה אור עיני אתי/ והיו אתי כל אומנותי/ ספרים עד אין מספר/ לא יאמינו כי יסופר/ מה שהיה לי מספר הזוהר והמאורות/ כפול ומכופל מכל מיני מהדורות/ ולא ידעתי ספורות/ בספרים מחודשים ממדרשות וספירות. (Gross, Saba, p. 220-21). The phrase "the light of my eyes" is to be understood literally, and not as referring to his son (Manor, Saba, p. 227). Saba's wide use of midrashic literature confirms the information he supplies here. (The same applies to his Qabbalistic library). Apparently he had in his possession midrashic sources that are no longer extant (L.

Ginzberg, *The Legends of the Jews*, Philadelphia (1954), index). One must note, however, that Ginzberg does not take into consideration the fact that Saba rewrote his book out of memory, hence it is not necessary to attribute every change from the known versions to a non-extant version that Saba supposedly owned. It seems to me also plausible to suggest that Saba had a midrash unknown to us on the story of Joseph and his brothers including Jacob's blessings, for this long section in Ẓ.M. contains a concentration of midrashic interpretations unknown from any other source. Compare a similar conjecture given by M.M. Kasher (*Torah Shelemah* vol. VII, New York (1950), pp. 1677, no. 47, 1679, n. 55).

Alongside many expressions of humility and talk in praise of this virtue, Saba's self-image was that of a scholar erudite in *Zohar* (Below App. C).

31 *Minḥat Yehudah*, Mantua (1558), introduction.

32 J. Hacker, "Some Letters on the Expulsion of the Jews from Spain and Sicily," p. 97. It is interesting to compare these figures with those of libraries in late Renaissance Italy which seem to have been smaller, despite the relative abundance of printed books in the 16th century (Z. Baruchson, *Private libraries of Jews in Northern Italy in Late Renaissance*, Ph.D. Dissertation, Bar-Ilan University, Ramat-Gan, 1985, p. 197).

33 In the same autobiographical passage he describes the manner of composing his books in Guimarães: הספרים שחברתי כתובים באצבע ידי/ חרוטים בעטי/ עד תום כחי/ ונוס ליחי/ הולך לאטי. Tishbi's interpretation of this phrase as describing his slow trip to Lisbon is not plausible (See Gross, Saba, p. 221, n. 29).

34 Saba tells us repeatedly that the second version of Ẓ.M. is much shorter than the first one, due to forgetfulness, shortage of books and lack of time (Ẓ.M. Gen. pp. 31b, 99a. Ex. pp. 21a, 32b. Deut. p. 56a. Also in his colophon at the end of Deuteronomy, (Manor, Saba, p. 230). See also below p. 41). He describes for us also the heavy supporting "footnotes" of Ẓ.M.: ועטרתיהו במרגליות הזוהר בכל פרשה ופרשה, ותקנתיהו בכל מיני מדרשות ואגדות, וציירתיהו בכל מיני טלוא ונקוד, מירושלמי ומכילתא וילקוט. (Gross, Saba, p. 220. The last word is missing in ms. Parma, but fits in the rhyme).

35 Ibid. p. 221.

36 ביתי נחלתי וכל מחמד עיני This seems to be the most explicit complaint about the loss of material possessions (See also above n. 19).

37 J. Osorio, *The History of the Portuguese during the Reign of Emmanuel*, London, 1752, pp. 28-9. The event was also described by Saba (below p. 23). Osorio continues his criticism of Emmanuel's "non-Christian" behavior following the description of the forced conversion in Lisbon (p. 30). For a detailed discussion of the major persecutions and of the Jewish reactions to them see: A. Gross, "The Ashkenazic Syndrome of Jewish Martyrdom in Portugal 1497" (*Tarbiẓ*, Forthcoming).

38 See Tishbi, Messianism p. 31-2.

39 On the fate of some of the books we read that in the fleet of Francisco d'Almeida, the first Portuguese viceroy in India, Francisco Pineiro also arrived. With the permission of King Manuel, he brought with him a box full of books. It was said that his father had collected them after the destruction of the synagogues and the forced-conversion. Thirteen Bibles or Scrolls of Torah (*brivias escritas em abraico*) were sold to the Jews in Kochin. The Jewish wife of the famous Jewish convert, Gaspar da Gama, was involved in that deal (E. Lipiner, *Gaspar da Gama; um converso na frota de Cabral*, Rio de Janeiro (1987), p. 193ff.). Some reached North Africa (A. Zacut, *Sefer Yoḥasin*, p. 220b). Others were saved by Jews (M. Benayahu, "A Source on the Spanish Refugees in Portugal and their Exit to Salonica," *Sefunot* 11 (1971), pp. 233-65))

40 Ibid. The phrase נהר פורטו as it appears in the printed edition of E.K. Esther (p. 22) is, no doubt, a scribal error.

41 ובאתי ללישבונה מחוץ לעיר וישבתי (Ibid.)

42 Ibid., and introductions to Ruth and Esther.

43 It seems clear that at this stage, without knowing its details, they suspected that a dark plot was being carried out against them.

44 Ibid. p. 222. In the introduction to Esther no help is mentioned (Printed edition p. 22, and ms. Warsaw 89/1, fol. 144). In the introduction to Ruth (p. 10b) we read:

והלכו עמי שני יהודים וחפרו תחת זית אחד וקברום שם (Cf. Genesis 22, 3. Could the biblical scene have influenced this version of Saba's account?)

45 It seems to me that he did not dig under the tree, but rather into a root of it, hoping that it be preserved there, ...וחפרתי בתוך זית גדול שהיה לו שרש גדול בארץ וטמנתי שם (ibid). Here we find an imprecision when compared to another version: ומיד הלכתי וטמנתי אותם תחת זית אחד זית רענן. (Introduction to Esther p. 22, and similarly in ms. Warsaw, and É.K. Ruth, p. 10b).

46. There seems to be another imprecision concerning the chronology. From the autobiographical passage in Ẓ.M. it appears that he lost his sons after the books, but in his introduction to Esther we read: לפי ששם קברתי כל מחמד עיני לפי שבהם הייתי מתנחם על שני בני שהיו קירות לבי שלקחום בעל כ־רחם להמיר דתם והייתי אומר הלא זה טוב לי מבנים ומבנות, ולא ראיתים יותר לפי שמיד השליכוני בבית הסוהר. (p. 22, and almost identically in his Introduction to Ruth p. 10b). From this it is clear that his sons were separated from him immediately, even before the burial scene. It is possible to say that he "comforted himself" in prison with the slim hope of somehow getting his books back. Nevertheless there is a consistent line of inconsistencies (albeit concerning minor details) in his autobiographical accounts. (See also above ns. 43, 44).

47 Presumably he means "daughters-in-law."

48 He might refer here to material belongings, like money. It is interesting to note that throughout his writings he mentions his wife only once - earlier in this passage, telling about the trip of the family to Lisbon. But whereas he mentioned the loss of his sons and daughters in Lisbon, there is no mention of his wife at all. It might be suggested that she converted without any outstanding resistance. This will help us understand two other problems: a. Saba does not note the special courage of the women in facing conversion as do Yaàvez (*Ór ha-Ḥayyim*, p. 32b), and the anonymous chronicler (A. Marx, "The Expulsion from Spain, Two New Accounts," *J.Q.R.* [o.s.] 20 (1908), p. 252); b. Saba's view of women is radically negative to an extent that one feels the need for biographical aid in explaining it (See mainly Ẓ.M. Gen. pp. 14a, 49b, 81a, 87b, 89b. Ex. p. 9b. Lev. p. 15a. Num. p. 20a).

49 The three additions of ms. Parma appear to be clarifying remarks by the scribe. An anonymous member of the group believed to be the direct cause of the King's special favour (Tishbi, Messianism, p. 35). Saba, who probably knew this, chose to ignore it, writing that the release was through the merit of Rabbi Shimon Meme who died in Lisbon as a martyr (Ẓ.M. Lev. p. 35a).

Herculano writes on the basis of a Portuguese source: "Tyranny recoiled before a constancy worthy of a better cause, and the government ordered that these seven or eight should be furnished a ship to carry them to Africa" (A. Herculano, *The Origin and the Establishment of the Inquisition in Portugal*, New York (1972), p. 124))

50 והייתי בכאן זמן רב חולה קלני מראשי ומעיני (סנהדרין מו א) To the best of my knowledge this text (together with the autobiographical story of Shem Tov Ibn Gamil) is among the earliest to prove the existence of a Jewish community in El Qsar el Kebir. Hirshberg's only note about the place in this period is that it was on the way to Fez. (H.Z. Hirshberg, *A History of the Jews in North Africa*, Jerusalem (1965) vol. I, p. 248). D. Corcos mentions it briefly ("Moroccan Jewry in the First Half of the 16th Century," *Sefunot* 10 (1966), p. 98, n. 236), as does J.M. Toledano, among other communities which were "taken over" by the *megorashim*. He does not refer to any sources and perhaps relies on later evidence. (*Ner ha-Maàrav*, Jerusalem, 1911, p. 69).

51 Two generations later it became the building of the Inquisition. Today it is the site of the National Theatre.

52 See the sources mentioned by Tishbi, pp. 29-30. The solution to the problem of how so many people could be put in so small an area becomes apparent from a 15th century drawing of the place, which also shows the huge yard behind the building. We also know the design of the interior of the building from its inquisitorial period (João P. Freire, *Lisboa do meu tempo e do passado*, Lisboa (1930?) vol. I, partes I, II]. That is not to say that the Jews felt comfortable there. The idea was to pressure them in every possible physical way. (Cf. Tishbi, p. 30 n. 51.)

[53] Tishbi, pp. 33, 35.

[54] Ms. Oxford, colophon in the end of Deuteronomy. He refers to the constant miracles God performs for those who cross the high seas (Ẓ.M. Deut. p. 5a).

[55] Ẓ.M. Deut. p. 69b, and see also ibid. Gen. p. 37a. The last phrase is from Job 33, 20. He uses the next verse to describe his sickness in Fez. See below n. 70.

[56] Corcos says that existed a small Jewish community in Arzila. However it is not clear whether he refers to the end of the 15th century or only to the 16th (Corcos, Moroccan Jewry, p. 74).

[57] J.M. Toledano, *HUCA* 5 (1928), pp. 403-409. It is not entirely clear whether it happened before or after the Expulsion from Navarre (1498). See Toledano, p. 408. Cf. J. Hacker, "The Nagidate in North Africa in the End of the 15th century," *Ẓion* 45 (1980), p. 119).

[58] Relying on the anonymous member of the group, they were sent off in the beginning of February, and Saba arrived at El Qsar el Kebir through Arzila between February-May 1498. His colophon in Ẓ.M. between Numbers and Deuteronomy (ms. Oxford) tells us that he started his commentary on the latter in Fez on the 22nd of Tamuz 5259 (30.6.1499). On the 2nd of Íyyar (2.5.1499), he finished the commentary on Exodus, still in El Qsar el Kebir. Thus he remained there 12-16 months. Most probably he wrote the commentary on Leviticus and possibly the whole commentary on Numbers before the move to Fez, for he tells us that as soon as he came there he took sick and lay in bed for 5 months until Hanukkah (28.11-5.12. 1499) (Ẓ.M. Deut. p. 126, and Manor p. 220, n. 57), which means that he lay in bed from the beginning of July; and if he commented on Numbers in Fez, then he must have arrived there at least a month before his illness (allowing a month for the writing, since there were two months between the end of Exodus and the beginning of Deuteronomy).

[59] Ms. Oxford, colophon in the end of Exodus. Here we find another inconsistency in the careless manner Saba recounts his life story: ועמדתי שם מרעיד קרוב לשישה חודשים. ואחר שזיכני השם ... והביאני למלכות פאס עלה בדעתי להחזיר עטרה ליושנה ולזכור קצת ממה שהיה כתוב שם. (E.K. Esther, p. 22). Thus, he skips altogether his stay in El Qsar el Kebir, saying that the thoughts of rewriting his works came to him only in Fez, unless he considers El Qsar el Kebir part of the "kingdom of Fez."

[60] R. le Tourneau, *Fez in the Age of the Marinides*, Oklahoma (1961), pp. 114-5.

[61] ibid., p. 119.

[62] Ross E. Dunn, *The Adventures of Ibn Battuta a Muslim Traveler of the 14th Century*, Berkeley (1986), p. 25.

[63] R. Brunschvig, *Deux Recites de Voyage inédits en Afrique du Nord au XV siécle*, Paris (1936), pp. 116ff.

[64] Rabbi Abraham Ardutiel, *Hashlamat Sefer ha-Qabbalah*, in *Two Chronicles from the Generation of the Expulsion from Spain* [A. David ed.], Jerusalem (1979), p. 38.

[65] ibid., p. 39.

[66] We are told that some returned to Spain and converted to Christianity. Others converted to Islam. Still, the rapid manner in which the majority returned to normal life and activities, cultural and literary included, is remarkable. This has not been sufficiently emphasized by scholarship that has stressed the long lasting traumatic effect of the Expulsion.

[67] Rabbi H. Gagin, *Èẓ Ḥayyim* [M. Amar ed.], Ramat Gan (1987), pp. 68-9. (Cf. Corcos, Moroccan Jewry, p. 100). Leo Africanus tells us that the number of the Jews increased tremendeously in the middle of the 16th century "since they were expelled from Spain." (*The History and Description of Africa* [R. Brown ed.], London (1896), p. 477). As to the estimated size of the Jewish population towards the mid-16th century according to non-Jewish sources, see Corcos, p. 100. We can learn that the number of the Toshavim around 1530 was probably less than 1,000 (Gagin, *Èẓ Ḥayyim*, p. 107 n. 53.) Generally on the situation described above see mainly the pioneering work of M.J. Toledano, *Ner ha-Maàrav*, Jerusalem, 1911 [reprinted, Jerusalem, 1973], and the Corcos article, pp. 93 ff.).

[68] He complains about his lack of books in El Qsar el Kebir: שאין לי ספרים מספרי התלמוד

והמדרשות והזוהר ולא ספר אחר זולת חמשה חומשי תורה. (Gross, Saba, p. 233, and also Gen. pp. 6b, 86b). He seems to have exaggerated a bit, for still in El Qsar el Kebir he writes: ובזה הייתי מתנבא ואיני יודע ... ועכשיו זיכני ה׳ ומצאתי מאמר אחד מסייע לדברי. (Ẓ.M. Gen. p. 124a). If this is a later addition in Fez, then he would have added it at the proper place in *Vayeẓe*. This seems to be the case with a similar statement one page later (p. 125a). Therefore these quotations have no bearing on the problem of the statement concerning *Ẓeror ha-Kesef* הלא הוא בפאס העיר הגדולה (Ẓ.M. Gen. p. 47a), which could not have been written in El Qsar el Kebir. See below p. 78).

69 See below n. 121.

70 He tells us about it in Z.M. Deut. p. 12b. Thus he wrote only a few pages prior to his illness.

71 Ms. Oxford fol. 348, at the end of the sermon he gave (in the printed edition of Ẓ.M. Deut. p. 15b): זהו מה שעלה בדעתי כשהייתי חולה ומוטל על המטה, למה נקרא זה המועד חנוכה. ודרשתי אותו שקמתי מחוליי במועד חנוכה של שנת ששים וראיתי לכותבו כאן בפרשת היחוד. The description of his illness survived in the Oxford ms.: ועמדתי כמו חמשה חדשים במטה מחולי מעיים בדם ואש ותמרות עשן, עד שכלה בשרי ועורי מרואי ושופי עצמותי לא ראו. (Ẓ.M. Deut. p. 12b). About its seriousness he writes that he ended his sermon saying: שכפי הטובות שקיבלתי מהי׳ שהחייני וקיימני ראוי לי לתת תודה להי׳ ולעשות הגומל... אחר שהי׳ עשה עמי ניסים גדולים והראה כי תחיית המתים בכח יכלתו וגבורתו. (ibid, p. 13a).

72 Ms. Oxford, colophon in the end of Deuteronomy.

73 In the end of the long colophon, he tells us that he completed it on the 2nd of Sivan 5260 (30.4.1500) (Gross, Saba, p. 224).

74 He arrived at El Qsar el Kebir in February-May 1498, and finished his commentaries probably around the High Holidays in September 1500. He was sick in El Qsar el Kebir "for a long time", and another five months in Fez, which leaves about one and a half years for his writing. He intended to write more: וברוך הי׳ אשר זיכני לחזור ולפרש... ופירוש מגילת רות ופירוש מגילת אסתר. ומהי׳ אשאל עזר לגמור פירוש שאר מגלות ושאר ספרים שדעתי עליהם. (É.K. Esther (introd.) p. 22). He seems to have indicated satisfaction at his fast pace, after writing less than half of his commentary on Genesis: לפי שזקני תורה כל זמן שמזקינים דעתם מתיישבת עליהם ויותר עושים בשנה אחת משני הזקנה ממה שעושים בכל השנים הראשונים. (Ẓ.M. Gen. p. 50a). At this point he was not young any more, and we should take his autobiographical declaration literally: והזקנה נתוספת בי (É.K. Esther p. 22). That would definitely be so if Saba had heard from Qanpanton himself the interpretation he quotes in his name (Ẓ.M. Gen. p. 38b. It is impossible to determine this from the text, but both men lived in Zamora and the possibility exists. Qanpanton died in 1463. Cf. Manor, Saba, p. 210).

75 His mental stamina is attested to by the relentless effort of rewriting his lost works. It would be a mistake to take his word at face value when he claims to have been comforted by his literary creation:.והייתי אומר הלא זה טוב לי מבנים ומבנות (É.K. Esther, p. 22 and Ruth p. 10b). Even in Lisbon, before his physical sufferings, it is hard to believe that he truly felt that way. In El Qsar el Kebir he sums up his weary state: משני גרושין על לוח לבי כתובות ושמורות/ עד אשר לבי ורוחי וכוחי עלי הומות/ ועיני כהות/ ולבגד ארגמן דומות. (Ms. Oxford, colophon at the end of Exodus). And at the end of his commentary on Avot, written in Fez, he repeats: אני הדל באלפי צעיר התלמידים אברהם סבע... המגורש בשני גרושים. (Gross, Saba, p. 229). The memory of his sons comes up in every extant introduction. Saba also left us the following poetic lines: וראיתי אותו כותב בפירוש זה המזמור שפירש יעקב בני אשר עליו לבי מאד חמרמר/ ואען ואומר/ הנה לשלום מר לי מר/ אשר גזלו אותי ואנסוהו בפורטוגאל. (É.K. Ruth, p. 42b).

76 Similar sentiments we hear from other contemporaries who had lost their children. On the problem and reactions of the Sefardim to the loss of children during the wanderings of the refugees and the special continuous awareness of it in the following generations, see J. Hacker, "Pride and Depression - Polarity of the Spiritual and Social Experience of the Iberian Exiles in the Ottoman Empire," in *Medieval and Society in Medieval Jewry, Studies Dedicated to the Memory of Haim Hillel Ben-Sasson* [M. Ben-Sasson, R. Bonfil, J. Hacker ed.], Jerusalem (1989), pp. 541-86.

77 See above n. 74.

78 See below our discussion of the themes of despair and consolation. One must also

admire his energetic activity as a preacher as soon as he arose from his sick-bed: וזה דרשתי בכל בתי כנסיות של קהל פאס אחר שעמדתי מחוליי, כי בעוונותי כשבאתי לכאן מיד נפלתי חולה. (Ẓ.M. Deut. p. 12b). The *megorashim* had four Synagogues in Fez in 1497. (Rabbi Abraham Anqawa, *Kerem Ḥemer* vol. 2, Livorno (1871), p. 3b).

79 See Libowitz, p. 36-7, and *Qiryat Sefer* 5 (1929), p. 176. (And see *Livnat ha-Sappir*, Jerusalem (1913), p. 2a. It seems that Saba wrote a commentary on Psalms).

80 Gross, Saba, p. 213 n. 39.

81 It is refered to by RaDBaZ in his *Responsa*, Livorno (1652), no. 55, p. 11a. (A. Gross, "The Qabbalistic Commentary on the Prayers Attributed to Rabbi Abraham Saba," *Asufot* 1 (1987), pp. 189-197). As to the identification of the above mentioned Alal, see Gross, Saba, p. 213, n. 39. M. Ḥalamish, in a bibliographical article, mentions another page Ms. British Museum 10521 fol. 2.) attributed to Rabbi Abraham Ẓaba. ("The Qabbalists of Morocco," *Daàt* 16 [1986], p. 94) It deals with the Qabbalistic meaning of *Kedushah.* Although the style is not characteristic of Saba and there is no discussion of this prayer in his writings, it is possible that it is authentically his

We know of one disciple of Saba's who wrote a commentary on the Torah twice as long as his master's (Ms. Budapest, Kaufman Collection, A 19). Many times he quotes Ẓ.M. starting "And my teacher wrote". (Gen. p. 76, 91. Lev. pp. 425, 617 and many more). It contains 2147 sides (and that is not all, for big parts of the commentary on Exodus and Leviticus are missing). If this author is not Rabbi Alal ben Alḥa'ikh then we know of two disciples. Although there is no evidence that Saba had a *yeshivah*, one short poetic passage, judging from its tone, seems to indicate that he had at least a small group of students whom he taught in Spain or Portugal (since the passage was written in El Qsar el Kebir): וזהו התענוג האמיתי כשהוא יושב בישיבתו וכל צבא השמים והתלמידים עומדים עליו מימינו ומשמאלו והוא יושב ושבע מקול הקורא. (Ẓ.M. Gen. p. 82b).

82 H.H. Ben-Sasson, "An Elegy on the Expulsion from Spain," *Tarbizẓ*31 (1961), p. 63.

83 A. Gross, "Rabbi Judah Khalaẓ in Tlemcen: Judeo-Iberian Culture in North Africa," *Exile and Diaspora, Studies in Jewish History Presented to Professor Haim Beinart*, Jerusalem (1988), p. 359.

84 Tishbi, Messianism, pp. 37-8.

85 A. Shoḥat, "Rabbi Abraham Zacut in Jerusalem," *Ẓion* 13-14 (1948-49), pp. 43-6. About Rabbi Abraham ben Eliezer Halevi's wandering from Portugal through Tlemcen see Tishbi, Messianism, p. 38 n. 89.

86 pp. 667-72. See also ibid., p. 694 n. 20.

87 pp. 668-9.

88 Toledano, p. 406.

89 M. Beit-Arieh and M. Idel, "Rabbi Abraham Zacut's Maámar al ha-Qeẓ veha-Iẓtagninut," *Qiryat Sefer* 54 (1979), pp. 174-94.

90 Gross, Khalaẓ, pp. 357-9.

91 מרנא ורבנא, נר אלוהים, אור ישראל וקדושו, רבי מורי ועטרת ראשי... זה לי עשרה ימים חליתי מחולי מיעיים והגעתי עד שערי מות, ומלאך מליץ וזכות קדושתך סגר הדלת בעדי. ברוך רופא חולים ברוך הוא... ואני נושק כפות רגלי קדושתך וכפות ידי קדושת הישיבה החבורה הקדושה. מאת קטן תלמידיך הקטנים נרצע אברהם צבע. *Mayyim Àmuqqim*, Berlin (1778), No. 25, 26 (and in the index no. 24, 25).

92 The spelling צבע is of no significance for we find besides סבע also צבע (RaDBaZ, *Responsa*, Livorno, 1652, no. 55, p. 11a. In the Warsaw edition 1882, vol. 2, no. 1127, it was corrected to סבע), and צבח (E.K. Ruth, ms. Warsaw, 89/1 fol. 14v. This is the only one to spell Lisbon in the correct phonetic form לישבואה).

93 Manor, Saba, pp. 221-24.

94 *Responsa Zera Ánashim*, no. 43. The responsum was written by Rabbi Jacob Ibn Ḥaviv. It is interesting to note the similarities in the fates of Saba and Ibn Ḥaviv. Rabbi Jacob Ibn Ḥaviv, who studied in the *yeshivah* in Zamora, came to Lisbon. In 1497(?) his son, Levi, was forcibly converted to Christianity. The father might have belonged to that elite group which was jailed in Lisbon (Tishbi, Messianisn, p. 46-9). If this is correct then he came with Saba to North Africa, but this chapter of his biography is not known. He reached Turkey, where his son eventually joined him after es-

caping from Portugal. It would appear that the experiences and itinerary of both were almost identical. (About the return of Saba's son to Judaism see below).

95 Ibid., p. 33b.

96 J. Hacker, "Rabbi Jacob b. Solomon Ibn Ḥaviv - An Analysis of Leadership in the Jewish Community of Salonika in the 16th Century," in *Proceedings of the Sixth Congress of Jewish Studies* vol. 2, Jerusalem, 1975, p. 121 n. 9.

97 *Èẓ Ḥayyim*, p. 50-1 n. 155.

98 Joseph Sambari, *Divrei Yosef*, Jerusalem, 1981, p. 143. Although Sambari tells quite a few stories, especially about 15th century Spanish rabbis, this story is unique. Moreover, as Manor has suggested, at least the fact of his death aboard ship seems to be earlier than Sambari's embellished account and was known as early as 1587 (Manor, Saba, pp. 224-6. His argument, however, is not without a measure of conjecture. See also M. Amar's corrections in *Èẓ Ḥayyim*, p. 50 n. 155).

The image of Saba portrayed in this story could be reflected in the scribe's Introduction to Saba's commentary on Ruth ms. Oxford (Bodley 2349): המובהק הענו המקובל האלהי

99 Ẓ.M., Ẓ.K., Ẓ.H.

100 This expression refers to western and central Europe, and especially, Italy and France. [See e.g. *Responsa Zera Ánashim*, no. 36, p. 23b].

101 Obviously he does mean Spain, but rather a burial in a Jewish cemetery.

102 This seems to be the biggest problem with this account, for Verona has no port, nor is it close to one. Venice, for example, would have been a much better choice.

103 The Biblical background of the book of Jonah is obvious as is the connection to the Day of Atonement, when this book is being recited in the afternoon. (The author of the story left it up to the reader's imagination to picture the captain of the ship entering the synagogue during the recital of the Biblical story...).

104 Rabbi Isaac Saba, *Qarnei Reémim*, Salonica (1802), p. 30a. Rabbenu ben Rabbi Eliyyahu of Qastoria, *Áderet Éliyyahu*, Venice, 1622 (See M. Benayahu, *The Relations between Greek and Italian Jewry*, Tel Aviv, 1980, p. 133). For a Rabbi Jacob ben Abraham Saba who signed a communal ordinance in Salonica in 1533, see *REJ* 41 (1900), p. 260, no. 19. He was of the community of Spanish exiles as is obvious from the text. (See also ibid. p. 105.) To round off the known Sabas in the first half of the century, we should make mention of Rabbi Isaac, Rabbi Joseph Caro's father-in-law, who lived in Adrianople. (*Beit Yosef* Ó.Ḥ., 425). According to S. Rosanes' conjecture, he was Rabbi Abraham's brother (*The History of the Jews in Turkey*, Tel-Aviv, 1930, p. 107. See also Manor, Saba, p. 244). Qaro does mention Rabbi Abraham Saba and Ẓ.M. in a homiletical passage, but he does not refer to him as a relative (*Ór Ẓaddiqim*, Warsaw (1902), p. 77). We find a Rabbi Samuel Saba, who appears to have lived in Adrianople and was an important scholar (*Responsa MaHaRIT* È.È. 3, part 2, Tel Aviv, 1959). Abraham Saba mentioned as a witness in a responsum from Damascus in 1589 is not identical to the subject of this study (*Responsa* of Rabbi Yom Tov Ẓahalon, Venice (1694), no. 104).

105. Z.M. Gen. p. 26a. In contemporary literature *ha-mayyim ha-zedonim* means baptism or the nations hostile to Israel (See Ẓ.M. Genesis, p. 7a. Due to censorship this edition is incomplete).

106 See above p. 78-9.

107 The conversion efforts on the part of the Crown started with the kidnapping of young children who were sent to São Tomé (unless their parents converted), as early as 1493. The island which was discovered by Portuguese navigators in 1470 is off the equator in the Gulf of Guinea. At that time it was volcanically active and densely forested. This was the second attempt to settle it. The first one (1485) failed. Most Jewish contemporary sources refer to it. Ruy de Pina connects it to the termination of the eight months' stay that had been given to most of the refugees. He tells us also about the colonial success of the move: "Moreover, because he commanded that all who were minors, boys and girls, were to be taken captives from among those Castilian Jews in his kingdoms and leave within the appointed time according to the conditions of their entrance; after commanding all of them to become Christians, he sent them to the said

island...so that being separated they might be better Christians. And it was as a result of this that the island became more densely populated and began to thrive exceedingly." (*Chronica del Rey Dom João II* [J. Correa da Serra ed.] in *Colleccao de livros ineditos de historia portugueza* vol. I, Lisbon (1790), ch. 68.)

108 This is correct for other refugees who also went through the Portuguese bitter experience. See e.g. A. Gross, "The Ten Tribes and the Kingdom of Prester John - Rumors and Investigations before and after the Expulsion from Spain," *Peàmim* 48, 1991, p. 31-3)

109 See above nn. 74, 78.

110 Introduction to Ruth (p. 10b), to Esther (p. 22), to *Sons' Glory* (Gross, Saba, pp. 220-3), as well as the colophon at the end of Ẓ.H. (ibid. p. 224) and in the end of Ẓ.M. (Ms. Oxford, Manor, Saba, p. 230).

111 Ẓ.M. Gen. p. 114b.

112 Ibid., Deut. p. 15b.

113 Ibid., Deut. pp. 47b, 85b. See also Ẓ.M. Deut. pp. 14b, 60a. É.K. Ruth, p. 23a.

114 ועל זה אמר אספדה ואילילה אלכה ערום בלבוש שק ולא אתנחם כל ימי וארד על בני אבל שאולה אחר שאני הרגתיו. (Ibid., Gen. p. 101b).

115 See below p. 23.

116 See S. Usque, *Consolation for the Tribulation of Israel* [M. Cohen ed.] Philadelphia, 1965, p. 201. Saba's presentation of the decree is more objective (Cf. above n. 106).

117 Ẓ.M. Deut. p. 46b. The anonymous chronicler interprets it in the same manner (Marx, *JQR* 20, 1908, p. 251).

118 See also Ẓ.M. Deut. pp. 14b, 60a. E.K. Ruth, p. 23a.

119 See above n. 67.

120 The literature on the use of psycho-analytical concepts in the service of literary and historical analysis is immense, as are the problems with this school. However we do not see our following attempt as part of such methods. All we do is use a commonsensical approach that does not have to agree with radical use of the psycho-analytical discipline.

121 On the psychological need of the survivor to recount his experience see Robert J. Lifton, *Death in Life, Survivors of Hiroshima*, New-York, Toronto (1967), p. 482. (In addition to the introductions and other relevant published passages, we read in ms. Oxford (in the Warsaw edition, Gen. p. 69a. The part in parenthesis was deleted): והנם כתובים בספרי הזוהר ואינם בידי כי נגזלו ממני בעונותי בגירוש פורטוגאל. [ואני הצעיר אברהם סבע נשארתי ערום מבלי רכוש ונמלטתי לארץ ישמעאל בחמלת ה׳ עלי ברוך הוא ומבורך. ועכ״ז אין ראוי שענין אלו הבארות ילכו ערומים בלי לבוש] ונראה שזאת הפרשה קשורה עם שלמעלה...

Although Lifton deals with reactions to physical death on a large scale as at Hiroshima, in the Holocaust, the Black Death, etc., it seems permissible to us to extend some of the generalizations to a spiritual disaster. This was the case with the Expulsions since a large part of the nation died a spiritual death by conversion (and in a way, a physical death too, since the number of Jews was reduced drastically). This is true not only of the Jews in Portugal, who were converted *en mass,* but also of the Jews of Spain, many of whom remained behind and accepted Christianity, while others who could not endure the tribulations on their way at sea and on land and in the places they reached, decided to return to their homeland and homes. (Bernaldes enjoys recounting at length the circumstances in Fez that caused many to return to Spain. But while he most probably exaggerated, this phenomenon cannot be questioned, for we do have references to it in Hebrew sources, and not only concerning Fez. The Spanish royal documents calling the Jews to come back were not detached from reality). The remnants must have felt like survivors. This is certainly true of a sensitive medieval Jewish preacher who survived all the calamities described above and who cared deeply for the fate of his people and religion. To be sure, some of the reactions described by Lifton are unique to the particular catastrophe he had investigated, but with proper caution and attention to the differences in circumstances and the nature of the disaster, it is possible to draw phenomenological parallels. For a study using tools similar to those suggested here, by F.

Talmage, "Trauma of Tortosa: The Testimony of Abraham Rimoch," *Mediaeval Studies* 47 (1985), pp. 384, 409.

122 see J. Hacker, "The Spiritual Image of the Jews in Spain in the 15th Century," *Sefunot* [n.s.] 2 (1983), pp. 29-35, 73-82. On preaching and history, see the general introduction in M. Saperstein, *Jewish Preaching 1200-1800: An Anthology*, New-Haven & London, 1989, pp. 79-89.

123 *Seder Éliyyahu Zuta* vol. I, Jerusalem, 1976, chapters 67-69. See also J. Hacker, "Some Letters on the Expulsion of the Jews from Spain and Sicily," *Studies in the History of Jewish Society in the Middle Ages and in the Modern Period* [E. Etkes, Y. Salmon ed.] Jerusalem (1980), pp. 90-2.

124 Also the historical fact was that the edict was signed in the month of Adar (Qapsali, ch. 68. Ben-Sasson, "An Elegy on the Expulsion from Spain," pp. 63, 67. Also see Baer, History, pp. 468-9).

125 I will describe Mordecai in the context of Saba's social criticism.

126 É.K. Esther p. 24.

127 Ibid. p. 23.

128 Ibid. p. 27.

129 Ibid. p. 28.

130 Ibid. p. 65. For the term *hafakhpakh* see B.T. Megillah 15b.

131 Ibid. p. 67.

132 Ibid. p. 29.

133 Qapsali, incidently, explicitly compares Ferdinand to Ahasuerus (Seder, ch. 67, p. 205). The influence of the Church and particularly of the Grand Inquisitor, Thomas de Torquemada, on the upholding of the decision is, apparently, an historical fact). Another identical point is that their claims to the kingdom were questionable unlike their queens (On Ferdinand and Isabel, see Qapsali, ch. 56, 57, 59, 67. On Ahasuerus, B.T. Megillah, 10b).

134 See B. Walfish, *Esther in Medieval Garb: Jewish Interpretation of the Book of Esther in the Middle Ages*, New York, 1993, pp. 183ff. The author sees the conflict in Saba's portrayal of Ahasuerus as a tension between midrashic and medieval influences (ibid. p. 189).

135 Gross, Saba, p. 220.

136 The sin of eating and drinking willfully at Ahasuerus' feast already appears in B.T. Megillah 12a, (Saba has also an exegetical problem for which this is a solution, namely, the connection between the feast and the main part of the book). Nonetheless, this is another similarity, since Jews in Spain on most social levels, partook in meals with Gentiles (e.g. H. Beinart, *Trujillo*, Jerusalem, 1980, p. 89). In some cases, despite some anger expressed against the Crown, we find that the Jews accepted the edict as a decree which the king had the right to issue, and saw in it a divinely ordained punishment by the means of the earthly king. (See Y.H. Yerushalmi, *The Lisbon Massacre of 1506*, Cincinnati, 1976, pp. 52-58. Tishbi, Messianism, p. 20 n. 29.)

137 E.K. Ruth, p. 10b.

138 E.K. Esther, p. 60. Saba follows here the Targum (Walfish, Esther in Medieval Garb, p. 161).

139 Ibid., p. 65.

140 Ibid., p. 66. This opinion is shared also by Arama, who says in the introduction to his *Àqedat Yiẓḥaq*: חכמיה שרים בכל חכמה ותושיה אלופים לראש הפילוסופיא, ופום ממלל רברבן על דתם ואמונתם. Similarly we find in *Kaf ha-Qetoret*, which was apparently written by a Spanish refugee: יכרות ה׳ כל שפתי חלקות לשון מדברת גדולות, אלו הכומרים הדורשים כנגד היהודים אשר בערי הפרזות ועל ידם בא קלקול גדול לישראל (fol. 16r). As for the two manifestations of hatred of the nations towards Israel, see Maimonides, *Epistle to Yemen* [ed. A.S. Halkin] New York (1952), pp. 9-11, 94-7. (Compare also ibid pp. 23-25 and Ẓ.M. Gen. p. 66a).

141 É.K. Esther, p. 23, 67.

142 Ibid. p. 28. Similarly, Arama in his commentary cannot comprehend this "naturally absurd" decree.

143 Ibid. p. 67. This is taken from Nachmanides' comments on Ex. 1,10.

[144] Ibid. p. 67. The notion that Mordecai was already a courtier is already expressed by Ibn Ezra (Esther, 2,9).

[145] Ibid. p. 68. This new motif is of special importance in the unfolding drama, taking place between the announcement of the edict and its annulment. Saba repeats this point several times, a fact that, as a rule, shows the significance of the idea for the author.

[146] Ibid., p. 86-7. Saba generalizes that "the common people hate Israel" (ibid., p. 73). Compare a similar view concerning the pogroms of 1391, P. Wolff, "The 1391 Pogrom in Spain Social Crisis or Not?" *Past and Present* 50 (1971), pp. 4-18 (and especially p. 16), and A. McKay, "Popular Movements and Pogroms in 15th century Castile," *Past and Present* 55 (1977), pp. 33-67. This notion also appears in the Hebrew literature of that period.

[147] É.K. Esther, p. 73.

[148] Ibid.

[149] Ibid. p. 84.

[150] Ibid. p. 68.

[151] In Spain we find an order to officials in Barcelona, which reflects the pressures (also physical) to which the Jews were subjected. (Baer, *Die Juden* vol. 1, no. 566). Qapsali relates that "In those frightful days, if a Jew owed money to a Gentile, they would hit him with sticks and lashes..." (*Sede*r, ch. 69, p. 210). We do not possess any information about the corresponding period in Portugal but there is no reason to believe that it was better.

[152] Saba, relying on the Aramaic translation, says that in the interim period the Jews were not allowed to occupy themselves with the study of Torah, nor to keep certain commandments such as the Sabbath, Phylacteries, etc. (É.K. Esther, p. 89). Some of it is identical to some of the decrees in the transition period in Portugal. See e.g. Ẓ.M. Deuteronomy, pp. 15b-16a. Tishbi, Messianism, p. 26-7.

[153] See e.g. *Sefer Ḥasidim* [J. Wistinetsky ed.], Frankfurt (1924), p. 84 no. 257.

[154] E.K. Esther, p. 23. See B.T Avodah Zarah p. 10b.

[155] Ibid. p. 73.

[156] Ibid. p. 75. Elsewhere he recommends intercession by bribery, "...for by means of presents and taxes [*ha-minḥot veha-árnuniot*] they can walk after them (i.e. the presents etc.) straight into the king's palace, and this is the meaning of 'I will appease him with the present,' as it says 'A gift in secret subdues anger; a present in private, fierce rage'" (Ẓ.M. Gen. p. 91a). Saba also learns from Jacob that submission and flattery of the strong Gentile is to be considered a positive political maneuver (Ẓ.M. Gen. pp. 62b, 90a,b).

[157] The plea for tolerance stressing the utility of the Jews is still the basis of Simone Luzatto's plea on behalf of the Jews of Venice in 1638.

[158] É.K. Esther, pp. 39-40. Rabbi Joseph Ḥayyun's answer is that the end of helping Israel sanctified the means (although this was prior to Haman's decree). He supports it even with an Halakhic source "Desecrate for him (a person in danger) one Sabbath so that we might keep many Sabbaths." (Ms. Moscow, Ginzburg Collection, 168/2. fol. 71a ff). This is a general justification for religious permissiveness by the courtiers (See below p. 119 n.79). "Saba's misgivings are the exception, and the general feeling among the exegetes is that Esther was placed in her royal position by an act of divine providence" (Walfish, Esther in Medieval Garb, pp. 123-4).

[159] Ibid., p. 22.

[160] Gross, Saba, p. 222.

[161] Esther, 8, 16.

[162] Ibid., 4,3, and Qapsali (Seder, ch. 69, p. 203).

[163] Esther, 8, 17.

[164] Qapsali (Seder, ch. 69, p. 210).

[165] On the way the Jews conceived of the "Royal Alliance" see, Y.H. Yerushalmi, The Lisbon Massacre, pp. 37ff.

[166] É.K. Esther, p. 91.

[167] Ibid. p. 97. This comes as the antithesis to Saba's repeated complaint about the overload of taxes, "...not like the kings of the nations who demand taxes from Israel, more than they are able to (collect and pay) and they strip their skin off them... and when they pay one (tax) they demand another." (ibid. p. 13).

[168] Ibid. p. 97.

[169] Ibid.

[170] See also the closing paragraph in A. Gross, "The Reflection of the Expulsions from Spain and Portugal in a Commentary on Esther," *Proceedings of the Ninth World Congress for Jewish Studies*, Section B vol. I, Jerusalem (1986), p. 158.

[171] Gross, Saba, pp. 220ff.

[172] Gross, The Ten Tribes, pp. 31-3.

[173] Hacker, pp. 25, 74.

[174] A. David, "An Unknown Dirge on the Expulsion from Spain," *Peàmim* 49 (1992), pp. 24-31. See also H. Shirman, "Elegies etc." *Qoveẓ àl Yad* [n.s.] 3 (1939), pp. 69-74. Rabbi David Ibn Yaḥya, a native of Lisbon, naturally mentions in his long elegy the Expulsion from Spain in a single line and then concentrates on the destruction of the community of Lisbon in almost forty (A.M. Haberman, *Óẓar Yehudei Sefarad* 5 (1962), pp. 11-16).

[175] The Ben-Ẓvi Institute ms. 2125 fol. 6r-6v. Ms. 2157 fol. 28v- 29r. See also ibid., fol. 63v.

CHAPTER TWO

THE EXEGESIS OF A QABBALISTIC PREACHER

Since in quantitative terms more than half of our study concerns itself with central issues and themes reconstructed from Saba's writings, notably Ẓ.M., a preliminary note of caution is in order. Beyond any particular issue or theme, Ẓ.M. is first and foremost an exegetical creation and therefore should be analyzed and discussed as such. The study of the literary form, content, and method is a prerequisite to any further attempt at a reconstruction of the author's *weltanschauung*.

But the inclusion of this chapter was not meant to serve only as a means for the external end of the last chapters dealing with Saba's thought and views of contemporary events and phenomena. Scholarship has concentrated, on the one hand, on exegetes of the classical period (11th-13th centuries including figures such as Rashi, Ibn Ezra, RaShBaM, RaDaQ and Nachmanides, and on the other, on the analysis of sermons in later centuries. There is almost no attempt to describe and analyze exegetes whose work was influenced by the fact that they were preachers.

An analysis of Saba's exegetical methods is of great importance. Beyond studying the literary *ouvre* of a fairly important preacher and exegete in his generation, an end unto itself, this should be of benefit also for the understanding of exegetical methods employed in Turkey and Palestine in the 16th century. Those trends had deeper historical roots than have been hitherto found.[1]

This chapter deals mainly with the following issues: The intended audience of the book (which will be discussed also in the chapter on Qabbalah), its main literary traits, some of the author's outstanding exegetical concerns and objectives, Saba's particular way of exegetical thinking, and the way he views his own commentary and its originality.

Beside the particular medieval exegetical tradition to which Ẓ.M. belongs, there are three major factors that shape Saba's commentary: Homiletics, Qabbalah, and Midrash. We attempt to characterize and assess the influence of these factors.

1. Ẓ.M. - The Name

The name Saba chose for his book is not accidental and is a multi-faceted one. Indeed, the various aspects of it could serve as mottoes for different chapters of our study.

We have already alluded to the Midrashic connection between Abraham and the "bundle of myrrh."[2] Qabbalah, an important component of the commentary and more so of Saba's personal spiritual life, is alluded to in the name of the book. This becomes clear if we examine the three commentaries he wrote in Portugal - *Ẓeror ha-Mor*, *Éshkol ha-Kofer*, and *Ẓeror ha-Ḥayyim*. Each of these phrases has Qabbalistic significance and refers to various *Sefirot*.

There are differing opinions as to the *Sefirot* that these expressions symbolize and, consequently, it would seem difficult to determine just how Saba conceived of them.[3] But we have one reference that might clarify the issue. We find in Ẓ.M. a long quotation from the *Tiqqunei Zohar*, concerning the Qabbalistic understanding of the problem of exile:

> [And since He is imprisoned with them in exile it has been said about Him: 'A prisoner cannot release himself from jail'],[4] and the *Shekhinah* is his jail. And the secret of it is [hidden] in the verse: 'My beloved is unto me as a bundle of myrrh [*ẓeror ha-mor*], that lies between my breasts.'[5]

Ẓeror ha-Mor according to this passage is the emenation of *Tiféret* and those that surround it. *Ẓeror ha-Ḥayyim* symbolizes, according to the *Zohar*, the emanation of *Malkhut*, and *Éshkol ha-Kofer* stands for *Binah*,[6] but it quite possibly for Saba symbolizes all three upper *Sefirot*.[7]

This Qabbalistic meaning is an esoteric one and comes as an addition to all the exoteric intentions made explicit by the author:

> ושכבר תמו הצרורות ובטלו ולא מצאתי צרור אחר קראתי שם זה החיבור אשכול הכופר לפי שהוא דומה קצת לצרורות כספי וזהבי, וכן לפי שיש בו ה׳ אשכולות הם חמש מגילות שיש באחת מהם אשכול הכופר דודי לי. וכן קראתי אשכול הכופר לומר שאעפ״י שבטלו האשכולות כאומרם איש שהכל בו מקרא משנה תלמוד אגדות, הכופר שמכפר עונותיהם של ישראל, עם כל זה מצאתי אשכול לאכול אע״פ שבכורה אותה נפשי.[8]

We note that Saba does not give any reason for the choice of the name *ẓeror ha-mor*, nor does he make mention of the fact that this expression and *éshkol ha-kofer* happen to be "neighbours" in the Bible,[9] which is presumably the reason Qabbalists took them as complementing symbols of the *Sefirot*. But one does not expect Saba to reveal the esoteric game of the names.

It would seem improbable that as a Qabbalist Saba chose names for the works written in Portugal that symbolize the totality of the *Sefirot* with no intent. Just as the works contain exoteric and esoteric commentaries, so do the names chosen by their author.

2. *Ẓ.M. - The Second Version*

It is evident from the text, as well as from the author's own admission, that

Ẓ.M. was written in a hurry.[10] The first version was much longer. The discussions were more detailed, included more references to other commentaries, and one could assume that his style was better. Saba apologizes several times for his clipped writing and, in one instance he describes the book as a mere outline of the original long version:

> ...I forgot all the things that were written there and with me (i.e. in my memory) there remained only these chapter headings [rashei peraqim] that I have written here.[11]

His haste can sometimes be traced. In one place Saba writes down the main points of the sermon he had given immediately after recovering from his long illness in Fez. Saba proved the point he was making from the Torah, the Prophets, and the Hagiographa. After recording the proofs in the proper order he adds about his original oral sermon:

> And in the Torah section I brought also (a proof from) 'For I will proclaim the name of the Lord...The Rock, His work is perfect...Is corruption His...Do you thus requite the Lord,' but I forgot to write it above (in its proper place).[12]

In other words, he did not have the peace of mind to insert the additional proof where it belonged.

There is some evidence that Saba made later additions to the text. In one case he writes an interpretation which originally appears in a Midrash. Saba concludes by saying, "And if I find it I will write it down."[13] While this attests only to his intentions, there is one place where he actually added a text that he wrote originally out of memory. In the story of the revelation of God to Moses in the Burning Bush Saba writes: "And about the reason(s) that He appeared in the Seneh, the Rabbis wrote twelve things parlleling the twelve Tribes of Israel I will write what I remember [*ézkor mah she-ézkor*] since I am in trouble."[14] Then he proceeds to write only nine of the twelve interpretations and says: "And the rest I have forgotten [*nifleú mimeni*]. Afterwards I found the whole Midrash and this is its (full) version..."[15]

3. Z.M. as a Guide for Preachers

Although Saba claims to have structured Z.M. in a way that everyone would find in it what his heart desires,[16] there is some evidence that Saba directed Ẓ.M. partially to preachers. In the Portion of Devarim which coincides with the Ninth day of the month of Áv, Saba suggested a "topic" [*nose*], and a "dictum" [*maámar*], two technical terms in the homiletical literature of the period:

> והנה יש מקום לדבר בענין שכתב איכה ובמעלת איכה. והנושא יכול להיות, איכה אשא לבדי. והמאמר, שלשה פתחו באיכה, תמצאהו במנורת המאור. וכן יכולים לדבר כאן בפרשת המרגלים דכתיב בהו, ויבכו בלילה ההוא, וכתיב, בכה תבכה בלילה, וכתיב בפרשה זו, ותשובו ותבכו לפני ה׳.[17]

In another instance, again relying on an association of words and again involving the *Haftarah*, we read:

> ובכאן יוכלו לדבר בענין שבת שמעו בענין המגילה, שמעו כי נאנחה אני, וכן, שמעו דבר ה' בית יעקב, בהפטרת היום. ואמרו במדרש, שמעו דברי תורה קודם שתשמעו דברי נבואה...נבואה קודם תוכחה...שמעו חיים קודם שתשמעו מתים דכתיב, העצמות היבשות שמעו דבר ה'.[18]

This seems to be at least a partial reason for the often excessive quotations from the Midrash. Thus Saba explains in one case:

> Since I saw in this section various interpretations by the preachers [darshanim], I have quoted this dictum because it contains all the interpretations they offer.[19]

Saba's objective was, then, to aid other preachers by enriching their sermons with Midrashic sources, and by guiding them in choosing a didactically proper topic. If this is true concerning the abundance of Midrashic material found in Ẓ.M., then we have here a beginning of the sixteenth century phenomenon of publications of Midrashic collections primarily for preachers.[20]

4. Preaching Symptoms in Content and Style

Ẓ.M. is a commentary on the Pentateuch. In form it follows the tradition started by Nachmanides. The latter dedicated the bulk of his commentary to an investigation of the plain meaning of the text [*peshat*], and occasionally added comments according to the mystical sense of the text [*derekh ha-émet*]. R. Baḥya ben Asher pursued this format but added two other methods of interpretation, namely, the Midrashic one, and interpretations utilizing the sciences [*derekh ha-sekhel*].[21] Baḥya inserted in his exegetical work an element that belonged to the sermonic literature: a general opening passage in the beginning of each Portion discussing a verse from Proverbs, which ties in with that Portion.[22]

It is to this trend in Biblical exegesis that Ẓ.M. belongs. It does not have the neat order of Baḥya, and the concept of *peshat* is radically different from that of Nachmanides and Baḥya,[23] but one can clearly see the initial discussion as *peshat*, after which follows the Midrashic explanation and finally the mystical. This is correct as a generalization, but not always do all three ways appear, and often the Midrashic interpretation is the *peshat*.

Saba does not comment on each verse and, when he does, his comment usually serves as a link in a chain of verses,[24] and the discussion as a whole is much more free-wheeling in nature than that of his two famous predecessors.

This is due not only to the turbulent circumstances under which the book was written, but also, and primarily, because of Saba's role in life as a preacher. Ẓ.M. is an exegetical work, following in the path of the two commentaries mentioned above. However, it is altered in content and style because Saba was a preacher and sermonic material was inserted.

Ẓ.M. does contain several sermons but they appear only in abbreviated form,[25] which makes their reconstruction difficult. On the other hand, the book is distinguished from other exegetical works by the addition of a great deal of material of a homiletical nature.

While Saba invests a considerable effort in his attempts to show that the Torah is constructed like a chain in which every ring is locked into the preceeding and following ones,[26] he does not comment on every verse in an orderly fashion. The general structure of each passage is of great importance to him and he focuses on the main theme of any given pericope, ignoring difficulties which do not fit his thought. On the other hand, he marshals all the questions he can, both good and not-so-good, if they can be answered by his interpretation. He does this in a manner similar to that of two disputants, in his own description. Saba says that if they argue with the intention of winning, they do not care if their logic is correct or faulty.[27] Similarly, we find that often the preacher (albeit perhaps subconsciously) tries to prove the truth by attempting to solve as many problems as he can amass.

Several times Saba uses the Haftarah as support for the points he is trying to make.[28] This is, of course, characteristic of a preacher. But the digressions go beyond the discussion of the *Haftarah*. Classical exegesis consists of short comments. This is true for Nachmanides and Baḥya, who might include longer comments than earlier exegetes, but nevertheless, like the latter, do not digress from the verse under discussion to introduce extraneous comments not directly related to the matter at hand. Such a style is a trait of the preacher.[29] The fact that we know both Nachmanides and Baḥya also to be preachers does not seem to have significantly effected their commentaries. When they wrote they restrained their personal homiletical drives. Saba, in this respect, is very different. Through the medium of word-association he goes far afield, interpreting, for example, a chapter from the Prophets or, more likely, a psalm, and only then does he return to the verse from which he started. Consequently, Ẓ.M. is much richer in extra-Pentateuchal material than most Torah commentaries.[30]

We have already discussed the fact that the preacher's commentary would be more likely than that of the exegete to be closely related to contemporary reality. It is not a question of differences in belief, for the Torah was seen generally as a holy text of eternal didactic value with lessons for each generation and each situation. The difference lies in the state of mind of each individual. The preacher's mind is geared towards the task of contemporary relevance to the audience. It is true that we can find preachers who directed their efforts towards philosophical or theoretical issues, like Anatoli and Arama but, in their case as well, one can sense a reaction to the reality of the contemporary philosophical or anti-philosophical milieu. Saba, however, seems in his sermons to have dealt with issues pertaining to the daily practice of the commandments[31] and contemporary events of national interest. His commentary is influenced greatly by reality and much of it cannot be fully understood if taken out of its historical context.[32]

In discussing the contents of Ẓ.M. influenced by Saba's vocation as a preacher, we pointed to long digressions as one of the features of the homiletical style. But there are more stylistic peculiarities in the book for the same basic reason.

The reader of Ẓ.M. is sure to notice Saba's repetitious style. While sometimes his writing is so clipped that only knowing his sources can help to understand his ideas, quite often, when he is excited by an idea or feels strongly about the importance of a certain point, the reader can expect a long repetitive passage.

This seems to be due largely to an awkward transition from the oral transmission form to the written one. It is quite obvious that, in our case, the ear can tolerate more than the eye. However, not every preacher can make this needed adjustment and divorce himself from his customary oral style.

The oral sermon thrives on rhetorical devices, but when those are put on paper in an identical form, their effect is lost and the reader is left with a repetitious text. The following example is one of many, where a word was taken and bent in all directions more than a dozen times (twenty-one to be precise) in the course of one short passage. We quote here only the concluding part of an apparent sermon:

> ולהזכיר חטאתם של ישראל *בין* ישראל *לבין* אביהם שבשמים נקרא איש *הביניים*. ולכן נקרא זה השבת שבת *בינתיים* לפי שבכח התשובה וסוד השבת שהיא תשובה, כמו שכתבתי, מסתלק איש *הביניים* מישראל ואינו שולט עליהם ביוה״כ. ולכן אמרו בסוף נדרים...ולכן אמר בכאן, ושמרו בני ישראל את השבת, הוא שבת *בינתיים*. לעשות את השבת, בפיך ובלבבך לעשותו. *ביני ובין* בני ישראל..., כי אני מכפר להם בזכות התשובה שהוא יום השבת. וזהו, *ביני ובין* בני ישראל. ואיש *הביניים* לא יבוא *בינינו* בזה היום בזכות שבת *בינתיים* שהוא סוד התשובה. ועל זה הטעם נקרא שבת *בינתיים* לפי שכתב בכאן בזה השבת הב׳, *ביני ובין* בני ישראל, מה שלא אמר בשבת הראשון. ולכן נקרא איש *הביניים* היצר הרע לפי שהוא עומד לעולם בין מערכות פלישתים ובין מערכות ישראל לעוות אדם בריבו, חוץ מיוה״כ שאין בו כח מכח שבת *בינתיים* והתשובה. ולכן סמך לכאן פרשת העגל שהוא יצר הרע...הנה רמז לאיש *הביניים*[33]

This passage also illustrates another stylistic trait, namely, the conclusion of a lengthy excursus in which Saba usually summarizes the main points, in accordance with the rule he himself suggested. He says that a person who writes or lectures at length should, at the end, repeat his main points in brief for the benefit of the readers or the audience, just as we find in Tractate Avot where the sixth chapter is really a summary of the preceding five.[34] This, of course, is necessary particularly in sermons that flow freely without any rigid limiting form of scholarly discussion.

Another stylistic influence of preaching on Ẓ.M. is the various means originally designed to arouse the interest of the audience. Saba brings the Biblical text to life by the use of direct speech. Instead of explaining what a character in the Biblical narrative says in a dry exegetical style, he turns the explanation into an elaborate speech in the first person which is included in the short verse allowed by the Bible for that character. When God, for example, curses Cain, Saba comments:

> 'And now you are cursed from the earth'(Gen. 4,11), namely, that your punishment for this continuous killing is to be grave as long as your brother's blood cries out from the earth...But for now I punish you that you will be cursed and homeless...the land will not endow you with its goodness even if you sow it, and also because you will be wandering all over the earth and have no time to plough and sow, your initial design will not materialize. Also you will be wandering expelled from one place to the next, just as your brother's blood wanders...[35]

In the course of the long explanation that God offers Cain concerning the curse, Saba uses another method of dramatization:

> ...so that your intention to remain the only one in the whole land in order to eat its fruit and be satisfied by its goodness, will not be realized. It shall not stand, neither shall it come to pass [ve-lo taqum ve-lo tihyeh]! For the land will not continue to give you of its strength...

The dramatic effect of the exclaimed phrase (taken from Isa. 7.7) is lost when put on paper, but can be powerful (and awakening...) when presented orally before a live audience.

This use of short phrases, borrowed or original, is highly developed by Saba. Sometimes he adapts a well-known phrase and uses it in an original manner, changing it to a humorous, ironic or sarcastic sense.

An episode in which many such elements of "special effects" appear together is the encounter between Sarah and Abraham concerning the problem posed by Hagar's stay in their household. Saba criticizes Sarah for offering Hagar to Abraham and for subsequently treating her harshly. For that, Saba says, Sarah's descendants were destined to fall into the hands of Ishmael. Then he adds: "For Abraham had told her: 'Do to her as you see fit' only in order to cool her anger, but she wrought and prospered (Dan. 8,12), [as it says]: 'And Sarah dealt harshly with her.'"[36]

The idea, as such, is already found in Nachmanides' commentary, but Saba's embellishment gives the idea a fresh, much livelier look. Saba also attacks Abraham for his behaviour with a series of provocative questions: "And where was his mercy? And where was the Torah he had studied...? And even without the Torah, his logic should have dictated...." Then Saba concludes it all with a vivid description of Hagar's tragedy, in which he has her speak in verse.[37]

In closing, we note one other stylistic influence of the oral sermon. In numerous places Saba concludes a long discussion by a short prayer-wish, usually for the speedy coming of the awaited redemption.[38]

5. A Qabbalistic Preacher's Peshat

The spectrum of comments described by Saba as *peshat* is possibly the widest imaginable. Indeed this exegetical term is assumed by him to have a meaning entirely different from the varyiously nuanced definitions of the classical medieval exegetes, which have been studied by scholars to date.[39]

Although on the mystical level "the entire Torah consists of the names of God," Saba is ready to interpret single words as coming from languages other than Hebrew: ולשון בגפו אמרו שהוא מצוי בעבודה המצרית בחלק כלי האומנים...לשון כלי אומנות, והוא לומר שאם הביא עמו כלי מכלי אומנותו שיוציאהו עמו ולא יעכבהו האדון.[40]

This is certainly a fine expression of *peshat* according to its strictest medieval definition. Indeed, if we had to define *peshat* according to this comment alone, we would have to put Saba's interpretation of this term on par with modern Old Testament scholarship.

But on the other hand we read:

> And he asked the shepherds about Laban's welfare [shalom]. And they answered: 'It is well [shalom], and behold Rachel his daughter cometh with the sheep' (Gen. 29,6). This (they said) in order to hint that Laban had no perfection [shelemut] other than Rachel who was coming with the sheep, since she was perfect in its absolute sense [shelemah be-takhlit ha-shelemut] in beauty and fear of God. And when he saw her he recognized her perfection, his soul coveted her, and he rolled the stone from the well's mouth and watered the flock of Laban. This is the *peshat* of this story.[41]

This association of Laban's welfare [*shalom*] and Rachel's perfection [*shelemut*] is but a trace of Saba's associative mind which is perhaps his foremost characteristic as a homilist, as we shall see below. Ibn Ezra, for example, would not need such an explanation to overcome any exegetical problem in the discussed verse.

In an introduction to a sermon[42] Saba says:

> 'Verily ye shall keep my sabbaths' (Ex. 31,13)...and it is repeated: 'Ye shall keep the sabbath therefore' (ibid 31,14), to tell us about the three Sabbaths which are hinted at in the section of Va-yekhulu (Gen. 2,1-3), and there I dwelled on it at length and also on the three meals. And according to the peshat it seems that he hinted here (in the word) 'sabbaths' to two special sabbaths in the year which are *Shabbat ha-Gadol* and *Shabbat Beinta'yim*.[43]

According to the *peshat* we are accustomed to in the 10th-14th centuries exegesis there is no problem at all with the plural form of "sabbaths" as Nachmanides comments: "...since there are many sabbaths during the year." Saba's is a pure homily of a preacher for whom these two particular sabbaths have a special meaning, being designated for sermons on themes connected with Passover and the High Holidays.

But the term *peshat* is stretched even further by Saba. On the verse which tells us that Abram gave "a tenth of all" to Malkizedeq, the king of Salem (Gen. 14:20), Saba gives several interpretations. Before turning to a mystical interpretation, he says the following:

> Or He hinted 'a tenth of all [mi-kol],' that God will add the letter *hei* and his name will be Abraham. And this is (the neaning of) 'a tenth of kol' for the numerical value of *kol* is fifty, and a tenth of it is five, which is (the letter) *hei*... and here He hinted to him that he was going to be perfect in the fifty Gates of Wisdom, for there is the seat of the first *hei* of the name of God. This seems to be the meaning according the way of *peshat*.[44]

Now this peculiar *peshat* involves no less than *gematria* and even a touch of mysticism [*sod*].

The problem of the development of *peshat* in the 14th-15th centuries is in need of further comprehensive research. At this stage, we can tentatively offer two factors that contributed to such a broad concept of *peshat*: a. the rise of Qabbalah as the one distinct and important method of interpretation, a fact that lumped together the other three traditional methods including *derash* and *remez* as being non-Qabbalistic; b. the rise of the sermonic literature that made the *derash* much more central. While in the classical period of exegesis in the 11th-13th centuries, the term *peshat* meant the delegitimization of homiletical interpretations, now came preachers who by appropriating the term and using it freely, blurred the differences and legitimized their homilies as *peshat*.[45]

6. Saba on Originality in Exegesis

When we come to assess an exegete's work we usually resort to an analysis of the exegetical methods he employed as well as studying his sources. We, however, would also like to find out Saba's own view of his endeavor as an exegete. This can be partially reconstructed from several references he makes with regard to orginality in exegesis.

Saba finds it important to emphasize his originality in expressions such as "This is what I think with the aid of neither a book nor a teacher."[46] The reason for this lies mainly in the need of the exegete as well as that of the preacher to be original.[47] This comes across clearly in the conclusion of his long interpretation of the names of Jacob's twelve sons. Saba, obviously elated, exults,[48]

> הרי לך מה שעלה בדעתי בענין לידת השבטים. וחקרתי ופשפשתי ומצאתי דברי חפץ מחופש / לא יערכם זהב ומופז / כאילו כבוד ה' עלי זרח / ומלתו על לשוני ערך / בלי מלמד ובלי ספר אלומותי אני מאלם / מי הקדימני ואשלם / ואם שכחתי או שגגתי פרסת העלם / המעיין בהם ידינני כנער ועלם / כי כפי הזמן והמקום אני ממשש בכל תלם ותלם / והשם יכפר בעדי כי שגיאות מי יבין.[49]

But besides praising his own originality, Saba seems to be at odds with the medieval exegetical tradition several times on this very issue. It is not that he has no reverence for some of them, like Nachmanides and especially Rashi,[50] but he simply thinks that at times they included in their commentaries ideas that had already been expressed in the Midrash or Talmud. Thus he says:[51] ובזה רבו הפירושים / וכל דבריהם בין דברי חז"ל מפוזרים Or similarly:[52] ומה שהקשו בכאן והאריכו המפרשים למשמש / אין כל חדש תחת השמש / ובמסכת סנהדרין פרק חלק הקשו זאת הקושיה...

While boasting of his own superior interpretation, Saba uses expressions denoting disrespect and lack of appreciation for his medieval predecessors:

> והנה כל המפרשים נבוכו בזה ופירשו בו פירושים שונים, איני חמור נושא ספריהם. וכבר הארכתי בהם בחיבור הראשון. ואף גם זאת כי לא נתחוורו דבריהם, הטוב שבדברים דברי הגדול הצרפתי שאמר תשובה על דבר כזה...ועתה שמע אמרי בזה וראה ועשה בני כחפצך כי אתה תבחר ולא אני...[53]

The above-quoted passages are comments taken from particular interpreted verses. In general references to his commentary, however, we hear a different tune. Saba apologizes for all the cases where it would seem to the reader that he claimed originality while this was not the case:

> And one should not suspect me when I mention some of the Sages' interpretations without naming my sources, for I have neither books of the Talmud, nor of the Midrash, nor of the Zohar, nor any other book save for the Pentateuch.[54]

And again:

> ואני מפיל תחינתי לפני כל יודע ספר / שאם ימצא בזה הספר אימרי שפר / או דבר טוב אחוזה ברשתי / ידוע תדע כי גנוב הוא אתי / מספרי המדרשים או מספרי איש עתי / הוא הקדוש רשב"י / ...[55]

As will become evident in the following chapters, there is a lot of factual truth in his apology, but there is also a great deal of convention. The main motive for saying this is the fear of being "caught plagiarizing." Saba did not want to be criticized as he criticized Nachmanides.[56]

There was yet another fear of criticism. Saba tried to avoid claims that he was "too original," and that his far-fetched interpretations are detached from the Biblical text. In one instance he praises his originality, summing up: "This is what came to my mind concerning the solution of this problem [*be-*

hatarat ẓeh ha-safeq] with the aid of neither a book nor a teacher, and it is 'a knob and a flower' [*kaftor va-ferah*]." But he feels that he must prove it in order to avoid the external criticism of people who might claim that although the interpretation is brilliant it cannot be considered the true meaning of the text, Saba adds:

> ולפי שבזה נראה שאני כמתנבא ואיני יודע ואני בודה מלבי דברים, והעיקר חסר מן הספר...בוא ואראך את הרשום בכתב אמת. כי הנה עדי לאותם שעל עקלקלותם מטים / וסהדי במרומים / בסוף פרשת משפטים.[57]

In the final analysis, in the struggle between the exegete and the preacher, between *peshat* and *derash*, it is largely owing to the awareness of such external criticism that the weight of the latter in Ẓ.M. is not even heavier.

So far we have examined external elements, questioning either the originality or the validity of particular interpretations. But there is here also an internal religious fear Saba had to reckon with, namely, the possible application of false interpretation to Scriptures.

To be sure, such feelings were shaped by the Midrashic dictum that "the Torah has seventy countenances." In general, this notion served as a permissive factor in exegesis, since it lowered the psychological barrier which the exegete would otherwise have had to face, namely, the responsibility of uncovering the one and only true sense of Scriptures, and the risk of being wrong.[58] This has been a contributing factor in the free development and spread of preaching, and it can actually be proven by a comparison to Halakhah, in which such an idea is not valid. The fear of misunderstanding is a dominating factor in the history of Halakhah and of Halakhic literature, because of its practical applications. It certainly served as a barrier for many, who avoided writing down their Halakhic decisions.

But despite this license, such feelings as hesitation, apprehension, or anxiety certainly existed in God-fearing exegetes. Saba was one of them.

He ventures to interpret Ruth 2, 8-17 in a Qabbalistic fashion, seeing Boaz' instructions to Ruth and to his reapers as the initiation of Ruth into the study of Qabbalah and the description of subsequent stages in her progress as a student.[59] In the conclusion of his long and highly original interpretation, Saba says:

> ואין להאריך בזה יותר כי כל הפרשה שמורה וערוכה לפי דרך זה, והשם יכפר בעדינו כי שגיאות מי יבין. ואעפ״י שנראה שאני מגלה פנים בתורה, מקום הניחו לי אבותי, לפי שכיוצא בזה מצאתי שדרשו במדרש הגלוי במ׳ רות...[60]

He goes on to quote the entire Midrash (Ruth Rabbah 4,11. 5,2) to show that his interpretation is not entirely novel but was concealed in the "Revealed Midrash."[61] Alongside the pride in the novel idea, we feel Saba's recoiling from being too original, too innovative. He therefore feels much better claiming that his originality lies in the understanding of the hints and the expanding of an already existing ancient Jewish tradition. Now his mind is set to rest, for there is no risk of committing an error.

We find similar feelings, though not so strongly expressed, concerning an idea which is not purely Qabbalistic. Saba explains that the Messiah was destined to come, on his mother's side, from Moab, since he would also need a streak of cruelty in order to fulfill one of his duties - taking revenge on the nations. Then Saba adds:

> האמת בעל הסברה הייתי ומלבי הוצאתי מלין, ואח״כ מצאתי רמז לזה במדרש ושמחתי כעל כל הון...הרי לך מה שפירשתי למעלה...וברוך ה׳ אשר זיכני למצוא מאמר זה מסכים עם מה שכתבתי.[62]

This is a perfect solution for Saba. He was original in that he arrived at the idea intellectually on his own. On the other hand, it is secured from a religious point of view by being supported by the Midrash.

While such expressions of relief at finding an ancient supporting source might seem more characteristic of innovation in Qabbalah, we can detect a similar attitude in the non-mystical layers of Saba's exegesis as well. Such is the case with his justification of the allegorical method of interpretation he applies to a series of laws in Deuteronomy:

> ובזה אין אנו מורים פנים בתורה שלא כהלכה כי מקום הניחו אבותינו להתגדר בהם. וכיוצא בזה אמרו במציעא, תשת חשך ויהי...זה העולם הזה...ומלבד זה מצאתי בזוהר בפרשה זו שאמרו, והיה מחניך קדוש...אלו איבריו של אדם, שנראה שמפרש מחניך על הגוף על דרך עיר קטנה...[64].

In other cases as well, we sense the feeling of relief and satisfaction when Saba says that after having thought of an original interpretation he found a Midrash that supported it.[65] However, the apologies for mystical and allegorical interpretations are the only explicit ones, and understandably so. The apology for allegorical interpretation of a commandment is to be understood against the background of similar Christian exegesis as well as of such interpretations by Jewish philosophers who were accused of antinomian tendencies.

On a more abstract level of thought Saba offers another justification for original ideas. He implies that one cannot be original because, in truth, there is no originality after Creation. All that exists or will come into actual existence was already created by God in the twilight which concluded the sixth day of Creation.

> ...and similarly 'the writing and the writing tool' (Avot 5,6), if we see a scribe or a wise man, doing some refined work...or composing new books, there is nothing new under the sun, for on the eve of the Sabbath this power was invested in the writing and the writing tool to do that.[65]

All ideas, as well as other creative work, come from God who has already created them, and consequently no man can claim absolute but at most relative originality in that he expressed it before other men.

In his quest for a license for intellectual freedom, Saba characteristically relies on a Midrash:

> באופן שנראה מזאת המגילה שניתנה לידרש ויש בה פנים ואחור כמו שאמרו ע׳ פנים בתורה...ואע״פ שאני בער ולא אדע כבר אמרו במדרש קהלת (י״ב, י״א), כלם ניתנו מרועה אחד ואפי׳ מה שתלמיד ותיק עתיד לחדש. ואמרו שם, ולא כשומע מפי תלמיד אלא כשומע מפיו של הקב״ה שהוא יחידו של עולם דכתיב, ה׳ אחד.[66]

The meaning of this Midrash is that one should accept novel interpretations of the Torah even from an ignoramus, as if God himself is speaking through that person. Conventions of humility aside, Saba seems to have interpreted this idea, at least as far as some of his Qabbalistic interpretations are concerned, very literally. His source of mystical originality is the result of a direct personal experience of *devequt*, or communion with God. Here are his opening rhymes to a Qabbalistic interpretation:

> ואם תרצה להכנס בהיכל המלך פנימה / ולשים בסלע קנך בדעת ובחכמה / ולעלות בין כוכבי עש וכימה / ולפרוץ בארבע רוחות צפונה ומזרחה נגבה וימה / ויזרח עליך אור ה׳ כלבנה וכחמה / ולהגיע אל השערה ולא תחטיא אפילו כמלא נימה / ותשמח על כל הון וכמוצא סימא / בהיותך עם ה׳ אחוז בחבלי בוץ ורקמה / הוא סולם מוצב ארצה וראשו מגיע השמימה / ...[67]

He tells us here, undoubtedly, of his own experience and source of knowledge. He shares the particular idea with the reader and invites him to join in and follow the route of the true wisdom.

We have seen, then, Saba's struggle with the problems of innovation. This notion according to him cannot be attributed to man, for everything has already been created by God. However, man may consider himself privileged if he is first to discover an interpretation. In practical terms, the Midrash is commended by Saba for originality, which is not always recognized by later exegetes. As far as Saba himself is concerned, he considers himself original in relation to his medieval predecessors, but on the other hand, the problems inherent in originality, particularly in non-conventional exegesis, namely, mystical and allegorical (of commandments) drive him to seek Midrashic origins for his innovations.

7. From Mystical to Literary Unity

The Qabbalistic idea that "the whole Torah is composed of the names of God" is well known,[68] and Saba maintains it too.[69] Consequently, the Torah is bound together as an inseparable unit. Moreover, the end of the Torah is tied to its beginning through the numerical value of *lamed* and *bet* - the letters with which the Torah ends and starts. In Saba's words: "Its end is linked to its beginning and its beginning to its end."[70] This phrase is borrowed from *Sefer Yeẓirah*, which thus describes the unity of the *Sefirot* and ends the sentence with the imagery "like the flame that is tied up with the coal."[71]

But this notion has its repercussions beyond the mystical sphere of exegesis, which is quite limited in Ẓ.M. It adds another dimension to all other levels of exegetical interpretations. Saba explains that the Sages derived new meanings out of the order of the sections [*darshu semukhim*], since "the Torah in its entirety (i.e. its sections) is bound together like flocks of sheep."[72] And while in this case it is not clear that the Qabbalistic concept is the factor behind the statement, we do find an explicit connection between the mystical unity and the non-mystical interpretation elsewhere. In the beginning of the sermon he says:

> And therefore it seems to me that we can derive a great idea from the section telling us about the generations of Esau...because even things that seem to us to be redundant and unnecessary contain great allusions. And therefore the entire Torah is tied together...and therefore it starts with a bet and ends with a lamed (constituting the word lev - heart) so that we should pay careful attention to the entire Torah,[73] for there is no difference between 'Hear, 0 Israel' and 'Timna was a concubine' (Gen. 36, 12). And therefore I applied my heart and eyes to understand why...[74]

He seems to be saying that the mystical profoundity of the entire Torah demands that the exegete try to assign significance to every detail, even on the non-mystical level, since what follows in that sermon is not Qabbalah.
The unity does not end in the Torah. Saba extends it to the book of Esther:

> ...for all its parts need each other and are tied to each other just like the parts of the Torah and therefore, it has been said that one is not to stop between the verses but should rather read all of them as if they were one verse, in order to teach us about the connection of all its parts and about the mysteries it contains.[75]

Sure enough, Saba looks for the connection between the first and the last verses of Esther, in order "to tie up the beginning of the Scroll to its ends."[76]

The overall picture of the Bible does not differ by much. Its twenty-four books constitute a unity shown by its numerical, symbolic significance:

> ...ולכן אמר כ״ה אמר ה׳ בתורה וכ״ה אמר ה׳ בדברי הנביאים והם כולם כ״ד ספרים ואחד של שם המיוחד לכולם הם כ״ה לפי שהתורה כולה שמותיו של הקב״ה, ולכן כמו שהשם נקרא ה׳ אחד כן התורה נקראת תורה אחת וישראל נקראים גוי אחד לפי שיש בהם סוד הייחוד.[77]

Again, using the imagery from *Sefer Yeẓirah*, Saba says:

> And this comes to show the superior nature of our Torah, that all of its parts are intertwined. And this is true not only of the Torah, but even

> the words of the Prophets and those who spoke with the aid of the Holy Spirit are all intertwined with the words of the Torah...And this is to show the superiority of the Bible[78] that all of its parts are connected together just like the flame that is part of the coal.[79]

But within the general framework there are smaller units with their internal cohesiveness. This applies to the Book of Esther, as we have seen,[80] to the Torah, and to each of its five books, which have their own themes. Saba, however, goes beyond this and believes that the weekly Portions have their internal themes that make their unity even more outstanding - a cohesiveness within a cohesiveness.

It is Saba's belief that the division of the Torah is mystically significant, and the number of the Portions even figures in the reason for the obligations to recite the *Shema* twice a day. The verse "Hear, of Israel" contains twenty five letters, "and therefore we ought to unify God twice... which is fifty as against the fifty Portions of the Torah, and the fifty gates of *Binah*...given to Moses."[81]

The prophet Jeremiah refers to two separate Portions:

> '...For I have not spoken...nor have I commanded them' (Jer.19,5), namely, 'I have not spoken' in Vayyiqra, which is the Portion of sacrifices, where it says: 'And God spoke to him.' 'Nor have I commanded [ẓiviti]' in the Portion of Ẓav...[82]

Saba generalizes:

> ולהודיענו עומק התורה וסתריה, ולא דבר רק הוא אלא ממנו, וכולה במספר במשקל. וכמו שיש סודות גדולים בתורה כן יש סודות גדולים בפרשיותיה...[83]

It comes as no surprise to us that the imagery from *Sefer Yeẓirah* is again used in this context:

> And He said...in order to seal the end of the Portion to its beginning and its beginning to its end, just like the flame that is connected with the coal.[84]

But although the root of the unity and cohesiveness of the Torah and its portions is the unity of God,[85] an idea of mystical character for Saba, the interpretations resulting from it are by and large non-mystical.

The preoccupation with connections is a dominant feature in Ẓ.M.. Utilizing a host of methods, Saba attempts to show the unity of the Torah by connecting each seemingly seperate part to the next (needless to say, these small units are the most cohesive), every Portion to the preceding one and to the one that follows. At the same time he attempts to show the cohesive nature of the Portion, and sometimes he ties up its beginning and end.[86]

It seems that the mystical idea of unity that stands behind his efforts as a "prime mover" influenced Saba to the point that he developed a literary analytic skill whereby he would look at a text as a cohesive unit even when there was no mystical idea to be demonstrated. This shows in his attempt at a similar conception in his non-Biblical commentary on Avot. In summarizing the nature of the tractate and his commentary on it, he makes no mention of any mystical unity, although he did believe that, in general, both the written and oral Torah were bound together mystically. Saba saw the novelty of his commentary in the connections between every single Mishnah and the following one, and indeed this was a novel approach to a tractate much commented upon.[87]

It seems to me that we have here a case in which the quest for unity rooted in mysticism was internalized by the exegete, who would now seek the unity of a literary text out of the inner quest for unity as an aesthetic value in literature.

8. Saba's Exegesis and the Midrash

The bond between Ẓ.M. and the Midrash is particularly strong.[88] Midrashic sources are a major component of the book and Saba is proud of it:

> ובניתיהו בכל מיני יופי וכן / להיות לכל שואל מוכן / ועיטרתיהו במרגליות הזוהר בכל פרשה ופרשה ותקנתיהו בכל מיני מדרשות ואגדות, וציירתיהו בכל מיני טלוא ונקוד / מירושלמי ומכילתא וילקוט.[89]

Saba admires the Sages as exegetes and is relieved when he finds support for a particular interpretation of his in one of theirs. Their advantage lies mainly in the oral tradition on which they draw:

> ורבותיי אמרו...ויש לנו להודות לדבריהם לפי שכל דבריהם דברי קבלה, ואנחנו הולכים ממשמשים כעורי קיר לסמוך עצמינו אליה. ואע״פ שיראה לנו דברינו כנים ואמיתיים יש לנו להשליך אמת ארצה לפי שהאמת אתם.[90]

However, Saba does not always follow his own instructions. Several times he gives his interpretations equal weight with those of the Sages and cites opinions of the latter as mere possibilities.[91] In rare cases, Saba prefers his own interpretations on the basis of textual evidence.[92]

Moreover, contrary to his statement concerning the authority of the Sages whose interpretations are all based on oral tradition, Saba seems to be aware of the phenomenon he terms "to make up a Midrash."[93] This touches upon the method of the Midrash which Y. Heinemann calls "creative exegesis",[94] and brings us to the discussion of the influence of Midrashic methods on Saba's own exegesis.

One can go through Heinemann's study and point to certain Midrashic methods employed by Saba. However, it is difficult at times to prove methodologically that Saba was not influenced by medieval exegetes. For example, the Midrashic principle that the deeds of the Biblical ancestors foreshadow the history of their descendants[95] is used extensively by Saba. But then, Nachmanides already does the same thing,[96] and Saba was greatly influenced by him.[97] Other factors to be reckoned with are Saba's personal background as a preacher, as well as personal ideological views that directed Saba in his endeavor as an exegete.

In general, however, the mass of Midrashic material quoted by Saba in Ẓ.M. and his own expressions of love for this body of exegetical literature (including his pride in his vast Midrashic library),[98] seem to indicate that almost of necessity he must have drawn directly from the Midrash, in which he was immersed, and not only in specific interpretations. Let us, then, examine which features of Saba's methods may be considered as directly influenced by the ancient Midrash.[99]

Some methods of the Midrash are not followed by Saba at all and others only to a certain extent. For example, the Sages, in their attempt to fill-in historical data missing from the Biblical text, give us the *sitz im leben* of certain psalms. "When did David compose this psalm? When he went to the Valley of Refaím."[100] They do the same thing in their famous story of David, who entered the bath-house and thought that he was naked of all the commandments until he realized that the precept of circumcision is inseparable from his body. Then he composed the psalm *la-menaẓẓe'aḥ ál ha-sheminit* (Ps. 12,1).[101] Saba goes on to explain that this story happened when David lived in circumstances under which he could not keep the commandments.[102]

Similarly, Saba interprets the Mishnah of "Ten people who sit and study Torah etc." (Avot 3,6) as having been said in times of decrees against the study of Torah.[103]

In both cases we see two influencing factors: a. Saba's frame of mind as a preacher that projects contemporary reality onto the text;[104] b. the influence of the Midrash which provides "historical" background for various literary parts of the Bible. However, in the Middle Ages it would have been considered an audacity for an exegete to place Biblical texts in a historical context.[105] Such interpretations by the Sages were mostly understood as based on oral tradition. Saba could not invent such background stories, but he could and did interpret the Sages in a similar vein.

While in the above mentioned cases we observe a compromise between the Midrashic method and the restrictions that prevented Saba from exploiting it to the fullest, there were areas which were completely out of bounds for Saba. He could not identify personalities, places and dates as the Midrash does every so often.[106] The age of "creative historiography" in its broader sense was past for the medieval Jewish exegete.

But if we cannot speak of "creative historiography" in its full Midrashic sense, we can speak of a creative historiographical imagination. Saba fills in historical lacunae penetrating deeply into the past and using his (sometimes medieval) imagination. This is reflected in the vivid descriptions of thoughts and emotions behind the actions taken by the Biblical characters - psychological insights - and his application of natural causation often taken from his own contemporary experience to the Biblical narrative.

When he fills in with facts omitted by the text, Saba is generally careful to open with "perhaps." "Perhaps the daughters of the Hittites were more beautiful."[107] "Perhaps the spring was far."[108] "Perhaps the old woman (Naomi) was hungry."[109] This illustrates the post-Midrashic hesitation in adding any background details to the Biblical narrative.

Saba knows, however, that Abraham could not sleep during the night prior to the destruction of Sodom, and describes it as if he were a novelist. In the following passage he does not add any hard facts but, after reading his description, the story gains an additional dimension of vividness.

> 'And it was when the camels finished drinking' (Gen. 24,22), that is, when he saw a small girl, beautiful and smart, who plucked up courage and strength to water ten camels who were tired from the trip, and each one of them needed ten buckets of water until the thirst of all the camels was quenched, as if she was twenty years old, he decided...[110]

His descriptions of the emotions of the active characters in various narratives are remarkable. Hagar in the desert;[111] Abraham, who cannot find a match for his son,[112] and Shimon and Levi fuming over Dinah's rape,[113] all get extra passages in Saba's script, which is rhymed for special effect.[114]

Saba has some psychological insights into the character of Biblical personalities. The brothers' hatred for Joseph was only enhanced because they did not vent their anger.[115] When they tore Joseph's tunic and dipped it in blood, they let out their frustration by doing to the tunic what they could not do to their brother.[116] Haman, interestingly, made a "Freudian slip," when he told the king, "Let the royal apparel be brought...and the royal crown which is set upon his head" (Es. 6,8). He was thinking of himself and thus revealed his real intentions of rebelling against the king and assuming the kingship.[117]

The general tendency of bringing the narrative to life in the manner described above is the result of three converging factors: a. the personality of the exegete; b. the preacher's mind; c. the Midrashic method of creative historiography within the permissible limits as defined above.

Indeed, the sketching of a personality "must be subject to rigid discipline if it is not to pass from the carefully lined notebook of the historian to the supple and suggestive canvas of the artist".[118] There is, however, one trait of Saba's personality that comes across clearly. The man was warm, compassionate and caring. His description of the emotional dimensions of various narratives, mainly in tragic situations, are touching. The love and attachment of parents to their children, in Saba's descriptions, are powerful.[119]

His treatment of contemporary issues on the national level reflect, and indeed magnify, the same impression.[120]

The second factor to be considered is Saba's preaching background. He seems to have had one of the talents which make for a good teacher and preacher, namely, the ability to give life to a narrative through the use of imagination in order to supply missing data concerning the thoughts and emotions of the characters.[121]

Therefore, if we seek to show a clearer influence of the Midrash on Saba's exegesis, we must turn to what has been termed "creative philology."

9. Chain Associations

A comparison of the Midrashic method and that of modern philology will show that while the latter, as a science, attempts to describe a difficult word by means of a word from the same root that appears in another context, the former attempts to connect the entire context of the second word in order to shed light on the context of the first. In other words, the second word is an indication planted purposefully as a clue in order for us to learn more about the first context. (Accordingly we are talking not of "creative" philology *ex nihilo*, but of a development of the existing clue from the state of epistemological potential into the actual).

There is another difference between the ancient Sages and modern philologists. The former were in no need of a concordance for they demonstrated a thorough individual mastery of the entire Bible. This was also true of medieval exegetes. But whereas grammarians such as Ibn Ezra and RaDaQ used their knowledge in a manner similar to the modern philologist, Saba uses his mastery of the Bible and his great associative talent for ingenious Midrashic sorts of associations.[122] In this respect we can say that his immersion in Midrashic literature influenced the direction of his exegetical effort. Let us cite two cases of chain associations.

In his commentary on Ruth, Saba connects the beginning of the book to what he considers to be its central theme, namely, the Messiah. We note also that he introduces what he is about to do as a *derashah*.[123]

> 'And a certain man of Bethlehem in Judah' (Ruth 1,1) and of Amram it says: 'And a certain man of the house of Levi went' (Ex. 2,1). Just as there, Moses our Rabbi who brought the light to Israel, was born, as it says: 'And she saw him that he was good' (ibid 2,2) and it says: 'And God saw the light that it was good '(Gen. 1,4). Also about the Messiah it says: 'Light is sown for the righteous' (Ps. 97,11), who is a righteous branch (Jer. 23,5) who is called light, and it says: 'Arise, shine for your light has come' (Isa. 60,1). And just as Moses was born to save Israel, so also the Messiah is going to save Israel from the oppression of the Kingdoms. And therefore, it says here: 'And a certain man...went,' and

> out of this going, the Messiah Son of David was born, just as of Amram it says: 'And a certain man...went,' and, from that, Moses our Rabbi, the Messiah of the God of Israel, was born.

If we look at Saba's comments on the verses describing the birth of Moses we will find a different chain of associations, a fact that underscores Saba's creativity in this area.

> ...'And she saw him that he was good' (Ex. 2,2) since he gave light to the world by the Torah. And this is (the meaning of the Midrash): 'that the whole house was filled with light' (Sotah 12a). It says here 'that he was good,' and it says above: '...the light that it was good'(Gen. 1,4), which is the light of the Torah, as it says: 'and Torah is a light' (Prov. 6,29). And it says: 'How great is your goodness which you stored up [ẓafanta] for those who fear you' (Ps. 31,20), and this is (the meaning of) 'And she hid [va-tiẓpenehu]' (Ex. 2,2). And since it alludes to the Torah that is called good, therefore it says: 'And she hid him for three months,' as against: '...the third month after the Children of Israel had left the land of Egypt' (Ex. 19,1).[124]

Associations of less complexity are very frequent. In interpreting Ps. 30, 12-13 as referring to the future redemption, Saba supports himself with two associations:

> ...'and girded me with joy', as it says: 'You shall go out with joy' (Isa. 55,12) and then they will 'sing the glory,' as it says: 'the glory of this latter will be greater...' (Haggai 2,9).125

Another example is the following:

> ...It seems that it refers to the future redemption, and therefore it says: 'Therefore it will be said' (Num. 21,14) in the future, 'in the book of the wars of the Lord.' What is 'the wars of the Lord'? This is the war of Amaleq, about which it says 'the Lord will have war with Amaleq' (Ex. 17,16). And there it also says: 'Write this as a memorial in the book' (ibid).126

10. Passage Parallelism (External and Internal)

Searching for parallels is one of the most unique features of Saba's exegesis. This is not to say that this technique is not to be found in medieval Jewish exegesis prior to Saba. We mean, however, a. to single out this element as a central one within our exegete's methods and b. to single him out as an exegete whose exegetical energy was channeled largely in this direction.

Parallelism of entire passages, narratives and chapters may be seen as a development of the single word association. It is, however, hard at times to retrace and determine the immediate association that sparked the entire parallel. Saba finds five parallel points between the story of Creation and the aftermath of the Deluge:[127]

> And after they paid for their sins, God wanted to renew the world...

And God made a wind to pass over the earth (Gen. 8,1).	And the wind of the Lord moved upon the face of the water (1,2).
And Noah opened the window of the ark (8,6).	And God said let there be light (1,3).
And he sent forth a raven (8,7). And he sent forth a dove (8,8).	And fowl that may fly above the earth (1,20).
The earth was dry (8,14).	And let the dry land appear (1,9).
...you and your wife (8,16).	Adam and his wife were created.

Did Saba have a preconceived notion of the historical significance of the Deluge which was to create a new beginning?[128] Was there an initial association of a word or words? Or was it, perhaps, Saba's vivid imagination and lyrical soul that created in his mind a *déjà vu* scene of Noah's family facing a humanless world as a parallel to Adam and Eve? All of the three are possible.

This sort of multiple literary parallel goes beyond the average Midrashic analogy of texts which is generally based on a single word association.

We find yet another type of parallelism which together with the associative factor, involves a new element - text analysis. In one instance, Saba actually tells us about the "windmills" of his mind. The text is that of Gen. 36 and the parallel is internal - in the shape of two ladders meeting at the top, as the chapter starts at the bottom of one ladder and ends at the bottom of the other.[129]

> ...I applied my heart and eyes to see what is behind the fact that this section starts with 'Esau, that is Edom' (36,1), and ends also with 'Esau, who is (the father of the) Edom(ites)' (36,43),[130] and also, why is it that in the beginning it counts 'the dukes of Esau' (36,15), and then 'the kings of Edom' (36,31), and then it says again: 'the dukes of Esau' (36,40), and the section ends with 'Edom who (is the father of the) Edom(ites)' (36,43).[131]

The initial spark was that of phrase associations, and the completion of the parallel was arrived at by a structural analysis.[132]

In his long exposition of Gen. 28, 11-15,126 Saba contends that God's speech (verses 13-15) is the full interpretation of Jacob's dream.[133] Out of the five parallel phrases, the first two have common words, which might have served as the initial attraction. (The rest have nothing in common and Saba has to show his homiletic ability in order to connect them).[134]

However, in this case, there is one additional factor, namely, Saba's conviction that the dream contains all the mysteries of the Torah,[135] and hence the extra-minute textual analysis which cannot be properly classified as genuine parallelism (Indeed, the two word-associations are not very impressive).[136]

Finding a parallel as a result of textual analysis and finding word-associations only in the following step is not a common trait of the Midrash where the dominant tool by which an analogy would be arrived at is a similarity of words.

But this fact itself, that Saba struggles to find associations even where they do not exist, seems to indicate how deeply he was influenced by the Midrashic method.

The final group of parallels is determined by the nature of the text. We refer to dreams, blessings and curses. One can guess with a great deal of certainty that Saba will find a parallel to any given dream or blessing. The dreams of Jacob and Joseph,[137] as well as those of Joseph and Pharaoh[138] match. Isaac's blessing to Jacob is parallel to God's curse of Adam,[139] as is Rebbecah's blessing (by her brothers) to that of the angel's to Abraham.[140] Last but not least, and indeed topping the list, is the long exposition of the names of Jacob's sons which match the blessings of Jacob and Moses to the tribes.[141]

Underlying this general attitude is the belief that dreams and blessings belong to the same category of prophecies, and therefore need to be studied carefully for clues. It manifests itself also in the fact that Saba uses these texts extensively for allusions to the Four Exiles.[142]

In conclusion, Saba extensively uses the Midrashic method of associating contexts. However, he goes beyond the Midrash in the complexity of the parallels he establishes. He is often led to it by other considerations which are justified *a posteriori* by the associations. In the course of our analysis we touched upon prominent features in Saba's exegesis whose existence might be attributed to Midrashic influence, but its extent cannot be determined conclusively because of other factors that apparently converged with the Midrash in shaping them.

NOTES

[1] S. Shalem in his study of R. Moses Alsheikh traces his methods back to the circle of his teacher R. Joseph Taitaẓaq in Salonika, while on the other hand, he shows the differences between Alsheikh and medieval Jewish exegetes up to Abravanel. (S. Shalem. *Rabbi Moses Alsheikh*, Jerusalem, 1966). A comprehensive study of Saba's exegesis would show that most of the traits found in the Salonica circle and in Alsheikh commentaries go back to the fifteenth century. In one instance, Shalem does recognize the possibility of deeper roots going back to Spain (Ibid, p. 133, n. 75). Such a connection in the area of homiletics was studied by M. Pachter in his Ph.D. diss. on the ethical and homiletical literature in sixteenth century Safed (Hebrew U., Jerusalem, 1976).

[2] See above p. 15.

[3] For example, R. Meir ibn Gabai, Saba's contemporary, writes: והז' כנום בלשון אשכול הכופר והעליונות צרור המור. (*Derekh Émunah*, Jerusalem (1967), p. 37). He does not refer to the symbol of *ẓeror ha-ḥayyim*. In the *Zohar* it is clear that the latter stands for *Malkhut* (*Zohar* II, p. 59a, 111, p. 25a. Cf. M. Idel, "'In the Light of Life' - A Study in Qabbalistic Eschatology," in *Sanctity of Life and Martyrdom, Studies in Memory of Amir Yekutiel* [Gafni and Ravitsky ed.], Jerusalem, (1992), p. 197 n. 25). *Éshkol ha-kofer* is *Binah* (Ibid. II, p. 27b). R. Ezra of Gerona in his commentary on Song of Songs (1,13) says: דימה לצרור המור הצורות שהם בכבוד נסתרים ונעלמים ולאשכול הכופר הגלויים...וכן נקרא הכבוד כמו כן צרור החיים על שם שהנשמות צרורות וקשורות שם... (*Kitvei ha-Ramban* [ed. Chavel], Jerusalem (1964), pp. 488-89).

[4] This was censored from the 1567 edition.

[5] Ẓ.M. Deut. p. 35b. This is a Hebrew translation of *Tiqqunei Zohar*, 6, p. 21b.

[6] See above n. 3.

[7] Ibid.

[8] É.K. Ruth p. 10b.

[9] Can. 1, 13-14.

[10] For the available dates see above p. .

[11] Colophon at the end of ms. Oxford (Manor, Saba, p. 230). See also Ẓ.M. Gen. pp. 31b,99a. Ex. p. 32b. Deut. p. 56a. On one occasion he says that he writes in short and therefore cannot repeat all that he would have liked to write down: לפי שארוכה מארץ מדה ואין לי פנאי However he does not explain the reason(s) for his lack of time (See above p. 12).

[12] Ẓ.M. Deut. p. 12b.

[13] Ibid., Ex. p. 14a.

[14] Ibid., Ex. p. 6b. Saba plays here humorously with the verse: "I will be with him in trouble" (Psalms 91,15), which is interpreted by the same Midrash on the Burning Bush as a promise of God to his people in Exile.

[15] Ibid., p. 6b-7a. (On this particular Midrash see M. Kasher, *Torah Shelemah*, Exodus, New York (1944), pp. 118-21). Although generally in literature such interpolations are not that unusual, the knowledge that Saba did in fact add to the original texts is important for it might be helpful in solving some textual problems (e.g. concerning *Ẓeror ha-Kesef*, see below p. 78-9).

[16] Gross, Saba, p. 220.

[17] Ẓ.M. Deut. p. 5a.

[18] Ibid., Num. p. 44a. In *Pinḥas*, Saba suggests: ובכאן יכולים לדבר בענין שבת דברי בחורבן הבית ותוכחות ירמיהו ובמעלתו. (ibid p. 40a, and also p. 41a). This Portion, as well as that of *Mattot*, fall around the seventeenth of Tammuz. All the explicit references to sermons are concerned with the "Three Weeks" period in which a solemn mood prevails because of the destruction of Jerusalem and the Temple that took place then. Interestingly, we find a sixteenth-century preacher in Salonica who in describing the contents of his sermons, writes: ...וקצת מגילת איכה בפרשת פנחס מטות ומסעי, ואביא בפרשת דברים מזמור על נהרות בבל...ואבארם כלם אל כוונת הפרשה ההיא אשר הם בה... (J. Hacker, "Intellectual Activity among

the Jews in the Ottoman Empire in the Sixteenth and Seventeenth Centuries," *Tarbiẓ* 53 (1984), pp. 583-4). This is exactly what we find in Ẓ.M. (with the exception of *Masèi*) including Psalm 137.

[19] Ibid., Gen. p. 125a. This could be behind the instructive tone in the following passage. It might be addressed to fellow preachers: ואני אקשה את לב פרעה. אין להאריך בפיי המפרשים ולא במדרשים אלא לברר וללבן האמת כפי מדרש הנעלם שכתבו שם... (ibid., Ex. p. 12b).

[20] See Hacker, Intellectual Activity, p. 585.

[21] See the introduction to his commentary (ed. Chavel, Jerusalem, 1974, p. 5).

[22] Ibid., p. 6 (See I. Bettan's chapter about Baḥya and preaching in, *Studies in Jewish Preaching*, Cincinnati, 1939). E. Gottlieb points out that Baḥya's inclusion of Qabbalah in his commentary was made possible by the precedent of Nachmanides, and that there is a development of the trend by Baḥya who presents Qabbalistic ideas in a clearer and less esoteric manner. (*Studies in the Kabbalah Literature*, Jerusalem (1976), p. 90).

[23] See our discussion below.

[24] For this tendency as connected to the belief in the unity of the Torah, see below pp. 52ff.

[25] E.g. Gen. pp. 98b-99a. Ex. 57b-58a. Deut. pp. 12a-13a, 14a-15a. An interesting comment on a homiletical flourish is found toward the end of Ẓ.H. Saba asks a series of five questions on the text and says: ואעפ״י שאין דרכי לעשות אלו הדיוקים, מפני כבוד סיום המסכתי רציתי בזה, ודיוקיי אחרים יובנו באלו.

[26] See below, p. .

[27] Ẓ.M. Ex. p. 15a (Compare Shalem, *Alsheikh*, p. 61ff).

[28] E.g. ibid Lev. pp. 9a, 16a-b. Num. p. 13b. Deut. pp. 52b, 53b, 54a.

[29] J. Dan, *Hebrew Ethical and Homiletical Literature*, Jerusalem, 1975, pp. 41-4.

[30] E.g. Ps. 93, 33, 30, 107, 121, 45, 122, 72, 23 (Ẓ.M. Gen. pp. 6b, 10b, 26b, 36b, 65a-b, 102b, 127a. É.K. Ruth p. 6a, É.K. Esther, p. 77). Saba, however, does not digress before interpreting the verse under discussion unlike the homiletical literature which, while retaining more of the aesthetic form of the oral sermon, might open by a discussion with no apparent connection to the Portion. For Saba, the exegete, digressions were án additional treat. One can reconstruct part of his commentary on Psalms (a commentary that might have existed. See above p. n.49). It was in style at this period not only to interpret Psalms in separate books but also in the homiletical literature (e.g. *Àqedat Yiẓḥaq*, *Ḥasdei ha-Shem* and others. Compare also C. Horowitz, *A Literary Historical Analysis of the Sermons of Rabbi Joshua Ibn Shu'eib*, Ph.D. Diss., Harvard U., 1979, p. 42).

[31] E.g. Ẓ.M. Ex. p. 57b.

[32] See chapters 1, 4, 6.

[33] Ẓ.M. Ex. p. 47b (See also ibid, Num. p. 8a). For the association of words as an exegetical technique, see below pp. 58-9.

[34] See below Appendix B.

[35] Ẓ.M. Gen. p. 19a.

[36] Ibid, p. 37b. For a sarcastic usage of a Biblical phrase see below p. 115). This usage of short Biblical phrases does not assume that Saba's sermons were delivered in Hebrew. In general, we believe that sermons in this period were delivered in Spain in the vernacular (with the exclusion of those delivered in small learned circles). However, Biblical and common Hebrew phrases were inserted. The reason for this was the lack of knowledge of Hebrew on the part of certain segments of Spanish Jewish society. This deficiency is reflected in the Valladolid Ordinances of 1432 which were written in Spanish (in Hebrew characters), with common Hebrew concepts and phrases interpolated where appropriate. (See Baer, *Die Juden* vol. 2, no. 287, pp. 280-97).

[37] ממדרש אמריה צועקת / ברוב כחה בוכה משתי עיניה ואומרת / אוי ואבוי כי הגביר הסגירני / והבעל והגבירה עיניתני / והשם שמע עצקתה / וראה דמעתה / ושלח אליה מלאך והשגיח בה / וזהו וימצאה מלאך ה׳ על עין המים / כמו מי יתן ראשי מים / ... (Ẓ.M. Gen. p. 37b). The use of rhymes to describe feelings of suffering people is very effective. (See below p. 57).

[38] E.g. Ẓ.M. Gen. pp. 67b, 69b, 96a. Ex. p. 58a (See also Num. pp. llb,12b).

39 An elaborately detailed study will show many similarities to the conclusions reached by Shalem in his study of the 16th century exegetes R. Moses Alsheikh and his teacher, R. Joseph Taitaẓaq (See above n. 1).

40 Ex. p. 37b, and see also ibid., p. 21b.

41 Gen. p. 68b.

42 It is partially quoted above p. 45.

43 Ex. p. 46b.

44 Gen. p. 35a.

45 See also Ẓ.M. Gen. pp. 13a, 35a, 73a. Lev. pp. 5b, 33b. Num. pp. 7b, 21b, 40b. Compare however, *Sefer ha-Émunah veha-Bitaḥon* in *Kitvei ha-Ramban* vol. 2, ch. 25, p. 364. Concerning the use of cognate languages in exegesis, compare C.B. Chavel, *Rabbi Moses ben Nachman*, Jerusalem, 1967, p. 147.

46 בלי ספר ובלי מלמד, בלי ספר ומדרש, בלי מלמד ובלי ספר (Ẓ.M. Gen. p. 86b, Ex. pp. 25b, 33b, Deut. p. 14a).

47 For the preacher, see J. Dan, *Hebrew Ethical and Homiletical literature*, p. 27ff. J. Hacker, "The Sefardi Sermon in the Sixteenth Century - Between Literature and Historical Source," *Peàmim* 26, 1986, pp. 116-18, and n. 23 there.

48 Rhymes by Saba are, generally, either an indication of satisfaction over an original interpretation (e.g. Ẓ.M. Gen. pp. 49a, 86b. Ex. p. 33b. Num. p. 46b. É.K. Esther p. 57), an introduction to an important issue (Ẓ.M. Gen. p. 46b. Deut. p. 36b, 74a. É.K. Esther p. 3), or a description of emotions (Ẓ.M. Gen. pp. 37b, 49b, 77b, 95b, 100b).

49 Ẓ.M. Gen. p. 86b. In the last rhyme Saba refers to his lack of books in El Qsar el Kebir. We learn of the competitive nature of oral preaching from the incident following Saba's sermon in the "gathering of the scholars in Castile," where one of the qabbalists in the audience said, hesitantly, that Saba had not been original and that the idea had been borrowed from the *Zohar*. Saba promised to provide a feast for the scholars if he would find the passage and send it to him (Z.M. Gen. p. 99a).

50 He calls Rashi המפרש הגדול, הרב הגדול, הגדול הצרפתי (Z.M. Gen. pp. 61a, 81a, 97a. Ex. p. 32b). The few places where Rashi left an unanswered question seem to present a special challenge for Saba (ibid, Gen. pp. 61a, 81a, 97a). On the total acceptance of Rashi's commentary in Spain in this period see A. Gross, "Sefardic Attitudes to Rashi's Commentary on the Torah," *Rashi - Studies in his Works* [Z.A. Steinfeld ed.], Ramat Gan (1993), pp. 47-55.

51 Ibid, Ex. p. 22b.

52 Ibid, p. 26b. See also Gen. p. llb.

53 Ibid, p. 32b. On this peculiar usage of the phrase חמור נושא ספרים and an earlier such usage, see Libowitz p. 34. Even the expression describing Rashi's interpretation is derogatory, for it is a paraphrase of טוב שבגויים הרוג

54 Gross, Saba, p. 223.

55 Colophon at the end of Deut. in ms. Oxford (Manor, Saba, p. 230).

56 עיין ברמב״ן ז״ל שתפס לרש״י ז״ל בפירושו ופירש הוא פי׳ המדרש ולא הזכירו (Ẓ.M. Gen. p. 117a). M. Kasher suggests that Nachmanides never saw that Midrash. (*Torah Shelemah*, VIII, New-York, 1950, p. 1677, n. 47). For an implicit criticism on similar grounds, see Ẓ.M. Gen. p. 115a.

57 Ibid, Ex. p. 33b. For the expression כמתנבא ואיני יודע see e.g. Nachmanides on Ex. 6,2.

58 Its importance for Qabbalistic exegesis was paramount, because of the grave dangers which might be caused by erratic interpretations. This is indeed RaDBaZ' explicit license: וכתבתי כמה פעמים שאין אני אומר שאין למצוות טעם זולת מה שאני כותב, אלא דעתי שכיון שמה שכתבתי הוא בנוי על הקדמות אותיות אשר מסרו לנו הראשונים ז״ל אי אפשר שלא יהיה זה מכלל ע׳ פנים של התורה וכולם כהלכה (*Meẓudat David*, Zolkiev, 1862, p. 62b, no. 435. See also below p. 52, for the same use of this dictum by Saba).

59 For a partial quotation see below p. 69.

60 É.K. Ruth, p. 21a.

61 Saba copies the Midrash in its entirety to show the parallels to his commentary,

thus claiming, in essence, that he is not commenting directly on the Biblical text but rather indirectly through interpretion of Midrashic text:

מדרש	*סבע*
עם נערותי, אלו הצדיקים	שבע הנערות הראויות לה מבית המלך. והיודע סוד הייחוד...היא כנסת ישראל עין יעקב יוכל להבין כל זאת הפרשה. וזהו,
עינייך בשדה...אלו סנהדרין וכתוב עינייך כיונים...על אבן אחת שבעה עיניים.	עינייך בשדה...היא שדה תפוחים...
לבלתי נגעך, שלא לרחקה.	רמז על מדות הדין, לבלתי נגעך.
וצמית...אל הכלים, אלו הצדיקים.	וצמית...אלו החכמים היודעים סוד ה׳.
ושתית מאשר ישאבון...זה בית השואבה שמשם שואבין רוח הקדש וחכמה...	ושתית...שהוא סוד הדיבוק ששמחים כשמחת בית השואבה. והנערים הם התלמידים.
ותפול על פניה...מלמד שנתנבאה בעצמה...	ותפול...שלמדה סוד הייחוד ונפלה על פניה לכסות עיניה בשעת הדיבוק.

62 É.K. Ruth, pp. 12b-13a. The source of the idea is *Zohar ‹adash,* Ruth, p. 96b.
63 Ẓ.M. Deut. p. 38b.
64 E.g. Gen. 86b, 124a, 125a, 132a, Num. p. 20a.
65 Ibid, Gen. p. l0a. In Z.H. Saba expresses this idea at length (fols. l0v-13v). Concerning exegesis, he adds an insight into the process of creativity: ומזה ניתן כח למחברים מפרשי התורה שיש להם כח לפרש דברים העמוקים מכח לבם ולשונם המסדר הדברים בפיהם. ולפעמים זה הכח לא ניתן להבין אלא מכח עט הסופר ואין יכולים לסדר הדברים ולהוציאן מן הכח אל הפועל...ומיד בהתחלת הכתיבה יד ה׳ עליהם השכיל והצליח ומלבן יוצאו מלין בכח הכתב והמכתב... In the same manner Saba explains the "miracle" of printing: וכן ציורי האותיות להוציאם בדפוס לעשות ספרים הרבה...אלו הדברים הם דברים גדולים ונראה שא״א להעשות בידי אדם. וזה הכח ניתן לאלו האומנים מששת ימי בראשית...ניתן כח לעושים דפוס האותיות ואח״כ מחברים אותם ויוצאים ספרים הרבה מכוונים בדפוס בכח יד ה׳ ובכח הלוחות, עד שנר׳ שיד אדם לא עשה דבר זה וכאילו מעצמם יצאו... (fol. 11r, 13v). He might already have seen printing in action in Zamora where Hebrew books were printed in 1485-87. (A.M. Haberman, *The History of the Hebrew Book*, Jerusalem (1968), p. 99).
66 É.K. Ruth, p. 21b.
67 Ẓ.M. Deut. p. 74a, and compare Gen. 86b, quoted above p. 49.
68 G. Scholem, *Elements of the Kabbalah and its Symbolism*, Jerusalem, 1973, pp. 41-3.
69 E.g. Ẓ.M. p. 72a.
70 Ibid, Num. p. 46a.
71 *Sefer Yeẓirah*, London (1902), ch. 2, p. 9. Saba uses it to describe the *Sefirot* (Ẓ.M. Deut. p. 74b).
72 לפי שדרשו סמוכים, לפי שהתורה כולה קשורה כעדרי רחלים הקשורים...
73 Already Nachmanides in his commentary on *Sefer Yeẓirah* forms the word "lev" out of the last and first letters of the Torah. However, there it is connected to Qabbalistic symbolism (*Qiryat Sefer* 6 (1930), p. 401). See also Baḥya on Deut. 34,12.
74 Ẓ.M. Gen. p. 98b. The identical idea appears in the works of many qabbalists like R. Ezra, R. Baḥya ben Asher (See Scholem, Elements, p. 48, and E. Gottlieb, *The Qabbalah in the Writings of Baḥya ben Asher*, Jerusalem (1970), p. 63). Compare Baḥya on Gen. 36, 39 (ed. Chavel) p. 302.
75 É.K. Esther, p. 94. The context is non-mystical.
76 Ibid, p. 24.
77 Ẓ.M. Deut. p. 13b. For the Redemption as the theme that unites the entire Bible, see below pp. 159ff.
78 Saba uses the term *Torah* but probably refers to the whole Bible.
79 Ẓ.M. Deut. p. 71a-b.
80 See also, É.K. Esther pp. 35, 37, 59.
81 Ẓ.M. Deut, p. 13b. That mystical mysteries are hidden in the division is an idea

that appears in the *Zohar* where it says that one must end the reading of each Portion in the exact place where Moses ended it (*Zohar* II, p. 206b, and see *Magen Ávraham*, Ó.Ḥ. No. 282).

82 Ẓ.M. Lev. p. 9a-b.

83 Ibid, p. 16b.

84 Ibid, Deut. p. 21a. This seems to be behind the ending of *Toledot*: אח״כ אמר וירא עשו כי ברך את יעקב, לחתום הפרשה ברשעתו ובהטעתו שהיה מטעה לאביו בדברים שקרים... (Ibid, Gen. p. 61b).

85 G. Scholem in the article mentioned above (n. 61).

86 A good example is the last paragraph of Behar which Saba tries to connect to the main theme of the Portion, and indeed to its beginning, while attempting to show its connection to the following Portion (see below p. 101).

87 Saba describes that commentary as follows: ...ובעמלי שטרחתי לפי מסי אבות ולקשרה כלה מראשה ועד סופה... (Ẓ.M. Gen. p. lla). We find the same tendency in a comment of his on the Passover Haggadah where in a short passage he attempts to connect five subsequent paragraphs (Ẓ.M. Ex. p. 20a). This "obsession" goes beyond the standard homiletical technique of finding connections.

88 We have dealt with one aspect of it in discussing the notion of originality as Saba viewed it.

89 Gross, Saba, p. 220. This description of the first version of Ẓ.M. also accurately describes the extant version.

90 Ẓ.M. Gen. p. 49a (See also Shalem, *Alsheikh*, pp. 121ff).

91 Ibid, pp. 19b, l00a, Ex. p. 45a.

92 כפי דעת חז״ל שאם נמצא ההורג אח״כ אין לחוס עליו וראוי להורגו. ולפי זה היה ראוי לומר, ואתה תבער דם החייב, איך אמר דם הנקי. אבל לפי הפירוש שפירשתי למעלה שחוזר לדם ההרוג יתיישב יפה. (ibid. Deut. p. 32a).

93 Discussing the justification for the killing of the people of Shechem Saba says: ...ורז״ל עשו מדרש (Ibid Gen. p. 95a).

94 It is divided into "creative historiography", and "creative philology" (Y. Heinemann, *The Ways of the Aggadah*, Jerusalem, 1954).

95 מעשה אבות סימן לבנים (Heinemann, p. 33).

96 Heinemann, p. 209, n. 86, and A. Funkenstein, "Nachmanides' Typological Reading of History," *Ẓion* 45 (1980), pp. 35-59.

97 It is true concerning particular interpretations, as well as in areas of thought such as *taàmei ha-miẓvot*. Nachmanides was the medieval exegete and thinker who most influenced Saba.

98 Gross, Saba, 220-1.

99 Let us note that the *Zohar* was considered by Saba as a Midrashic book, and in style and content it should be considered as belonging to this genre (e.g. Heinemann, p. 176).

100 Heinemann, p. 23.

101 B.T. Menaḥot, p. 43b.

102 See below p. 108.

103 Ẓ.M. Deut. p. 14b.

104 See above p. 18-9. Both cases are to be connected to persecutions in Saba's own generation.

106 This phenomenon is not completely non-existent. We find interpretations of prophecies directed to certain heretical beliefs (e.g. Ẓ.M. Deut. p. 53a. Yaàvez̧ in *Ór ha-Ḥayyim*, p. 73, and earlier by Nachmanides on Ex. 13, 16), but this cannot be compared to the full scale historicizing by the Midrash.

106 Heinemann, pp. 39-32.

107 Ẓ.M. Gen. p. 60b.

108 É.K. Ruth, p. 21b.

109 Ibid, 26a. See also Ẓ.M. Gen. p. 53b, 55b, 103b.

110 Ibid, p. 52b.

111 Ibid, p. 37b.

112 Ibid, p. 49b.

113 Ibid, p. 45b.

[114] The rhymes could very well be an influence of the maqamah literature.
[115] Ibid, p. 99b.
[116] Ibid, p. 101b.
[117] É.K. Esther, p. 81.
[118] I. Twersky, *Rabad of Posquières*, Cambridge, Mass. 1962, p. 39.
[119] E.g. Ẓ.M. Gen. p. 85b, Deut. p. 48b.
[120] See below chapters 4,6.
[121] Indeed this is behind the close ties between the Bible and the reality of Saba's period, for the imagination projects one's own existence onto the distant text. (This is true, by and large, for the medieval mind and is reflected in descriptions of Biblical stories and characters in art).
[122] This tendency of Saba's goes much beyond the use of this method by preceeding medieval homilists.
[123] אני רוצה לדרוש אותו לשבח... (É.K. Ruth p. 11b).
[124] Ẓ.M. Ex. p. 4a.
[125] Ibid, Gen. p. 27a.
[126] Ibid, Num. 32a. Saba continues to expound the verse in the same fashion, using interesting associations (For more examples, see ibid. Ex. pp. 3b, 9b).
[127] Ẓ.M. Gen. p. 25b.
[128] See below p. 124.
[129] For the idea derived from this parallel see below p. 129-30.
[130] Saba's quotation of this verse is inaccurate. (This is by no means his only misquotation).
[131] Ẓ.M. Gen. p. 98b. Saba tells us that he embarked on that intellectual effort due to the conviction that even what seems unimportant in the Torah, such as the generations of Esau, contains profound teachings.
[132] We had the occasion to discuss Saba's view of the totality of units leading to the structural analysis of units such as the Pentateuch, including its internal parallelism (E.g. Genesis-Leviticus, Exodus-Numbers. See below p. 126) and inter-book parallelism (E.g. Lamentation-Pentateuch, Avot-Pentateuch). This should be taken into account as a factor behind the search for order in any given scriptural unit. However, the immediate method of finding the key to the structure and understanding of our chapter is that of phrase-association.
[133] Ẓ.M. Gen. p. 63a-76a.

י״א. וישכב במקום ההוא	י״ג. הארץ אשר אתה שוכב
י״ב. סולם מוצב ארצה	י״ד. זרעך כעפר הארץ
וראשו מגיע השמימה	ופרצת ימה וקדמה...
והנה מלאכי אלהים	ונברכו בך כל משפחות..
י״ג. והנה ה׳ נצב עליו	ט״ו. והנה אנכי עמך ושמרתיך...

[134] Ibid, p. 65a.
[135] As a secondary factor we might add that Saba has a special "weakness" for dreams (See below).
[137] Ẓ.M. Gen. p. 99b.
[138] Ibid, p. 105b.
[139] Ibid, p. 59b.
[140] Ibid, p. 53a-b.
[141] Ibid, pp. 72b-86b.
[142] This, incidently, is a clear symptom of Midrashic influence (See our discussion of this point below p. 171-2). There is yet another set of internal parallels in Saba's analysis of the Reproof sections. He claims that the blessings in the opening parts are qualitatively not inferior to the curses (Ẓ.M. Lev. p. 33b, Deut. p. 47b). Those parallels are neither neat nor well arranged, nor is there any aesthetic dimension of associations. His motive for undertaking this exposition is explicitly polemical. (See also below p. 155). The same applies, apparently, to the long passage of equations in the Song of *Haázinu*, where Saba attempts to show that the punishments for Israel's ingratitude are parallel to the favours God has bestowed on them. The aim there is to show that God is just and does not over-punish His people (ibid, Deut. p. 67a-b).

CHAPTER THREE

QABBALAH

Ẓ.M. is basically a non-esoteric commentary, but it does contain Qabbalistic material which cannot be ignored. Even if one would agree that Saba's Qabbalah cannot be characterized as extremely innovative - which is presumably the reason why scholars of Qabbalah have not devoted more than a few sentences to him - it would be a mistake to assume that his works have no significance for the history of Qabbalah. It is incumbent upon us to determine: a) what is the nature of the Qabbalistic passages included by Saba and the reason for their inclusion; b) what is the meaning Qabbalah had for Saba personally. In the course of our study we shall touch upon two topics somewhat neglected by scholars: popularization vs. esotericism, and the role of Qabbalah in the Jewish religion and in the perfection of the individual. These are major issues that must be investigated in order to understand the history of the expansion of Qabbalah and its power as a spiritual force within the framework of later medieval Judaism.

1. Saba's Knowledge of the Zohar

In general, Saba's Qabbalah is that of the Zohar. His many references to the *Zohar* and the long quotations, mostly from memory, from this vast literature throughout the Ẓ.M., are the best proof of this.[1] Saba himself also states this explicitly:

> And now listen to what the holy one, Rabbi Shimon bar Yoḥai, wrote about this...and all that I say in this book revolves around his words and his opinion, since it is a true teaching.[2]

Saba acknowledges his indebtedness to the *Zohar* again, this time in rhyme:

> ואני מפיל תחינתי לפני כל יודע ספר / שאם ימצא בזה הספר אימרי שפר / או דבר טוב אחוזה ברשתי / ידוע תדע כי גנוב הוא אתי / מספרי המדרשים או מספרי איש עתי / הוא הקדוש רשב״י / ...[3]

From a source examination of his references and quotations, as well as from his ideas in general, it is clear that Saba read and, indeed, possibly mastered the entire *Zohar*, including *Zohar Ḥadash*, *Tiqqunei Zohar*, and *Sitrei Torah* - not such a common phenomenon in the 15th century.[4]

The following quotation, even after allowing for conventional exaggeration, gives us some insight into the extent of his library of Qabbalistic works. Mourning over his lost paradise in Portugal, he writes proudly about his library and its contents:

לפי שהיה אור עיני אתי / והיו בידי כלי אומנותי / ספרים עד אין מספר / לא יאומן כי יסופר / מה שהיה לי מספרי הזוהר והמאורות / כפול ומכופל בכל מיני מהדורות / ולא ידעתי ספורות / בספרים מחודשים ממדרשות וספירות.[5]

2. The Ultimate in Mystical Study

What was the ideal form of study of the Qabbalah for Saba? It was not the recital of the *Zohar* by heart but, rather, a two-stage study similar in a way to that of the Talmud, in which innovation followed the mastery of the available knowledge supplied by tradition.

In a unique interpretation of Ruth 2, 14-16, Saba depicts Ruth as a student of Qabbalah being initiated into its mysteries by Boaz' reapers:

> Therefore he said that when she would confront such things and not be able to eat bread, 'and dip your morsel in vinegar' (Ruth 2, 14), just a little dip, but that she should not try to penetrate into the inner things, as it says, 'You have no business with the things that are secrets' (B.T. Ḥagigah 13a). And she did so 'and she sat beside the reapers,' and not among them. 'And he offered her parched corn,' things that suit her, to feed her from the light things. And since understanding that one deduces one thing out of the other, and that after he has the basics 'A wise man will hear and will increase learning' (Prov. 1,5), therefore it says that he commanded them: 'Let her glean even among the sheaves and do not reproach her,' (Ruth 2,15) although she might try to penetrate into the inner things. And since it is possible that she would err in the understanding of those things...therefore he said: 'And let fall also some of the handfuls,' (ibid. 2,16), namely, that even though she would penetrate in order to understand the profound things which are bound to each other like sheaves, nevertheless, do not rebuke her.[6]

The student starts slowly, sampling only the "light foods" and assuming only a passive role. Then he enters the circle and may study deeper issues, taking on a more active role, albeit under the supervision and coaching of the members of the circle. As we have no other sources that support this description it is hard to draw from here any historical conclusions concerning the joining of newcomers into the fold of a qabbalistic circle in 15th century Spain.

The ultimate goal is independence and complete detachment from the master, since only through the development of one's own ability to solve problems without consultation with the master can one reach the true understanding of the hidden mysteries. This is, indeed, what Elijah told Elisha, his disciple, before ascending to heaven:

> 'If you see me being taken away from you' (II Kings 2,10)...so that whenever you have any doubt you will not say: I will go to Elijah and he will interpret for me the secrets, than 'it shall be so unto you'

> (ibid..), for when you will know that I am not with you, but that you have to ceaselessly devote days and nights to concentrated study, only then will you be able to attain everything and 'it shall be so unto you.'[7]

3. Popularization vs. Esotericism

The impetus to reveal the esoteric usually derives from a conflict between the traditional element which demands discipline and prohibits the members of the exclusive group from spreading their knowledge to the multitudes, and the individual's inner need to share the "truth" with others. The fruit born of these conflicting factors is popularization of one form or another. Therefore, a great deal of the enormous body of Qabbalistic literature belongs to this category of literary compromise. Moreover, one can possibly argue for the inclusion of the whole body *en bloc*, for Qabbalah by its very nature is an oral teaching and no one doubts that some elements are omitted even from the most explicit books and remain concealed.

The difference between writers would only be in quality and quantity. Therefore, one must characterize the particular limits and methods of the popularizer, as well as the extent to which he was able to be consistent with his guidelines and follow them through accordingly.

The element of esotericism fluctuates in accordance with the aims of the author and the nature of his intended readers.[8] Consequently, the definition of "popularize" as "render suitable or intelligible to the common people...,"[9] is correct only for an extreme sort of popularization.

While the tension described above is usually at the root of the phenomenon, it would be insufficient to leave it at that. One must also seek the secondary reasons (or excuses) by which the writer justified his endeavor. To put things into perspective, let us take a few examples that will illustrate the variety between the poles.

Rabbi Isaac Sagi Nahor, writing in the 13th century, when Qabbalah was still limited to a small circle of mystics, was very cautious. His more esoteric traditions were committed to writing only in "hidden epistles" (*megillot setarim*) which were not sent out lest they fall in undeserving individuals. Such things were taught by him to his disciples orally.[10] Moreover, his Qabbalistic writings contain what appear to us as contradictions due to the different intended audience.[11]

Concealing the secrets from unworthy people is characteristic of the period and is very conspicuous in another Geronese mystic's writing - Nachmanides. His commentary on the Pentateuch, which also contains Qabbalistic interpretations, is so unclear to the uninitiated that it seems to have been a direct reason for its failure to gain popularity, despite Nachmanides rabbinic over towering stature, and it being succeeded by the Qabbalistic system of the *Zohar*.[12] Nachmanides' students continued the strategy of their master keeping the secrets within intimate circles, and when faced the outburst of the new outgoing attitude of the new school "the 'timid' Kabbalah of Nachmanides' school was doomed to colapse."[13]

The Zoharic school of Qabbalah is indeed much more aggressive in writing. But even in the case of such a prolific writer as Rabbi Moses de Leon, who was the main to propagator of mysticism in the later part of the 13th century, we find the need to apologize for committing a mystical oral teaching to writing. In *Mishkan ha-Èdut* and *Sefer ha-Rimmon* he claims that the influence of rationalism which caused a spiritual and religious deterioration of the generation under up to the point of scorn at the commandments and antinomianism must be countered by Qabbalah.[14]

Two hundred years later, in the generation following the Expulsion, we find several popularizers. Let us survey some of them. Rabbi Moses Cordovero's short treatise *Ór Neèrav* is an example of extreme popularization. Moreover, this treatise includes an outright plea for the study of Qabbalah. Not only is it allowed and not harmful, claims Cordovero, but it is also a religious duty. This message is conveyed in the first part of the book. The second part is an "Introduction for the Beginners," where basic ideas and symbols of the Qabbalah are discussed. Cordovero concludes with an abridged dictionary of symbols and the Qabbalistic terms they represent. This book was to serve as a guide which would attract the uninitiated, enable them to continue beyond the book's limited scope and to delve into the depths of the study of Qabbalah. As the excuse for his popularization, Cordovero says that the spread of Qabbalistic knowledge could hasten the redemption.[15]

Rabbi Judah Ḥayyat's *Minḥat Yehudah* is a commentary on an earlier Qabbalistic treatise named *Maàrekhet ha-Élohut*, which Ḥayyat, a contemporary of Saba's, tries to make intelligible. Although in comparison to the above mentioned *Ór Neèrav* it is not so systematic and clear for the beginning student of Qabbalah, it is, nevertheless, designed for non-Qabbalists interested in the esoteric teachings of the Qabbalah.

Ḥayyat relates in his introduction that he was approached by Rabbi Joseph Yaàveẓ, a Spanish refugee, and some distinguished people from Mantua, to explicate the mysteries for them.[16] It would seem that Yaàveẓ, who was singled out by Ḥayyat, pushed the leaders of the Mantuan community to ask Ḥayyat to write his commentary (and probably to finance it).[17] Ḥayyat says, however, that he had his own reason for doing so, - his belief that the study of Qabbalah would hasten the redemption.[18] In the same category we may put Rabbi Meir Ibn Gabai who discusses freely the doctrines and details of Qabbalah in his works *Tolaàt Yaàkov*, *Àvodat ha-Qodesh* and in *Derekh Émunah*, his very explicit treatise on the *Ten Sefirot*. He expresses the hope that someone would be influenced by his writings, apologizes in a routine manner for doing something that might be more befitting a great person, but does not seem to be bothered at all by his act of revealing mystical secrets.[19]

Rabbi Moses Alsheikh's commentaries on the Bible are different from the works mentioned above. Though from the same *milieu* as Cordovero, Alsheikh chose not to deal with Qabbalah in his commentaries. Although they contain Qabbalistic traces, they are rare, and when the author does refer to an interpretation along such lines, he no more than alludes to it without really saying anything that would be comprehensible to anyone who does not have the proper background. Indeed, one might question the validity of terming it a "popularization,"[20] since popularization has a clear target and audience while here the material is vague. Some popularization is found in Alsheikh's thought which is based on Qabbalah but without referring to it or to its technical terminology.[21]

Now let us examine the nature of the Qabbalah contained in Saba's writings in general and in Ẓ.M. in particular.

3.1. Between Esotericism and Popularization

Saba acknowledges the validity of the accepted rule that there are profound religious ideas that should not be discussed in public. This is true not only for mystical teachings, "for ideas told in public might be misinterpreted or even understood contrary to their initial intention."[22]

Consequently, the people of Israel were divided at the foot of Mount Sinai into two groups:

> ...and therefore the majority of the people do not need to be told about secrets and wisdom, but rather things that comfort the hearts, like Aggadah and stories...'So you shall tell the house of Jacob,' who are the majority of the people, things that attract the hearts. But 'to the Children of Israel,' who are the wise and the elders, you should tell secrets and wisdom...and hidden things from the mysteries of wisdom.[23]

This division applies also to the commandment of *Haq'hel*:

> '...in their ears' (Deut. 31,11), to allude to the secrets of the Torah which are handed down to them in a whisper...and since the masses...do not need this, therefore it says, 'so that they will hear...' (ibid. 31,12), to teach that for them hearing will suffice, so that they will learn to revere God by observing the actual commandments such as Ẓiẓit and Tefillin.[24]

In light of Saba's unquestioned awareness of the need for esotericism in Qabbalah, there are two obvious questions with regard to Ẓ.M. which need to be dealt with: a) why did Saba insert Qabbalistic passages in the book?; b) to what extent did he remain loyal to his own sense of esotericism as reflected in the passages quoted above?

Saba claims that the knowledge of Qabbalistic reasons for the commandment is valuable for everyone since one who understands that there are mysteries behind these seemingly physical acts will keep and observe them more carefully. This does not necessitate any profound understanding of the particulars but only a general awareness of the meta-Halakhic significance that is imbedded in the acts performed.[25]

However, there is more to it than this and a case in point is the commandment of *Ẓiẓit* in which every detail is shown by Saba to have its symbolic significance. The general idea is that God creates unity in the universe. Now, what ought a person to know?, Saba answers:

> And this unity [ha-yiḥud veha-qishur] every man who is called a Jew and wears these fringes should have in mind that he is connected and tied wondrously to the (only) one God and thus becomes a part of God.[26]

Saba, who started by explaining the cosmic significance of this commandment, ends by emphasizing a different dimension altogether. Above and beyond the cosmic effects and the need for special care in performing the details of a commandment, there is a personal dimension as well. Saba says here that the person is rewarded with spiritual ascent for "since he has a wing [*kenaf ẓiẓit*] he is united with God...by the means of that wing which enables him to fly up...." In other words, every simple Jew has the opportunity to taste some of the bliss that is the lot of the Qabbalist. Here, then, we have the manifestation of the inner need to share the true religious experience with the masses who are, after all, the Qabbalist's co-religionists.[27]

How popular is the Qabbalah in Ẓ.M.? At the outset of Ẓ.M. Saba makes a conservative declaration, stating that the story of Creation contains mysteries which the Sages forbade to be expounded.[28] He remains loyal to this prohibition and does not deal with any Qabbalistic doctrines concerning the Creation [*maàseh bereshit*]. His restraint can be exemplified by the fact that he quotes the *Targum Yerushalmi* on the first verse "With wisdom God created,"[29] ignoring completely the Qabbalistic connotations of the word "wisdom [*ḥokhmah*]."[30] His references to the *Zohar* are devoid of any mystical value and, thus, he consistently upholds his opening statement throughout the first chapter.

Saba does elaborate on the creation of the *Sefirot*, but not in Ẓ.M.[31] The closest he comes to a theoretical discussion of their number is in the following passage which will illustrate just how far Saba was ready to go in an explicitly theoretical discussion of basic esoteric doctrines:

> ...and therefore they said that He enumerates here thirteen items, gold, silver, copper etc. to symbolize the thirteen attributes which are identical with the ten Sefirot and the three which are hidden, and we do not know their names. And so you will find that in the prayer of Yishtabbaḥ

> there is a variety of thirteen types of praises...but one should not dwell on this at length.[32]

When he refers to the *Sefirot* and the unity among them he does not use the names that were generally used in this period but rather equivalent terms that would not be understood by reader unfamiliar with Qabbalah. The following passage concerning the need to unite the *Sefirot* in a symbolic act is characteristic:

> ולכן צריך לאגוד כל אלה הדברים ולטבול אותם בדם הציפור השחוטה ולא יהיה נרגן מפריד אלוף, ולא יהיה מפריד בין אחים, אלא לחבר האהל להיות אחד.[33]

After commenting briefly on the structure of the Tabernacle and its furnishings, Saba summarizes:

> And similarly all the sizes...and numbers are precise and intentional, containing allusions to the numbers of the Holy Names, the fifty gates of Binah...And one should not dwell on this at length, because these are the mysteries of the world (and I wrote this) only in order that you would know in a general manner that all the items of the Tabernacle are symbols for supernal things and for the Creation [maàseh bereshit].[34]

He presents a general Qabbalistic outline so that the reader will be aware of the mystical level of the Torah and that the interested one would go and search for that knowledge by himself. It is clear that Saba does not intend Ẓ.M. to be a textbook for a beginner's course in Qabbalah.

Another means of popularizing Qabbalistic material is by making it available to the public through the dissemination of hitherto unavailable esoteric writings. In the context of Qabbalah, the case that might come to mind is the publication of the *Zohar* in the sixteenth-century Italy. This was an attempt to make esoteric texts available through the medium of printing. The inclusion in Ẓ.M. of long passages quoted almost verbatim from the *Zohar* can be considered an effort, albeit on a limited scale, along the same lines.[35]

Saba quotes very often either from the *Zohar*, *Midrash ha-Neèlem*, or *Tiqqunei Zohar*, in the same manner that he quotes the Midrash. Usually he cites the "Revealed Midrash" [*midrash ha-galui*], and then goes on to say "and in the Hidden Midrash [*midrash ha-neèlam*] it is written..."

As we have already mentioned, he quotes *almost* verbatim. There are two reasons for this: a) many a time, mainly in the first parts of his book, he relies on memory alone (a fact that not only teaches us about his dedication to the study of the *Zohar* before the expulsions but also attests to his extraordinary memory); b) Saba translated some passages into Hebrew.[36] Hence we have here a popularization in two senses: Saba made esoteric material available and also more intelligible by eliminating the difficulties presented by the *Zohar*'s original Aramaic.

The idea of quoting Zoharic material in the context of an exegetical work is not new. We already find R. Joseph Angelino, in his *Livnat ha-Sappir* quoting from *Midrash ha-Neèlam*. The translation of Zoharic passages is not novel either. R. David ben Judah he-Ḥasid, who wrote 150 years before Saba incorporated such translations in his Book of Mirrors, although those are not as long as those in Ẓ.M.[37] Saba, however, differs from them on in that Ẓ.M. is basically a non-mystical commentary and hence his audience is wider.[38]

We must, however, qualify the impression of Saba's popular tendencies in Ẓ.M.. In actual fact, the majority of Zoharic passages referred to or quoted by Saba, are not of an esoteric nature and can be read in the same manner as the many Midrashic interpretations quoted in Ẓ.M.[39] Here too, Saba tries to minimize his revelation of the esoteric.

Comparing Ẓ.M. with another treatise by Saba will underscore the conservative attitude of the author to the use of mystical material in Ẓ.M.

As we have seen, Saba does not usually talk about the *Sefirot* by the more known names, but feels more comfortable referring to them by other names given them by Qabbalistic tradition. He also avoids any technical discussion of the divine Emanations. He does so, however, in a short treatise devoted to this very issue. It was written for Rabbi Alal ben Alḥaikh who apparently was his disciple (at least in Qabbalah).[40]

Only when we read this treatise written for an individual can we appreciate Saba's restraint in Ẓ.M.[41] It explains the system of the *Sefirot*, the balance between right and left - *Din* and *Raḥamim*, a short reference to the differing opinions concerning their number (thirteen or ten) and the status of the first *Sefirah* [*keter èlyon*], which is above the ten knowable to humans, as well as a detailed survey of the nature of each. There is a short explanation of the manner of their emanation. There is a special emphasis on their unity which is incomprehensible to the human mind.[42] The Sefirot are referred to by their common names (*Ḥokhmah*, *Binah...Tiféret...Malkhut*), which are not used generally by Saba in Ẓ.M..

When compared to the elaborate interpretation of the *Sefirot* by Ibn Gabai we see again how cautious Saba was. Although it was written for an individual he writes: "And behold the emanation of these *Sefirot*, hoe they emanated, how they were, and how they count ten, it is very profound [*àmoq àmoq mi yimzaénu*] and no human mind can contain it. The only thing you should know is that after They emanated from Him, They and Him and their Name and His are one"[43] And even in a treatise written for an individual Saba comes to the point where he says:

> And concerning this point one should not explain more in writing, for it is of the things which are transmitted orally, and I have already revealed this mystery to you orally on the Sabbath.[44]

In summation, the fact that Saba advocates an oral esoteric teaching of the Qabbalah does not prevent him from explaining particulars in a Qabbalistic manner nor even from quoting long passages from the *Zohar*, for he distinguishes between profound mysteries to which he only alludes, and other teachings that may be communicated via the less esoteric written medium. However, even script retains a measure of esotericism in comparison with a public oral sermon. In addition, Saba employs a "half esoteric" method of reference to Qabbalistic terminology.[45]

Can his Qabbalistic endeavor be called popularization? Yes, but only to a certain extent. The mystics would gain more knowledge of particulars through short comments or references to the *Zohar*. The uninitiated reader might become curious enough to seek that esoteric knowledge which Saba did not really provide. In other words, the Qabbalah in Ẓ.M. is seldom "rendered suitable or intelligible to the common people," but is designed to attract the interest of the reader.[46] One might say that it is the first step toward popularization. It is Saba's *Introduction to the Ten Sefirot* that better qualifies as such, but that treatise was apparently not intended for popular use but for an individual, who has been a close private student of his. To him Saba imparted some of his Qabbalistic traditions. However, the more esoteric doctrines he did not commit to writing even for him, and others he only explained to him in a very superficial manner.

When we take a look at the writing of Qabbalistic works by the Qabbalists exiled from Spain, and the straight forward discussion of major mystical doctrines, they seem to fit very well with the tradition of the Zoharic school from late 13th century and on, Saba does not. After the Expulsion they had all the more reasons to write down Sefardic Qabbalistic traditions so that they not be forgotten. Most of the Qabbalists copied works they owned due to the lack of books in the wake of the Expulsion, which might also be the reason for Saba's inclusion of Zoharic texts. The meeting with other forms of Qabbalah in Italy and in the East served for them as a stimulus to answer, criticize, integrate, and reconcile.[47] Saba's attitude to writing of Qabbalah seems to be outdated and out of place. He wanted to spread the light of Qabbalah, but in a limited and controlled manner. This might reflect Saba's conservative character, a fact that seems evident in his stand on other issues such as Messianism.

4. Halakhah and Qabbalah

Qabbalah, unlike philosophy, its spiritual counterpart, has exercised a profound influence on the Halakhah. The first major breakthrough of the Qabbalah into the world of the latter occurred with the appearance of the *Zohar*.[48]

However, in broad national terms, its influence did not start to become apparent until two centuries later.

This mystical trend was naturally of an esoteric character and, therefore, it might seem, at first glance, that it should have been the exclusive concern of small esoteric circles. But Qabbalah is comprised of two elements - intellectual study of the mysteries of God hidden in the Torah, and the prescription of intentions one should have while performing any given commandment. The first element, which is of a theoretical nature, has no direct contact with the more practical Halakhah; while the second, being the practical arm of the mystical theory (though involving only the mind through the specifically prescribed *kavanot*), complements the Halakhic act by providing it with a symbolic Qabbalistic content. The contact with Halakhah was slowly widened and deepened through the development of a body of additional customs and Halakhic decisions based on the mystical-theoretical element. This development of Qabbalistic Halakhah and customs, contrary to the semi-practical element of *kavanot*, must have been aimed, to a certain extent, at the Jewish people at large even if the Qabbalists did not claim so openly. (This accounts for the fact that several Qabbalistic customs were accepted by Spanish Jewry quite early).

After the initial penetrations of the Qabbalah into the realm of Halakhah, significant inroads do not seem to have been made until the fifteenth century. These were deepened in the sixteenth century when the main carriers of the Qabbalistic tradition - the Jews of Spain - were dispersed. Only then, when the influence of its arch-rival, philosophy, had seriously been limited and Qabbalah started to emerge as the dominant spiritual complement to Halakhah, and only when its legitimacy almost ceased to be in question, historical conditions were ripe for a major Qabbalistic attempt to descend from the heights of esoteric elitism and influence the way of life of the nation as a whole.[49]

For the "neutral" Halakhic authorities Qabbalah was a spiritual-religious force which may have been authentic and supreme in its distinct realm but which should not be interfering with Halakhah, which belonged to the practical-religious realm and had its own internal set of rules and dynamics traditionally separated from any meta-Halakhic trend. However, if the details of Halakhic practice contain mysteries as the Qabbalists claimed, and if these are of supreme cosmic importance, then it follows that Qabbalah should have a say in the Halakhic decision-making process and should even be empowered to alter laws which hitherto were, "unfortunately," based solely on the exoteric processes of the Halakhic legal system.[50] If this claim was to be accepted on a national level, it had to be made on the basis of authority entrenched in historical reality. This could take place only when this argument was not to counter a total denial of the supremacy of Qabbalah, as was claimed by some individual Halakhists.[51]

In the following pages, we will discuss both aspects of Qabbalah, the intellectual and the practical-Halakhic in Saba's commentaries as they relate to the traditional value of Talmudic study and normative Halakhah.

4.1. Ẓeror ha-Kesef - A Lost Book

À propos the contact of Qabbalah and Halakhah in the practical legal realm, Saba tells us that in his youth he wrote a book on Jewish law[52] called *Ẓeror ha-Kesef*. He refers to it several times, and on the basis of these references we can describe its contents in general terms.

It dealt with the application of Qabbalah to Halakhah. It explained commandments as well as Halakhic details in a Qabbalistic light. It added Qabbalistically-oriented customs and presented a code of law whose Halakhic decisions took Qabbalah into account. The references to some sections of the book can teach us about its scope. It contained laws of Circumcision, *Rosh ha-Shanah*, Mourning, *Hanukkah* and *Purim*, Day of Atonement, *Tefillin*, Prayers, Levirate Marriage and *Ḥaliẓah*, and Laws of Idol Worshippers.[53]

Judging from the fact that Saba usually refers his readers to Ẓ.K. for lengthier discussions of the topics at hand, and from the fact that some of the material included in that work was of a homiletical nature, we can assume that it was not small. Most of the customs Saba mentions, as well as the reasons for the commandments can be traced back to the *Zohar*.[54] It seems that Ẓ.K. was much more explicit in revealing mystical secrets, because in Saba's Commentary on the Prayers he presents the reader with a detailed description for meditation on the *Sefirot* while reciting the first verse of the Shema) Saba tells us that it was included in Ẓ.K.[55]

The question of whether or not Saba rewrote this work in North Africa is based on one problematic reference to it. After discussing the esoteric meaning of the commandment to hear the sound of the horn [*shofar*] and of some of the prayers on *Rosh ha-Shanah*, Saba concludes "...as I have explained in Ẓ.K. in (the section of) the Laws of *Rosh ha-Shanah*, behold it is in Fez the great city."[56]

This statement could not have been written when Saba wrote this section of Ẓ.M. since he was still in El Qsar el Kebir. Furthermore, we know that he did not write Ẓ.K. until he had completed his commentaries on Avot, Ruth and Esther, since he gives us a precise time-table of his literary activity up to the beginning of the commentary on Esther. The most logical solution is that it was added later when Saba rewrote Ẓ.K., since we have already seen a similar interpolation.[57] The only difficulty with this is that there are two earlier references to Ẓ.K. in Ẓ.M. However, the statement indicating that there is a (single?) copy only in Fez sounds authentic, and one familiar with Saba's style and manner of writing would not be surprised at this. It would be uncharacteristic of Saba to check carefully for the first reference to Ẓ.K. for this interpolation.

The loss of Ẓ.K. is especially to be regretted for it might have saved scholars a great deal of speculation concerning the Qabbalah-Halakhah relationships in this period. We do not know for whom this book was intended, but the mere fact that a young Qabbalist sat down in fifteenth- century Castile to write, possibly for the first time, a compendium of Jewish law totally inseparable from and dependent upon Qabbalah, might suggest a certain readiness on the part of Spanish Jewry to adopt Qabbalistic practices and accept, in principle, a role for the Qabbalah in its Halakhic system beyond any particular customs (such as the repetition of the last three words of the Shema, which was apparently widely accepted in Spain).[58]

There is another remarkable point which one can gather from what Saba tells us about the book. He never characterizes it as a Qabbalistic book, although Qabbalah was its novel element and his reason for writing it. It was a book "concerning the laws [*dinnim*]," divided into sections called "Laws of [*hilkhot*] Circumcision" etc. in the tradition of the normative codes. In other words, in Saba's library the book was classified under "Halakhah" and, for him, its primary Qabbalistic component apparently was an integral part of Halakhah.

4.2. Qabbalah as Halakhah

There are a few relevant passages in Ẓ.M. that help us determine, however partially, Saba's position on the relationship between Halakhah and Qabbalah.[59] One concerns the laws of meat and milk.

The prohibition of eating meat and milk together was extended in the Jewish tradition to include eating dairy products after meat. Opinions vary as to how long must one wait between them. The most stringent opinion maintains that only six hours after eating meat may one have dairy products. Concerning the eating of meat after milk, most medieval *posqim* are of the opinion that one may eat meat immediately after eating dairy products or after a short wait. R. Joseph Caro cites the *Zohar* as saying that one may not eat meat after milk at the same meal.[60] Saba, however, says:

> ...that one is prohibited to eat milk after meat, as well as meat after milk. And although the scholars set various time limits, nonetheless R. Shimon ben Yoḥai has already written that just as it is prohibited to eat milk after meat, so one must not eat meat after milk, and the time limits in both cases are equal - until the food is digested in one's stomach which is about six hours, which is (also) the time between meals....And since there are stomachs that digest at a slower pace, those who fear God... should not eat cheese and meat on the same day, and certainly not cheese after meat. And this is the custom of those who are rigorous in the observance of the commandments [medaqdeqim be-miẓvot] and men of good deeds [anshei maàseh]. And the reason for it...[61]

The reason behind this custom is that meat represents Judgement while milk represents Mercy, and these two should not be mixed. Saba says that the Zohar maintains that the two cases are equal, and since for Saba the six-hour wait after eating meat is given, therefore it follows that one must also wait six hours after milk.[62] After relating this stringent ruling based on the combination of Halakhah and *Zohar*, Saba tells us of an even greater stringency, namely, the custom of some Qabbalists to avoid eating cheese and meat on the same day. This opinion, although mentioned in the Talmud (B.T. *Ḥullin* 105a), is rejected, and to the best of my knowledge is not repeated by any Halakhic authority in the Middle Ages.

What is important for our discussion is Saba's casual Halakhic decision based on the *Zohar*, directed not only to Qabbalists (who are expected to be more stringent).

A similar case, in principle, is the case of a bailee who claims that the depositor owes him money. Saba says that he has no right to retain the deposit as a payment for the debt owed to him.[63] Again, this is a stringency not mentioned by the codifiers, and Saba says unequivocally that "one may not retain it under any circumstances." He uses the Zohar to support an opinion that seems to have hardly been known in Spain.[64] We see here, however, that Saba felt the need to find Halakhic support for this Qabbalistic decision.[65]

On another Halakhic question Saba sides with the Halakhah against some Qabbalists who, according to Saba, do not understand that they are contradicted by both the Halakhah and the Qabbalah. The problem concerns the time of the third Sabbath meal:

> And therefore one must be very careful...especially with the third meal which is the most important of them all...and the mystics [ha-yodìm] hasten to fulfill it immediately after the first meal of the day but they do not know...and its time has not arrived yet, and consequently they do not fulfill that duty, as it is mentioned by the codifiers, and especially R. Yonatan of blessed memory, proved it conclusively. And (moreover) it is proven by the nature of the meal itself that it must take place after (the prayer of) Minḥah, for we pray then "You are one," and we unify all three Sabbaths...and after we have prayed to unify all things we have to cause all things to rejoice through the happiness of the three meals...[66]

In this case there is perfect harmony between Halakhah and Qabbalah. Moreover, Saba criticizes some Qabbalists for not knowing that there are no Halakhic disagreements on this point, which is apparently true in this period.[67] This is sufficient for Saba to decide the issue. He adds, however, that this Halakhic ruling "makes sense" from a qabbalistic perspective as well.

There are several opinions concerning the days on which the laws of lesser mourning during *Sefirat ha-Òmer* apply. According to one opinion only do these laws apply to the whole period between Passover and Pentecost.[68] However, Saba considers this opinion to be correct and Halakhically binding, since the real reason for the mourning is not the widely accepted view that the death of R. Akiba's disciples occurred then, but the mystical one that up to thirty-three days the force of Judgement reigns. This is his interpretation of the Halakhic decision that the mourning stops after the thirty third day-laborers Here too, Saba sides with a Halakhic opinion, albeit a minority one, basing the Halakhah of mourning on Qabbalistic grounds.

In the following case, Saba, basing himself on Qabbalah, sides with Maimonides against Rabbenu Asher ben Yeḥiel, who was considered the Halakhic authority in Castile in this period.[70]

> ...And therefore one must recire the blessing over wine at all three meals (of the Sabbath) and in the format used in the morning, namely qidusha rabba...so he must do in the third meal...and on this issue the opinion of Maimonides is correct, not that of Rabbenu Asher, of blessed memory. He (i.e. Maimonides) wrote that just as in the morning one recites a benediction over wine, so also must he do at the third meal...since it is the most important.[71]

In Ẓ.M. there is one further Halakhic detail based on the Qabbalah. Saba claims that it is prohibited to stop the reading of the Torah during the account of the travellings of the Children of Israel in the desert,[72] due to the symbolic number of the trips - forty two.[73] Ẓ.M. seems to be the lone source for this Qabbalistically based prohibition.[74]

As one can readily see, all of Saba's Qabbalistic decisions are quite "harmless". In general, there are no cases of leniency as the result of Qabbalistic influence. A notable exception is the case of the repetition of the last three words of the *Shema* in order to bring the count of the total number of words to two hundred and forty eight (ReMaḤ).[75] However, one must consider the apparent fact that this was already an established custom in Spain, although there are no authoritative Halakhists of the period who discuss its Halakhic problematics, and RaDBaZ has to rely on Saba.[76]

While it is clear that Saba was a Qabbalist, we do not know to what extent he was involved in the study of Halakhah. One cannot expect to find an abundance of Halakhic material in an exegetical work, and Saba's literary emphasis on exegesis over Halakhah is not conclusive evidence for the superiority of the former over the latter in the writer's personal life. In the few references to Halakhah that we find we seem to detect an authoritative tone.[77] However, we tend to think that Saba, if asked, would have classified himself primarily as a Qabbalist. This can also be supported by the fact that his library seems to have been Qabbalistically rather than Halakhically oriented.

The contacts between Qabbalah and Halakhah can be divided into the following categories: a) new customs; b) decisions with some measure of Halakhic foundation; c. stringencies without any Halakhic foundation; d. leniencies with no strong Halakhic basis. In the cases found in Ẓ.M. Saba seems to strive towards harmony between Halakhah and Qabbalah and, accordingly, he finds it important to mention the Halakhic opinion corresponding to the Qabbalistic stand on a particular issue. The fourth category, the touch-stone for measuring his attitude towards the problem, does not exist in Ẓ.M. The casual tone with which Saba deals with the Halakhic-Qabbalistic issues raised in Ẓ.M. might perhaps indicate that Saba felt that his audience was well disposed to Qabbalah.

5. Halakhah, Qabbalah, and Man's Perfection

Although the centrality of the Halakhah in Judaism is well known, an ideal religious person was always conceived of as one who occupied himself with the spiritual dimension of religion as well. A combination of *vita activa* and *vita contemplativa* was the ideal for which one should strive. The nature of the spiritual complement to Halakhah was a bone of contention between philosophy and Qabbalah. The synthesis between the active and the contemplative was subject to various formulations by philosophers and Qabbalists. In order to examine Saba's stand on this issue, it is important to examine his view on the dual nature of the Torah, of the commandments, and of man.

5.1. Carnal and Spiritual

Saba, as a Qabbalist, claims that the entire Torah has two senses - exoteric and esoteric, or revealed and hidden [*nigleh ve-nistar*] - and he tries to show that the esoteric sense exists even when the text might seem to be a simple narrative.[78] Saba expresses this oft-repeated notion in rhyme:

> ...שיש בה לחם אבירים / מתוק מדבש ונופת צופים / ובה כל מיני מאכל מקישואים ואבטיחים / וחציר ובצלים / קליפה על קליפה ופנים בתוך פנים / מאכל דק וגס נגלה ונסתר...[79]

The "agricultural" or "food" imagery is not novel.[80] But what is interesting is that he describes the two senses of *peshat* and *sod* as "coarse and light foods," because elsewhere these expressions are used by Saba to signify the carnal and spiritual existence of man.[81] This is not to say that Saba sees *peshat* in a negative light as did a few radical Qabbalists,[82] for this sense of Scripture is represented generously in his commentary. It is definitely legitimate but, at the same time, inferior.

This duality applies not only to the narratives found in the Torah but also to the *miẓvot*. Saba emphasizes that the commandments have esoteric meanings but does not neglect to comment from time to time on the exoteric reasons for certain *miẓvot*.[83]

The commandments themselves are divided into two types, active and contemplative - corresponding to the carnal-spiritual division - for they are supposed to shield man's body and ṣoul which are partners in sinning:

> Therefore our Torah is divided into active commandments [miẓvot maàsiyyot] for the body, eyes, hands and legs - and contemplative commandments [miẓvot ìyyuniyot] for the soul, in order that we may know and understand God. An example of the latter is 'I am the Lord your God etc.,' which are dependent upon the intellect [sekhel] and acceptance [qabbalat ha-lev]. And this is 'If you will listen to the voice of God' (Ex. 15.26), namely, the acceptance, 'And will do that which is right in His sight' (ibid.) - the action. And this is 'And know the God of your father and serve him' (I Ch. 28,9).[84] And these two parts are directed towards the two parts of man, the soul and the body. And they correspond to 'We shall do, and we shall listen' (Ex. 24,7). And this is also 'The conclusion of the matter, everything being heard' - corresponding to the listening, 'and keep His commandments' corresponding to the action. And these two (aspects of the commandments) correspond to the two components of man - the soul and the body... and this is 'for this is the entirety of man [ki zeh kol ha-ádam]' (Ecc. 12,13).[85]

This passage reminds us of Maimonides' division of the commandments based on the welfare of the body [*tiqqun ha-guf*] and of the soul [*tiqqun ha-nefesh*],[86] although its emphasis is on the spiritual preventive treatment by the *miẓvot*, contrary to Maimonides; for whom *tiqqun ha-guf* is an earthly well-being of the body and of society as a whole. Saba's conception is much closer to that of R. Baḥya ibn Paquda, who divides the commandments into "duties of the limbs" [*ḥovot ha-évarim*] and "duties of the hearts" [*ḥovot ha-levavot*].[87] Therefore it would be worthwhile to investigate whether, for Saba, the contemplative *mizvot* enjoy the same superiority over the active *mizvot* that they do in Baḥya's scheme.

5.2. The Active, Contemplative and Antinomianism

Baḥya Ibn Paqudah's emphasis on the spiritual *miẓvot* and of the spiritual component of *ḥovot ha-évarim* is so overwhelming, that it might lead someone following his system to neglect performing the acts themselves in favour of concentrating on his spiritual development. Indeed, philosophy was accused in the following centuries of promoting antinomianism.

In Saba's works, despite the same division of the commandments, we find an adamant insistence upon the active *miẓvot* as the basis of Judaism. Is the knowledge of God through study and contemplation superior to the active *miẓvot*? Ultimately, yes. The "true wisdom" for which Israel deserves to be called "a wise and understanding people" is that of "understanding and knowing me" (Jer. 9,23).[88] More explicitly Saba says:[89] וירמוז בזה כי עיקר התורה תלוייה באמונה כאומרו, השכל וידוע אותי.

There is no doubt that Qabbalists are the religious elite, although all Israel have a share in *Òlam Haba*.

Nevertheless, we find a statement which seems to flatly contradict this notion, asserting, in the same phraseology, the superiority of the active *mizvot*.

> לפי שעיקר התורה תלוייה במעשה כמו שפירשתי למעלה וכמו שאמרו, גדול תלמוד שמביא לידי מעשה, אבל אם אינו מביא לידי מעשה אינו גדול.[90]

This idea is repeated again and again but mostly in the context of a polemic against antinomianism. In this context, when the choice is between the active and the contemplative, Saba never tires of stressing the importance of the former. However, the religious ideal is not to fulfill the *mizvot* without investing them with spiritual content.

The active *mizvot* have, according to Saba two aims: a) to facilitate the endurance of the ideas behind the *mizvot* (an example is the commandment to eat and drink on Purim;[91] and b) to influence the beliefs of the person performing the commandments.[92] This latter might be identical with Saba's contention that antinomianism leads to heresy and a disbelief in Providence. In other words, the knowledge of God arrived at by study and contemplation is possible only as a second step, i.e., only if, at the same time one also performs the active commandments which direct his beliefs into the right channel. In this sense, the simple physical act has a point of contact with the spiritual, which is the real measure of one's religious level.

This view of Saba's comes across very clearly in his interpretation of God's speech to Israel before they received the Ten Commandments (Ex. 19,3-6). The people understood the priority of the active *mizvot*, and therefore first said "We shall do", and then "We shall listen." This teaches us,

> כי עיקר התורה תלוייה במעשה. ואע״פ שהעיקר הוא הידיעה כמאמר השכל וידוע אותי, הכל הולך איר המעשה כאמרם כל שחכמתו מרובה ממעשיו אין חכמתו וכו׳. והמעשה ג״כ צריך תלמוד כאומרו, דע את אלהי אביך ועבדהו. אבל המעשה יועיל בלא תלמוד, מה שלא יועיל התלמוד בלא המעשה.[93]

Despite the awkward style, the idea is clear. From a spiritual point of view *maàseh* (action) needs *talmud* (study),[94] so that one may know how to perform; but, in essence, *maàseh* by itself is valid from a religious point of view. *Talmud*, in comparison, is not worth anything, religiously speaking, if it is not accompanied by *maàseh*, since the importance of *talmud* is in its application to *maàseh*. In addition, the study of meta-Halakhah must be sustained by the actual *mizvot* or else heresy will result, as the Mishnah states: "He whose wisdom is greater than his deeds, his wisdom will not endure".[95]

After Saba pours out his wrath on the antinomians who are also heretics, he divides the people of Israel in accordance with the dual nature of the *miẓvot*. The knowledge of God was given to the Elders and the active *miẓvot* to the masses, who were incapable of doing more. Taken out of context, this is a daring distinction that a philosopher could not have expressed without being accused of antinomianism. For Saba, this statement is an expression of elitist feelings as a Qabbalist but, at the same time, it is mitigated and balanced by stressing, both before and after, the centrality of the act (from which even the Elders are not exempt).

This, of course, agrees with the basic contention of the Qabbalah that the understanding of the mysteries of the *miẓvot* is the means for the performance of the latter with proper intentions.[96] The antinomians Saba has in mind would seem to be students of philosophy. Saba's harsh language seem to indicate this.[97] Also his expression "those who set an alien fire" is the expression Alami uses to refer to antinomian philosophers.[98] But one would have expected Saba, in refuting their theory concerning the sufficiency of the knowledge of *taàmei miẓvot* and of God, to lash out at their false philosophical approach and raise the banner of Qabbalah. His failure to do this raises the suspicion that the antinomians are not necessarily identified exclusively with philosophers.

We find that Yaàveẓ addresses a similar problem with an explicit reference to students of Qabbalah. Claiming that the study of Qabbalah must be balanced by deep roots in action, Yaàveẓ says:

> And it seems to me that those scholars whom Jeremiah rebuked mastered not only the sciences [ḥokhmot ḥiẓoniyyot] but also true wisdom...*maàseh bereshit* and *maàseh merkavah* they knew very well, as well as uttering the (holy) Names ...All they missed was the great foundation of performing the commandments rigorously [be-diqduq] ...and they relied on their esoteric wisdom [ḥokhmatam ha-penimit] to utter the Names in order to be saved from the enemies.[99]

And while here he talks about Jeremiah's generation, it might very well be that it reflects contemporary reality, for we read elsewhere, "...and even if you find people who know it (i.e. Qabbalah), unless they possess piety [*ḥasidut*] they cannot truly know it, and it only seems that they know it...."[100]

Again, in justifying Maimonides who wrote against the use of amulets, he writes, "...and those who were in his time did not possess piety [*ḥasidut*] and sanctity any more..."[101] The piety [*ḥasidut*] those people lack is the proper performance of the active *miẓvot*.

It seems that the following passage in which Saba directs his criticism at people who neglect the active commandments, should be understood in a similar manner:

> ...and perhaps one might say...that it is unnecessary to perform miẓvot actively, but rather to study Torah day and night and know the reasons for the commandments and His unity and greatness, as it says, 'understanding and knowing Me' (Jer. 9,23), and, consequently, he need not bother himself [yatri'aḥ aẓmo] with performing the commandments since 'no one possesses honor but the scholars [ḥakhamim].'[102]

The origin of such a claim is not heretical philosophy, and the study of the unity of God as well as that of *taàmei miẓvot* are not philosophical either.

The study of these, as such, is legitimate and Saba does not oppose it. It seems, then, that the neglect of the observance of the *mizvot* alluded to by Saba is not restricted to philosophical antinomians but was also found among certain students of the Qabbalah. On the other hand, it is not a result of outright scorn at and degradation of *ḥovot ha-évarim*, of which R. Moses de Leon accuses the philosophers in *Sefer ha-Rimmon*, but rather due to the preoccupation with mysticism in a way that absorbs the individual's attention and energy and causes neglect of all other aspects of religion, which become secondary.[103]

5.3. The Study of Halakhah and Qabbalah

So far we have dealt with the importance of the active commandments,Dthe ultimate superiority of the contemplative ones, and that those who perform the *miẓvot* have the theoretical knowledge of God and of *taàmei miẓvot*. In the last part of this chapter we shall examine Saba's views on the relation between the study of Talmud (or Halakhah) and Qabbalah.

We have seen that occupation with meta-Halakhah must be accompanied by performance of *miẓvot*. However, the Qabbalist must not neglect the study of Halakhah as well, in order to ensure his spiritual and physical well being. In fact, the Qabbalist must immerse himself in it. The pre-occupation with Qabbalah might be harmful to the individual, witness the fate of three of the four who entered the mystical *Pardes*. R. Akiba was the only one to emerge in peace because he was immersed in Halakhah, which preserved his spiritual balance and enabled him gradually to reach the deepest mysteries and without danger.

> ...for he was rich in Torah (i.e. Halakhah)...and was content with his share (of mysteries), and did not go beyond his limits. Therefore, he finally reached the ultimate depth of the mysteries without confusion or insanity.[104]

This seems to be connected with the idea that antinomianism leads to heresy. In the case of R. Akiba, the study of Halakhah led him through the spiritual labyrinth without his being hurt in any way.

There is another advantage to the study of Halakhah. Saba does not address this explicitly but it seems to follow from his insistence on the importance of the act.

> And although the study of the mysteries of the Torah and the reasons for the commandments is a great thing.[105] Nonetheless, the purpose of study and understanding[106] is exclusively the act itself. And this is the meaning of '...greater is talmud for it leads to *maàseh*' (B.T. Qiddushin, p. 40a), since through the talmud one would know how to perform them.[107]

In this passage Saba says that the purpose of the study of Qabbalah is to attain the knowledge necessary to perform the *mizvot*. It seems to follow logically that the *study* of Halakhah has priority over Qabbalah since it deals with the much more basic knowledge of "how to perform them." Indeed, this is an inescapable conclusion from the basic Qabbalistic belief that the Halakhic details of the commandments are based on the mysteries of Qabbalah.[108] Therefore, one must know "how to perform" in the plain Halakhic fashion, while the Qabbalistic instructions are only secondary.[109]

We have observed that according to Saba there exists a duality on several levels. The Torah contains outer and inner meaning, and although the former is corporeal while the latter is spiritual both are legitimate. The commandments are divided into active and contemplative, paralleling man's body and soul. Each active *mizvah* is comprised, in its ideal form, of a formal act and a spiritual intention. These two aspects are provided by Halakhah and Qabbalah respectively. It is true that the latter is religiously superior and attainable by a minority of people, however only the former has a legitimate independent status. The active *mizvot* steer the contemplative ones in the right direction. Otherwise correct beliefs could not endure. The spiritual knowledge one attains through Qabbalah is, in the final analysis, not detached from the active *mizvah*, for it reaches down, so to speak, in order to elevate it. Therefore, the study of Qabbalah as an end in itself without application to the act is useless. It follows, then, that one's efforts should be directed to the study of Halakhah, which ensures the knowledge of *what*, *how* and *when* to do. The knowledge of *why* (i.e. Qabbalistic intentions) is superior but only of secondary consideration. The study of Qabbalah which supplies this information is, therefore, superior yet secondary not only to the active observance of the commandments but also to the study of Halakhah.

This attitude, we must emphasize, does not distinguish Saba from his contemporaries and possibly from the great majority of Qabbalists throughout history. He represents the conservative mainstream of Sefardic Qabbalah.

The real image of Qabbalists could be easily and completely distorted if we are to rely solely on their writings. Based on his literary output, R. Abraham ben Eliezer Halevi could be mistakenly understood as a person who devoted his entire intellectual energy to mysticism and apocalyptic activities. An incidental remark in one of his epistles from Jerusalem, where he describes the centrality of halakhic studies in his *Yeshivah*, radically alters this impression.[110] The same is true of R. Joseph Yaàveẓ who has been known mainly for his outspoken polemic against philosophy, his support of Qabbalah as the spiritual alternative, and his activity as a preacher. This is a correct picture if we consult his writings. Here again, an incidental biographical note by his son shows that his primary occupation in Italy after the Expulsion was with Halakhah.[111]

NOTES

[1] Long verbatim quotations (mainly from *Tiqqunei Zohar* and *Zohar Ḥadash*) characterize his writings after his arrival in Fez, i.e. his commentaries on Deuteronomy, Ruth and Esther.

[2] Ẓ.M. Lev. p. 20a. This statement discloses the level of importance he attributes to the mystical part of his commentary, for by no means can most of the book be connected in any way to mysticism. Saba means to say here that even when he expressed a novel mystical idea, it is either based on basic Zoharic doctrines or is traceable to a particular idea of the *Zohar*. Indeed, the roots of his thought should be sought in the *Zohar*, as we shall often see below.

[3] Ms. Oxford. Colophon at the end of Ẓ.M. This apology has a great deal of truth to it, although one must balance it with the realization that this humility may, in part, be considered a literary convention. (see above pp. 48ff.).

[4] We have some doubts concerning his knowledge of the *Raàya Mehemna*) (He quotes from it in Ẓ.Ḥ. fol. 43r.) saying that he found it in an "ancient manuscript of the *Zohar*", apparently in Portugal (A. Gross, "R. Abraham Saba's Abbreviated Messianic Commentary on Haggai and Zechariah," *Studies in Medieval History and Literature* II, [I. Twersky ed.], Cambridge Mass., 1984, p. 401 n. 152.) About the rarity of Zoharic texts such as *Tiqqunei Zohar* and *Raàya Mehemna* in this period see: M. Idel, "Sefardi Qabbalah After the Expulsion," *The Sefardi Legacy* [H. Beinart ed.], Jerusalem, 1992, p. 507.

[5] Gross, Saba, p. 220-1. About the use of Light [*ór*, *óra*, *meórot*] in order to describe the *Zohar* or other Qabbalistic literature, see e.g. D. Ruderman, *The World of a Renaissance Jew*, Cincinnati, 1981, p. 233 (see also Tishbi, Messianism, p. 142 n. 47).

[6] É.K. Ruth, p. 21a. Saba's idea here is a development of teh Zoharic identification of the reapers (*meḥaẓdei ḥaqla*) as Qabbalists: ואעלת בחולקא חדא ואוליפת אורחיה וידעת ביה מאינון מחצדי חקלא, תלמידי חכמים איקרון קוצרים. ומאן נינהו (*Zohar Ḥadash, Midrash ha-Neèlam* Ruth 85d). See a discussion of these theme in Y. Liebes, "the Messiah of the *Zohar*," *The Messianic Idea in Jewish Thought*, Jerusalem, 1990, pp. 146-148 n. 224. Rabbi Meir Ibn Gabai, Saba's contemporary, sees himself as going after the "reapers in the fiels of apples" (*Tolaàt Yaàkov*, Jerusalem, 1967, p. 8). On Cordovero's reference to the study of Qabbalah by those "reapers" see: B. Zack, "Cordovero's Attitude to the Zohar and to Rabbi Shimon bar Yoḥai and his Circle," *F. Talmage Memorial Volume* I, Haifa, 1993, p. 71.

[7] Ẓ.M. Ex. p. 6a. Saba does not mean literally "everything," since he emphasizes time and time again that this is impossible for the human mind.

[8] E. Gottlieb distinguishes between Baḥya ben Asher's commentary on the Pentateuch intended for more scholarly readers and his *Kad ha-Qemaḥ*, written as a guide for preachers. The latter, intended in the final analysis for the masses, contains much less Qabbalah. (*The Qabbalah in the Writings of Baḥya ben Asher*, Jerusalem, 1970, p. 25).

9 *Webster's Unabridged Dictionary*, Toronto, 1976. 10 G. Scholem, "A New Document on the Beginning of the Qabbalah," *Sefer Bialik* [J. Fichman ed.], Tel Aviv, 1934, p. 161. In the Geronese circle itself there existed tension, dilemmas and controversy concerning the revelation of mystical secrets. Rabbi Isaac apparently rebukes Rabbi Ezra and Rabbi Azriel who made public secrets "in books and epistles" (ibid, p. 146).

11 H. Fedaya, "The Spiritual vs. the Concrete Land of Israel in the Geronese School of Kabbalah," *The Land of Israel in Medieval Jewish Thought* [M. Ḥallamish and A. Ravitzky ed.], Jerusalem, 248-9.

12 M. Idel, "We have no Kabbalistic Tradition on This," *Rabbi Moses Nachmanides (Ramban): Explorations in His Religious and Literary Virtuosity* [I. Twersky ed.], Cambridge Mass., 1983, pp. 67-73.

13 ibid, p. 72.

14 G. Scholem, *Major Trends in Jewish Mysticism*, New York, 1961, pp. 202-3.

15 See I. Robinson, "Moses Cordovero and Kabbalislic Education in the Sixteenth Century," *Judaism* 39 (1990), pp. 155-62. Cordovero's permissiveness can be seen also with respect to the interdiction against the study of Qabbalah before the age of forty. He did not accept it, while the circle of the Ari (also in Safed) did. For the history of this interdiction see M. Idel's article in *AJS Review*, 5 (1980), (Hebrew part), especially p. 13.

16 *Minḥat Yehudah*, Mantua (1558), p. 3a.

17 *Tolaàt Yaàkov*, p. 8.

18 Yaàveẓ' motivation was to present and propagate the Qabbalah as a spiritual alternative to philosophy which, he believed, had been the major reason for the fall of Spanish Jewry. (To this thesis Yaàveẓ dedicated his polemical treatise *Ór ha-Ḥayyim*.) Cf. Idel, Sefardi Qabbalah, p. 505.

19 ibid., p. 2b. Ḥayyat's introduction also reveals his purpose of neutralizing false Qabbalistic trends such as that of Abraham Abulafia which was influential in Italy.

20 S. Shalem, Alsheikh, p. 77-84.

21 ibid., p. 81.

22 Ẓ.M. Gen. p. 27b.

23 ibid., Ex. p. 33a.

24 ibid. Deut. p. 57a. Similarly he says: וזהו רמז על סודות התורה שראוי שיהיו בחשאי ולא בקולי קולות. וזהו ושפוני טמוני חול, כי החול אם תמצא כלי מנוקב לא ישמיע קול מה שאין כן בדברים אחרים

25 Ẓ.M. Gen. p. 55a. É.K. Esther p. 46. (This point comes up in the controversy surrounding the publication of the *Zohar* (See Y. Tishbi, "The Controversy about the Zohar in the Sixteenth Century in Italy," *Peraqim* I, Jerusalem, 1967-68, p. 179).

26 Ẓ.M. Num. p. 25b.

27 We note, however, that unlike those who saw in the spreading and dissemination of Qabbalah a means for hastening the Redemption or at least a fulfillment of a prerequisite for its coming (Tishbi, The Controversy, pp. 141, 153-56 and above p. 95), Saba apparently held no such belief. Redemption, to be sure, can be brought about by the acts of the Qabbalists, who are also those who sustain the world in the present (Ẓ.M. Ex. p. 18a, and see the context of the quoted verse from Isa. 32,17) but, as far as the people as a whole are concerned, he says only that "at that time" (*Òlam Habba*, which is to come after the Days of the Messiah) Israel "will be crowned by the knowledge of the Name of God, and the ten *Sefirot*." (ibid., Deut. 43b).

28 Ẓ.M. Gen. p. 3a.

29 בחוכמתא ברא ה׳ (ibid.).

30 E.g. *Zohar* I, 30b, Nachmanides, Baḥya ben Asher, and Recanati (on Gen. 1,1).

31 See below p. 102?.

32 ואין להאריך בזה (Ẓ.M. Ex. p. 40a). Similarly he says elsewhere: כן תמצא שהיו בקטורת י״א סמנים...ואחד כנגד אדון יחיד על הכל ועולה על העשר והמשכיל יבין (ibid., p. 46a). The different opinions concerning the number of the *Sefirot* are discussed by him in his short treatise on the *Sefirot*.

33 ibid., Lev. p. 19a. The context shows that the allusions here are to the *Sefirot*.

34 ibid., Ex. p. 41a.

[35] We do not know whether Saba made an effort to publish his book. He did leave us some beautiful lines describing the "miracle" of printing (see above p. 65 n. 65).

[36] E.g. Ẓ.M. Deut. p. 34b-36a (This is a translation of *Tiqqunei Zohar* 6, pp. 21a-23a). In É.K. Ruth (pp. 40b, 41b) Saba translates passages from *Zohar Hadash* (p. 95b, 105a) as a digest of the different interpretations found in the *Zohar* on Ruth. He omits, therefore, all the digressions found in his source. (There are some differences between the text used by Saba and the printed editions of *Zohar Ḥadash*. See also É.K. Ruth pp. 12b-13a).

[37] *The Book of Mirrors: Sefer Marót ha-Ẓovót* [D.C. Matt ed.], Chico, California, 1982, p. 13. M. Idel, "The Translation of the Zohar by R. David ben Judah he-Ḥasid," *Àlei Sefer* 8, 1980, pp. 60-73.

[38] Angelino, aware that the very act of putting the mysteries of the Qabbalah down on paper would be tantamount to publicizing the esoteric, says: ועל כן ראוי להסתיר ספר זה ואין ללמדו אלא לזקן שקנה חכמה והוא בן מ׳ לבינה, ואז״ל דברים שהם כדבש וחלב יהיו תחת לשונך (See M. Idel, The History of the Interdiction, p. 11).

[39] Indeed, this is the reason that Saba mentions the Midrash and the Zohar together (above p. 68).

[40] See above p. 13.

[41] Ms. Sassoon 919/20, pp. 85-9. It is entitled: הקדמת הר״ר אברהם סבע בפירוש עשר ספירות שכתב לה״ר עלאל בן אלחאיך ז״ל מארץ תלמסאן Saba also wrote for his a treatise on the mystical secrets of the prayers: פירוש התפילות על דרך הסוד.

[42] ואם רץ לבך לומר היאך הוא אחד ומתחלק לעשרה החזירהו למקומו כי זהו מגדל הפורח באויר שאין המחשבה תופסת בו (p. 87).

[43] ibid. p. 85.

[44] ibid. p. 86. One could only conjecture why R. Alal asked Saba to write that commentary for him, since Saba had communicated higher mysteries to him orally.

[45] We must note, however, that it is difficult to define conclusively what Saba considered permissible to be written and what was to be taught exclusively orally. For example, the passage from *Tiqqunei Zohar* (Ẓ.M. Deut. p. 34b-36a) seems to be very explicit and daring notwithstanding Saba's apology for writing it (ibid., p. 36b).

[46] E.g. והיודע סוד הייחוד בסוד דלת של אחד היא כנסת ישראל עין יעקב יוכל להבין כל זאת הפרשה (É.K. Ruth p. 21b). The elaboration of this, including the precise prescription for meditation on the *Sefirot* while reciting the *Shema*, can be found in the extant folio of Saba's commentary on the prayers (See above n. 41 and A. Gross,D"The Qabbalistic Commentary on the Prayers Attributed to Rabbi Abraham Saba," *Asufot* 1, 1987, pp. 189-197.

[47] Idel, Sefardi Qabbalah, p. 41.

[48] See J. Katz, "Halakhah and Kabbalah - First Contacts," *Y. Baer Memorial Volume*, *Ẓion* 44 (1979), pp. 148-72, and idem, "Halakhic Statements of the Zohar," *Tarbiẓ Jubilee Volume*, 1980-81, pp. 405-22.

[49] In this explanation we are not trying to negate the opinion according to which the acceptance of a custom into the Halakhah was conditioned upon its prior acceptance by people in practice. Beyond the acceptance of a particular custom lay the acceptance of the sovereignty of the Qabbalah in the spiritual domain. (Compare J. Katz, "Post-Zoharic Relations between Halakhah and Kabbalah," *Daàt* 4 (1980), pp. 60-61).

[50] Compare Katz, First Contacts, p. 159. This claim is behind R. Tam ibn Yaḥya's criticism of the Qabbalah (see following note).

[51] E.g. הקבלה היא חכמה רמה איומה כנדגלות...אך בזמנינו זה אפס המדע הזה וסתרי תורה נעלמו...ובזמנינו זה תם זכות אבות ואין מחזיק בצדק בחכמי הזאת, אדרבא הם הורסיי פנות התורה ועמודיה יתפלצון. ואם איש מבני ישראל ירצה לעיין בקבלה ראוי לעשותה כלי חמדה לעצמו...לא יחזיק טובה לעצמו להורי׳ לזולתו ליחד וכ״ש לציבו׳ (R. Tam ibn Yaḥya in R. Elijah Mizraḥi's *Responsa*, no. 1).

[52] חיבור צרור הכסף שמדבר בדינים שחברתי בימי נעורי... (É.K. Ruth p. l0b).

[53] Ẓ.M. Gen. pp. 38a, 47a, 116b. Ex. p. 18a, Lev. p. 22b. Deut. pp. l0b, 13b, 40a, 66b. (See also ibid. Gen. pp. 9b-lOa).

[54] The custom of walking around the grave seven times in order to drive the ghosts away (Gen. pp. 9b-l0a) is an exception. (See G. Scholem, *Elements of the Kabbalah*, pp. 149-50). Also see now M. Benayahu, *"Maàmadot u-Moshavot," Studies in Memory*

of the Rishon le-Ẓion Rabbi Y. Nissim, vol. 6, Jerusalem (1985), pp. 105ff. Concerning Saba's demonological view of Christianity (Ẓ.M. Deut. p. 66b) see below pp. 131-7.

55 Gross, Commentary on the Prayers, pp. 195-7.

56 כמו שפירשתי בספר צרור הכסף בהלכות ראש השנה, הנה הוא נצמא בפא״ס העיר הגדולה (Ẓ.M. Gen. P. 47a).

57 See above p. 42.

58 E.g. Mizraḥi, *Responsa*, no. 1.

59 The relevant cases in Ẓ.M. discussėd below are not mentioned as being included in É.K. However, it is highly improbable that some of them were not discussed there. The fact that Saba neglected to mention it does not prove the contrary.

60 *Beit Yosef*, Ó.Ḥ. no. 173 (*Zohar* II, p. 125a). Caro's own opinion is not clear.

61 Ẓ.M. Ex. p. 37b-38a.

62 Although we find in RaMA's gloss (Y.D., 89,2 in parentheses) that according to the *Zohar* one must wait six hours before eating meat, this does not seem to be the case (at least in our printed version of the *Zohar*. Compare *Siftei Kohen* on Y.D. 89,16). The source for Saba's stringency is a custom which was never even discussed as a potential Halakhic norm in B.T. Ḥullin 80a)

63 וכן אין להאריך בזאת הפרשה לפי שהיא מפורשת בדברי המפרשים והפוסקים בדיני נזיקין וחבלות ודיני השומרים, אלא שבדין פקדון אכתוב לך מה שכתבו בסתרי תורה כי מי שמשימין בידו פקדון לשמור צריך להחזיר הפקדון לבעליו ולא יעכבנו אצלו בשום תביעה. ואפי׳ אם בעל הפקדון חייב לו ממקום אחר אינו יכול לעכבו בחובו בשום ענין אלא שיחזיר לו פקדונו ואח״כ יתבענו. וכן הסכימו קצת מהמפרשים והוא דין ישר. ואע״פ שיש חולקין יכריע האמת... (Ẓ.M. Ex. p. 36b) *Zohar* III, p. 119a and also *Zohar Ḥdash*, pp. 23b, 108a-b).

64 Margaliot in *Niẓẓozei Zohar* (*Zohar* III, p. 119a, n. 6) refers to RITBA and *Kolbo*. The latter attributes its origin to an ordinance by Rabbenu Tam (See also idem on *Zohar* (II, p. 198b, n. 8). Concerning R. Tam and this ordinance see his responsum in *Sefer ha-Yashar*, Berlin (1898), no. 34a, p. 55, n. 4. However, one should note that RaDBaZ (*Responsa* III, no. 481) was not aware of any Halakhic support for the *Zohar* (Saba might have referred to the RITBA since he defines his sources as *mefarshim*, namely Talmudic commentaries

65 In this case, it seems that the Halakhic sources influenced Saba's understanding of the Zohar, for he refers to legal right while the plain sense of the *Zohar* refers only to propriety. (However, cf. *Zohar Ḥdash*, p. 23b).

66 Ẓ.M. Gen. p. 8b. The Halakhic authority mentioned by Saba might be identical with R. Jonathan of Cuenca, and see B. Septimus, "'Kings Angels or Beggars': Tax Law and Spirituality in a Hispano-Jewish Responsum," in *Studies in Medieval Jewish History and Literature* [I. Twersky ed.], Cambridge Mass., 1984, p. 311, n. 5.

67 Cf. Tur Ó.Ḥ. No. 291. On the 12th century controversy between R. Meshulam and R. Tam, who used to eat the third meal before *Minḥah*, see: I. Ta-Shema, "Miriam's Well," *Jerusalem Studies in Jewish Thought* 4, 1985, pp. 254-63.

68 See *Beit Yosef*, Ó.Ḥ. No. 493 (The number of thirty-three is reached by deducting holidays and Sabbaths from the total of fifty days).

69 Ẓ.M. Lev. pp. 27b-28a. This Qabbalistic opinion attributed to R. Isaac Luria (*Shaàrei Teshuvah*, *Shulhan Arukh*, Ó.H. No. 493) is, then, much earlier. This, Saba claims, is also the reason we do not say *she-ḥeheyanu* for *Sefirat ha-Òmer* (For the reasons hitherto known, see Talmudic Encyclopedia 4, p. 436.)

70 ובפרט סמכנו על הרמב״ם...ובתנאי שלא יחלוק עליו הרב הגדול רבינו אשר...ומאשר שמנה לחמו... (Baer, Die Juden II, no. 360, p. 385).

71 Ẓ.M. Gen. p. 9a. The two opinions are cited in Tur Ó.Ḥ. no. 291. Also see Katz, Post-Zoharic, p. 67 and compare *Beit Yosef*'s interpretation of Maimonides.

72 In the Portion of *Masèi*, Num. 33, 1-49.

73 Ẓ.M. Num. p. 46a.

74 It found its way into the standard editions of the *Shulhan Arukh* through the *Magen Ávraham* (Ó.Ḥ. no. 428, 8).

75 *Zohar Ḥadash*, Ruth, p. 95a.

76 See S.Z. Havlin, *Tarbiẓ*, 40 (1970), pp. 106-9. M. Benayahu, "Qabbalah and Ha-

lakhah - a Confrontation," *Daàt* 5 (1980), pp. 70-72. Katz, Post-Zoharic, p. 66. RaDBaZ refers to Saba's Commentary on the Prayers for support (See I.M. Goldman, *The Life and Times of Rabbi David Ibn Zimra*, New York, 1970, p. 70).

77 See also his short comment where he disagrees with RABaD's opinion concerning a special benediction over the change of bread during the meal [*shinui ha-pat*] (Ẓ.M. Num. p. 43a) RABaD's opinion is quoted by Rabbenu Nissim on Pesaḥim p. 10lb and in *Shittah Mequbbeẓet* on Berakhot p. 59b).

78 E.g. Ẓ.M. Gen. p. 49a.

79 ibid. Num. p. 18a. Saba here implies multiple esoteric meanings, but at the same time there is only one basic distinction between *nigleh* and *nistar*. Such a division seems to have contributed to Saba's broad definition of *peshat* (See above p. 47-8).

80 E.g. *Zohar Ḥadash* Ruth p. 10lb, and R. Joseph Giqqailla who uses a nut [*egoz*] to describe the inner and outer sense of the Torah (in his introduction to *Ginnat Egoz*).

81 Ẓ.M. Deut. p. 18a.

82 See e.g. I. Tishbi, *Mishnat ha-Zohar*, Vol. 2, pp. 376ff.

83 This topic obviously cannot be exhausted in one footnote. Let us, however, illustrate extreme cases of *peshat* as applied by Saba to *taàmei miẓvot*. The first example is that of the Passover Sacrifice, a commandment historicized by Saba á-la-Maimonides. The second case is concerning some of the gifts to the priests [*matnot kehunah*]. Saba envisages the practicality of those gifts: ...להרחיקם מחוקי מצרים...הם לקחו טלה לממונה עליהם ובעבורו אין אוכלים בשר, אתם תקחו אותו לשוחטו ולצלותו ולאכול את בשרו ולשרוף את הנותר. הם מקטרים אליו בריחות ומרקדים לפניו, ואתם תתנו דמו במשקוף כדי שיהיה נראה ולצלות בשרו כדי שיריחו ריחו ולאכול בשרו על מצות ומרורים יאכלוהו...ואולי שעל זאת הכוונה בעצמה צווה לעשות העבודה הזאת במילוי הירח עת תוקף שמחתם והקרבתם למזל טלה הממונה עליהם. (Ẓ.M. Ex. p. 17a).

...ולפי שהם יחפים על גבי הרצפה ומתקררים צוה לתת להם ראשית דגנך תירושך ויצהריך בענין שיתחממו ביין. וכן ראשית גז צאנך, לכסותם בבגדים ויחם להם (ibid., Deut. p. 27a).

The same scheme seems to be correct for the Oral Torah as well. Commenting on Deut. 33,19 Saba says: "And in those two seas, which are the Written and the Oral Torah, there are the mysteries of the Torah covered and hidden". (ibid. Gen. p. 83a).

These two parts of the totality of the Torah are inseparable, "...just like the flame that is tied to the coal," (Ẓ.Ḥ. fol. 13v). Following Saba's parallelistic way of thinking, it seems to us that just as the Written Torah contains narratives and laws, so the Oral Torah also contains Halakhah and Aggadah. Just as the mysteries of the Written Torah are hidden in both of its components so it also is with the Oral Torah. Indeed we find mystical interpretation by Saba of Aggadah as well as of Halakhah (E.g. above p. 51. Concerning Halakhic details, see Ẓ.M. Gen. pp. 15b, 16b, 96a. Ex. pp. 16a, 36a. Lev. p. 24a. Num. p. 25b. É.K. Ruth p. 23a.

84 In a slightly different manner R. Joseph Yaàvez, Saba's contemporary, divides and interprets this verse (*Ór ha-Ḥayyim*, p. 23-5).

85 Ẓ.M. Lev. p. 7b. See also ibid. Gen. p. 34b, Ex. p. 24a.

86 Guide III, 27.

87 See: *Hebrew Ethical Literature* [ed. Tishbi and Dan], Jerusalem - Tel Aviv (1970), pp. 115,124.

The notion that man's existence has two components which are supposed to be perfected by the commandments is repeated by Saba and applied to several biblical figures. The midwives in Egypt "feared God" in their hearts, "and did not do"- actually, what Pharaoh told them to do. (Ẓ.M. Ex. p. 3b). Malkizedeq, the King of Shalem, was perfect [*shalem*] in the dual aspects (ibid., Gen. p. 34b), and so was Mordecai (É.K. Esther, p. 98).

88 Ẓ.M. Deut. p. 9a.

89 ibid., p. 21b.

90 ibid. Deut. p. 59a. A survey of Jewish thought on the Talmudic dictum גדול תלמוד שמביא לידי מעשה can be found in N. Lamm, *Torah Lishmah*, Jerusalem, 1972, pp. 100-132.

91 É.K. Esther p. 93.

92 Ẓ.M. Ex. p. 31a (See e.g. *Sefer ha-Ḥinnukh*, no. 20).

[93] Ẓ.M. Ex. p. 32b.

[94] Saba takes *talmud* to mean the study of meta-Halakhah. He may be following *Tiqqunei Zohar* (Livorno, 1854, p. 6a), but he does not follow the latter's Qabbalistic symbolism in our case (See also É.K. Esther, p. 11, and below App. B).

The idea, included in the same passage in Ẓ.M. that the knowledge of Qabbalah would prompt "fear of the Lord" seems to be expressed by Saba elsewhere: "'If you seek it as silver and search for it as for hidden treasures' (Prov. 2,4), which is the hidden meaning [*nistar*], 'Then you will understand' (ibid. 2,5), the revealed - 'the fear of the Lord' (ibid.), namely, that you will be careful in (performing the commandments of) *Ẓiẓit* and *Tefillin*, which are 'the fear of the Lord' (ibid.), although you will not know their mysteries and reasons [*taàm*]." (É.K. Esther p. 46, and similarly in Ẓ.M. Gen. p. 55a).

[95] It is not clear here whether it is meant to be a logical conclusion that follows from the denial of the *miẓvot*, or if it is a natural consequence of not having to occupy themselves with *maàseh*, which, if observed, directs one's beliefs.

[96] See I. Tishbi, *Mishnat ha-Zohar* 2, pp. 42ff.

[97] See especially É.K. Esther p. 10-11.

[98] *Íggeret Mussar* [ed. A.M. Haberman] ,Jerusalem (1946), p. 43. Saba knew Alami's treatise. Yaàveẓ also uses the same phrase quoted from Alami (*Ór ha-Ḥayyim*, p. 30).

[99] *Ór ha-Ḥayyim*, p. 73.

[100] Commentary on Avot, Warsaw (1880), p. 60.

[101] *Ór ha-Ḥayyim*, p. 94.

[102] Below App. B.

[103] This phenomenon of a disturbance of religious balanced behavior could be found already in the Talmud concerning the tension between daily prayers and the study of Torah (Halakhah). See B.T. Sabbath p. 10a. Rosh ha-Shanah p. 35a. Lamm, *Torah Lishma*, pp. 121ff.

[104] Ẓ.M. Gen. p. 32b.

[105] דבר גדול This refers to the relevant Talmudic expression דבר גדול מעשה מרכבה דבר קטן הוויות דאביי ורבא (Sukkah p. 28a). For a discussion of this phrase including references to various medieval interpretations of it, see I. Twersky, "Religion and Law," in *Religion in a Religious Age* [S.D. Goitein ed.], Cambridge, Mass. (1974), pp. 73, 82.

[106] השכלה This alludes to the verse השכל וידוע אותי a status which is achievable through the study of Qabbalah.

[107] É.K. Esther p. 11. (See also below App.).

[108] See our general introduction above p. 76-8.

[109] Saba does not talk about the study of Talmud for its own sake, and its importance seems to lie in the pragmatic realm of daily observance of the commandments.

[110] A. Yaàri, *Epistles from the Land of Israel*, Tel Aviv, 1943, p. 163.

[111] R. Joseph Yaàveẓ, *Ḥasdei ha-Shem*, New York, 1934, p. 5. It is also interesting to note that *Kaf ha-Qetoret*, the apocalyptic commentary on Psalms by an anonymous contemporary Qabbalist, is replete with references to the study of Halakhah.

CHAPTER FOUR

SOCIAL AND RELIGIOUS CRITICISM

Criticism of immoral behavior in Jewish society has been an integral part and an essential ingredient of the Jewish traditional sermon. The preacher saw himself as the successor to the prophets in the dual role of reprover, on the one hand, and consoler, on the other. His aim as both was, of course, to improve the lot of the Jewish people and ensure the survival of the suffering nation by trying to elevate its moral standards and by "strengthening weak hands" tired of bearing the heavy yoke of exile. This had become a major problem in Spanish Jewry, especially from the last decade of the 14th century, and was exacerbated a hundred years later by the Expulsions from the Iberian Peninsula.[1] The tension in Saba's works between the two functions creates a blend of criticism, with sorrow and anger on the one hand, and understanding, even justification, on the other.

1. General "State of the Nation" Critique: Disunity

Scattered in his writings we find criticism of Jewish society. The deficiencies and shortcomings of which Saba speaks are well-known not only to his readers but are even recognized by the Christians. Saba does not deny the problems. On the contrary - and while emphasizing Israel's superiority - he remains loyal to his mission, telling the people what must be told.[2]

Mordecai, as an exceptional leader, succeeds by his diplomatic excellence in being accepted by all his brethren:

> ...'even though they were many [le-rov éḥav]' (Es. 10,3), and it is a great virtue to be able to confront the differing opinions of each one of them.[3]

And Saba generalizes:

> And this characteristic of the Jews is well-known, that due to our sins, there are among us jealousy, hatred and, in particular, envy of one's neighbour.[4]

The extreme expression of the lack of unity is the phenomenon of informers [*malshinim*], which, it seems, was not rare at all:

> And you surely know the phenomenon that exists in Israel, that when one knows of another who killed a man, once they quarrel, he will reveal what he knows and even what he does not know.[5]

The state of disunity, as opposed to Saba's theory of the unity of all individuals within the abstract body of Israel,[6] hurts him greatly, especially since the Jews, in exile among enemies, need to assist one another. Thus, Saba chose to interpret Haman's characterization of the Jewish people as follows:

> 'There is one nation,' namely, although it seems as if they are one unified and loving nation, nevertheless, they are 'scattered and disunited,' and there is disharmony because of senseless hatred [*sinát ḥinam*], despite the fact that they live in exile among the nations.[7]

Saba is not alone in this criticism of Hispano-Jewry. Already in the 12th century we hear harsh words from R. Abraham ibn Ezra concerning the internal disunity.[8] But one may safely say that this trend to criticize gained momentum in the 15th century and reached its peak in Saba's generation.

R. Isaac Arama, on the same verse in Esther says, "and dispersed, for their disunity separates between brothers and friends, and they are happy at each others misfortune." R. Isaac Caro also reminds us of Saba's sarcastic critique:

> 'Thinkest thou to kill me' (Gen. 2,14)...and it is well known that when Jews quarrel, each tells the other all the bad things he knows about him back to the tenth generation.[9]

While Caro does not mention denunciation, we do hear an echo of Saba's accusation in *Kaf ha-Qetoret*, apparently written by one of the exiles from Spain: "And this alludes to Israel in their exile, concerning the informers who exist in (our?) generations. And so it is written, 'thy destroyers... shall go forth from thee'."[10]

Perhaps the best expression of frustration at this internal state of affairs is to be found in Ibn Verga's *Shevet Yehudah*. Thomas, the Christian scholar, tells the king:

> If you want to destroy them (i.e. the Jews), order them all into one city with no foreigner amongst them and let them appoint their own leaders. You will then see that they will never agree on anything, and over disputes they will kill each other.[11]

Except for Arama, all the others wrote after the Expulsions. It would seem that these hard times - before the Expulsions, and even more so after them - brought about some serious soul-searching in the ranks of the scholars who, by and large, saw their tragedy as a divine punishment for religious and moral sins and corruption.

As for the facts, one must realize that the unique mentality of Hispano-Jewry - which made its Jews so different from their Franco-German brethren in so many respects - also found its expression in individualistic behavior within Jewish society. Some factors, related to the general Hispanic mentality, concepts, behavior and mannerisms, influenced, and eventually characterized, that Jewry.[12]

It is in Spain that we hear again and again of violence in the synagogue. In Catalunia, at the end of the 13th century, we are informed of a fight in a synagogue on the Sabbath that involved swords.[13] Late in the 15th century, we read of such a case in an inquisitorial document.[14] Similarly, we are told by Ibn Verga that "due to the conceit of some of our people... a fight took place concerning seats in the synagogue, and each one took off the torches that stood before the Ark, in order to hit one another."[15] This took place no less than on the eve of the Day of Atonement.

Obviously, the cases mentioned were not isolated. As Ibn Verga concludes: "And there are many such incidents among us." The specific cases that have come down to us serve as illustrations for some of the background to the critical comments of Saba and his contemporaries.[16]

So much for Saba the castigator. The impression is that his criticism is restrained and somewhat muted. Considering the historical circumstances and the external pressures of the Gentiles, he could not but show a forgiving and understanding attitude. This, coupled with one of the major aims of his writings - helping his people to overcome the deep despair and depression caused by the Expulsions and their aftermaths[17] - might have been the background for the following passage dealing with another aspect worthy of serious rebuke. It is difficult to imagine it being written in peaceful times:

> ...and this alludes to the exiles and the future redemption. For during the exiles he is called Yaàqov - derived from deceit [ùqbah], since as a result of their hard life which in turn results from the troubles of living in exile, one finds among them cheating and deceit, because otherwise they would not be able to survive in the world. Therefore, this is a manifestation of the Divine Providence and He blessed them with it...for in exile his name is Yaàqov and either by deceit or by honesty he shall pass his term in exile.18

We find a like complaint by R. Solomon Alami: "We dealt with them in fraud and deceit...to the point that they despise us they hold us to be thieves and cheaters...and every work that is abhorred and contemptible they call a 'Jewish work'."[19] Now this is an open, harsh internal criticism in a treatise devoted to a comprehensive review of the socio-religious faults that supposedly brought about the just and divinely ordained catastrophe that befell Spanish Jewry in 1391.

Noteworthy in Saba's passage is the fact that we cannot detect any tone of rebuke for immoral behavior, although there is no doubt that Saba did not condone this kind of dealing with the Christians. As he says elsewhere: "...But among the nations they are scattered and disunited, each one for his own end, to wrong and steal from the nations with permission [*be-heter*]"[20]

Interestingly, we find a similar idea in the intriguing book *Shevet Yehudah*, written about twenty years after Ẓ.M. by another Spanish refugee who moved on to Portugal, converted to Christianity in 1497, and eventually fled from there and returned to Judaism:

> The Viceroy answered: There cleverness [*piqḥut*] is mere shrewdness, and they inherited it from their source, their Patriarch Jacob...
>
> Said Thomas: ...This shrewdness is also a result of their special need for it, more than any other nation, therefore they must think hard...in order to earn their living.[21]

What this might mean is that such an apologetic idea circulated in that generation in Iberia. But the surprising element which distinguishes Saba's idea is that he goes further by actually transforming a fault into a positive phenomenon and a manifestation of Divine Providence, which, in its infinite wisdom, endowed the Jewish character with a "survival mechanism" to ensure Jewish survival in exile. This phenomenon Saba considers to be temporary for the transition period of exile, which unfortunately lingers on for 1500 years. This negative characteristic is no less than a divine blessing!

We do not know of such an apologetic idea in medieval Jewish literature, and we believe that it should be understood, as already indicated, in light of the historical background, namely, the low morale of the audience to which Saba's writings were directed, coupled with an immense hatred for Christianity triggered by the troubles that culminated in the Expulsions.[22] It was the preacher's dual and conflicting role, as pointed out in our introduction, that produced two virtually contradicting views concerning the immoral behavior of the Jews toward the Gentiles.

2. *Class Criticism: the Rich, the Courtiers, and the Leadership*

Thus far we have indicated Saba's criticism of the divisiveness, disunity and individualistic tendencies that constitute the underlying cause of immoral acts. But his primary and most vehement social criticism, unrelenting and harsh, is reserved for the wealthy class within the community.

Saba's strong identification with the poor finds a poetic expression which reflects a deep emotional involvement.[23]

> And it is known that the poor, all his days are pain and frustration. He does not have food, always lifts his eyes to Heaven, and his life hangs in doubt before him. In the morning he says 'would it were evening,' for the fear of his heart, and his poverty...What should the poor do, a man who saw only grief and never any good, and his eyes are lifted to Heaven and to people, for his infants ask for bread but no one gives it to them.[24]

This explains his characterization of the precept of *Shemitah* as "the root of the Torah, and the foundation of the whole world," because it was given, in his opinion, so that the rich will "lift his eyes to Heaven," and thus will better understand the needs of the poor in regular (non-*Shemitah*) years.[25]

The situation in reality is one a of less than ideal relationship between the rich and the poor and Saba correlates this fact with the ineffectiveness of Israel's prayers. He suggests a causal relationship between these two factors:

> ...since we see many a time that, due to our sins, we are wrapped in prayer-shawls and still are not being answered. But the meaning is: 'As long as Israel keeps all that is contained in this prayer [*seder*] of the Thirteen Attributes (Ex. 34,67) as I do, namely, to pity the poor...and practice charity with each other.' ...But if they are cruel and evil-doers...[26]

The reader can easily imagine and vividly visualize Saba explaining in a sermon the rationale of the stingy rich whom the Torah warns:

> For the man who closes his hand does consult his heart first, and the latter tells him: 'You have at home very poor people. It would be much better if you gave it to them.' Moreover, his heart tells him: '...But you work day and night without sleep in order to earn your living and now will you give it as food to the inhabitants of the wilderness? Let them go and gather straw for themselves from wherever they find it, as you yourself used to do!'[27]

The situation is even worse. Not only do the rich not give the poor charity but they also take from them illegally. This probably refers to tax collectors - whose task it was to provide the Crown with the taxes to be collected from the community - who do not display any compassion towards the poor.[28]

His criticism of the wealthy class is not a sweeping generalization which admits no exceptions of rich people who are not guilty of the desire to exercise domination over the poor, but Saba's heart lies with the poor, to whom he promises justice in their reward of spiritual wealth:

> ...for before God there is no regard for the rich more than for the poor, and it is possible that someone whom we consider great, is in truth very small, and vice versa...and there (in heaven) there is no domination and superiority [*serarah u-maàlah*] but (God is) with the oppressed and the lowly, who is (analogous to) 'half a sheqel,' which is a broken thing...so that they should not be arrogant and pursue domination and superiority...and the one who cleaves to God is the broken vessel, the broken and depressed heart, this is 'half a sheqel' and not a whole sheqel.[29]

Indeed, Saba sees in the pursuit of social domination the animating force of those rich Jews. Expressions such as arrogance, domination and superiority [*gaávah, serarah, maàlah*] appear again and again in the passages where he castigates the rich. The biting sarcasm in the following passage reveals the contemporary significance in pre-Expulsion Spain and epitomizes his opinions and emotions concerning the prevailing social injustice through his distinction between Moses and other people:

> All people do not want anybody else to have domination besides themselves. Moreover, they are jealous when they see others having domination, and this is more pronounced if they think that a certain man used to be their equal and now has domination over them.[30] And this is (the meaning of) 'man's envy of his neighbour.'[31] They do not want anyone to have any domination and superiority but that everybody will know that the land was given only to them, and that they have the ability to let die or to maintain, to feed people or to take their livelihood away from them.[32]

Here, then, we have an eloquent testimony to the struggle for social power among the more influential people within the community as well as the concomitant suffering of the poor which Saba claims comes as a direct result of the compelling human desire for domination over one's fellow man.[33]

The people who achieved leadership by their ambition for power proved to be failures when they could not respond responsibly to the challenges that arose. The leader must devote himself to his people, make personal sacrifices for them and show readiness to sanctify the Name.[34] This the leaders could not do for they were not leaders of truly religious and moral stature.[35] Saba is very persistent in his emphasis on the nexus between social corruption and religious laxity "between man and God." This is clearly evidenced in Saba's description of the ideal Jewish courtier - mainly in his comments regarding Mordecai. By implication we can deduce his veiled criticism of the contemporary courtier class.

The courtier's duty is two-fold and can be summed up as utilizing his unique status to promote the welfare of the Jewish community. One sphere of activity is that of representing the Jews at the King's court, and the other is inner-directed, i.e. within the community itself. His ultimate success will depend on the degree to which he displays outward pride and esteem in his religion by means of which he will gain respect and honor, even at the court.

Mordecai spread a lot of charity, which helped him to become popular among the Jews.[36] He used his elevated status, political experience and diplomatic wisdom to promote peace among people so that they accepted his opinion and judgement.[37] On the other hand, he did not use his power to rule by intimidation. His veneration "was not forthcoming because he was violent [*álam*] or because he imposed an excessive fear, but was rather due to respect resulting from his greatness."[38] His communal activity also had a spiritual dimension for he served as a religious preacher and cared not only for his personal religious perfection but also for his people's religious welfare.[39]

But beyond the perfection of his personal religious life and his devotion to his people, he openly and proudly exhibited his origin and faith, and despite this "he was the viceroy, and beloved by all the courtiers [*sarim*]".[40] The secret of Mordecai's success lay in the fact that he was able to overcome the disparity between his pronounced Jewishness and the prevailing hostility towards Jews which existed in the court. Indeed it was his Jewish behavior which gained everyone's respect and friendship. Saba emphasizes the demonstrative fashion of Mordecai's Jewishness:

> 'A Jewish man' (Esther 2,5), as if it said: 'Look what a wonder! Having a worthy [*kasher*] Jew in Shushan the capital, who was standing at the king's gate and was an important courtier in the palace, circumstances under which one would normally adopt their ways and become defiled [*yitgaèl*] by their foods...in spite of this he was a worthy 'Jewish man' separated from any impurity as was the case with Joseph.[41]

We do not find here an unequivocal condemnation of the majority of the courtiers but rather an understanding of the circumstances which are the reason for Mordecai's uniqueness.

It is tempting to identify the characterization of Mordecai with Don Isaac Abravanel who participated actively in public Torah study, whose grandson was sent to Portugal before the Expulsion from Spain,[42] and seems to have been the symbol of a "worthy Jew" in the king's court.[43]

When the Jewish courtier represents his people and religion properly, it remains up to God to cause the other courtiers to respect him, as happened with Moses who, in spite of the plagues he brought upon Egypt, "was very great in the eyes of Pharaoh's servants and advisors although, as a rule, every craftsman hates his colleague..."[44]

Mordecai's greatness caused the status of the Jews in the country to be superior to the rest of the population.[45] Thus, Saba recognizes, as did the rest of Spanish Jewry, the importance of the courtiers' role in shaping the destiny of the communities. Saba's criticism is mild, taking into account the objective circumstances which made it difficult to meticulously keep to the letter of the Halakhah.[46] But the courtier's success depends not on the sciences he possesses - and Mordecai possessed them all - but on his personality which should be shaped at its roots by one dominant characteristic:

> Even though he (Mordecai) was crowned with various qualities and wisdoms, he obtained the quality of humility which is the greatest of all qualities.[47]

Thus, consistent with his criticism of the leaders, Saba sees the source of the courtier's religious and moral perfection - and ultimately the key for his success - to be humility, the quality that the Jewish leadership actually lacked.[48]

Now we are in position fully to understand one of the better known passages from Ẓ.M. in the broad context of social and religious criticism. In this short passage Saba explains the reasons for the Expulsions, starting "And in the first book I here explained at length the reason for the Expulsion [*gerushin*]." Here we have in a nutshell his critique of the upper class. Let us, then, analyze this concise passage:

And He said: 'You shall make for yourself no idols' (Lev. 26.1), to hint that *Shemitah* is equal to the rest of the commandments and everyone who denies it is considered as one who believes in idolatry. And all this comes from covetousness [*ḥemdah*], since he coveted the fruits of the seventh year. And it is to this that He alluded in 'neither shall you place any figured stone [*even maskit*] in your land' (ibid.), as He said: 'and upon all the beautiful crafts [*sekhi'yot ha-ḥemdah*]' (Is. 2,16). And since all this comes out of the *Shemitah*, which is included in the Sabbath, He concluded the (weekly) Portion with 'You shall keep my sabbaths' (Lev. 26,2).

And in the first book I explained here at length the cause for the Expulsion (saying) that the arrogance and domination [*ha-gaávah veha-serarah*] that existed in Israel as though they were living in their own land brought it upon them so that they were building ruins for themselves, and houses panelled with cedar and with beautiful crafts like kings' palaces, for the sake of which they bowed down and worshipped idolatry. Also the Expulsion was a result of the desecration of the Sabbath, and controversies [*maḥloqet*] and quarrels in synagogues on Sabbaths and holidays, so that by their sin they caused them to become houses of idolatry as they (the Sages) tell us (B.T. Yevamot 96b): A certain rabbi saw a synagogue in which there was a controversy and he said: I am afraid that it will become a house of idolatry, and indeed, after a short while it was taken away (from the Jews) for idolatry. All this resulted from their lack of reverence of the sanctuary. And this is the meaning of 'You shall keep my Sabbaths and reverence my sanctuary, I am the Lord.'

From the exegetical point of view, Saba here tries to show the relationship between the last two verses of the Portion (*Behar*) and its central theme - *Shemitah*, on the one hand, and on the other, to the "Reproof Section" (which follows), in which the Torah promises the punishment of exile if Israel will sin. Saba solves the problem of the seemingly dislocated verses by equating the severity of transgressing the *Shemitah* with the sin of idolatry and by showing that the Sabbath is the foundation of the *Shemitah*. The connection to the following Portion - something Saba never fails to discuss - lies in the fact that the commandments mentioned in the last two verses were the causes for the Expulsion alluded to in the Reproof Section.

We have, then, four points: covetousness and idolatry (which are interrelated), Sabbath, synagogue. But the first two seem to be the decisive sins since a) Saba talks about "the *reason* for the Expulsion," and b) repeats only the first one in the Reproof Section.

In order to understand this short passage fully we must look at Saba's Biblical expressions with which he plays masterfully.[49] In addition it is necessary to check his main medieval literary source - R. Solomon Alami's *Íggeret Mussar*, and finally, fill in gaps or verify our reading of the passage from Saba's own writings.

Biblical Sources:

Isaiah 2,16: (12-13: For the day of the Lord of hosts shall be upon everyone that is arrogant [*geéh*] and lofty... and upon all the cedars of Lebanon...)...and upon all the beautiful crafts [*sekhi'yot ha-ḥemdah*] ...(20: On that day a man shall cast his idols of silver and idols of gold [*élilei khaspo ve-élilei zehavo*].

Job 3,14: ...with the kings and counsellors of the earth who built ruins for themselves [*ha-bonim ḥoravot lamo*].

Jer. 22,14: (13: Woe to him who builds his house by unrighteousness, who uses his neighbour's service without wages and gives him not for this work). Who says I will build myself a great house with spacious upper rooms... paneling it with cedar [*ve-safun be-érez*]...[50]

While it is already apparent from these sources that we have here a critique directed at the upper class including the courtiers, it becomes definitive when we compare it with Alami's critique in the wake of the massacres of 1391 and its aftermath.

> Those who sat in their paneled houses were expelled from pleasant palaces. And for building in our exile, despite the destruction of our Temple, wide houses with spacious upper, beautiful rooms, we were expelled.
>
> The great ones of the community...who stood before kings in their courts and their castles...and became arrogant...and Israel has forgotten his Maker and built palaces. And they grew proud to their destruction, everyone has corrupted his way upon the earth pursuing domination.[51]

The root of the problems lay mainly in social corruption and immorality. Those rich Jews who walked in kings' palaces (Job 3, 14), who held in their hands all the power, mercilessly exploited the lower classes (Jer. 22,14). This same idea is elucidated in another place:

> 'But Yeshurum waxed fat...you did wax fat...' to hint that the great and the distinguished ones [*ha-gedolim veha-yeḥidei segullah*] kicked their King many times over in comparison to the masses [*haàm*], since it says only 'But Yeshurum waxes fat,' but the distinguished ones and the dignitaries [*ha-yeḥidim veha-sarim*] used to steal, rob, and perpetrate injustice upon the simple people [*qetanim*] in order to become rich and to gather fat upon their loins.[52]

In the next stage, money became the idol which they worshipped (Isaiah 2,20). The material security and comfort on Spanish soil (where they felt as though they were on their own land) brought them to the point that in trying days when they had to choose between Judaism and wealth they "bowed down and worshipped idolatry." This refers clearly to conversions for economic gain either during the 15th century or at the time of the Expulsion. This idea appears elsewhere:

> ...in the end of days the nation will decline ...and will proceed from evil to evil [*me-raàh él raàh*] and immediately when they will realize their trouble they will say: 'Have not these evils come upon us because our God is not among us,' and they will recognize their sin, but then they will go from evil to a greater evil, [*me-raàh él raàh gedolah yoter*] namely, that they will turn to alien gods...[53]

The first evil, then, was while they were still Jews, and only in the second stage did they convert to Christianity. The expression "from evil to evil" is borrowed from Jer. 9,2. The context there is one of social immorality including deceit, lying, slander, etc.[54]

Again, it all began with internal immorality, arrogance and domination.[55] All evil points back to one single root, and although the criticism is scattered all over Saba's writings and appears in different contexts, we find unity and consistency on this subject as well as on other topics, where - very characteristic of him - he has a definite tendency to focus on one single point, from, or to which, everything flows.

One must also note in conclusion what Saba does *not* say. Although he criticizes antinomian tendencies several times,[56] he does not tie voluntary conversions to the influence philosophy. There is only one place that can be interpreted this way. Commenting on chapter 13 in Deut.,[57] he analyzes the three ways of tempting an individual to convert to idolatry. The Torah counts those three ways according to their degree of danger: a) a prophet who claims a new revelation nullifying the old one;[58] b) relatives;[59] c) "I am not afraid so much of this (relatives)...but I am afraid that...evil people..." The description of these people is as follows: בני בליעל עזי פנים בני בלי עול תורה ומצוה מוטבעים בטיט היון חזקים וגבורים לפרוץ הגדר ולהדיחך בחלקת אמרים רכו משמן. Saba sometimes uses the expression *tit ha-yeven* to denote foreign beliefs,[60] and he uses the term *ben beliyaàl* to describe Aristotle, but this is not the exclusive use.[61] But even if this interpretation is correct,[62] it would explain, according to Saba, only a limited part of the phenomenon of voluntary conversion. In this respect Saba's stand does not reflect extreme opinions such as that of Yaàveẓ, and others who address the problem of conversions to Christianity since 1391, for whom philosophy is the main factor to blame for the conversions.[63]

3. *The "New Christians" - The Historiographical Problem*

The historical study of the New Christians64 has advanced greatly in the past three decades. Its importance for the understanding of Jewish history in 15th-century Spain and outside of the Iberian Peninsula in subsequent centuries has been widely recognized. Scholarship has been enriched by new avenues of research as efforts were made to make use of the various literary genres in all relevant languages and of archival documents of all sorts, primarily inquisitorial. On the other hand, great efforts were invested in attempts to uncover the methodological vulnerabilities of the different studies.[65]

B. Netanyahu deserves special mention in the history of the modern historiography of this field for a daring comprehensive study in which he tried to prove, from the different genres of Hebrew literature in the 15th century, that the New Christians - who converted to Christianity at the end of the 14th century in Spain - assimilated rapidly into Christianity and lost any Jewish identity and practice. The violent campaign against them which started in the mid-15th century was primarily of a social and racial nature and not a religious one. This is also true of the establishment of the Spanish Inquisition in the last quarter of the 15th century, which should be viewed as an institution created in order to fabricate accusations against "judaizers," who did not exist in reality. Even the Inquisition did not cause a profound and prolonged Jewish awakening among the multitudes of the already Catholicized New Christians.[66] Netanyahu did much in that volume to reopen serious discussion of the historiographical problem. It certainly brought about a more critical attitude in the examination of Hebrew sources. The publication of that admirable revisionist attempt promoted scholarly ferment and much was said and written in reaction to it, mainly on the methodological level, and was devoted by and large to Netanyahu's discussion of the *responsa* literature.[67] The homiletical literature did not draw as much attention from scholars. In the following pages we intend to put under close scrutiny the view and attitude of R. Abraham Saba, to whom Netanyahu devoted a very short discussion.[68]

Netanyahu divides the subject into two: a) Saba's attitude to martyrdom; b) his view of the New Christians. It is worthwhile to follow this order and compare our conclusions concerning details, generalizations and methodological rules. To present a complete picture it will be necessary, however, to add a section concerning Saba's attitude to the life of the converts as Marranos.

3.1. Martyrdom

Concerning Sanctification of the Name [*qiddush ha-shem*], Netanyahu states:

> Like Caro,[69] Saba emphasizes the duty to sanctify the Name and, like Caro, he found no extenuating circumstance that might justify conversion. But in Saba's writings this attitude is brought into sharper relief and, in fact, raised to the position of an Article of Faith. There is no sign here of the flexibility with which the rabbis treated the rule 'Let him be killed and not transgress...' One should give his life and not convert; one should suffer imprisonment, hunger, and torture - and not convert. In fact, to undergo the death of a martyr is, in his opinion, no torture but the attainment of real peace through complete union with God.[70]

This judgement relies almost solely on a passage which constitutes part of a sermon revolving around Hanukkah.[71] Saba explains that the Maccabeans won because of their readiness for self-sacrifice in the Sanctification of the Name. Their mental ability to do so was a result of their daily *devequt* during the recital of the *Shema*, and at this point Saba recommends a way for the individual to die as a martyr without fear:

> And this is the meaning of 'And you shall love the Lord your God' (Deut. 7,5), For the one who does it out of love, his longing and love cause him not to value himself, his wife and his children, but he rather cleaves [*mitdabbeq*] to God when he says 'the Lord is One.' He shuts his eyes from seeing evil as if he died by a kiss, and out of his burning longing he says 'Let Him kiss me with the kisses of his mouth' (Cant. 1,2). And about this it has been said, 'For Your sake are we killed every day' (Ps. 44,23), for every day we sacrifice ourselves to die for the Sanctification of the Name at the time of the declaration of the unity of God...until your souls will ascend upward to the *Shekhinah* as a result of the longing and the happiness, and you will attain the secret of union [*ha-dibbuq*] in life...Therefore everyone must be in a state of great happiness during the declaration of the unity of God, to remove from in front of his eyes all sadness and worry together with the wordly happiness, so that the subject of his happiness will be God alone...In addition one should sing [*le-naggen*] during the *Shema*...so should do all those who face troubles and exile...and give their soul for the Sanctification of the Name during the *Shema* when he says, 'and with all your soul' - even if He takes your soul away. And so, when it happens that one will be told either to transgress the Torah or be killed, he will choose to die...since every day he sacrificed himself during the recital of the *Shema*.[72]

Saba later continues to say that one should educate his children on a daily basis to believe in the unity of God so that on a trying day they will also choose martyrdom.

Tracing the history of such an idea might prove helpful. The initial connection between the daily recital of the *Shema* and martyrdom is ancient and can be traced back to the Midrash which states that every day one can fulfill the act of martyrdom through the recital of the phrase "and with all your soul" (with the proper intention), and this is the meaning of the verse in Psalms 44,23: "Nay, but for Thy sake are we killed all the day."[73] This idea of the *Sifrei* is mentioned and developed in the middle of the 13th century by R. Jonah Gerondi, whose main education was Ashkenazi-oriented and his consequent pattern of thought and action followed in the spiritual and pious footsteps of the Ashkenazi Ḥasidim.[74] The *Zohar* repeats the same idea with minor changes in style and content.[75] R. Asher ben Yeḥi'el, an Ashkenzi rabbi, emigrated to Spain from Germany in the beginning of the 14th century and exercised great influence on the Toledan community and on Castile as a whole in the spheres of Talmudic study and religious piety. He finds this idea important enough to include in his Rule.[76]

The 15th century in Spain brings about a different emphasis. The reality of massacres and, eventually, death sentences by the Inquisition for "judaizing" brought the idea in contact with the real prospect of martyrdom. R. Abraham Halevi, a contemporary of Saba's, (again following an Ashkenazic tradition) goes one step further in his *Megillat Ámrafel*. Directing his words to potential *relaxados* to be burnt at the stake, he says that the daily recital of the *Shema* in a certain manner and intention would ensure the martyr a painless death.[77]

The same basic idea is developed by Saba in our passage in direct connection with the possibility of forced conversion, experienced in Portugal by the Jews including Saba himself. He emphasizes its educational end, namely, the preparatory significance of the *Shema* for martyrdom, and shows how to achieve the ultimate spiritual heights through its proper recital. He does not go as far as Halevi, who promises physical immunity to pain, but only that this daily practice would eventually eliminate the fear of physical death. Saba's idea, then, is but one of several notions trying to encourage people to overcome their fears and become martyrs rather than betray their Jewish faith in an age when martyrdom was no abstract idea.

Now even if we had only this passage alone and posed the question whether it constitutes a proof that Saba raises the principle of martyrdom to the position of an Article of Faith, the answer would be definitely in the negative. As a preacher who believed in this commandment, Saba tried to do everything within his power to advocate martyrdom and encourage those Jews who might be deterred from achieving the acme of religious faith because of the physical pain involved. He found a way to circumvent the physical obstacle by cultivating a daily state of ecstatic *devequt* as preparation for actual martyrdom. Indeed, from this passage we detect Saba's profound understanding of the human fear of physical torture and death. He might have been disappointed with the limited number of a few dozen Jews, of the 10,000, who were not converted in Lisbon, but it would be unimaginable to claim that Saba rejected the converts because they did not live up to the religious demand of the ultimate sacrifice of one's own life.

But we have other sources to aid us in clarifying his stand on the issue of martyrdom[78] and while the above passage, detached from his biography and the Portuguese context of that sermon, might be misunderstood to mean that we are dealing with an Article of Faith, we find that this principle is not absolute and is qualified by changing circumstances. When a person's actions can endanger the public's safety, it seems that one should not sanctify the Name even if it is a case of idolatry. Mordecai probably would not have acted in the pious way he did had he foreseen the consequences:

> ...for he wanted to sanctify the Name and give his life by abstaining from bowing down to Haman and the image on his clothes, and this is

> of the items about which the Sages said, 'Let him be killed and not transgress.' But for the fact that he encountered an unfortunate consequence, since Haman wanted to uproot everything...and the king was persuaded by him...for himself, he (Mordecai) would not have cared whether he died or lived.[79]

Saba is well aware of the difficulty of choosing martyrdom over Marranic life. He was present in Lisbon when more than 99% of the Jews converted during four days of continuous pressure. On the individual level he questions the validity of Esau's sale of his birthright to Jacob:

> And since all this (sale) was under complete duress, for a man would give everything he has for his life and you do not have a better annulment (of the deal between Jacob and Esau) than that...and you have here a claim of compulsion [*ónes*].[80]

That is why he calls Mordecai repeatedly "a righteous and a pious man who was ready to sacrifice himself."[81] His sensitivity to this human element in its conflict with a religious command is also behind the repeated emphasis that acceptance of a covenant (Judaism included) under duress or under "half a compulsion" [*ḥaẓi ónes*] is worthless, and so the Israelites did not have complete responsibility for keeping the Torah, neither in Moses' time, nor in Joshua's "...since because of Joshua's honor they did not reveal their true thoughts, because they were ashamed(!) of him for he would use arms against them...only at the time of Mordecai and Esther...because then there was no compulsion, and they accepted of their own free will without any trace of compulsion [*beli ẓekher ónes*]."[82]

Now we can put in perspective what Saba thought of forced conversions to Christianity. Saba understood the mental and social pressure when the public or national atmosphere is one of religious laxity and claims that one must be strict sometimes and forgive at others, according to the changing circumstances:

> ...for they did not sin out of their own free will, but were compelled to do so [*ával ánusim hayu*]...but the sin of the crowd caused them (Aaron and Miriam) to sin, for it was a potentially dangerous time [*èt mukhanah le-purànut*] after Israel went from evil to evil, from murmuring to lusting [*mi-mitónenim le-mitávim*]...for the punishment must be in accordance with the time and place.[83]

In summation, we can say that Sanctification of the Name is not an Article of Faith but rather the highest manifestation of the love of God. It is a supreme religious state, the peak which not every believer reaches and conquers; nevertheless, he may remain a believer. And so, while Saba cannot over-emphasize the religious importance of martyrdom and is very emotional about it,[84] he does understand those who believe in this principle but find it too difficult to achieve in practice.

3.2. Marranic Life

In all his writings, Saba avoids attaching labels to the New Christians. He never calls them *mumarim* or *meshumadim*. Only once does he refer to a small group of them as *ánusim*.[85] Moreover, he prefers to allude to the problem of living as Marranos rather than discussing it explicitly, even when the actual implications of his discussion are quite transparent. In the following passage Saba offers an interpretation of the midrashic story about King David, who entered the bath house, and upon feeling depressed that he was "naked of all commandments," remembered his circumcision and was comforted by it. Saba talks explicitly about previous generations and only implicitly about his own time:

> ...and the forced conversions [*shemadot*] are alluded to by the 'entering the bath house'... they were happy when they saw the circumcision in their flesh, something that no king could take off, and because of (the existence of) this commandment which contains in it the name of God, they put God at their head saying, 'This is my God and I will glorify Him' (Ex, 15,2), and gave their lives for the sanctification of the Name...and he (David) cleaved to God by the means of this commandment...And by this he taught his descendants that when they would be in trouble and exile in times of forced conversions, they would be comforted by the circumcision in their flesh and would go on observing it since it is equivalent to all the rest of the commandments.[86]

In the 15th century circumcision achieves a special mystical-nationalistic significance. While the roots of the idea are deep and reach back to R. Judah Halevi,[87] there is in this period a general shift to this position particularly as a result of the general shift away from rationalism,[88] but also because of the historical reality of the Marranos.[89] Saba adds that the Qabbalistic dimension inherent in circumcision[90] raises its importance to the point that it is "equivalent to all the rest of the commandments," and, in addition, serves as a means for mental preparation for martyrdom. This is a significant parallel to the section concerning the *Shema* and martyrdom. Indeed, if we go back to the sermon, part of which we have quoted earlier,[91] we find that the parallel is perfect also in terms of the *Shema* as a substitute for the inability to study Torah:

> And since God foresaw the length of the exile and the extent of the troubles, which would result in the Torah's almost being forgotten from Israel, He wanted to give them a short section that comprises most of the fundamentals of the Torah [*rov gufei torah*], so that if, God forbid, the Torah would be forgotten as a result of the multitude of troubles, one small section would remain for them - the section of unity [*parashat ha-yiḥud*], with which they would occupied themselves, and it would be considered as if they occupy themselves with the Torah in its entirety. And if it happens that there is a decree against the study of the Torah - as

> happened in the time of Rabbi Akiba and in other times - at least they will have the verse, 'Hear, 0 Israel,' in their hearts and it will be considered as though they are occupied with the whole Torah...[92]

The two paragraphs complement each other. Saba says that one can attain perfection through the Torah a) by study [*ìyyun*] and b) by the commandments [*maàseh*].[93] In periods of forced conversion Israel was given two things to keep. These symbolize the Torah in its entirety and would contribute to the survival of the *Ánusim* as Jews.

Saba's understanding of Marranic life is again clearly evident. He sympathetically takes into consideration the dangerous conditions and perilous situations and claims that the observance of two commandments, which are actually only passive, would suffice. The recital of the *Shema* may be done in thought,[94] and circumcision is certainly no daily act.

Clearly one should try to keep as much as he can, but Saba though he does not insist on it, recommends that they "commemorate" some of the commandments in a special way in order to remember the Jewish faith, so that if one has to choose between Christianity or martyrdom he will choose the latter:

> And if they will decree against putting on phylacteries, you should, as a symbol [*siman*], tie around your hand a thread of scarlet in memory of the blood of the covenant...similarly you should put symbols on your doorposts and your gates so that you will remember your exit and entrance to the world, so that you will give your soul for the sanctification of the Name. And this is like 'Erect for yourself markers' (Jer.31,4).[95]

3.3. Marranos and Conversos - On the Historicization of Exegetical Texts

We have thus far examined Saba's attitude to the problem of martyrdom and Marranic life. We found that he is far more solicitous than we were led to believe. The remaining question is whether we can find in his writings any criticism of the New Christians at all. Let us again use Netanyahu's analysis of the most relevant passage for the question under discussion as a point of departure.[96]

The context is an exegetical one, the background of which is "what they (the exegetes) ask; how is it possible that after they repented saying, "'(Are not these evils come upon us) because our God is not among us' (Deut. 31,17), He said, 'And I will surely hide My face,' (ibid, 18)?" Saba gives six possible answers to this question.

Netanyahu dwells on the fifth answer. Saba says that God will hide His face because they repented as a result of misfortune and adversity and, therefore, their repentance is not complete and unacceptable. That is why the verse makes mention of the troubles prior to their repentance. This also explains the phrase "And they will say on that day," namely, in the period of troubles. The problem is that when the troubles are over, "they might go back to their corruption [*yashuvu le-qilqulam*]."[97]

This, theoretically, could reflect the conditions of the Marranos in Spain after the establishment of the Inquisition. But then, one may ask: Is there a justification for an "historical midrash" on a passage that does not make any explicit mention of any historical relevance and appears in a strictly exegetical context? Is there any hint that it alludes to historical reality? One might consider an external support for the historicization of this interpretation, namely, that R. Isaac Caro - a contemporary of Saba - gives the same interpretation, relating it explicitly to the Marranos.[98] Similarly we find it in a fragment written by another contemporary who apparently spent time with Saba in prison in Lisbon.[99] One might claim, therefore, that this was a widespread and accepted interpretation during this period.

However, a careful reading of the continuation of Saba's comments on verses 19-21 will prove conclusively that a historicization in our case would be incorrect. Saba shows that verses 20-21 are parallel to verses 16-18 both in the detailed sins and their respective punishments. Consequently, he asks, "Why was this section repeated?" His answer deserves to be quoted fully to clarify the methodological problem we are dealing with and since it is central in reaching a more balanced understanding of Saba's view of the New Christians:

> And I think that God foresaw their actions and knew that in the end of days this nation [*ha-úmmah*] will go from bad to worse [*mi-dḥi el deḥi*] and from evil to evil, and when they will realize their trouble they will say, 'Are not these evils come upon us because our God is not among us'(17), and they will recognize their sins. (But) after that, they will proceed from evil to a greater evil, namely, that they will turn [*she-yifnu*] to other gods and will anger Him and break His covenant. (And) although many evils and troubles will befall them, they will not recognize their sin and will not admit their transgressions, neither out of trouble [*ẓarah*] nor out of comfort [*revaḥah*]. Therefore He said that this is the reason for writing this song (19), so 'that this song shall testify before them as witness' (21). Thus the song itself will warn them concerning their belief [*tatreh bahem àl daàtam*], although they will not repent of their own volition. And this is a great benevolence on the part of God, that although they will not want to, they will return to God and He will be their God against their will, as He says elsewhere, 'surely with a mighty hand and with fury poured out will I be king over you' (Ez. 20,33).[100]

His answer, then, is that the seemingly redundant verses (20-21) refer to what would happen in "the end of days";[101] consequently the earlier verses (16-18) are not to be understood as referring directly to his generation.

But, instead, we have a harsh and quite explicit reproof of the New Christians. Let us try to analyze on the basis of this passage, how Saba viewed the recent past, the present and the future. "The nation went from bad to worse and from evil to evil" in the material as well as the spiritual sense. He alludes here, also, to the reason for that. The insertion of the phrase "they will proceed from evil to a greater evil," borrowed from Jer. 9,2, refers in its context mainly to social corruption and immorality, sins which Saba mentions in other places. As a direct result of their troubles they realized their state of sinfulness but, finally, decided possibly because of Christian polemical influence, that God removed his Providence from them and out of despair proceeded from one evil to a greater evil, namely, turning to other gods. By this they tried to escape the harsh fate of "the nation."

Saba does not talk here about forced converts but about Jews who decided to convert to Christianity on their own. The process of conversion seems to be identical to the conversion of the upper-class as described by Saba in the passage on the reasons for the Expulsion. Those Conversos, despite the troubles they will encounter, will not recognize their sin. The source of the troubles could be social, something the New Christians certainly faced in the second half of the fifteenth century. But it seems that here Saba refers more specifically to the Inquisition, for the verse he quotes from Ezekiel is interpreted by several others of the period as referring to the Inquisition and the Conversos, and it seems that this interpretation became standard in this period.[102] The phrase "the nation" is not to be interpreted in its broad sense since "the nation" did not convert.[103] If this is the subject of the entire passage, (note that Saba uses it only once - before the conversion stage.) than it should be understood as referring mainly to a segment of the leadership, for we do not know of a large scale voluntary conversion in Spain in the second half of the fifteenth century which could be described as "the nation,"[104] and Saba does not seem to allude here to conversions due to the Expulsion from Spain. There is, however, one more interpretation to be considered, namely, that Saba refers here to the mass voluntary conversions in the wake of the disputation of Tortosa in the second decade of the fifteenth century. In view of the great influence of Alami on Saba this suggestion seems plausible (and Alami wrote his *Íggeret Mussar* soon after that disputation). Saba, like Alami, castigates the upper-class and connects social corruption with conversion.

Now, what is the substance of Saba's criticism of those converts? All he says is that "...they will not recognize their sin and will not admit their transgressions." In this statement Saba seems to reprove them for remaining in Spain where they must live openly as Christians although they probably do not believe in Christianity This would be identical with Alami's demand, which is the accepted halakhic view and is repeated by many other rabbis in this period: that they flee Spain

The process of religious deterioration described here explains an ambiguity in another passage on Deut. 32,15-17, where Saba sees the repetition of "'And Jeshurun waxed fat...you did wax fat'...as referring to the masses, but with particular emphasis on the distinguished ones, who stole, robbed and wronged...in order to get rich...."[107] The beginning refers to social justice and corruption by the leaders, while the end of the verse talks about forsaking God and turning to other gods. These two sins could occur simultaneously in Biblical times, but if there is any allusion here to Saba's time, or at least a projection of prevailing contemporary conditions onto the Biblical period, then we must read it as referring to religious deterioration, beginning with social corruption and ending in conversion which broke the tie with the Jewish community.[108]

Saba's criticism here is directed mostly toward the wealthy people who were also leaders in the communities. Money and power were their goals and, therefore, they did not prove themselves worthy of leadership when the external pressure became more intense. Saba tells us about the leader who is to be ready to sacrifice himself for his people. Gideon is a proto-type of such a leader: "Now look and understand...how he sacrificed his life for Israel."[109] The Biblical proto-type of the unworthy leader - with what seems to be a transparent allusion to the contemporary reality - is Elimelekh, who abandoned his people in difficult times when they needed him: "...for since he was the leader of the people [*nesi ha-àm*], it was suitable for him to die first rather than leave Canaan."[110]

Those people's "end proved their beginning." They kept their Jewish faith as long as it was worthwhile, consequently they were the first to abandon the sinking ship of Spanish Jewry.[111] It is clear that he addresses two types of New Christians. His instructions concerning the Sanctification of the Name obviously could not be directed to the group of Conversos mentioned above while, by the same token, he would not castigate all those Marranos who converted under some measure of force, although, like other rabbinical authorities, he could not approve of their stay where they could not practise Judaism in its fullest sense.

One might be tempted to make a neat distinction between Spain and Portugal, claiming that references to martyrdom and to Marranic life refer to Portugal, where the Jews were converted under duress - although it must be stressed that Saba, who was among the few faithful and withstood the pressure, did not condone that conversion - while Saba's condemnation is directed to the Conversos of Spain. This, we believe, would be only partially correct. Saba's instruction to the Marranos to keep observing the commandment of circumcision, for example, seems to be partially grounded in the reality of the observance of this commandment by Marranos in Spain.[112] Most of his anger is directed at a group of Conversos. To the extent that the criticism is directed to the New Christians as a whole, it seems to be limited to the common rabbinic demand that they "return to God" by leaving Spain.

There seems to be one more location, which has not been discussed to date where Saba refers to the Marranic problem. It appears right after Saba's reference to the demonic origin of the customs and rituals of the Christian clergy thus allowing us, from the methodological point of view, to see in it a reference to Jews whose sin is their conversion to Christianity:

> 'Of the Rock that begot thee thou wast unmindful' (Deut. 32,18), namely that this is a great evil since you know that they (the gods) have no power to do either good or harm, while God, blessed be He, is a Rock and is omnipotent and you desert Him. Moreover, 'And didst forget God that bore thee' (ibid), so that you would have deserted Him for a short time [*zeman muàt*] and then return to His worship it would not have been so bad, but you 'forget' forever [*la-àd le-òlam*] the great God.... and therefore He said: 'I will hide My face from them, I will see what their end shall be' (32, 20), because by hiding the face they will be destroyed at once.

If we are indeed to historicize this passage, we must try to identify the motives of those converts. God could "understand" and forgive them had they left Him for a short time and then return to Him. This could be expected of Jews who converted out of pragmatism, not of conviction. Saba says explicitly that the converts know that the "idols," i.e.,. the crucifix, can do no good nor harm to anybody. The wrath they deserve will come upon them because they forget God "forever." Their unforgivable sin is the fact that they do not leave the *terra idolatria* in order to return to full pledged Jewish life. Saba's words could not be directed at good Catholics of Jewish origin, but to such Marranos who did not renounce Judaism even after many years of outward life as Christians, but still would not do the ultimate religious step expected of them by Halakhah - leave everything behind and rejoin the living body of the nation.

The following passage reads as follows:

> And it is also possible that He said: 'And the Lord saw and spurned because of the provoking of His sons and His daughters' (32, 19), that God wanted deal with them mercifully, getting angry at them not like He gets angry at sensible people [*benei daàt*] but like one who gets angry at his young sons and daughters...since they are small and change their minds, and therefore I want to know how far will they go...and just as they have forsaken Me and have taken alien gods so they might forsake them and return to God. But they did not do so and 'stayed on their guard' and 'roused Me to jealousy with a no-God, and I will rouse them to jealousy with no-people' (32, 21), so that they not be my people...

Again one should ask whether there is a justification for the historian to assume a contemporary relevance in this passage. It is a new interpretation and therefore not necessarily connected to the previous one. In the interpretation itself there is no hint to the Iberian situation. If we take a look at the opening of the following comment, we will find that Saba seems to see the whole Portion as referring to the past. In short, if we are to try and remain methodologically on solid empirical grounds our starting point should be that we are dealing here first and foremost with a Biblical commentary, and consequently if the commentator himself does not mention explicitly the contemporary historical relevance, we ought to look for internal evidence in the passage that will make it difficult to be understood without taking into consideration the commentator's own *ambiance*.

Of course one might still insist that even if Saba intended to comment on the biblical situation he must have been influenced subconsciously by his generation's experience. Admittedly this is possible and sometimes likely. But even if this is true in the passage quoted above it will lead us only to the point that has been already proven, namely, that it seemed to Saba that those New Christians who remained in Spain for a long time, perhaps for generations, were not returning to God by fleeing that land of idolatry, and that he was very angry at them for it. This does not give us any empirical data about their private religious lives and beliefs.

To sum it up, even if we cannot describe Saba's attitude to the New Christians as "warm and friendly", one certainly must not use terms such as "unusual coldness and aloofness,"[114] as the dominant features characterizing his feelings towards them. It is remarkable that even the criticized group is not abandoned by God who will, by force if necessary, bring them back to their source. One tends to think that Saba does not refer to Catholics who did not know of their Jewish origin but rather to a majority who kept some measure of Jewish life or beliefs. Due to the remaining sparks of Judaism in their hearts Saba did not see them as a limb completely detached from the body of the Jewish people. He foresaw the complete and physical return of the group to the bosom of ancestral Faith.

If we are to generalize about the rabbinic attitude toward the New Christians, we must first realize that it was a complex one and that it was conditioned by various factors such as subjective feelings, personal experiences, religious conviction and responsibility. We always find criticism, sometimes outright hate, very often a touch of ambiguity, and always the belief that they still are an organ of the body of Israel which is severed temporarily but has not lost completely its Jewish vitality and therefore is destined to be reunited with Judaism.[115]

NOTES

[1] See our separate discussion of problems resulting from these historical circumstances as reflected in Saba's writings, below, chapter 6.

[2] On Israel's superiority see below, pp.138ff. The sad state of the nation after the Expulsions might have reduced the criticism.

[3] É.K. Esther p. 98.

[4] É.K. Esther, p. 96 and similarly Ẓ.M. Ex. p. lla-b (see also n. 31).

[5] וכבר ידעת הסגולה שיש בישראל שאם יודע אחד מחבירו שהרג את הנפש אם יפול ריב ביניהם יגלה מה שידע ומה שלא ידע (Ẓ.M. Lev. p. 29b). Note the sarcastic use of the word *segullah* which usually has positive connotations. It is possible that there is an echo here of his brother's trial (See above Ch. 1 n. 9). Although Baer contends that the term *malshin* applies only to an informer who endangers the community and not to slandering of individuals, (Baer, History vol. 2, p. 456) Saba does use it in the latter sense (Ẓ.M. Ex. p. 4b).

[6] See below p. 139.

[7] É.K. Esther, p. 66. For some Midrashic interpretations of this verse see, M.D. Herr, "The Hatred of Israel in the Roman Empire According to the Sages," *The De Vries Memorial Volume*, Jerusalem, 1969, pp. 149-59.

[8] In his commentary on Esther 3,8.

[9] *Toldot Yiẓḥaq*, Jerusalem, 1959, p. 115.

[10] Ms. Paris 845, fol. 67r. There should be no doubt that at times the Jews felt that the problem of informers assumed dimensions of a plague. In the famous Ordinances of Valladolid in 1432 there is a large section devoted to this issue. See Baer, History vol. 2, index, and especially pp. 64-9, 263-6).

[11] *Shevet Yehudah* [A. Shoḥat ed.], Jerusalem (1947), p. 42, and also p. 40.

[12] Y. Assis, "Crime and Violence Among the Jews of Spain (13th-14th Centuries)," *Ẓion* 50 (1985), pp. 221-2, 239.

[13] J. Regné, *The History of the Jews in Aragon*, Jerusalem, 1978, no. 1316. Baer published an ordinance from 1305 that deals specifically with fighting in the synagogue (Die Juden vol. 1, p. 952).

[14] H. Beinart, *Trujillo*, Jerusalem (1980), p. 30. Compare also Juan de Prado's alleged words in J. Kaplan, *From Christianity to Judaism*, Jerusalem 1983, p. 123. People occasionally came into the synagogue in Amsterdam armed, if we are to believe contemporary drawings.

[15] *Shevet Yehudah*, p. 128. Compare also J. Shatzmiller, "Tumultus et Rumor in Sinagoga: An Aspect of Social Life of Provencial Jews in the Middle Ages," *AJS Review* 2 (1977), pp. 227-55, especially the author's conclusion on pp. 240-41. The sources in Ashkenaz are silent on such an issue, which, in our opinion, shows that this phenomenon was, indeed, rare or non-existent there.

[16] About cases of violence (including in the synagogue) and murder up to the 15th century see, Asis, Crime and Violence, pp. 227-34.

[17] Ẓ.M. Gen. p. 97a.

[18] *Íggeret Mussar* [A.M. Haberman ed.], Jerusalem (1946), p. 47. While here it is not absolutely clear whether Saba refers mainly to internal immoral behavior or in their dealings with Gentiles (as A. Shoḥat maintains in *Shevet Yehudah*, p. 179). But in another place he clarifies this point (See next note).

[19] É.K. Esther, p. 66. Compare *Shevet Yehudah*, p. 29. The comment on p. 45 might be internal). Compare R. Moses of Coucy in *SeMaG*, Venice (1547), Negative Precepts, no. 74, p. 152c., and *Shevet Yehudah*, p. 127 (But there Ibn Verga claims that the Christians generalize on the basis of very few cases).

[20] *Shevet Yehudah*, p. 155.

[21] The fact that Saba's attitude towards the nations is very negative and degrading cannot by itself account for this idea. As for the history of the idea, we find that Rabbi Moses R. d'Aguilar (17th c. Amsterdam) responds in the exact same fashion in a *respon-*

sum to a Marrano who left the Iberian Peninsula, resided in Antwerp, and had not yet joined a Jewish community. However, d'Aguilar does not go so far as to suggest that this negative characteristic is a divine blessing. (See J. Kaplan's article in the *Proceedings of the Sixth World Congress for Jewish Studies* vol. 2, Jerusalem, 1973, p. 98). An astounding sentence we read in *Kaf ha-Qetoret:* ...והקב"ה שהיו משועבדים לו לא היה מצרי כי אם יהודי רמאי ופקח והיה מבין אותם (fol. 165b). However, the word *ramai*, which is applied to God could not be but a synonym to *piqe'aḥ*, namely, clever, shrewd.

Another expression of the contrast between the double duty of the preacher can be found in another context. Saba rebukes his generation: ולפי שישראל בעוונותיהם אין רואים ואין שומעים החזיקו בתרמית מאנו לשוב בסוף גלות האחרון יותר מבכל הגלויות ומרו ועזבו את רוח קדשו (Ẓ.M. Deut. p. 69b). On the other hand he praises the Jews: היטבת חסדך האחרון, בגלות האחרון בצרות גדולות מן הגלות הראשון, לבלתי לכת אחרי הבחורים, הם הע״ז אשר בחרו הראשונים ברוב ההצלחות (É.K. Ruth, p. 42a, and compare Ẓ.M. Lev. p. 32a).

22 An emotional outpouring can be detected in Saba's works very easily. Many a time he uses rhymed prose, which often expresses either exultation or deep sorrow (notably in discussing parents' relations to their children). See above p. 57.

23 Ẓ.M. Lev. p. 31a.

24 Ibid.

25 Ibid, Ex. 54b. Here he discusses "annulment of divine decrees." Public prayers for rain he mentions in Lev. 32b, and 34a, where he tells the story about R. Hisdai Crescas. Yaávez seems to refer to the same story in *Ór ha-Ḥayyim*, p. 96. Similar stories about different rabbis were common at this period (See S. Bernstein in *HUCA* 1945-46 [Hebrew part], pp. 6-7. J. Avivi in *Peàmim* 38 (1989), p. 65. *Shevet Yehudah*, p. 142, 158. Toledano, *Ner ha-Maàrav*, pp. 80-1. One can add few more stories told by E. Qapsali (*Seder*, ch. 40, p. 145), A. Gavishon, J. Sambari and others. However, it is found already in *Sefer Ḥasidim* [J. Wistinetzky ed.], Frankfurt, 1924, no. 402, p. 121. (See also, Jose C. Astrain, "Los Conversos Aragoneses segun los Procesos de la Inquisicion," *Sefarad* 18 (1958), p. 282.

26 Ẓ.M. Deut. p. 24a.

27 See quotation below by n. 52.

28 Ẓ.M. Ex. p. 45b. For an earlier use of *gaava u-serara* see R. Jonah, *Shaàrei Teshuvah*, 3, 163. For the contemporary reality background of his criticism see Bernard Septimus, "Piety and Power in Thirteenth Century Catalonia," in *Studies in Medieval Jewish History and Literature* [I. Twersky ed.], Cambridge, Mass. (1979), pp. 217-18. Saba is more explicit and harsher .

29 Saba changes from singular to plural. This as well as change of gender is common in his writings. (Many times they are Hispanisms).

30 Often, Saba's not so clear ideas can be fully understood by using another location which contains the same idea or interpretation. The expression קנאת איש מרעהו (Ecc. 4,4), is used in his commentary on Esther (see note 4) and is usually interpreted as jealousy over material achievements. But here Saba is more explicit and says that the phrase refers more specifically to jealousy over power and domination.

31 Ẓ.M. Num. p. 18b.

32 Saba extends the struggle for domination even to the field of Torah study, saying that the greatness of Hillel and Shamai lay in the fact that their controversies were not for the sake of domination and superiority (Ẓ.Ḥ. fol. 17b).

33 Ẓ.M. Gen. pp. 24a, 42a. É.K. Ruth, p. 10a.

34 This will be discussed further in the context of martyrdom and forced and voluntary conversion.

35 É.K. Esther, p. 98. The original rise of a courtier is attributed by Saba to three possible causes. Only one of them is a direct divine cause (ibid, p. 90). This would support the opinion of those who do not see in belief in the "Natural Cause" [*ha-sibbah ha-tivìt*] any heresy. See I. Twersky, "Joseph ibn Kaspi, Portrait of a Medieval Jewish Intellectual," *Studies in Medieval Jewish History and Literature*, Cambridge, Mass. (1979), p. 248 note 6. (See also Ẓ.M. Num. p. 35b about the causes for survival of a nation in war).

36 É.K. Esther, p. 98.

37 Ibid, p. 90.

38 Saba also depicts Moses as a preacher (Ẓ.M. Deut., p. 3a).

39 Ibid, p. 97.

40 Ibid, p. 38. It is worthwhile noting that concerning Joseph he uses the same key-word which he uses to condemn the leaders: לא *נתגאה* ולא חטא בשפתיו להתגאל בפת..וביין משתיו (Ẓ.M. Gen. 103b).

41. Saba expected Mordecai to do the same with Esther. See above p. .

42 See *Kesef Mishneh*, on *Mishneh Torah*, Berakhot 3,8, Baer, History vol. 2, p. 437 and above p. 24), and contemporary chroniclers and historiographers.

43 Ẓ.M. Ex. p. 16a.

44 See our discussion of Saba's commentary on Esther in light of the historical experience of the period (above pp. 18ff).

45 This agrees with Ben-Sasson's analysis (Generation, pp. 28-34). But while Saba understands the Halakhic problems that the courtier faces, he cannot forgive this class of distinguished Jews for their failures in the internal social sphere and for not being able to face the external religious challenge.

In general, we detect a soft line of sensitivity in Saba's personality. He also takes into account the difficulties in discussing martyrdom (see below pp. 104ff). He actually, frees the courtier from the obligation of Torah study Ẓ.Ḥ. fol. 25b).

46 É.K. Esther, p. 97.

47 Cf. *Shevet Yehudah*, p. 128.

48 Ẓ.M. Lev. p. 32a.

49 The following analysis relies on the fact that when a man with an outstanding associative mind like Saba's used Biblical expressions or phrases, he at least had in back of his mind the whole biblical context, namely, the immediate verses before and after the phrase or expression he borrowed. (See above pp. 73ff).

50 Another relevant verse, especially for Alami, is: "Is it the right time to sit in your panelled houses while this house is in ruins."(Hagai 1,4).

51 *Íggeret Mussar*. The four quotations can be found, respectively, in pages 39, 40, 44, 4. We also find there "And the leaders of the people [*rashei àm*] do not mind...and ignore (acts of) desecration of the Sabbath" (p. 28). Saba echoes such a complaint saying: "...and they are also accustomed to the fact that most of them go out as soon as the Scroll of the Torah is taken out, in order to do their work or to talk gossip." (מיד... יוצאים רובם למלאכתם או לדבר לשון הרע) He notes there: "And this I have preached many a time before the Expulsion" (Ẓ.M. Ex. p. 57b)

Concerning the quarrels in the synagogue on sabbaths and holidays and lack of "fear of the sanctuary" Saba says, "...The Scroll of the Torah stands open on the Sabbath, and they do not want to have an *àliyyah*...and thus degrade the Torah for their own honor, for they say: I do not want to be but third or seventh, and if I agree to go up, who will come after me" (ibid, p. 58a). The problem of *àiyyot* has a parallel by Alami: כאשר תעלה לקרות בתורה עלה בכלל העולים ואל תפנה אל האלילים להיות מתחיל או משלים (*Iggeret Mussar* , p. 31).

52 Ẓ.M. Deut. p. 66b. For examples of ruthless tax-collectors see H. Beinart, "The Image of Jewish Courtiers in Christian Spain," *Elites and Leading Groups*, Jerusalem, 1964. pp. 60-61, 68-69. One should pay attention to the use of several synonyms which indicates that the pulse of the writer beat faster as he wrote it... The upper class continued in their sinful way of life after the Expulsion from Spain to Portugal as Saba tells us in the Reproof Section: "And about the verse 'And I shall bring them,' (one might ask) but they were there already? It would seem though, that God brought them into their enemy's land so as to make them suffer, but when He saw that they added transgressions unto their previous sins, he brought them 'to their enemies' land' - who is even crueler than the first. Just as we saw that the Jews were expelled from Castile because they behaved there like kings, and they came to Portugal... 'And I shall bring them to their enemies' land,' which refers to the second coming [*biáh sheniyah*] when He brought them to Arzila..." (Ẓ.M. Lev. p. 35a).

53 Z̧.M. Deut. p. 59b.

54 For a more detailed analysis of this passage see the section about conversions below, p. 110.

55 Arrogance was seemingly also the cause for assimilation through mixed marriages (either as a cause for conversion or after it by the Conversos), as Saba understands the reason for Elimelekh's sons' intermarriage. They came to Moab, "where they became great people and became arrogant to the point that they married foreign women." (É.K. Ruth, p. 12a).

56 Z̧.M. Ex. 32b. Deut. p. 51a. É.K. Esther, pp. 10-11. Z̧.Ḩ. fol. 30b.

57 Z̧.M. pp. 22b-23a.

58 To this Saba gives an answer close to that of Maimonides in *Mishneh Torah, Yesodei ha-Torah*, ch. 8. See also *Shevet Yehudah*, p. 38, The contemporary polemical context is evident.

59 Concerning familial influence compare Arama, discussed by B. Netanyahu, *The Marranos of Spain in the 15th Century According to the Hebrew Sources*, New-York (1966), p. 148.

60 Z̧.M. Ex. 19b, 21b.

61 Z̧.M. Gen. 18a, 72b. See, however, ibid, Deut. p. 24b.

62 For one thing, the expression *benei beliyaal* appears in the verse itself (Deut. 13,14), and is not added by Saba.

63 See also Netanyahu, Marranos, pp. 163-4.

64 We use three terms for the sake of convenience and precision: New-Christians - All the Jews who converted to Christianity. Conversos - New Christians who identified themselves with Christianity. Marranos - New Christians who identified in practice or belief with Judaism (Cf. Y.H. Yerushalmi, *From Spanish Courts to Italian Ghetto*, New-York, London, 1971, Preface p. xv, and pp. 39-40).

65 See for example the bibliographical article by G. Nahon, "Les Marranes espagnols et portugaise et les Communautes juives issues du Marranisme dans l'Historiographie recente (1960-1975)," *REJ* 136 (1977), pp. 297-367, and the recent essay by Y. Kaplan, "The Problem of the Anusim and the New Christians in the Historical Research in the Last Generation," *Studies in Historiography* [M. Zimmerman, M. Stern, Y. Salmon ed.], Jerusalem (1988), pp. 177-44.

66 B. Netanyahu, The Marranos, pp. 3-4.

67 E.g. G. Cohen's review in *JSS*, 29, 1967. pp. 178-84, and a more recent and comprehensive discussion by Y.H. Yerushalmi in From Spanish Court to Italian Ghetto, pp. 21ff. And see now B. Netanyahu, "On the Historical Meaning of the Hebrew Sources Related to the Marranos," *Hispania Judaica* (1980), pp. 79-102.

68 Netanyahu, Marranos, pp. 162-172.

69 Rabbi Isaac Caro (a contemporary of Saba's) in his book *Toldot Yizḥaq*.

70 Netanyahu, Marranos, p. 169.

71 In the Oxford mss. folio 348a. Saba ends that passage saying: זה מה שעלה בדעתי כשהייתי חולה ומוטל על המטה, למה נקרא זה המועד חנוכה. ודרשתי אותו כשקמתי מחוליי במועד חנוכה של שנת ששים, וראיתי לכותבו כאן בפרשת הייחוד (See the chapter about his biography above p. 11?).

72 Z̧.M. Deut. p. 15a-b. As to the history of the Spanish exegesis of Psalms 44 and the change of direction in the third quarter of the 15th century in light of historical reality see J. Hacker, "'If we have forgotten the Name of our Lord' (Psalms 44:21) : Interpretation in Light of the Realities in Medieval Spain," *Zion* 57 (1992), pp. 247-74.

73 *Sifrei*, Vaéthanan, 7.

74 *Íggeret ha-Teshuvah*, p 24. (see Y. Ta-Shema, "Ashkenazi Ḩasidism in Spain: R. Jonah Gerondi - The Man amd His Work," *Exile and Diaspora* (H. Beinart's Festschrift), Jerusalem (1988), p. 187 and n. 50.

75 *Balaq*, p. 195b, and see E. Azkari, *Sefer Ḩaredim*, 1,16.

76 I. Abrahams, *Hebrew Ethical Wills*, Philadelphia (1976), p. 125. For a full survey of the use of this idea in Spain see now: J. Hacker, "Was Qidush Hashem Spiritualized towards the Modern Era?" *Sanctity of Life and and Martyrdom, Studies in Memory of Amir Yekutiel* [Gafni and Ravitzky ed.], Jerusalem (1992), pp. 221-32.

[77] See G. Scholem, "New Studies Concerning R.A. Halevi," *Qiryat Sefer* 7 (1930), pp. 153-55, 441-42. D. Tamar, *Qiryat Sefer* 33 (1958), pp. 376-78, and ibid. 34, 1959. p. 397. R.J.Z. Werblowsky, *Joseph Caro, A Lawyer and a Mystic*, Oxford (1962), p. 152. On the martyrological legacy of the Hasmoneans as reflected in *Megillat Ámrafel*, see H.H. Ben-Sasson, *Trial and Achievement*, Jerusalem (1974), pp. 213-15. For a collection of Midrashic homilies about love of God and martyrdom in Tannaitic Thought see S. Safrai, "Martyrdom in the Teachings of the Tannaim," *Y. Baer Memorial Volume* (*Ẓion* 44) (1979), pp. 34-5.

In ms. Oxford, Bodley, 464, fol. 49b (16th century, Balkan or Palestine), we find another version of this idea: ...תדע כי כל המייחד שמו של הב״ה ניצל מאש. הלא תראה כי בזה הפסוק רמוז אלף מאחד ושין של שמע הוא אש ומם ועין של שמע הוא מישאל ועזריה, חת ודלת מאחד חנניה ודניאל. לפי שאלו ייחדו שמו של הב״ה בכל לבבם ולכן ניצולו מן האש Here, then, one is promised to be spared altogether from the actual experience of martyrdom. In other words, the writer tries to convince his reader not to be afraid of performing acts that under regular circumstances would put him in danger of being burnt at the stake. In the reality of the 16th century he could have referred only to the Marannos. To be sure, the origin of the idea seems to be in the book *Qene Ḥokhmah Qene Binah*, but there the phrase reads: ...תדע כי כל המייחד שמו של הב״ה ניצל מאש. הלא תראה כי בזה הפסוק רמוז אלף מאחד ושין של שמע הוא אש, ומם ועין של שמע הוא מישאל ועזריה, חת ודלת מאחד חנניה ודניאל, לפי שאלו ייחדו שמו של הב״ה בכל לבבם ולכן ניצולו מן האש (Kracow, 1894, p. 821). The last two words were deleted in its 16th century version.

[78] Netanyahu only used Saba's commentary to Deuteronomy. One should note that his pagination belongs to that book, for in the 1879 edition which he used, each of the five books has separate pagination.

[79] É.K. Esther, p. 71. Here we have, in fact, the rationalization of the special license for courtiers to deviate from some Halachic norms as we find in R. Joseph Caro "...for the survival of Israel [*mishum haẓalat yisraél*]...because when there are Jews who are close to the king they step into the breach to annul the decrees (against Israel)." (*Beit Yosef*, Tur Y. D. *Ḥuqqot ha-Goyyim*, no. 178. This very attitude could be surmised from Saba's description of Mordecai's pietism concerning eating Gentile food. (See above p. 100. Ben-Sasson, Generation, p. 34. Gross, Saba, p. 218 n. 61).

A remark which might be relevant to our discussion and could be considered quite permissive is found concerning the bows Jacob took in the process of welcoming his brother, Esau: "...when Jacob bowed down to Esau seven times including his wives and children, so that he almost transgressed the prohibition of 'Thou shalt not bow down to an alien god,' (Ps. 81, 10), but his intention was (to bow down) to Heaven, since it says: 'And He passed before him and he (Jacob) bowed down to the ground,' (Gen. 33,3) - to God who is called He." (É.K. Esther, p. 61). In other words, since his intention was holy, though his outwardly actions were contradictary to it, it was not considered a sin. Although the idea already appears in the *Zohar* (Ẓ.M. Gen. p. 98a-b), if we translate this to the historical reality of 15th-century Spain, we get a description of, and a religious rationale for, Marranic behavior of coming to church, bowing down to Christian images while directing their prayers to the God of Israel. While many of the Marranos tried to avoid going to Mass, when they did go, they either said different prayers or intended at least to direct them to the God they believed in. (See, for example, H.P. Salomon, "The De Pinto Manuscript: A 17th Century Marrano Family History," *Studia Rosenthaliana*, 9 (1975) p. 43 and n. 135. C. Roth, "Religion and Martyrdom Among the Marranos," *Holy War and Martyrology*, Jerusalem (1968), p. 96). It is not that Saba would recommend this sort of religious life in any way, but it is quite possible that he would say that under duress this is not considered idol worshipping.

[80] Ẓ.M. Gen. p. 56b.

[81] É.K. Esther pp. 39-40. The whole question that Saba develops at length as to why Mordecai allowed Esther to be taken to the king's palace is based on his piety (see above p. 23).

Martyrdom is supposed to be a supreme act proving the religious man's love for his God. In addition, says Saba, the act is outwardly directed to gaining the respect of the Gentiles. "...and they (the Gentiles) will praise them" for "they gave their lives for the

Sanctification of the Name." (Ẓ.M. Deut. p. 43b. Similarly says Yaávez̧, talking about the contemporary problem of apostasy and martyrdom, adds: "And we have heard such words from their [i.e. the Gentiles] mouths in the generation of *shemad*" [*Ḥasdei ha-Shem*, New York (1934), p. 36-7]). On martyrdom in this period see A. Shoḥat, "Martyrdom in the Thought of the Spanish Exiles and the Qabbalists of Zafed," *Holy War and Martyrology*, Jerusalem (1968), pp. 131-45. Shohat quotes from Saba's well known sermon in Deut. (pp. 15-16), following Ben-Sasson, Generation p. 42. His assertion that "the demand of the pietistic Qabbalists for martyrdom was absolute," needs refinement, especially in Saba's case. One cannot agree to this rigid presentation. There was certainly a difference between preaching the ideal and understanding the reality of human condition.

We do side, however, with Shohat's objection to J. Katz' notion concerning this period, that supposedly the association between the recital of the *Shema* and martyrdom brought about a weakening of the latter through its "spiritualization" (p. 143. Saba was left out of the list). A similar criticism also appears in J. Hacker's article about R. Solomon le-Beit ha-Levi's view of Israel among the nations, *Tarbiz̧*, 1969, p. 78, n. 197. For a more complete critisicm of Katz' thesis see Hacker's recent article, "Was *Qidush ha-Shem* Spiritualized etc.," [above n. 76] For a further analysis of, and additional material for Shoḥat's discussion, see above n. 77.

82 Ẓ.M. Deut. p. 50a,b. É.K. Esther, p. 3-4. Although the idea is built on a Midrashic foundation, the emphasis that finds its expression in the excessive length of presentation and in repetitions, shows how strongly Saba feels about accepting any religion out of necessity.

83 Ẓ.M. Num. p. 20a. One could note, at least in the "way of *derash*" that the grave religious situation of "proceeding from evil to evil" is also Saba's description of the Jews in Spain (see below pp. 110ff.).

84 This seems to be mainly a result of his experience in Lisbon. The thought of so many Jews who did not have the religious courage to resist conversion by risking their lives occupied him during the long months of his illness in Fez and produced an idea which connected the coming holiday (*Hanukkah*) with the problems that bothered him so much. We find that this subject had an impact on Saba's commentary in other instances. For example, when Ruth told Naomi: "Wherever you will die, there I shall die too," she meant to say "even to give my life for the Sanctification of the Name." (É.K. Ruth, p. 16a).

85 Ẓ.M. Lev. p. 35a. It is the group that helped with the burial of R. Shimon Meme. The verb המר does not necessarily have a strong negative connotation, for Saba uses it in connection with the Castilian refugees who left Portugal by ship during the winter of 1493 many of whom returning to Spain and after tremendeous hardships converted to Christianity; as well as concerning the forced conversions in Portugal in 1497, while it is clear that he could not criticize those victims to the same extent as the voluntary *mumarim*: ואמי הוי הוי ונוסו מארץ צפון, שזה רמז על המגורשיי שבאו מפורטוגאל שלא יעמדו שם וילכו להם. ואמי הוי על אותם שהלכו באניות משם ונאבדו רובם והמירו דתם, והוי על אותם שנשארו שם שכולם המירו דתם ועליהם אמי, ונוסו מארץ צפון. ועכ״ז הבטיחם שלא יפחדו וזהו, כי כדי רוחות השמים פרשתי מארץ צפון. ועכ״ז הבטיחם שיעברו עליהם צרות רבות ששללו אותם ובזו אותם והרגו אותם הי ינקום דמם (Gross, Messianic Commentary, p. 396).

86 É.K. Ruth, p. 23a.

87 *Kuzari*, 2,34, 3,7.

88 E.g. J. Guttmann, *Philosophies of Judaism*, N.Y., Chicago, San Francisco (1964), p. 242.

89 While in the 13th and the 14th centuries we find many followers of Maimonides (Guide 3,49) like Anatoli (*Malmad ha-Talmidim*, sermon on *Lekh Lekha*), R. Menaḥem ben Aharon ben Zeraḥ (*Z̧edah la-Derekh*, 1,4, chapter 22), R. Nissim of Marsaille (*Maàseh Nissim*, *he-Ḥaluz̧* 7 (1865), p. 140), we find in the 15th century a different trend in P. Duran's *Qinah ve-Hesped* (appended to the volume of *Maàseh Éfod*, Vienna (1865), p. 195), Crescas (*Ór ha-Shem* 2, 22, chapter 5), Albo (*Ikkarim* 4,45), R. Abraham Shalom (*Neveh Shalom* 4, 8), and Abravanel (Commentarv on *Lekh Lekha*). Note-

worthy is R. Isaac Caro's unprecedented radical view, that one who is not circumsized is not considered to be a Jew, a view which has no foundation in Halakhah (*Toldot Yiẓḥaq*, p. 104). See A. Gross, "Reasons for Circumcision: Trends and Historical Influences," *Daàt* 21 (1988), pp. 25-46.

90 See mainly *Zohar*, Gen. 89a-93b. Lev. 14a-b.

91 See note 72, that passage deals with the *Shema* as a preparation to martyrdom.

92 Ẓ.M. Deut. p. 14b.

93 É.K. Esther, p. 98. For a full discussion of this see above pp. 82ff.

94 See also the passage concerning the possibility of praying in one's thought when conditions are such that one cannot pray openly (É.K. Esther p. 11). There too, Saba does not explicitly express the transparent actuality of the idea.

95 Ẓ.M. Deut. p. 16a. It is possible that Saba's permissive attitude concerning Jewish practices by the Marranos stems from his view - following Nachmanides - that the duty of keeping the commandments in exile is only that they should not be forgotten. Indeed, Saba relies on the same verse "Erect for yourself markers." (É.K. Ruth p. 19b. See Nachmanides, (and his sources) *Derashah le-Rosh ha-Shanah*. in *Kitvei ha-Ramban* [ed. Chavel], Jerusalem (1963), p. 251). Actually here Saba dangerously approaches the Marranic theological excuse that in time of danger it suffices to remember the commandments. C. Roth, (article cited above p. 119 n. 79). See now: A. Ravitzky, "'Waymarks to Zion': The History of an Idea," *The Land of Israel in Medieval Thought* [M. Ḥallamish and A Ravitzky ed.], Jerusalem, 1991, pp. 1-39, and esp. 19-25.

Inter alia, Saba's information in the same sermon (p. 15b) that the synagogues were taken away as part of the religious campaign against the Jews during 1497 is affirmed by Portuguese documents. Since the spring of that year the Crown seized communal property such as synagogues and cemetaries from the Jews (Pimenta Ferro Tavares, Os judeus, p. 489).

96 Most of the passages discussed by Netanyahu are not relevant. Netanyahu translates Saba's comments on Deut. 6, 14-15 (on p. 170, n. 74): "If you do not want to worship God out of love," says Saba, "worship him out of fear, 'for he is a jealous God who will not forgive the sin of conversion and who will wipe you off the face of the earth.'" The original reads as follows: ואם לא תרצו לעבוד מאהבה עבדו מיראה כי אל קנא ה' אלהיך בקרבך והשמידך מעל פני האדמה In addition, if we read carefully we will see that the sermon on the recital of the *Shema* and the extra religious importance it assumes under conditions of forced conversion ends in the paragraph just before the paragraph from which Netanyahu quotes. The subject of this paragraph is the entrance to the Land of Israel in the time of Joshua and the life in the land thereafter. There is no justification for historicization of this passge.

Another passage centers around Deut. 22,8. כי יפול הנופל ממנו (Ẓ.M. p. 37a). For some reason Netanyahu identifies the adjectives *ha-nofel* and *ha-ḥote* as referring to the Conversos. Again there is no shred of evidence for it. On the contrary, Saba discusses those sinful people who do not repent despite the Day of Atonement and the "days of repentance," which God gave them, because they do not believe that such a concept of repentance is possible. Saba spent almost three whole pages refuting this erroneous idea in what seems to be a sermon for the Sabbath of the "Days of Repentance." (Ẓ.M. Deut. p. 53a-55a. It is located in the *Niẓẓavim* Portion which supports our conjecture, aside from details of content which point in the same direction). In the opening of that long discussion Saba quotes the verse כי יפול הנופל ממנו (p. 53a).

97 Ẓ.M. Deut, p. 59a.

98 *Toldot Yiẓḥaq*, p. 156.

99 Tishbi, Messianism, p. 112.

100 Ẓ.M. Deut. p. 59b.

101 Saba clearly thought of his days as the last (and lowest) stage of the long exile and possibly the beginning of the Redemption (See below ch. 6).

102 See Abravanel in his commentary to this verse. S. Usque, *Consolation for the Tribulation of Israel*, Dialogue 3, chapter 25, p. 199. R. Solomon le-Beit ha-Levi interprets it similarly (J. Hacker, "Israel Among the Nations As Described by SheLaH of

Salonica," *Tarbiẓ*, 38, 1969, p. 61). The belief that the New Christians will return to Judaism was also widespread. P. Duran believed so (loc. cit., in note 89). R. Abraham ben Eliezer Halevi (G. Scholem, *Qiryat Sefer*, 7 (1930), p. 444), and others. (The author of *Kaf ha-Qetoret* says with reference to the forced converts in England: ...רובם לא עמדו בנסיון ויתערבו בגויים עד כי יבוא אליהו ז״ל (ms. Paris, 845, fol. 139a).

103 See É.K. Ruth, p. 42a.

104 See Netanyahu, Marranos, p. 162, n. 63.

105 See below n. 107.

106 This goes back to Maimonides' *Íggeret ha-Shemad.*

107 For the full quotation see above p. 102.

108 The same applies to another passage that seems to be relevant to our discussion (Ẓ.M. Deut. p. 67a). Saba implies a pragmatic motivation for conversion although the converts realize that their new deity is powerless. God is angry at them for not returning to Him. (This passage follows an explicit reference to Christianity and therefore seems to be of contemporary relevance, although Saba goes on to show the parallels between the favors God had bestowed upon Israel and the punishments given to them in the distant past).

109 Ẓ.M. Gen. p. 24a, 36b. Abraham and Moses belong to the same category (ibid, 42a).

110 Ruth p. l0a. (*Nasi* in our period meant a leader of the community, usually by virtue of money and lineage.) Noah belongs to this negative category (Ẓ.M. Gen. p. 24b).

111 See above p. 102-3.

112 See H. Beinart, *Conversos on Trial*, Jerusalem (1981), pp. 11-12. See also Saba's description of Esther's clandestine observance of the dietary laws through the help of Jewish girls (É.K. Esther, p. 42).

113 Ẓ.M. Deut. 67a.

114 Netanyahu, Marranos, p. 172. It seems that a careful study of Abravanel's references to this issue will also disclose a more balanced view of the New Christians than that presented by Netanyahu. Abravanel, using precise terminology, differentiates between Conversos and Marranos.

115 See generally, Ben-Sasson, Generation, pp. 34-43.

CHAPTER FIVE

THE MEANING AND COURSE OF HISTORY

The search for the meaning of history, its scheme and course through the study of the Bible was not a rare phenomenon in the Middle Ages. Delving into the Holy Scriptures in order to elicit any allusion to the division of human history, the nature of the present in the divine historical plan and, (for the millenarian) ultimately, to gain an insight about the date of the coming *eschaton*, was widely accepted as a legitimate method.[1] The Bible was a supreme epistemological source and one needed only to decipher its concealed secrets. The Messiah was coming, and in the not too distant future. Most people, Jews and Christians, believed it. Both religions had been waiting for him too long.

If Christians had good reasons to await the Second Coming impatiently, how much more so did the Jews (for the First Coming, of course). The Jews awaited his coming not only as individuals but also as members of a generally condemned religion. Endowing history with structure and meaning would give the Jew not only a glimpse of the ray of light at the end of the long and dark tunnel called "Exile," but would also give him some understanding and appreciation of the significant and central role, albeit extremely passive, that the Jews are playing currently.

This subject occupied Saba's thoughts incessantly, and themes such as Israel's superiority, the place of Christianity in world history and related topics, coalesce into a cohesive unit. We omitted from our discussion Saba's periodization of history because he has "multiple divisions," inconsistent with each other, a fact that renders any specific division meaningless. In a fine homiletical traditional manner he divides the history of Israel into three or four-fold divisions,[2] as the particular Biblical text allows. It is clear that concerning this specific point he is eclectic, and his novelty usually lies only in the exegetical application of well-known schemes. Only once does he attempt a periodization of the entire world history.[3]

1. Good and Evil in History

Looking at history as an arena for the war between Good and Evil is the notion that Saba develops. Such an idea is not new and already appears explicitly in the Dead Sea Scrolls, but as a systematic presentation we encounter it first in Christianity with Saint Augustine, whose dualistic historical view of *civitas dei* and *civitas terrena* is based on the belief that humanity is divided into two groups, "believers and "disbelievers." He was the first to apply this thesis to history, starting from its dawn in Genesis, identifying Biblical figures and classifying them.[4] This continuous "Good-Evil battle syndrome" is the basis for our discussion.

The scholarly studies of the problem of evil as a Qabbalistic theme deal primarily with its cosmic manifestation, or with the philosophical problems such as the divine origin of Evil, its existence and its nature.[5] The following reconstruction includes some notions scattered throughout the *Zohar*, which exerted a great measure of influence on Saba. However, Saba seems to be independent, more elaborate, and conscious of the overall picture of human history. Saba does not seem to be concerned with the theosophical problems of Evil but almost solely with its earthly manifestation.[6]

Evil came with the creation of Eve,[7] was actualized with the infamous Sin and, ever since, Samael "hounds Israel" until the Redemption, which will liberate Israel and the world from it.[8] Samael is an abstract cosmic satanic force which tries to tempt man to do evil [*yeẓer ha-ra, naḥash*] but is represented throughout history by real people who are evil by "virtue" of heredity. (This is one of the reasons that Saba struggles repeatedly with the problem of determinism implied by this theory.[9])

Cain was the direct result of his parents' Sin and was born to carry the flag of Evil.[10] After the deterioration of the first ten generations, God decided to put an end to it. The Deluge was to sever the course of history and thus cause a new beginning after humanity had "paid its debt;" and Saba shows this through his favorite method of philological and content parallelism.[11] Noah himself sinned immediately after the "new creation" and Saba interpreted "the man of the earth" [*ish ha-ádamah*] as "the man because of whom the earth was lost."[12] Noah, apparently, inherited a nature that was a combination of good and evil, and the latter was actualized by Ham and Canaan who represent Evil.[13] Shem was to balance the scales.[14] Isaac representing Judgement [*Din*], albeit of the Forces of Holiness, was the vehicle through which Esau came into being while Jacob inherited the characteristic of Mercy [*Ḥesed*] from his mother.[15] From here on until the end of the book of Genesis, we are given the continuation of the "dualistic history." Chapter 36 informs us of the descendants of Esau, all of whom "are wicked and bastards," and from Chapter 37 to the end of the book we read of Jacob's sons who were all "righteous and of pure conception," which Joseph's biography exemplifies.[16]

Aside from their duty to create a "balance of the super powers," the righteous had their hands full trying to prevent a disaster which was made possible by the cause of all evil in the world - the Sin. There was a need to produce some good acts of symbolic value to balance the residue of sin, for "the world was unstable and almost crumbling," and Scripture tells us that "the righteous is the foundation of the world" (Prov. 10,25).[17] This was the task of Noah,[18] and then of Abraham,[19] who, through doing good deeds, tried to negate the deleterious effect of the Sin and consequently bring about a restoration [*tiqqun*] of the world: "Adam and Eve sinned by eating, so he fed people and converted them, as against the Tree of Knowledge he planted a tree...and called it by the name of God..."[20] Jacob helped by giving blessings that paralleled the curses Adam had received.[21] So did other righteous people, seven in all. But evidently all these efforts were minor, and only produced temporary relief. The crucial event that restored the world's stability was the building of the Tabernacle and its consecration by Aaron and his sons during the seven days' Consecration ceremony.[22]

This last point seems to be one of Saba's major original Qabbalistic thoughts, which he repeats several times and at considerable length. Going back to the Midrash we find that the first sin in human history, which became known in Christianity as the Original Sin, brought upon humanity the punishment of death. That sin did not effect the human condition in that it became the basic cause for all of one's sins.[23] A notion similar to the above mentioned Christian dogma seems to be contained in the Midrashic saying that the presence of Israel at Mount Sinai and their participation in the Revelation erased the effects of the Original Sin, cleansing them from the filth [*zuhamah*], expressed in a natural tendency to lustfulness, that had been transmitted from the Snake through his intercourse with Eve, and that had clung to her descendents ever since that sin.[24] Saba deviates here from the regular understanding of the Talmud and *Zohar* concerning the restorative effect of Israel's presence at Mount Sinai. To be sure, Saba does use this saying in positing the superiority of Israel over the Gentiles,[25] but this great happening had its lasting effect only in the national realm. It did not have the requisite global effect of ensuring the world's permanent existence. The reason could possibly lie in the need for a symbolic parallel act of great magnitude, like the creation and consecration of the Tabernacle. Another explanation may be surmised from Saba's comment that the Tabernacle was to atone for Adam's sin as well as for the sin of the Golden Calf.[26] This might mean that the latter nullified the potential atonement of the Revelation at Sinai. However, if Saba indeed does not rate this event as high as one might expect, it could be due to his emphasis of its coercive nature.[27] One can also think of possible exegetical reasons. Saba saw such a detailed line of Creation-Tabernacle parallels that he was convinced that this, and not the acceptance of the Torah, was of great significance for the Sin and its effect on the world. Besides, as a rule Saba prefers to see a pattern of progression in any series of events or acts.

2. *The Restoration of Adam's Sin*

According to Saba, the Torah, which is comprised of five books, contains in essence only four.[28] Books one and three, two and four, are parallels. In Genesis we have the story of the Sin and its effects, and in Leviticus of its restoration [*tiqqun*] through "the creation of a new world in the seven days of consecration [*milluím*]...which came to replace [*le-male*] the original days and fill the hole (created by Adam)."[29]

The mystical meaning behind the Sin, the "crumbling world" and the restoration is explained by Saba. Adam and the wicked generations that followed chased the *Shekhinah* out of the lower world and all seven heavens. The world, consequently, could not exist in such a state so Abraham and six other righteous men (the Patriarchs, Levi, Qehat, Amram, and Moses) brought the *Shekhinah* down again. This process culminated in the Sinaitic Revelation. But this was not enough. In order to complete the process and have the *Shekhinah* remain permanently, there was still a need for a series of positive acts of a specific nature, parallelling that which had happened to Adam and his sons.[30]

In that ritualistic drama, Aaron and his sons acted for Adam and his sons. The sacrifice of the bullock as the sin-offering (Ex. 29,2) was on behalf of Adam; the two rams - for Cain and Abel; and the unleavened bread and cakes were to represent the Tree of Knowledge which was wheat.[31] The garments, and especially the tunic, corresponded to Adam's "garment of skin" (Gen. 3,21).[32] In this vein Saba interprets all the details of the ritual to be performed with the blood of the animals. (Ex. 29,20).[33]

Being fully aware of the loose Midrashic method which he employs, Saba says, "And since all this would seem (to some readers) as if I say it intuitively [*ke-mitnabe*] but I do not know (it to be the true interpretation), He revealed it by saying, 'And from the door of the tent of meeting you shall not go out for seven days' (Lev. 8,33), against the seven days of Creation, which were colapsing because of the Sin..."[34]

But all this did not suffice, for the sinful beginning of human history was just too heavy an iniquitous burden for the world to bear. At this point, Nadav and Avihu became the main heroes with the crucial, albeit passive, role in what seemed to be a tragedy but in fact was a happy ending.

This notion assumes such an important and central place for Saba, that he does not tire of repeating himself, emphasizing time and again the same basic point, with the very same expressions and phrases.[35] In discussing this idea, there is, however, a problem which must be addressed, namely, the presence of some minor as well as some major and (or) implicit, inconsistencies and contradictions. Some of these will be treated as we proceed.

The death of Aaron's two older sons on the eighth day was not an accident but rather the climax of the entire event, and was intended and ordained by God without telling even Moses.[36] Saba states several times that the purpose of the seven days of *milluím*, including the death of the two sons, was to strengthen and give a proper base [*le-vasem*] to the world that was "crumbling" because of the first Sin.[37] In other places he says, however, that it was to atone personally for Adam (or also for his son, or sons, or only for his sons).[38] What Saba apparently means is that through the atonement for Adam's Sin the pristine situation of a world with a sinless Adam was restored.

The confusion in Saba's different references concerning the question of who they were to atone for (Adam, Adam and Cain, Cain and Abel, or all three) should be seen as an inconsistency resulting from the problem of "symmetry." The entire idea is constructed around the double parallels, Creation-Tabernacle, Sin(s) - Rituals of the seven days. The thesis in its entirety fits with a remarkable elegance...until the final act. There we have two people who throughout the seven days acted as Cain and Abel. However, the number two does not fit. Ideally, Saba also needed Aaron to die for Adam in order to create a perfect parallel. On the other hand, the main sin was Adam's and it would, therefore, make more sense to die for him, rather than, say, for Abel.[39] So Saba seems to have changed his mind, and we get all possible combinations of atonement; for Adam, for Adam and his sons, for Adam and Cain, and for the sons only.[40] This is also why Saba had to justify their death by saying that they were the greatest people since Adam and Cain and, therefore, were chosen. It would seem logical enough under the terms of the parallel drawn between the sons of Adam and Aaron. But since they died not only for the son(s) but mainly for Adam, it was necessary to add an explanation for God's choice.[41]

The most glaring contradiction in this matter is Saba's insistence in several places that Nadav and Avihu were the four Biblical prototypes who entered the *Pardes*, the other being Adam, Noah, and Abraham. Their parallels in the Mishnah were, respectively, Elisha ben Avuyah [*Áḥer*], Ben Zoma, Rabbi Akiba, and Ben Azai. Nadav and Avihu, like Ben Azai, "looked at what they were not permitted to". They "separated the *Ẓaddiq* and the *Shekhinah*" (*Ẓaddiq* - usually stands for *Yesod*), or, "they did not seek unity with their Master" (= *Rav* - usually *Tiféret*), or, "they did not seek unity with a woman (and consequently with a Woman - *Shekhinah*).[42] Saba contends that all the differing opinions expressed by the Sages concerning Nadav and Avihu are, in the final analysis, identical and invested with esoteric meaning.[43] Following the Sages, he does actually call what they did a sin [*ḥet, àvon*], but this does not prevent him from saying that they died sinless, and only because the ancient account of Adam had to be credited and balanced:

> ...for the sons of Aaron died to atone for the sin of Adam...since those two were sinless [*be-lo ḥet ube-lo àvon*], but just wanted to cleave to God through their wisdom (i.e. Qabbalah), and 'coming close to him' (Lev. 16,1), they died, and not for any other sin.[44]

Proceeding to interpret Lev. 16,2, Saba makes his only attempt at resolving the apparent contradiction.

> ולפי שעון בני אהרן כבר רמזתי למעלה שהוא רמוז באמרו, וישימו עליה קטורת (ויקרא י׳, א׳), ולא אמר עליהם שזהו, נרגן מפריד אלוף (משלי ט״ז, כ״ח). וחטאו בזה הע״ת שהוא עת לעשות לה׳ (תהלים קי״ט, קכ״ב), שלא ידעו לחברה להיות האהל אחד. ולכן הזהיר לאהרן, ואל יבוא בכל עת...בזאת יבא...ולפי שבני אהרן נכנסו בעת רעה מתו.

Saba here uses an idea found in the *Zohar* to say that they did not commit a sin but rather a mistake, namely, entering at the wrong time, *èt*; for there is a positive *èt*, which is *Zot*, i.e. *Malkhut*, and a negative one which is the *Sitra-Áḥra*. Nadav and Avihu did not know that, and for switching positive and negative they were, so to speak, electrocuted.[45] It only remains now to reconcile this "mistake" and the sins Saba attributes to them elsewhere. This seems to be a problem of reconciliation that already exists in the *Zohar*, which contains multiple interpretations.[46] But while the latter can allow multiple sins expressed in one act, Saba must trace all of them to a common "sin-mistake." Significantly, he omits one Zoharic explanation, namely, that they offered incense although they were not allowed to do so during their father's lifetime. All the other interpretations can be explained as resulting from wrong mystical timing.

As to the idea itself, seeing death as an atonement for the Original Sin, for humanity, seems *prima facie*, to be of Christian origin. This is only partially correct since we find the roots of such an idea in Jewish thought as early as the Midrash which states: "The death of the righteous atones."[47] Admittedly, this saying is limited to a narrow national scope, but the basic difference in the nature of Judaism and Christianity would lead to this specific difference in the notion under discussion. Indeed, in principle, there is no difference whatsoever; the death atones for the members of the faith.[47a]

The major difference (aside from the nature of the dead) lies in the purpose of the atonement. According to Saba, the grave Sin created a residue of Evil that caused the world to lose its equilibrium. This idea is completely different from that of the Christian Original Sin because the affected object is the world and not individuals and consequently the atonement affects the world.[48] In this sense Saba's notion is much more universal than the Christian one according to which the atonement is conditioned by the individual's faith. This was partially corrected by the seven righteous, by the revelation on Sinai and by the construction of the Tabernacle and its consecration. The final act of restoration was the death of Nadav and Avihu. The impending universal catastrophe vanished. The circle had been completed and terminated. For all practical purposes this particular effect of the Sin remains an episode of the past.

3. Israel and Amalek

While the cycle of the Sin and its restoration in one dimension ran its course, arriving at the finish-starting line of renewal, another consequence of the Sin - the manifestation of Evil in history-was to continue its own existence on a permanent basis without a chance for its elimination. This was to be accomplished only through the final Redemption.

From the birth of Jacob and Esau history revolves, basically, around the repetitive encounters between these two twins and their descendants - Israel and Amalek. In accordance with his view of the meaning of history, Saba says that the latter's aim is to destroy Israel as a means to the destruction of the world, which was created for Israel. When Amalek attacked Israel in the desert his aim was

> to uproot Israel, so that they not go up there (to Jerusalem) and thus return the world to a state of chaos by destroying Israel, which is the purpose of the Creation.[49]

The course along which this power-struggle occurs is a history whose structure is a combination of two basic characteristics. It is linear, as the views of history of all western religions can be described. But it also contains the idea of recurrence, and while the linear aspect is an expression of the hope that history has an end and shows some kind of direction, Saba adds to it two wave-like lines which cross each other. When one of them is up, the other is down and *vice versa.* Israel and Amalek travel through time and history on these two parallel lines. In terms of time, one must of course, allot to Amalek more time on top, and more in terms of the height of the waves. Every recurence of the encounter begins with the ascent of Amalek, and concludes with his downfall.[50]

> ...And if you will ascend to high-heaven...even there bad (fate) will reach you, until you will be destroyed. This is because you desired to attack Israel before whom your ancestors already started to fall, as we have seen that Esau fell before Jacob, Amalek before Joshua, and Agag before Saul, and so will you fall before him.[51]

This general view already appears in the Talmud, where about Jacob and Esau we read that when one rises the other falls and about Jerusalem and Caesaria that when one prospers the other lies in ruins. However, there we are not given any pattern of the recurring encounters.[52]

Indeed, the idea of recurrence of history is inherent in the belief to which Saba adheres that "whatever happened to the Patriarchs is a sign for their descendants (*maàseh ávot simman la-banim*)." However, the difference is that here we have a scheme for understanding not only single isolated ocurrences in the future of the people's history, hinted at by different incidents that have happened to the founders of the nation, but an overview of history as a whole.[53]

Saba gives us more data for our graph by discussing the nature of Edom's ascent and descent and the final ascent on the Israeli line. This description constituted the sermon he delivered before "the gathering of the scholars in Castile," which shows again the centrality of this theory in his thought, even before the Expulsions.[54]

Historically he brings us up to date on this issue by substituting *Malkhut Édom* for Amalek saying, "And remember, do not forget, the wickedness of the kingdom of Edom who turned upwards and says every day: 'Where is your God?'"[55]

The of identification between the shrewd and cruel tactics Haman used in his attempt to annihilate Israel and those of contemporary "Edomites" strengthens the idea of historical recurrence in one more aspect.[56]

This view of history explains two things: a) The "personal" involvement of God in the war against Amalek; b) The centrality of Purim and the reading of the Book of Esther which, according to a Jewish tradition, renders them eternal in contradistinction to other holidays:[57]

> ...so the matter of Amalek is a clue for the Days of the Messiah...and God will sit for eternity in peace and rest. For as long as the seed of Amalek exists, God has, so to speak, sorrow and war... And therefore the issue of Amalek (i.e. the command to remember and destroy him) is a great thing in our Torah and is compared to the Sabbath. And therefore the holiday of Purim is greater than all other holidays.[58]

The final victory over Evil will eventually occur with the coming of the final Redemption, when Amalek-Satan-Samael-Yeẓer ha-Ra, etc., will cease to exist.[59] And this is the reason for the centrality of the story told in the book of Esther:

> ...for the foundation of the Days of the Messiah is the annihilation of the seed of Amalek, something that Mordecai and Esther started.[60]

The "Four Sections" [*Árba Parshiyot*] correspond and allude to the Four Exiles, and are read two before Purim and two after it, in order to underscore the centrality of this event for Jewish (and consequently for world) history "since this Scroll is built and founded upon the theme of Amalek and Haman whose their fall is the foundation (or model) for all exiles and redemptions."[61] That period was "the lowest one for Israel and the highest and greatest possible one for Haman."[62] This is, therefore, portentous for the survival of Israel, which has already survived the worst.

About the present state of the "waves" or "scales" Saba says, "for now Israel is in a state of deterioration [*yeridah*]."[63] About Edom he tells his audience in the "gathering of the scholars in Castile" that, "the wicked kingdom stands as high as high heavens."[64] The corrective rise and fall of Israel and Edom, respectively, is therefore close at hand. The fall of Edom will be sudden and hard while the rise of Israel will be slow and gentle.[65]

The structure and meaning of history, then, serves as a means to the end which we have discussed in the introduction, namely, to be able to interpret the significance of the present. From the dark abyss of historical reality Saba viewed Jewish and world history and found a pattern and meaning from which he extracted a message of consolation for a troubled people. The ascent is imminent and, until then, Israel's task is to represent the cosmic Good in the world against Edom.

This general view of history uses for its periodization the recurring encounters between Israel and Edom which occured before and after the Exile. The present constitutes the first of the two-part standard encounter. It is the last in the historical chain and happens to be the longest and harshest one of all. But the second part of the encounter is yet to come.[66]

4. On the Devil, Demons, and Christ

As a Jew who lived in the 15th century, a period when the Jews of Spain were under great pressure and severe strain from continuous religious polemics and conversions to Christianity, one might have expected to find in Saba's writings a polemical attitude, both defensive and offensive, with occasional scorn for the persecuting religion. Such elements would be only strengthened by the Expulsions.[67] On the other hand, the dialectic relationship between polemics and influence is well-known and might explain a certain "carelessness" in using expressions which, taken out of context, resemble some Catholic ideas.[68]

In the realm of ideas we find that Saba's comments on Moses' death and burial seem to be implying the possibility of notions that Jews tried so desperately to refute. After logically examining the relevant verses, Saba concludes that there were no death and no burial whatsoever:

> Therefore I say that as all the stories about Moses were wondrous, so also were his death and burial...And if he was an appointed angel since the creation of the world...he did not die and was no man...but an angel.[69]

To be sure, Saba is not the first one to suggest that Moses did not die. This idea appears to have had deep roots in Jewish tradition.[70] This is also true concerning the idea that Moses was an angel.[71] However, all those sources talk about Moses' ascent from his original state of human to the spiritual height of angel.[72]

Thus Moses, the savior of Israel, only *appeared* in human form and, by implication, Yokheved, his mother, could have theoretically been a virgin (if not for Aaron and Miriam). It is true that we find a free use of a similar expression elsewhere: "And when he told him 'You shall no longer be called Jacob,' (he meant) because you are no man but God [*él*]."[73] But regarding Moses, Saba does not talk Qabbalah and seems to mean what he says, literally.[74]

It would appear to us that the explanation of this phenomenon, as radical as it might sound, fits in with Saba's overview of history as discussed above. One passage has particular relevance to us. This is Saba's censored comment on Deut. 32,17, which is to be found in manuscripts and the first and second printed editions of Ẓ.M.:[75]

> And perhaps He alluded in '*lo seàrum avotekhem*' (Deut. 32,17) to that which the Sages said, that the demons [*shedim*] have no hair...And since the people of Edom and all their abominations and vanities come from the Force of the Demons [*mi-ko'aḥ ha-shedim*], therefore their monks and priests[76] shave off their hair leaving on top of their heads a spot like a stain. And those who are even more impure, like the bishops and the pope, shave all their hair like a circle and leave only a little hair around, close to their ears. And just as there is no blessing in demons, likewise they plant by their churches [*beit taùam*] a fruitless tree. And so it is fitting that they would not bear sons and daughters.[77]

Since Saba did not leave us any neat and detailed thought concerning Christianity, we must ourselves proceed one step further and ask: If this is the way Saba views the representatives, how then does he view the one they represent, namely, Jesus? It is certainly conceivable that Saba sees in him the incarnation of the highest order of impurity, of Samael. If so, the Christian doctrines could basically be correct with one "little" modification: Jesus was not the Son of God but the Son of the Alien God [*él zar*] - Satan! If we want to pursue this line of thinking a little further, we can draw another parallel between Good and Evil in the world: Moses, the angelic being who did not die, the savior of Israel from Egypt who brought the Torah down for them to save their souls and, on the other hand, Jesus, with similar "personal" characteristics, only that his purpose on earth was the very reverse - to draw people into the service of the Forces of Impurity.

While this reconstruction might, at first sight, seem radical in its novelty, it can be supported by several contemporaries of Saba. A fairly recent study of the two anonymous authors of *Sefer ha-Meshiv* and *Kaf ha-Qetoret* is of great importance to us.[78] It seems that Samael is substituted for the Holy Spirit in the story of the conception of Jesus.[79] Samael is the representative of Christianity and, according to one passage in *Kaf ha-Qetoret*, Jesus is one of Samael's incarnations.[80]

Some of the Messianic ideas in *Sefer ha-Meshiv*, which carry with them a definite Christian flavor, are quite intriguing. According to this author, the Messiah is a product of the contact between Jacob and the *Shekhinah*.[81] Finally, in *Sefer ha-Meshiv* we even find a Virgin, albeit a heavenly one of fire (*Shekhinah*), as the mother of the Messiah, who is (probably) divine.[82] Saba does not go this far in his description of the Messiah but, on the other hand, while the above mentioned authors cloud their ideas with equivocal expressions and heavy symbolism, Saba seems to acknowledge the earthly possibility of a virgin giving birth to a heavenly being, as we have shown above concerning Moses' angelic origin.

Interestingly, the identification of Christianity with Samael is to be found in the work of another of Saba's contemporaries, the famous Qabbalist and Messianic enthusiast R. Abraham ben Eliezer Halevi. In his introduction to the Messianic treatise *Meshare Qitrin* he says:

> And those young children...fell into the hand of the evil Samael and worship and bow to him...Synagogues became houses for foreign worship, Torah Scrolls burnt in flames, and pious and righteous people died in all the troubles that came upon them.[83]

Halevi here no doubt describes what happened in Portugal between 1492-1497. He says that young children "fell into the hand of the evil Samael and (since then) worship and bow to him." His words are unequivocal - the forced conversion to Christianity brought about the worship of Samael by those pure unfortunate children.

The similarities in some basic notions concerning the demonic nature of Christianity seem to indicate that such views were to be found in some Qabbalistic circles late in 15th-century Iberia. Saba, however, did not belong to the Qabbalistic-apocalyptic circle where the demonization of Christianity was popular.[84] Contrary to those eccentric authors he was tremendously influenced by the *Zohar*.[84a] Saba also seems to have been far from pursuing a "wild" course of Qabbalistic Messianic speculations as did the two anonymous authors. As we shall show, he apparently did not at all engage in *ḥisuvei qeẓ*, unlike Halevi, for whom this was a central occupation. Therefore, assuming that such ideas were not necessarily a 15th century creation *ex nihilo* one should try, at least in Saba's case, to trace within the main trend of Spanish Qabbalah the early stages of the demonization of Christianity which may have served as the possible basis of his notions in this respect.

We have an idea of Jewish origin which connects Jesus to Qabbalah already in the 14th century. Profiat Duran tells us that "in his youth" (about the middle of that century) he heard from an Ashkenazi scholar that Jesus and the Apostles were mystics who had an erroneous tradition in Qabbalah and used the Forces of Impurity to perform miracles.[85] This is a late development of the ancient polemical claim that Jesus was a magician and reflects, in part, the Christians use of the Qabbalah in the 14th century in their polemical writings to validate and vindicate their faith.[86]

This developed notion says that, in essence, the Qabbalah uses terminology and expresses ideas that were misunderstood ,misinterpreted and accordingly misused by Christians.[87] It is unlikely that the Jews had to invent the Qabbalistic interpretation of Jesus' miracles in order to refutate Christian argumentns in the context of Jewish-Christian polemics. If we have here a Jewish reaction to the study of Qabbalah by Christians, it seems plausible to suggest that one and a half centuries later, after continuous Christian use of Qabbalah (oral if not written),[88] Qabbalists, under the influence of pre- (and post-) Expulsion historical circumstances, would go one step further, saying that Jesus did not only use the Forces of Impurity but was, rather, Samael's actual incarnation on earth.[89]

However, in light of Nachmanides' great influence on Saba, one might see in the latter's demonic view of Jesus and Christianity a direct development of the former's implicit view of that religion:

> However, the Holy One, blessed be He, commanded us, that on the Day of Atonement we should let loose a goat in the wilderness to that 'prince' (i.e. power) ...and destruction and waste emanate from that power, which in turn is the cause of the stars of the sword, wars, quarrels, wounds, plagues, division and destruction. In short, it is the spirit of the sphere of Mars, and its representative among the nations is Esau (Rome), the people that inherited the sword and the wars, and among animals (its portion consists of) the *seìrim* and the goats. Also in its portion are the devils called "destroyers" in the language of our Rabbis and in the language of Scripture *seìrim* (satyrs, demons), for thus he (i.e. Esau) and his nation were called *seir*...[90]

The "prince" associated with Esaw is Samael, as apparent from that passage. Cosequently, the demons are connected to Christianity and its power source - Samael. Nachmanides reveals no more. Saba's view of Christianity, of its demonically oriented customs and of Jesus, might well be taken as an interpretation or a development of the Nachmanidean understanding of Christianity.[91]

At this point, one could make a case for the interpretation of Saba's comments on Ps. 87,4 as alluding to Jesus.[92] Saba says that the second part of the verse "This one was born there [*zeh yulad sham*]" refers to Hiram, who was the only wise person among the nations. He was from Tyre, which is mentioned in the first half of the verse. Of his "wisdom" Saba tells us that Hiram, through magic, "made himself God," flew in the air, and king Solomon could not overcome him until God gave him wisdom. This, Saba says, is found in the *Zohar* on *Terumah*.[93] In fact Hiram is mentioned there, but there is nothing like this story there. In another location, however, one finds the following story:

> Solomon caused Hiram to descend from that stage. For he (Hiram) said: 'I sit in the seat of God's etc.' (Ezekiel 28:2). As we have been taught by the Sages: 'Hiram made himself God.'[94] After Solomon came he caused Hiram, using his wisdom, to come dow ...and we have learnt also that he (Solomon) sent him a demon that took Hiram down through seven sections of Hell...[95]

We have here most of the elements of Saba's account except for the aerial battle. This seems to have been taken out of the anti-Christian polemical treatise *Toldot Yeshu*. There, the author describes Jesus as a magician who performed miracles by using the Name [*hashem ha-meforash*] until Judah the Gardener (or Iscariot, according to other mss.) overcame him in an aerial battle.[96]

Now we do not have any explicit references by Saba to Jesus that would clarify his view of Jesus' birth, life, and miracles. But Saba's view of the different Church officials seems to indicate that he believed Jesus to have been either a man who allied himself with the Forces of Evil or, even more radically that he was the incarnation of Samael, "agreeing" with some Christian doctrines. This seems to fit in with Hiram's description here. Moreover, the verse under discussion was used by Christian Christological interpretations in polemics against the Jews.[97] We might add that Saba refers to the subject of this verse at the end of his discussion, as איש אחד פרטי שהוא האיש הרמוז, the numerical value of which is the equivalent of ישו. This *gematria* appears in *Toldot Yeshu* as well.[98] Tyre figures in Jesus' life[99] but more importantly, from the Midrashic period it is identified with Rome.[100]

If this analysis is correct, it would mean that Saba wrote on two levels, with the exoteric expressions covering the esoteric meaning by contradicting it. Since a) he identifies the subject of the verse with Hiram, saying that he is the only Gentile throughout history to attain "wisdom," and b) Jesus was considered to be Jewish.[101] For our discussion this would imply that Saba's view of Jesus was rather "conservative": Jesus was not a god who became a man, but a man who became a god for a while, probably through the knowledge of Qabbalah, as the opinion cited by P. Duran,[102] and this was his "wisdom."

There are more references associating Christianity with demons. In one place Saba translates and expands a story related in *Zohar Ḥadash* about a cave where blind and limping Gentiles went to be cured as well as a Jew who took his ill son there. In the cave the father saw a demon [*shed*, in the *Zohar*: *ḥad sitna*),[103] curing them.[104] G. Scholem, in a personal letter to Libowitz, suggests that Saba alluded to Santiago de Compostela.[105] It seems that even if Libowitz is right, and he did not have that place in mind, Saba would still classify it as cure by the aid of the Forces of Evil.[106]

An unequivocal statement about Jesus, without mentioning him by name, would clinch the Jesus-demon issue:

> And therefore He said: 'If the plague be spread in the garment, or in the warp, or in the woof [*ó ba-sheti ó ba-èrev*]' (Lev. 13:51), since it is known that a garment is comprised of warp and woof. But He meant to hint here to that demon [*shed*] which rules the warp and woof (according to the Christian faith).[107] And therefore He ordered: 'And he should burn the garment...,' since it is an abomination[108]

The "demon that rules the Cross [*sheti va-èrev*], according to the Christian Faith," could be only the crucified image of Jesus.[109] The expression "according to the Christian Faith" means: according to Saba's understanding of Christianity. This becomes clear when we read another passage in the continuation of the censored passage about the Church officials' custom of head-shaving. There Saba generalizes about Christianity and the origin of its rituals:

> And I have (explained) at length all the customs of idolatry in the Laws of Idol Worshipers in my book Ẓ.K., (saying) that all of them have to be explained that way, and they (i.e. Christians) do not know the real reasons and their flavor changed (i.e. they have forgotten the origin of their own customs).[110]

At this point we can interpret the following passage and identify its subject:

> And He said: 'He shall bruise thy head.' (Gen. 3:15). He hinted here to the matter of the primordial Snake which is Samael...and he is identical with Esau, and Edom, and 'the Head whereto they bow' (2Sam. 15:32)...[111]

Samael is identified with the "Head" whom "they bow down to."[112] This "Head" is idolatry. The end of the passage discusses the harm and injury the Jews suffer due to Samael, and Saba refers us to another place where he says that they are "Nadav and Avihu, and the ten martyrs, and every generation..."[113] Here Saba includes the cosmic Samael with the earthly one - Christianity, the head of which is the "Head."[114]

To sum up, then, Christianity, viewed by the Jews as the realization of Evil in the world, was connected to Samael very early. The demonological aspects of it were developed in Qabbalistic circles at least as early as the 13th century. Such ideas were highly esoteric and primarily transmitted orally. Thus what we know from the written tradition might be only the tip of the iceberg. In this respect one must emphasize the limitations of the attempt to reconstruct the history of the demonologization of Christianity.

The 15th century is characterized by the development of earlier concepts to more extreme conclusions, and by additional measure of bluntness in style. Saba himself had a detailed demonological interpretation of Christianity and herein lies his main original contribution to the history of the idea. The Church, for him, represented the demons, and both were the representatives of Powers of Impurity in the world. Christian rituals in their totality were to be understood accordingly, but Christians simply do not know their source and the original reasons for their customs anymore. Jesus himself is not described adequately enough to characterize his demonic nature, but he fits into this scheme as definitely a major demon, perhaps the incarnation of Samael. Historical factors, as well as the use of Qabbalah as a framework for understanding the meaning, structure, and dynamics of history, contributed to what seems to have been a natural background and a fertile soil for the growth of such a demonic view of Christianity. One can only regret that Saba's book Ẓ.K, written long before the Expulsion and which held a detailed account of the author's view of Christianity, is not extant because of the persecutions in Portugal.

Finally, aside from what has already been mentioned about the internal development of the idea, we should consider one further possibility as an external catalyst which contributed to the crystalization of the demonologization of Christianity and Christ. The discussion of devils, demons and religion, reminds us of a Christian author, earlier than the Jewish sources discussed above. The similarity between this 10th-century description of the mythical Jewish Antichrist, by Adso of Montier-en-Der, and the later Jewish notions is suggestive. This popular account was to shape Christian view of the Antichrist in the coming centuries. Norman Cohn summarized it as follows:

> He is to be the offspring of a harlot and a worthless wretch and, moreover, at the moment of his conception the Devil is to enter the harlot's womb as a spirit, thereby ensuring that the child shall be the very of incarnation of Evil.[115]

In other words, Jesus have become, for our Qabbalists, the Jewish Antichrist according to the Christian popular view. Such views that became part and parcel of medieval Christianity contributed in on small measure to the creation of the frame of mind in which Jews have molded their ideological reaction.

5. Between Israel and the Nations

If we attempt to compare the general attitudes of the rational philosopher and the Qabbalist concerning this issue, we will find them to be radically opposed to one another. The former tends to minimize or eliminate any differences in the natural-human realm, limiting them exclusively to the religious one, namely, that Israel possesses the only true revelation, and he will try to demonstrate other religions' errors both in theory and in practice. The Qabbalist, in sharp contrast, tends to widen the gap in every possible direction.

The reason for this major difference between these two trends is that philosophical eminence is attained through intellectual achievement and, of course, nobody can claim exclusive national rights to the intellect, especially since Jewish philosophy relied openly on non-Jewish sources. Qabbalah, on the other hand, thrives on the Hebrew letters of the Torah, their numerical combinations, order and shape, as well as on the secrets imbedded in the commandments which are exclusively Jewish. While the Torah and, in turn (to a certain extent), the Talmud became the object of study of Christians, Qabbalah nevertheless remained, generally speaking, an esoteric teaching (even within Judaism). This was the "wisdom" that made the difference. It was a Jewish possession and a Jewish discipline nationally and individually. The abstract body of the people as well as individuals within it possessed it - the former in potentia, and the latter in actuality.[116]

Through this system of thought, the differences between Israel and the Nations assumed a new dimension and were expressed in a new realm - the mystical. For the Qabbalist the gates to the world of symbolism opened the way to new and richer possibilities for expressing the uniqueness and superiority of Israel, and concomitantly the base nature and inferiority of the Nations.

Saba himself sees the differences mainly in the mystical realm. In the beginning all were equal and all nations were afforded equal opportunity to accept the Torah, an old rabbinic notion. But the historical fact was that Israel was elected and won the Torah. The apparent contradiction between this idea and the division of humanity into Good and Evil, with its inherent determinism, is resolved by saying that free-choice is still possible on a meta-rational level which is above human understanding. "For God's knowledge does not force anything to happen in the future, in a wondrous way...although to us it seems an impossibility...because our knowledge is limited."[117]

In the desert, Israel underwent a short period of rigorous training to serve as preparation for the upcoming Sinaitic Revelation. This included lack of food and water,[118] and a new diet consisting of manna. That "bread of angels [*leḥem ábbirim]*," was "a very light food," and was given to them in order to purify their minds [*le-ẓakkekh sikhlam*]," because they departed Egypt "fat with full belly from bad food, which causes their minds to be heavy [*àvim be-sikhlam*], because of eating fish, cucumbers, and onions." That period was a torture and torment for them due to their habit of eating "heavy foods to full satisfaction."[119]

While Saba is clearly opposed to any sort of radical asceticism,[120] he views the "manna diet," as well as the imposition of dietary regulations and restrictions, as a necessary physical instrument for cultivating spirituality and attaining a state of holiness.[121] For Israel, therefore, the body's loss is the spirit's gain, while the reverse is true of the Gentiles who are "the mighty and the strong, who eat pig's meat."[122]

The Revelation on Mount Sinai, says Saba, cleansed Israel of the lustfulness [*zuhamah*] that attached itself to the human race from the episode of the Snake and Eve.[123] But the Gentiles who were not present there remained with the negative effects of the Sin and consequently "go after their desires..."[124]

The spiritual ascent reached its peak neither at Sinai nor at the consecration of the Tabernacle[125] but with the arrangement of the camp through its division into four units under four flags. By this symbolic mystical imitation of the Divine Camp in heaven, they attained union with God, and Saba concludes: "This dedication of the flags surpassed all spiritual heights."[126] The three stages of the spiritual ascent of Israel are symbolized by the parallels of Sinai-Exodus, Tabernacle-Leviticus, Flags-Numbers.

The nature of the mystical attachment [*dibbuq*] of the nation to God created an initial union of God-Israel, but the direct consequence of that oneness is a mystical unity of all the individuals within the national body. Expressing this idea in a context which seems to have been a sermon about the mutual responsibility of Israel, Saba says:

> And therefore just as He commanded Israel that due to their holiness they should have nothing but perfect unity and love... 'And thou shalt love thy neighbour as thyself,' that it is not suitable that there would be any division [*ḥilluq*] among them... And this is an advantage that the nation of Israel has over all other nations, in that all of them are considered as one, due to their Master and due to their soul. Due to their Master (meaning), since He is one. And due to their soul (meaning),[127] that it was carved from His Throne of Glory, and since all their souls are carved from one place, it is suitable that their bodies would be one (i.e. that people should treat each other accordingly).[128]

Aside from the additional responsibility that this idea mandates, it has also an existential advantage which manifests itself in the fact that Israel, as a whole, is a "wise and understanding nation" (Deut. 4,6).

Saba distinguishes between two kinds of wisdom which Israel possesses or is capable of achieving.[129] The only true wisdom of Israel is Qabbalah and Israel is termed "wise and understanding" by virtue of that knowledge of God and not on account of their observing the commandments. It is true that most people are not "wise" but the "foundations of wisdom" are present, and this creates at least a potential that allows many individuals to "hold fast to the Lord" (Deut. 4,4). The Gentiles, conversely, do not have this capacity for "wisdom." As a matter of fact, throughout history only one of them attained "wisdom," namely, Hiram, King of Tyre. The manifestation of that wisdom was the ability to perform magic through the use of the Forces of Impurity.[130] Within Israel, contrastingly, there are many such preeminent individuals [*yeḥidei segullah rabbim*]. It seems, then, that Saba refers here to "practical" Qabbalah [*qabbalah maàsit*]. This, however, becomes unclear because in the following paragraph he says that the difference between Israel and the Nations lies in the fact that through the observance of the commandments the Jews can influence the natural order, a fact which renders them a "wise and understanding nation" in the eyes of the Gentiles (although the true wisdom is the knowledge of God):

> And 'they will say, what a wise and understanding people this great nation is' (Deut. 4,6), alluding to the fact, that even though true wisdom is 'understanding and knowing me' (Jer. 9,23) ...and not the observance of the commandments will they be called 'wise and understanding,' nevertheless He promised them that by keeping and fulfilling them they will be rendered 'wise' in the eyes of the nations, although (in truth) this is not so. When the nations see Israel observing the commandments,[131] and going out, wrapped in prayer-shawls, reciting the Thirteen Attributes, and thus bringing rain when it is due or stopping a plague (in the same manner), then they (i.e. the nations) will say that, in this respect, they (i.e. Israel) are all very wise as a collective [*bi-khlal*]...they are all wise, clever and knowledgeable of the Torah so that by the means of the commandments God is close to them and responds to their prayers.[132]

Saba says, then, that Israel as a collective can perform acts which the Gentiles cannot. The emphasis here is clearly on the prerequisite of closeness to God by virtue of the simple observance of the commandments. But the second element he mentions is the collective nature of the act of prayer that causes rain to fall and plagues to stop. This seems to connect with the idea of the unity of all the individuals of Israel. This is the secret of their special capacity to influence the course of nature through God by means of the commandments and collective prayer.[133]

There is one more area of Israel's superiority which is totally divorced from mysticism, namely, their way of life. The morality of the Jews is superior to that of the nations.

The Torah is interested that the Gentiles be aware of it and thus commanded Israel to offer peace to a besieged city about to be attacked by it. The aim was

> ...so that the nations will realize the greatness of the Torah that commanded the initiation of a call for peace, even though they would not have to do so (according to the nations' moral standards).[134]

One's dealings with a Gentile should be so conducted as to sanctify the Name through actions that go beyond the mere intention to satisfy Halakhic norms. Through this, the Gentile will think positively of the Jewish faith. Saba adds, however, that in the present state of exile there is an additional pragmatic reason for such behavior: "...and therefore one must sanctify the Name, now more than in earlier times, for the sake of peace [*mi-shum darkei shalom*]."[135]

Saba envisages the future when Israel will be redeemed:

> ...And they will win a name and praise and glory in the mouths of all nations, who will praise them for the attainment of a good name [*shem tov*] during their exile, by clinging to the Torah and giving their lives for the Sanctification of the Name.[136]

Underlying these calls for acts of demonstration or the investment of a commandment with such an intent, is the wish to show the superiority of the Jewish religion. This can be demonstrated in the common field of morality and ethics which, in general terms, are accepted by both religions. Such issues, indeed, are raised in polemics throughout the Middle Ages.[137]

There is here neither an echo of the desire to attract converts,[138] nor a long term plan for reaching a state of tolerance and the elimination of anti-Jewish sentiments by suggesting an improved code of moral behaviour.[139] It is first and foremost the expression of a deep need of the lowly and lonely for some measure of recognition and respect from their foe and oppressor.[140]

NOTES

1 The only real opposition to it was the school of thought questioning the long-range results after disappointments. This tension between the inner need to reveal and share the knowledge of the awaited date and the inherent dangers of it was expressed by many individuals who struggled with it. So we find, for example, R. Abraham ben Eliezer Halevi trying to justify his stand in face of the Jewish traditional opposition to it (starting with B.T. Sanhedrin, p. 97a), as well as against healthy instincts. (*Maámar Meshare Qitrin*, Jersualem, 1977, p. 4a ff.). Most of the known Jewish calculations (in print) were collected by A.H. Silver in *A History of Messianic Speculation in Israel*, Boston, 1929.

2 Usually, we find the traditional four-fold division of the Four Kingdoms, or Four Exiles. An example of a threefold division can be found in Ẓ.M. Ex. p. 25b.

3 He parallels six thousand years to the six days of Creation. To summarize the history of this periodization one must start with St. Augustine, who was apparently the first to use this scheme in the very end of *The City of God* (XXII, 30). This notion was upheld for a long time (partially because of Augustine's authority and in part due to its flexibility, for it did not fix a definite date for the *parousia*). After the year 1000 it gradually started to lose ground, but was picked up by Joachim de Fiore (end of 12th c.), the most influencial figure in Christian millenarianism in the High Middle Ages. (On the history of the division of history up to Joachim see: M. Reeves, "The Originality and Influence of Joachim of Fiore," *Traditio* 36, 1980, pp. 269-97.) The first to adopt

this scheme on the Jewish side was apparently R. Abraham bar Ḥiyya in the first half of the 12th century, who got it either through Isidore of Seville or St. Augustine. (See J. Guttmann in his introduction to *Megillat ha-Megaleh*, Berlin, 1924, p. XIII and see A. Funkenstein, "Nachmanides' Typological Reading of History," *Ẓion* 44, 1980, pp. 53-4). In the 15th century we find Abravanel using the same scheme referring to R. Abraham bar Ḥiyya and to Nachmanides as his sources (For an analysis see Netanyahu, *Abravanel*, p. 223-24). Saba is mainly influenced by Nachmanides (Ẓ.M. Gen. pp. 6b-7a). There is one deviation from the latter in that Abraham is the central symbolic figure of the second millennium. According to *Seder Òlam Zuta*, Abraham was born in 2048. It is worth noting that Abravanel sides here with Saba. But this "chronological squeeze" into the historical scheme is forgivable in comparison to Saba's description of the fifth day-millennium: ביום החמישי היו אומרים, הרנינו לאלהים עוזנו, כנגד האלף החמישי שבו תהיה הגאולה. ולכן צריך לשוב בתשובה ועבור הרנה במחנה כדכתיב, קומי רוני בלילה. ואנו מובטחים שהשם יגאול גאולתנו כמו שגאל ליוסף והצילו מצרתו ומגלותו Since Saba lived in the sixth millennium how could he have used the future tense to describe the fifth? Even if we apply Abravanel's distinction between the period before 4250 which was "non-Messianic" in potentia, and after this date which was a "potentially Messianic" period but which Israel did not merit, and the present final, absolute, and unconditioned period of Redemption (Netanyahu, p. 223), it would not solve the seemingly logical absurdity without a radical amendment of the text. Saba's main contribution to the history of this historical scheme lies in his interpretation of the daily psalm sung by the Levites in the Temple in accordance with the nature of each day-millennium. (Several lines, related to Edom and to the forced conversions in Portugal, are missing from the 1567 edition and on, due to censorship. The same lines were to be expurgated from the two earlier editions but some unharmed copies are still extant. Ẓ.M. happened to be the first book on the list of the infamous *Sefer ha-Ziqquq* from 1596 (Ms. Paris, Alliance, 49 (H80A) fols. 2r-3r. Ms. Vatican, 273, fols. 25r-26r). See N. Porges, "Deux Index Expurgatoires de Livres Hébreux," *REJ* 30, 1895, pp. 261-62. Idem, "Der Hebraische Index Expurgatorius," *A. Berliner Festschrift* 1903, p. 291. A. Berliner, *Censur und Confiscation*, Berlin, 1891, pp. 26, 35, 41, 45. M. Benayahu, *Copyright Authorization and Imprimatur for Hebrew Books Printed in Venice*, Jerusalem, 1971, p. 207).

[4] It is important to note that Augustine's idea of two "Cities" and the conflict between them is not limited to communities or individuals, but also within one's self there could exist those two forces "Jerusalem in his heart and Bybelon in the rest of his body." (G.L. Keyes, *Christian Faith and the Interpretation of History, A Study of St. Augustine's Philosophy of History*, Lincoln, Nebraska, 1966, p. 160. See also R. Bultmam, *History and Eschatology*, Edinburgh, 1957, p. 61. For bibliography see C.A. Patrides, *The Grant Design of God, The Literary form of the Christian view of History*, London, 1972, p. 24 n. 23). One major difference between the Qabbalistic parallel notion and that of St. Augustine is that while the latter seems to talk more about the division between the existence of the two groups and their separate routes, the Qabbalists, Saba included, emphasize more the constant clash between the two and the belligerence of Evil. (e.g. T. Mommsen, "Augustinus on Progress," *Medieval and Renaissance Studies*, Ithaca, New York, 1959, pp. 295-98. Mommsen describes the two "Cities" as two parallel lines).

[5] G. Scholem, *Elements of the Kabbalah and its Symbolism*, pp. 187-212.

[6] In this respect, on the Qabbalists' view of historical reality as an aspect correlated with Qabbalistic *weltanschaaung* and specific ideas, scholarship is still wanting.

[7] Ẓ.M. Gen. p. 14a.

[8]. Ibid, pp. 16b, 57a.

[9] E.g. Ẓ.M. Gen. 27b.

[10] Ibid, p. 18b. The straight line of Cain-Esau is emphasized by the author of *Tiqqunei Zohar* who says that Cain's sons were to shed Israel's blood, and God showed him "all that his future descendants would do to Israel every generation" (69, p. 114b).

[11] Ẓ.M. Gen. p. 25b. He finds five such parallels between the story of creation and the immediate aftermaths of the Deluge, which is compared to the original state of thin-

gs (See above p. 60). The idea, as such, appears already in Nachmanides' sermon *Torat ha-Shem Temimah* (*Kitvei ha-Ramban*, ed. Chavel, Jerusalem, 1964, p. 145).

[12] Ẓ.M. Gen. p. 28b. But there is no over-emphasis of this point.

[13] Ibid, p. 29a. Canaan seems to be the evil one. Ham represents *Din* (ibid, p. 20b) and therefore carries with him the potential for a son like Canaan. (See *Zohar* I, pp. 73a, 228a, II p. 236b, *Tiqqunei Zohar*, 18, p. 37a Augustine, *City*, XVI, 2, 3).

[14] Ẓ.M. Gen. p. 29a. Japheth is somewhere between the two (See also Saba's attempt to fit him into the scheme on p. 20b). Abravanel, who has a three-fold division of human life: the animal, political, and rational, has these three sons-as well as Cain, Abel and Seth set perfectly into his scheme (Netanyahu, *Abravanel*, pp. 139-42). But later he must change it into a two-fold division (ibid, p. 143). Saba has his own problems in the early stages of history.

[15] Ẓ.M. Gen. p. 56a. See also *Zohar*, III, p. 215a, and *Tiqqunei Zohar*, 70, p. 128b.

[16] Ẓ.M. Gen. p. 99a.

[17] The *Zohar* connects this verse only with circumcision (I, p. 93a, *Ẓaddiq-Yesod*-Circumcision).

[18] Ibid, p. 20a.

[19] See *Zohar* II, p. 245a.

[20] Ẓ.M. Gen. p. 51b (quoting from *Midrash ha-Neèlam*).

[21] Ẓ.M. Gen. pp. 58b, 59a.

[22] Saba was inspired apparently by the parallel Creation-Tabernacle which appears in the Midrash (*Tanḥuma*, *Pequdei*, 2. A modern elaboration of it can be found in M. Buber, *The Way of the Bible: Studies in Biblical Literary Style*, Jerusalem, 1964, pp. 54-6. Buber does not mention the Midrash. See also N. Leibowitz, *New Studies in the Book of Exodus*, Jerusalem, 1970, pp. 348-52). The *Zohar* seems to have a similar idea concerning the seven days of consecration (e.g. I, p. 34a). But that could have been at best only a source of inspiration since a) it atoned only for the Golden Calf; b) The word *millu'im* is interpreted in an eschatological vein.

[23] E.E. Urbach, *Ḥazal*, Jerusalem, 19, pp. 372-7.

[24] B. T. Sabbath, p. 146a. This theme is picked up by the *Zohar* (I, p. 54a, II, p. 168a). According to Urbach this saying has an anti-Christian over-tones, since it actually negates the need of the Jews for salvation through Jesus in order to overcome the Original Sin (*Ḥazal*, pp. 377-8). One should make mention of the other version of the Christian Original Sin, namely, that the Sin's eternal effect was not to automatically doom to Hell all humans who are not saved through Jesus, but only to cause a tendency to sin, similar to the notion in the Midrash concerning the *zuhamah*. As is evident, one does not have to look for medieval Christian sources for that idea, as found in the Zohar, just as Crescas, who maintains that circumcision saves one lustfulness and thus from Hell, was not in need of adapting this idea from the parallel Christian notion of the Original Sin and baptism (See D. Lasker, "Original Sin and Its Atonement According to Ḥisdai Crescas," *Daàt* 20, 1988, pp. 130- 5)

[25] Ẓ.M. Deut. p. 19b.

[26] Ibid., Ex. p. 41a.

[27] See above p. 107.

[28] Ẓ.M. Lev. p. 4a. Deuteronomy essentially repeats and summarizes things which were included in earlier books.

[29] Ibid. The rest of Leviticus is explained accordingly. (See also ibid., p. 21a).

[30] Ibid., p. 3b-4a. The notion that the *Shekhinah* was brought back down by the seven righteous men appears in the Midrash several times (e.g. *Shir ha-Shirim Rabba* 5,1. *Pesiqta de-Rav Kahana* 1,1). Saba, however, brings a Midrash saying that the restoration took place prior to the building of the Tabernacle. The part played by Aaron, Nadav and Avihu in the process of restoration does not appear in the Midrash.

[31] Ibid., Ex. p. 44a. The Sages identify that tree with several trees (vine, fig, or wheat). The Zohar contends that all the interpretations are true (*Tiqqunei Zohar*, 24, p. 69a) so Saba feels free to identify it later on with the vine (Ẓ.M. Lev. p. 13a. There, Moses recounts to the priests the prohibition to serve God after drinking wine).

[32] Ẓ.M. Ex. p. 42b, and in greater detail in Lev. p. lOb-lla.

[33] Ibid, Ex. p. 44b.

[34] Ibid, Lev. p. lla.

[35] One good reason for it is its originality.

[36] Concerning the seven days prior to their death in which Aaron and his sons were to stay inside the Tabernacle, Saba says that it was in accordance with the period of mourning in Jewish law. (Ẓ.M. Lev. p. lla-b). Saba cites it from a Midrash but uses it to show that their death was pre-meditated.

[37]. E.g. ibid., p. 13a.

[38] בענין שבזה היו ממלאין החסרון והפחת של אדם הראשון ומשלימים אותו...לפי שבני אהרן מתו למלאות חסרון של אדה״ר ובניו (ibid, Ex. p. 44b. Also in Lev. pp. lla, 21b. Num. p. 15a).

[39] Abel's need for atonement is problematic, although he was not a perfectly righteous person. (*Zohar* II, p. 168a).

[40] Ẓ.M. Ex. p. 44b, Lev. p. 14a, Lev. p. 13a, Num. p. 15a, Lev. pp. 4a, lla.

[41] This would seem to be contrary to the conventional notions concerning Abraham's and Moses' greatness. Although Saba finds fault with Abraham (Ẓ.M. Gen. p. 37a-b), he believes him to be the parallel of R. Akiba who was the only one to survive the supreme mystical test of entering the *Pardes*, unlike Nadav and Avihu who died like Ben Azai (see above p. 86).

[42] Ibid., Lev. p. 12a-b.

[43] He seems to mean that the general esoteric meaning of the sin is identical and the interpretations differ only in the technical details as to how and why they separated between the *Sefirot*. (See also Nachmanides on Lev. 10,2, and on 16,2, to which Saba refers). It should be noted that it was already Rabbi Moses Isserles who pointed to the problem of contradictions mentioned above (J. Ben-Sasson, *The Philosophical System of Rabbi Moses Isserles*, Jerusalem, 1984, p. 324).

[44] Ibid., p. 21a-b.

[45] The source of this idea is the *Zohar*, II p. 155b, III, p. 58a. Saba belabors this point.

[46] *Zohar* III, pp. 5b, 33b, 34a, 37b, 57a.

[47] B.T. Moèd Qatan, p. 28a. *Vayiqra Rabba*, 20. (The latter is connected explicitly to Aaron's sons). Saba also says that Nadav and Avihu atone for the sin of the Golden Calf, especially after the destruction of the Temple and this is the reason for reading, on the Day of Atonement, the section about their death (Ẓ.M. Lev. p. 21b. The idea is borrowed from the *Zohar* III, p. 57b).

[47a] It should be mentioned, however, that the Zohar does talk about the suffering of the righteous that atones for the world (Zohar III, pp. 217b-218b). Concerning this Zoharic idea and its further evolution by Rabbi Moses Cordovero (especially in connection to the Ten Martyrs) see: B. Zack, "RaMaQ and the ARI," *Jerusalem Studies in Jewish Thought* 10, 1992, pp. 313-5.

[48] Also the Talmudic notion adopted by the Qabbalah about the lustfulness which stuck to mankind ever since the Sin (see above nn. 23, 24) differs from the Christian dogma of the Original Sin in that one's fate is not completely controlled and predetermined by it. It is only a bad tendency that was caused by that Sin. (See G. Scholem, *Kabbalah*, Jerusalem, 1974, p. 154).

[49] Ẓ.M. Deut. p. 40b.

[50] One might prefer to describe this view of history as a balance-scale travelling along a straight line with Israel and Edom on the opposite scales.

[51] É.K. Esther, p. 82. The view of the story of Purim as representing the battle between Good and Evil already appears in Baḥya's *Kad ha-Qemaḥ*, Warsaw, 1878, pp. 148ff. (See I. Bettan, *Studies in Jewish Preaching*, p. 109). There, however, it is in an astrological context.

[52]. B.T. Megillah, p. 6a. (See also below n. 100).

[53]. About the theme of recurrence in history, including an exhaustive bibliography, see G.W. Trompf, *The Idea of Historical Recurrence in Western Thought* (lst of two volumes), Berkeley, Los Angeles, London, 1979.

54 See below App. C. The structure of the book of Esther is similar to that of Gen. 36 but consists of twelve stages (É.K. Esther, p. 88).

55 Ẓ.M. Deut. p. 70a. The phrases he uses here are Biblical and Midrashic concerning Amalek. Compare also: ...שמחרפים ומגדפים אותם בכל יום על קדושת שמך...אבל חרפו אויבך ה' שאומרים אייה אלוהיך, וכן חרפו עקבות משיחיך ואומרים לשחק בנו, מדוע אחרו פעמי מרכבותיו אחר אלף ות"ק שנה. (É.K. Ruth, p. 36a. Similarly in *Kaf ha-Qetoret* fol. 77b. But already in the *Zohar* II, p. 188b. (See W. Bacher, "Judaeo-Christian Polemics in the *Zohar*," *JQR* .[o.s.] 3, 1891, pp. 782-83).

56 É.K. Esther, p. 68. (See the quotation above p. 22).

57 *Midrash Shoher Tov*, Proverbs, 9. See also RaSHBA in his *Responsa*, Rome edition 1470(?) (reprinted in Jerusalem 1977) no. 53. Saba's reference to the Talmud Yerushalmi confuses this idea with another (Megillah, 1,4).

58 Ẓ.M. Deut. p. 40b-41a. On God's involvement, compare *Zohar* II, p. 67a.

59 ואנו מובטחים שהשם ישבר ראשי לויתן על המים ויפל ראש סמאל למטה... (Ẓ.M. Gen. P.16b).

60 É.K. Esther, p. 12.

61 Ibid, p. 14.

62 Ibid, p. 95 (Compare Baḥya's idea, above n. 51).

63 Ẓ.M. Num. p. 32b.

64 Below App. C. Ben-Sasson sees in it a reference to the recently united Spain, but on this point he is not convincing (Ben-Sasson, Generation, p. 56).

65 The idea of a slow progressive redemption is first found in J.T. Berakhot, 1,1, and ibid Yoma 3,2. Compare also *Zohar*, I, p. 170a (albeit through a slightly different metaphor, and an altogether different idea about Esau). This might have been the passage to which one of the "knowledgeable scholars of the *Zohar*" referred (See the conclusion of that sermon).

66 To be sure, Saba uses the traditional schemes of the Four Kingdoms and Four Exiles, and very frequently, but as far as the substantial meaning of history they have no weight and are used by Saba mostly in a superficial way for other purposes.

67 Although rewritten in North Africa, Saba's writings carry with them a definite Spanish "flavor." He addresses himself, for example, to the problem of philosophical antinomianism that as far as we know did not exist in Fez (see Abraham Ardutiel's description of Fez in *Avnei Zikkaron*, published by G. Scholem, *Qiryat Sefer* 7, 1930, p. 458. See also J. Gerber, *Jewish Society in Fez*, Leiden, 1980, p. 101). Some defensive polemical arguments can be found here and there (e.g. Ẓ.M. Gen. pp. 5b, 126b. Ex. pp. 35a, 50a. Deut. pp. 9a, 22b, 54b).

68 About the name of Leah's third son Saba says: ואולי על זה נקרא שמו לוי על סוד החיבור שנתחבר השם עם לאה (Ẓ.M. Gen. p. 71b). Therefore, the name Levi is comprised of his mother's name, and two letters of his "Father's." We can already find a similar notion in a more concealed manner in the Passover Haggadah: וירא את ענינו - זו פרישות דרך ארץ וירא אלהים את בני ישראל וידע אלהים Nevertheless it is still surprising to find such a notion written very explicitly in a Christian *milieu* and, particularly, in the fifteenth century when the religious tension and polemical confrontation between Judaism and Christianity reached its climax in Spain. (see Daniel J. Lasker, *Jewish Philosophical Polemics Against Christianity in the Middle Ages*, New York, 1977, pp. 105-134 (Incarnation), 153-59 (Virgin Birth). Such a mode of expression is surprising even after allowing a measure of permissiveness, taking into consideration that as a Qabbalist, Saba should not be expected to be as careful in the use of expressions relating to God as we would expect of a philosopher. (One can feel Saba's delight when he is able to employ a daring anthropomorphic expression and relate it to God. Discussing Jacob's dream, Saba turns to his readers saying: הראיתם אדם ישן והמלך ממתין עליו מתי יקיץ, ובעוד שהוא ישן המלך בעצמו מפריש ממנו הזבובים והיתושים (Ẓ.M. Gen. p. 65a). Inserting some humor into old Sarah's reaction to the news about her future son, he comments: צחוק עשה לי אלהים, כי מרוב שמחתה אמרה אני יודעת כי יושב בשמים ישחק ממני לפי שאני זקנה (ibid. p. 45a). In another instance he falls just short of calling the Messiah "Son of God:" זה כלל המגילה להודיענו בן מי הילד הזה...ויד השם עשתה זאת בדרך נס עד שלזאת הסיבה תמצא שכנה התורה למלך המשיח כאילו הוא בן כאמרו, ה' אמר אלי בני אתה (E.K. Ruth, p. 8a). Here, however, there might be an implicit anti-Christian exegetical polemic, sin-

ce this verse (Ps. 2,7) was interpreted christologically. But even if this was the intention, Saba, by relating the verse to the Messiah, deviates from the Jewish tendency to identify the "son" with Israel or David (e.g. Jacob ben Reuven, *The Wars of the Lord* [J. Rosenthal ed.], Jerusalem, 1963, pp. 64-5. RaDaQ in his commentary on this psalm. *Joseph ha-Meqaneh* [J. Rosenthal ed.], Jerusalem, 1970, p. 99-101).

69 Ẓ.M. Deut. p. 81a-b. Saba identifies Moses with Metatron (ר״ת: מטטרון שר הגדול) and with God (משה בהיפוך אותיות השם). This is different from the relevant passages in the *Zohar* that does not deny Moses' death despite some equivocal statements (See especially I, pp. 37b, 131b. III p. 280a). However, see below n. 71.

70 On Josephus, for example, see S.A. Loewenstamm, "Moses' Death," *Tarbiẓ* 27, 1958, p. 149. On a much later expression of this tradition see Y.L. Weinberger, "A Lost Midrash on Moses' Death," *Tarbiẓ* 38, 1969, p. 287.

71 The relevant medieval material from Maimonides onward was gathered by M. Idel (*Abraham Abulafia's Writings and Thought*, Ph.D. Diss. Hebrew University, 1976, p. 93). Abulafia's influence on Saba seems to be limited to the use of hermeneutical methods applied to the name Moses (See above no. 69).

72 In Samaritan literature we do find notions according to which Moses existed before the world and, accordingly, Yokheved's pregnancy is explained as a miracle (James A. Montgomery, *The Samaritans, Earliest Jewish Sect*, New-York, 1968, pp. 225-9).

73 Ẓ.M. Gen. p. 92b.

74 Ben-Sasson's conclusion that under the tremendous polemical pressure, some Christian ideas penetrated into Jewish thought in this period (Ben-Sasson, Exile, p. 216-17), is acceptable and could account for minor influences, but not for major theological points of contention.

75 Venice, 1523, 1547. Its location in the 1879 edition is before the words וכבר הארכתי בהלכות עכו״ם.

76 כמרים וגלחים Usually the two words are synonymous.

77 Ẓ.M. Deut. p. 66b. In the *Sefer ha-Ziqquq* we read the following comment on this passage: וצריך עיון בזה כי הוא דבר רע נגד הגלחים שלנו. The nicknames of *seirim* and *shedim* for priests are not a novelty. The term *seirim* is found in a *responsum* of R. Ẓemaḥ ben Shimon Duran written several years before the expulsion from Spain: ויעשו נשואיהם ע״י השעירי (*Responsa Yakhin u-boaz*, Livorno, 1782 vol. II, no. 19, p. 73b). This term was also applied to the Franciscans (*fratres minores*) already in the thirteenth century as a play on words (*minores* in Hebrew: *ẓeìrim*). See J. Shatzmiller, "Towards a Picture of the First Maimonidean Controversy," *Ẓion* 34, 1969, p. 141). For the term *shedim* as applied to them see Libowitz, p. 27. (Originally, Kayzerling, "Sefardim," *he-Ásif*, 6, 1893, p. 79). This, however, is alleged in Hamburg as late as 1647. Approximately at the same time we have a similar reference in Amsterdam. Interestingly, that author interprets the exact same verse as does Saba (Deut. 32,17), and says that it refers to officials of the Inquisition. (J. Kaplan, *From Christianity to Judaism*, Jerusalem, 1983, p. 298). We find such expressions against Christianity, the Inquisition and, perhaps, Jesus among the Marranos. (H. Beinart, *Conversos on Trial*, Tel Aviv, 1965, p. 229 n. 16, and see also ibid. p. 233 n. 33). Although these might be cases of mere popular customary curses, the distance between this and actual beliefs could be very short. However, the roots of the expression go back to the 13th century and can be already found in the commentary of R. Baḥya ben Asher on Gen. 17,1: עו״ג ערלי לב וערלי בשר שהם מצד השדים וישראל מצד אל שדי This referred to Christianity as a whole and is not connected to any specific Christian custom. It is in Saba that all three elements come together: the nicknames of the clergy, the comprehensive idea as to the origins of Christianity, and the specific illustration of the shearing of the hair.

As to the latter idea we find RaDBaZ, Saba's contemporary, telling us the following: כי כולם נמשכים אחרי עבודת הצלמים...וכגון כומרי ארם (קרי: אדום) שמגדלין סביבות הראש ומניחין באמצע פנוי (*Meẓudat Ẓiyyon*, Zolkiev, 1862, no. 59). It seems to us however, that RaDBaZ found it in Ẓ.M. which he probably read (In his *Responsa*, Livorno, 1652, no. 65, p. 7b) he refers to Saba and his Qabbalistic books. A different reason for the priests' particular hair style appears as early as *Toldot Yeshu*: כי נקרח ראש ישו כשנסחב (Krauss, *Das Leben*, p.

130), and in a slightly different form in J. Dan's, *The Hebrew Story in the Middle Ages*, Jerusalem, 1974, p. 130 (Quoted from Isaac Troki, *Ḥizzuq Émunah*, [M. Wexler ed.], New York, 1932, p. 277). An idea that might be somehow connected to that of Saba is found in R. Menaḥem Recanati's *Commentary on the Torah*: וזהו סוד לא יקרחו קרחי בראשם, כי היא אזהרה לכהנים הבאים ממדת החסד. אמנם ללוים שהם ממדת הגבורה נאמר, והעבירו תער על כל בשרם, להחליש הכחות ההם שלא תראה, כי הגוים אשר מדת הדין שופעת עליהם ובפרט לכומרי ע"ז שרוח הטומאה שורה עליהם משחיתים הפאות בהקפת ראשם אף כי הם בזה כסומי' בארובי' וכן מנהגם גם בכתובת קעקע. (Venice, 1523, p. 104b).

It is interesting to note that the connection between the hair-shearing and magic is found within Christianity. Generally the origin and reason for the clergy's tonsure are not known. One of the conjectures is that it is symbolic of Jesus' crown of thorns (Cf. the reason given above in *Toldot Yeshu*). As to the demonic connection, we find that the Celtic Druids had their own particular version of the tonsure. Contrary to the "Tonsure of Petrus," adopted by Rome and described here by Saba, they used to shave the anterior of the head leaving a little in the front above the forehead. The Druids occupied themselves with magic. Rome saw in Simon Magus their spiritual father, and their tonsure was named after him (J.A. McCulloch, 'Tonsure,' *Encyclopedia of Religion and Ethics* vol. 12 [J. Hastings ed.], Edinburgh, 1921, p. 386a-b). We have no way of determining whether such information reached Saba. (The last information we possess on such local custom is from the beggining of the 9th century.) However it is of interest to point out another association in that we are told that Simon Magus flew in the air with the help of demons until he was brought down by the prayer of the Apostles. A similar story by Saba is discussed below. We do not have any source as to alleged difference according to Saba between the tonsure of the low clergy and that of the bishops and the Pope.

78 M. Idel, "The Attitude to Christianity in the Sefer ha-Meshiv," *Ẓion* 46 (1981), pp. 77-91.

79 Ibid, p. 79.

80 Ibid, p. 81. One might add the following passge: והסוד גדל את המן, הוא סמאל, וינשאהו וישם את כסאו מעל כל השרים אשר אתו וכל עבדי המלך כורעים ומשתחוים לישו הנוצרי יש (ימח שמו), והוא עשו הרשע בסוד גלגול (fol. 215a. See also ibid. fol. 130b, and cf. fol. 212a. The author of *Kaf ha-Qetoret* also draws the parallel of the heavenly conflict between Good - God and Israel, and Evil - Samael, Christians and Moslems [ibid., p. 82]).

This seems to have influenced the author of *Galya Raza*, who writes similarly: ותדע שד' פעמים היה נגזר עליו משׁשת ימי בראשית שיתגשם בילוד אִשה ובפרצוף אנושי...הראשון היה שר האופים ולבסוף נתלה, השניה בהמן ולבסוף נתלה, השלישי בישו הנוצרי ולבסוף נתלה, הרביעי עתיד להיות בארמילוס (*Galya Raza* [R. Elior ed.], Jerusalem, 1981, p. 11 and n. 68. See also Idel's article n. 32, which refers to *Sefer ha-Peliáh*, and M. Oron's article in *Daàt* 8 (1982), p. 88 n.17.) The author of the *Galya Raza* might have been influenced by the apocalyptic legend of Armilus, who is the Jewish equivalent of the Christian Antichrist. According to one version he will be the son of a marble statue of a beautiful woman with whom Satan will have intercourse. He is called בן שטן in several apocalyptic treatises, particularly in *Sefer Zerubbavel*, from the 7th century and on (Y. Even Shemuel, *Midreshei Geúlah*, Jerusalem and Tel Aviv, 1954, pp. 72, 79, 80, 380, 383). In other words, the origin that had been attributed to Armilus was transferred to Jesus. This could also be said of the two other anonymous authors who should be viewed and studied as belonging to the apocalyptic tradition. (We find also in *Kaf ha-Qetoret* the notion that the first *gilgul* of Esaw was in Jesus and the second in השטן ארמילוס (Idel, p. 81. G. Vayda, "Passages antichrétiens dans 'Kaf ha-Ketoret'," *Revue de l'Histoire des Religions* 197, 1980, p. 48).

81 Ibid, p. 86.

82 Ibid, pp. 88-90. In Idel's article there is no reference to any discussion of the Davidic, and at the same time divine, origins of the Messiah. It is possible that the author of *Sefer ha-Meshiv* means to say that God will be an additional partner to the natural parents contributing the divine character of the Messiah. A similar notion we find in various Christian traditions concerning the nature of the Antichrist (See e.g. B. McGinn, *Visions of the End*, New York, 1979, p. 85).

[83] והנהו ינקי זערי עוללי טיפוחים...נפלו בידא דסמאל רשיעא ופלחי ליה וסגדי קמיה וינקי ראש פתנים אכזר. בתי כנישתי איתעבידו בתי פולחנא נוכראה, ספרי אוריתא אתוקדו בנורא, חסידי וזכאי קשוט מיתו בכמה עקו על עקו דאתא עלייהו (*Meshare Qitrin*, p. 2b.) The author seems to have been in Portugal in 1497, as Scholem suggests (ibid., Introduction, p. 13. The description seems to be that of Portugal and, therefore, has bearing on the question of the destiny of some of the confiscated books there. See M. Benayahu in *Sefunot*, 12 (1971-78), p. 245. See also, A. Gross, "The Ten Tribes and the Kingdom of Prester John - Rumors and Quest Before and After the Expulsion," *Peàmim* 48 (1992), p. 27 n. 82). See also Abravanel's final short remark on Genesis 27, 40.

[84] I. Idel, Introduction to A.Z. Aescoli, *The History of Jewish Messianic Movements*[2], Jerusalem, 1988, p. 22. Idem, "Sefardic Qabbalah After the Expulsion," in The *Sephardic Legacy* [H. Beinart ed.], Jerusalem, 1992, p. 504.

[84a] "Also the Zoharic material in the spiritual world of this circle (i.e. of *Sefer ha-Meshiv*) is very limited." (M. Idel, "Neglected Works of the author of Kaf ha-Qetoret," *Peàmim* 53, 1993, p. 82).

[85] *Kelimmat ha-Goyim*, in *The Polemical Writings of Profiat Duran* [F.E. Talmage ed.], Jerusalem (1981), p. 11.

[86] Ibid, n. 2, and bibliography on p. 12 n. 10.

[87] Ibid, pp. 12-13.

[88] G. Scholem, "Considerations sur l'Histoire des Débuts de la Kabbale Chrétienne," in *Kabbalistes Chrétiens* [A. Faivre and F. Tristan ed.], Paris (1979), pp. 30ff. One may assume a wider oral use of it, although we know of only one or two authors who put things down in writing (Pedro de la Cabaleria and Paulus de Heredia). This is reinforced by Abraham Farissol's report about a group of a dozen apostates who tried to convert others through the use of Qabbalistic writings (See S. Lowinger, "Recherches sur l'0euvre Apologetique d'Abraham Farissol," *R.E.J.* 105, 1940, p. 43, and note on p. 50. Also, Scholem's article pp. 36-9. D. Ruderman, *The World of a Renaissance Jew*, Cincinnati, 1981, pp. 51-2. It seems that the evidence, scanty as it is, shows that the Christian use of Qabbalah in the 15th century this was not a rare phenomonon. On a Jewish reaction which associates Christian Qabbalah Evil with in the 16th century see M. Idel, "The Magical and Neoplatonic Interpretation of the Kabbalah in the Renaissance," *Jewish Thought in the Sixteenth Century* [I. Twersky ed.], Cambridge Mass, 1983, n. 65).

[89] The notion found in *Klimmat ha-Goyim* is repeated by the author of *Kaf ha-Qetoret*: אין פחד...זה כשפעל בסוד שם המפורש [דברי פיו] און [ומרמה] שרמה כ״כ עמים רבים (p. 93a). He resorts to this idea although Jesus should have possessed super-natural powers by virtue of being the incarnation of Samael (See above n. 80).

[90] Nachmanides' commentary on Lev. 16,8 (I owe this reference to Prof. B. Septimus). See also Baḥya ben Asher on Lev. 16, 7. Cf. Nachmanides' comment on Num. 24, 20. The history of the identification of Esaw-Edom-Seìr-Christianity was discussed in graet detail in G. Cohen, "Esaw as Symbol in Early Medieval Thought," *Jewish Medieval and Renaissance Studies* [A. Altmann ed.], Cambridge, Mass. 1967, pp. 19-48, and esp, p. 27 n. 31. Here we deal with the later stage of the association Seìr-*seìrim* (-demons).

[91] Dr. Fedaya tends to interpret the above-quoted Nachmanidean passage as part of the author's astrologic scheme. Even if this is true, it could well serve as an ideological basis for Saba.

As to the identification of Samael with Christianity, one can find it hinted in pre-Nachmanidean Qabbalah, while its roots can be traced back to the Midrash (H. Fedayah, "*Pegam* and *Tiqqun* of the Divinity in the Qabbalah of Rabbi Isaac Sagi Nahor," *Jerusalem Studies in Jewish Thought* 6 (1987), pp. 275, 220 n. 117). It seems that also Abraham Abulafia, who attributes to Jesus the expression אל נכר and refuses to commit this סוד to writing saw him in demonic light (See: M. Idel, "Abulafia on the Jewish Messiah and Jesus," *Immanuel* 9, 1980, p. 78). Yet, Nachmanides' influence on Saba is much more plausible.

[92] Ẓ.M. Deut. p. 8b-9a.

93 *Zohar* II, p. 149a.

94 B.T. Ḥullin, p. 89a (and Rashi). *Bereshit Rabbah*, 96,5. *Tanḥumah Vaéra*, 8 (Buber's edition: 9). For other ancient sources on Hiram, see L. Ginzberg, *The Legends of the Jews* vol. 4, Philadelphia, 1954, pp. 335-6, vol. 6, Phil., 1959, pp. 424-6.

95 דשלמה עבד דנחית לחירם מההוא דרגא דהוה אמר, מושב אלהים ישבתי וגו' (יחזקאל כ"ח, ב'). דתניא, חירם מלך צור עבד גרמיה אלוה. בתר דשלמה אתא עבד ליה בחכמתיה דנחית מההוא עיטא ואודי ליה לשלמה...ותנינן...דשדר ליה חד שידא ונחית ליה שבעה מדורין דגיהנם. (*Zohar*, III, p. 61a). This image of Solomon could have been nourished, in part, by the popular medieval view of him (See J. Trachtenberg, *The Devil and the Jews*, Philadelphia, 1961, p. 63). It does not seem likely that the author of the *Zohar* had Jesus in mind. It might be that R. Ḥayyim Vital thought so. He uses the exact same phrase that describes Hiram and applies it to Jesus: בכל ימי העולם לא נמצא כענין שני אנשים שהאחד עשה עצמו אלוה והוא ישו הנוצרי (S. Horodetzky, "R. Ḥayyim Vital on Jesus and Mohammed," *ha-Goren*, 10, 1928, pp. 159-60). If this is indeed an interpretation of the *Zohar*, it would indicate that he probably received it as an oral teaching. However, it seems that there is no hint in Vital's words of the demonologization of Jesus, and "made himself God" means only that he pretended to be God. This entire notion might go back to the New Testament where it is claimed that the Jews accused Jesus of "making himself equal with God" (John, 5, 18 and similarly ibid. 19,7).

96 For the different versions, see, Samuel Krauss, *Das Leben Jesu*, also idem, "Fragments arameens du Toldot Yeschou," *REJ* 62, 1911, pp. 28-37, and Louis Ginzberg, *Genizah Studies* (*Ginzei Schechter*) vol. 1 New-York (1928), pp. 324-38.

97 See Jacob ben Reuven, *The Wars of the Lord*, pp. 72ff, R. Joseph Qimḥi, *Sefer ha-Berit* [ed. F.E. Talmage ed.], Jerusalem (1974), p. 52. RaDaQ in the end of his commentary on this psalm in the edition of 1477 (In the edition of *Sefer ha-Berit*, p. 76-7). Saba's comment on verses 4-5 is similar to that of RaDaQ but more radical and with a mystical redirection). See also Menaḥem Meiri on this psalm, and *Joseph ha-Meqaneh*, p. 113.

98 Krauss, *Das Leben Jesu*, p. 71.

99 Matt, 15, 21. Mark 7, 24.

100 *Tanḥumah Vaéra* 13, Bo 4 (Compare to the verse in Ez. 28,2). See also B.T. Megillah 6a, and the versions in *Diqduqei Sofrim* n. 9. On the sources in the ancient *piyyut* see: L. Zunz, *Die Synagogale Poesie des Mittelalters*, Berlin, 1855, pp. 441, 444. S. Krauss, Die hebraischen Benennungen der modernen Volker," *Jewish Studies in Memory of George A. Kohut* [S. Baron and A Marx ed.], New York, 1935, p. 407. This identification is found many a time by Rashi: Genesis 25,23. B.T. Pesaḥim 42b. Y. Baer, "Rashi and the Historical Reality of His Time," *Tarbiẓ* 20 (1949), pp. 330-2. See also *Zohar* II, 238b. For the the 15th century see S. Bernstein, "The Poems of Don Vidal ben Lavi," *Tarbiẓ* 8, 1937, p. 364. Baer, *Die Juden* I, pp. 798-9. Abraham Zacut, *Sefer Yoḥasin*, London, 1924, p. 88b. Isaac Abravanel, *Commentary on Samuel*, Jerusalem, 1976, p. 325. *Commentary on Isaiah*, Jerusalem, 1979, p. 131.

Again, Saba might have interpreted a relevant passage by Nachmanides in the same vein. The latter alludes to Christianity by referring to Tyre and its king, Hiram. In his *Vikku'aḥ* he writes: והיה הענין שלא רציתי לומר להם מה שאומר בהגדה שהמשיח יעמוד ברומה עד שיחריב אותה...וכמו שנאמר בחירם מלך צור, ואוציא אש מתוכך היא תאכלך (יחזקי כ"ח, י"ח) (*Kitvei ha-Ramban*, I, p. 310). Hiram and Jesus might have been deduced from the equation of Tyre and Christianity.

101 Saba is aware of esoteric writing on two levels, when the real intention is only alluded to. This is the way he interprets the Mishnah in *Avot* (4,1): איזהו מכובד המכבד את הבריות. כנגד אלישע אחר שקיצץ בנטיעות הגן והפריד אלוף ונפק וחטא, לפי שחשב ח"ו שהיו שתי רשויות ומיעט כבוד המקום ולא חס על כבוד קונו. ולכן לקח הדבר ברמז. כנגד כבוד השם לקח כבוד הבריות ואמר, איזהו מכובד משום כבוד אלהים הסתר דבר. אבל מן הראייה שהביא תוכל להבין הענין שאמר, כי מכבדי אכבד ובוזי יקלו (שמו"א ב, ל), והוא מאמר השם על בני עלי שהיו מבזים את השם ואת משבחו וזהו, כי מכבדי אכבד ובוזי יקלו, כי בוזי השם ומכבדים עצמם יקלו מעצמם. וזה נאמר על אלישע אחר. (Ẓ.M. Gen. p. 32b).

In other words, the nature of the reference is meant to draw the attention of the careful reader and discloses the real intended meaning of the saying, which taken literally cannot agree with the esoteric truth. Although Saba wrote Ẓ.M. in a Moslem country he might have thought it wise to conceal radical elements of his his attitude to Christianity assuming that the book will eventually reach Christian domain.

102 See above n. 85.

103 It seems that the terms שד and שטן are interchangeable, as for instance, in the *Zohar* III, p. 282b, where Samael whom we would expect to be called שטן, is named שד.

104 Ẓ.M. Lev. p. 20b, *Zohar Ḥqdash*, p. 14b.

105 Libowitz, p. 38. On that pilgrimage center see, Marilyn Stokstad, *Santiago de Compostela*, U. of Okalahoma Press (1978) (especially the updated bibliography).

106 It is highly improbable that Saba did not know of the place, a route to which passed not far away, north of Zamora (and Scholem is probably right). Benito Garcia said in his inquisitorial trial that he had gone to Santiago to see the devils (*los diablos*. Baer, History, p. 407.)

107 These words were omitted by the Jewish internal censorship.

108 ולכן אמר, והנה פשה הנגע בבגד או בשתי או בערב (ויקרא י״ג, נ״א), כי ידוע הוא שהבגד הוא השתי והערב. אבל רמז בזה על השד הזה השולט (במהדורת ווארשא נדפס בטעות: הטילם) בשתי ובערב כפי אמונת הנוצרים, ולכן צוה, ושרף את הבגד או את השתי או את הערב, לפי שהוא תועבה. (Ẓ.M. Lev. p. 18a).

109 This, again, appears in one version of *Toldot Yeshu*, where the two parts of the Cross are Edom and Samael (Krauss, Das Leben, p. 297). In Germany, we find what seems to be a potential background for Saba's comment: והבגד אשר תהיה בו נגע צרעת, אע״פ שאין מקרא יוצא מידי פשוטו מכל מקום ליכא מידי דלא רמיזא באורייתא. והבגד, בגדי כומרי ישו שיש להם שתי וערב על בגדיהם. והיה הנגע, עתידה אומה הרשעה שתלקה בצרעת (M.R. Lehman, "Allusions to Jesus and Mohammed in the Commentaries of the Ashkenazic Hasidim," *Sinai* 87, (1980), p. 39). All the relevant medieval sources might, ultimately, be traced back to the Midrash which states צרעת זו אדום (*Vayiqra Raba*, 15, 9, *Tanḥuma, Tazria*, 11).

110 For another limited attempt at interpreting monastic and monkish rules according to the images of the constellations, see R. Abraham ibn Migash, *Kevod Élohim*, Costantinople, 1585, (reprint Jerusalem, 1977), 3, 23, p. 143a.

111 ואמר, הוא ישופך ראש (בראשית ג׳, ט״ו). בכאן רמז ענין נחש הקדמוני הוא סמאל...והוא סמאל הוא עשו הוא אדום הוא הראש אשר ישתחוו שם (שמו״ב ט״ו, ל״ב), דכתיב, ויצא הראשון אדמוני, הוא אופן מרכבותיו שעולה מספרו ק״ל כמספר סמאל וזהו, הוא ישופך ראש, לפי שהוא ראש הפעור... (Ẓ.M. Gen. p. 16b).

112 The Talmud interprets "Head" as idolatry (B.T. Sanhedrin, p. 107a).

113 Ibid, p. 92b.

114 One might add a possible allusion to Jesus in the first part of the word ישופך The connection between the snake and Jesus is explicit in an Ashkenazic source: ערום בגי׳ ישו, כי נחש וישו לאבד את העולם נתכוונו, זה בגוף וזה בנשמה. (loc. cit. above n. 111, p. 38). On the wall of one of the houses in Seville there remained an inscription on ceramic: הוא ישופך ראש. Could it be explained in light of our interpretation?

115 N. Cohn, *The Pursuit of the Millennium*, London, 1970, p.78. See also Trachtenberg, *The Devil*, pp. 34-35. Jeffrey B. Russel, *Lucifer, The Devil in the Middle Ages*, Ithaca and London (1984), p. 77. The most recent edition of Adso's "Letter on the Origin and Life of the Antichrist" was based on 170 mss., a fact which attests to its popularity. As to Adso's early Christian sources see, Mcginn, *Visions of the End*, pp. 82-3. The description of the mother could be, however, a reaction to the Jewish tradition concerning Jesus' mother. The suggestion to describe our *ecclesia diaboli* as a reaction to the image of *synagoga diaboli*, was made by M. Idel (see above n. 78). See also: R. Bonfil, "The Jews and the Devil in Christian Consiousness in the Middle Ages," *The History of Jews' Hatred* [S. Almog ed.], Jerusalem, 1980, p. 119. There could also be a transfer here of the popular demonic conception of Moses, onto Jesus (See Ruth Mellinkoff, *The Horned Moses in Medieval Art and Thought*, U. of California Press, 1970, pp. 135-6, and Norman Cohn, "The Horns of Moses," *Commentary* 26, 1958, p. 228).

116 We do not mean to exclude pre-Qabbalists like Judah Halevi. But in our typology he belongs to the mystical camp.

117 וזה בהכרעה סגוליית נפלאה משאיר כל הדברים על מציאות (Ẓ.M. Gen. l0b-lla). Saba felt it necessary to explain this at length several times, e.g. ibid, Deut. p. 56b.

118 Ibid, Ex. p. 26b.

119 Ibid, Deut. p. 18a. Compare a similar idea in the *Zohar* II, p. 183a-b.

120 Ẓ.M. Gen. p. 39b. Num. p. 9a. Deut. pp. 30b, 33a, 39b. (See, however, Num. p. 6a, and compare it to Saba's comment concerning the Christian priests who have no children, above p. 132).

121 Ẓ.M. Lev. pp. 14b, 24a. Saba disagrees, then, with the opinions that see in the dietary laws as a physical safeguard from bad foods. (See ibid, p. 13b. The influence of food on the mind is expressed elsewhere (ibid, Gen. pp. 13a, 27b).

122 Ẓ.M. Deut. p. 28a-b. The derogatory term אוכלי בשר החזיר is very common in this period (e.g. *Àqedat Yiẓḥaq*, 60, p. 33b. *Magen ve-Romaḥ*, p. 91. Abravanel on Lev. 11 (Jerusalem, 1964, p. 65b). But we already find this motif in Baḥya's *Kad ha-Qemaḥ*, p. 119, and indeed it goes back to the early *piyyut* (L. Zunz, *Die Synagogale Poesie des Mittelalters*, Berlin, 1855, p. 448).

123 See above p. 125.

124 Ẓ.M. Deut. p. 19b (See above n. 48).

125 See above p. 173?.

126 Ẓ.M. Num. p. 3b. This notion appears in R. Menaḥem Recanati (*Sefer Taàmei Miẓvot*, London, 1963, pp. 5a ff).

127 See ibid, Gen. pp. 3b, 4b.

128 Ibid, Lev. p. 24a-b. This plea for unity repeats itself in Deut. pp. 13a, 21b. (See also above p. 132 ?). This notion appears in the sixteenth century by RaDBaZ (*Meẓudat David*, no. 13, p. 3d). Z. Greis refers to Cordovero (*Tomer Devorah*, New York, 1960, pp. 8-11) as the oldest source known for this idea ("The Ḥassidic Conduct Literature from the Mid-Eighteenth Century to the 1830's," *Ẓion* 46 1981, p. 220).

129 The main discussion is in Ẓ.M. Deut. p. 8b-9a.

130 See our discussion above, pp. 134ff.

131 The constant reiteration of the importance of the commandments is explained in Ẓ.M. Lev. p. 34a: כי כבר כתבתי כי גאוננו ותפארתינו ועוזנו ביד שובנו היות לנו הכח להוריד הגשמים בעתם בכח תפלתנו. ודבר מפורסם הוא כי על זה התנאי קבלו אותנו בארץ העמים כשגלינו מארצינו. וכבר קרה כזה כי במלכות ארגון בזמן עצירה השליכו היהודים כולם מחוץ לעיר וסגרו השערים בעדם עד שיביאו המים, ודרש הרב ן' חסדאי קרשקש זצ״ל וכה אמר בתחילת דבריו, לנו המים. והשי״ת פקד את עמו...ואח״כ בעונתינו היינו צועקים וצווחים ולית מאן דישגח בן, לפי שנתקיים בנו בעונותינו, ושברתי את גאון עוזכם... And more specifically in Ex. p. 54b: ...שהרי אנו רואים הרבה פעמים...שאנו מעוטפים בטלית ואיו אנו נענין. אבל הרצון כל זמן שישראל עושין כסדר בזה... (Here, however, the emphasis is on commandments of social ethics).

132 Ẓ.M. Deut. p. 9a. Saba arrives at this interpretation of the verse because he had to satisfy two requirements: a) "wise" implies wisdom; b) the Gentiles should appreciate it, i.e. it should be universal. The natural choice of Qabbalah does not satisfy the second, and other sciences are not exclusively Jewish and are nothing to be proud of anyway, especially philosophy. Therefore he finds a Jewish phenomenon which, although not the true wisdom, is a wisdom "in the eyes of the nations," and this interpretation is supported by the next verse. (Compare *Kuzari* 3, 39. For Halevi, natural sciences and philosophy are still worth being proud of in showing the nations that they are included in the Talmud). It is only in the sixteenth century that we hear the claim that knowledge of Qabbalistic reasons for the commandments would render the Jews a "wise and understanding people" (Tishbi, The Controversy, p. 180). That could be due to the spread of Christian Qabbalah. For a fuller discussion of the interpretation of this verse, see I. Twersky, *Introduction to the Code of Maimonides*, Yale U. Press (1980), pp. 381-87.

133 In Ẓ.M. Ex. p. 31b Saba expresses the same idea, emphasizing again the metaphysical power of Israel by virtue of practice alone (see also ibid, p. 26b).

134 Ibid, Deut. p. 30a.

135 Ibid, p. 34. For a proper background see *SeMaG*, Positive 74 (Venice, 1547, p. 152 c-d) and *Sefer Ḥasidim* [Wistinetzki ed.] Frankfurt, 1924, no. 1003. But Saba does not over-emphasize the pragmatic aspect, as does *Sefer Ḥasidim*. (See J. Katz, *Exclusiveness and Tolerance*, New-York, 1962, p. 101.)

136 Ibid, p. 43b. There is here a faint echo of *SeMaG* (previous note). Also see below n. 140.

137 E.g. R. Joseph Qimḥi in *Sefer ha-Berit*, p. 26. There the Jew attempts to show the inferiority of Christianity through the apparent fact that they do not practise the Decalogue, including the five social commandments. (On principle, this was the claim of the priest who confronted R. Menaḥem Meiri when he attacked the latter in a "common" religious zone, namely, the issue of repentance to which the Jews did not devote even one treatise. See the introduction to *Ḥibbur ha-Teshuvah*). Similarly R. Ḥayyim ibn Mussa tells us: ואמר החכם הנזכר לפתות, אדוני הלא ידעת אם לא שמעת שאין ליהודים אלא ספר אחד באלהות ששמו מורה נבוכים, ולנו יש ספרים באלהות שלא יכילם היכל גדול כזה מתהומא עד גבול רקיעא (*Magen ve-Romaḥ*, p. 133). In a long passage Saba gives us a unique description of the "daughters of the Gentiles," including their make-up from head to toe (literally) and characterizes their behavior as follows: ...לפי שבנות הגויים הם מופקרות והם פרוצות בעריות ואין להם בושת פנים ומצחיהם נחושה, והולכות בשווקים וברחובות ואצל כל פינה יארובו לצוד נפשות נקיים ולדבר עם אנשים (Ẓ.M. Deut. p. 32b. Cf. R. Solomon ben Shimon Duran, who writes in 1437 in detail about Christian sexual perversion, in *Milḥemet Miẓvah*, Jerusalem, 1980, p. 32a). Elsewhere we read: ברוך תהיה מכל העמים, לפי שאתה נזהר מרציחה וניאוף וגניבה וחמדה...שהם פרוצי'... (ibid, p. 17b). It is not clear whether this passage is purely exegetical or carries an allusion to present reality. It seems to refer to the low morals of Christians à-la-Qimḥi, but not necessarily to any ideal state of affairs on the Jewish side. As a result, we spare a possible contradiction between this passage and his criticism of the Jews on some of these accounts [See above ch. 4 n. 27). But the truth of the matter is that contradictions of this sort are "permissible" for Saba as a preacher who assumes the dual role of castigator and consoler, which may bring out two contradicting views on the same issue by the same man.

138 Despite the undoubted influence of *SeMaG* on Saba, in this as well as in other issues, the latter is clearly against proselytes, of whom he does not think highly (Ẓ.M. Ex. pp. 35b, 50b).

139 See *Shevet Yehudah*, particularly his summary in ch. 63.

140 It seems that the long passage about Crescas and the rain (above n. 133) betrays the same emotions of the desire to be accepted and recognized for contributing to the host country. (That passage is longer than our quotation and includes a few rhymes, a fact that, as a rule, reveals Saba's emotions.

CHAPTER SIX

DESPAIR AND CONSOLATION

Despair of redemption can be considered a central motivating force behind individuals who chose to abandon Judaism for other religions during the Middle Ages, or for secularism in modern times.[1] This force has been present in varying degrees of intensity throughout Jewish history.

The study of this theme during the last phase of Jewish history in medieval Spain has its import for the understanding not of only that period, but also of the post-Expulsion "migration" of Sefardic ideas and mentality to other parts of the Diaspora. It seems that from the turn of the century on, the profound feelings of despair which found their expression in numerous writings became part and parcel of post-Expulsion Jewish thought, and the term "despair" [*yeúsh*] appears with more frequency. This mood spread to Ashkenazic Jewry in Eastern Europe and surfaced, even in times that were not tragic, as the result of generations weighed down by the burden of the continuous national tragedy of Exile which became heavier with each passing year and every "minor" persecution. Pondering and contemplating the status of Israel and its future, essentially a characteristic of Sefardic thought, thus became more of a national characteristic, as East met West.[2]

1. General Historical Background

G. Scholem has proposed a relationship between the Qabbalistic doctrine of R. Isaac Luria in Safed in the third quarter of the 16th century and the Expulsion from Spain:

> Only gradually, as the Expulsion ceased to be regarded in a redemptive light, and loomed up all the more distinctly in its catastrophic character, did the flames which had flared up from the apocalyptic abyss sweep over wide areas of the Jewish world until they finally seized upon and recast the mystical theology of Kabbalism.[3]

This relationship between the Expulsion and Luria's doctrine as cause and effect has been reconsidered in recent scholarship.[4] If this is to be maintained, the relationship should be considered at best an indirect one, through the historical mediation of the apocalyptic writings and Messianic expectations regenerated throughout the 15th century and in the wake of the Expulsion.[5] The natural reactions to thwarted expectations can range from mild disappointment to extreme religious despair. The latter could be accentuated if specific dates for the arrival of the Messiah were introduced by authoritative individuals. However, the euphoric peak from which the fall is most painful occurs when Messianic activity seems to take shape and then eludes its believers. This factor also existed to an extent with the Reuveni-Molkho episode in the third decade of the 16th century.

All of this contributed in the final analysis to the perpetuation of the tragedy which was kept alive in people's hearts. Moreover, the more intense the expectations so, proportionally, also was the subsequent measure of despair for an already demoralized people. The need for a theological solution was, therefore, urgently needed. It was this the sequence of Messianic expectations and disappointments that might have led to Luria's innovative myth.

However, we are here concerned with Saba's writings whose second version was written in the first decade after the Expulsion from Spain and 2-3 years after the Portuguese "Expulsion." At that time both past and present despair intermingled with hope for the future, creating an atmosphere of confusion.[6] This was the stimulus for some of the writings of the period dealing with the problems of Exile, suffering and redemption.

2. *Shades of Despair*

Moving closer to our more specific issue at hand, one can distinguish shades of despair. In its light shade, despair of reality constitutes a wish for redemption. The awakening of Messianic hopes as a consequence of hardships inflicted by history is evident. There is, however, a lighter shade of such despair that carried with it negative religious manifestations. Such despair weakens the readiness to wait for Redemption, blurs sensitivity to the reality of Exile; in other words, it decreases religious awareness.[7] This religious despair of Redemption is nourished by the length of the Exile and is enhanced by a good material life, the ability to live peacefully and even luxuriously among the nations. Thus did R. Ḥayyim ben Beẓalel understand this phenomenon:

> ...this bitter Exile..., for many of our people who almost despair of redemption, and consider themselves as residents [*ke-toshavim*] in the land of their enemy, and build for themselves beautiful houses (there), not in the Holy Land.[8]

There is yet another shade of religious despair, the darkest of them all. It is rooted in extreme mental and/or physical pressures and its results range from mild scepticism to renouncing one's religion and embracing a more convenient one.[9] The same historical conditions that might enhance hope and apocalyptic expectations in some, might also bring about extreme despair in others, depending on one's particular make-up.

The loss of the sense of *galut* by the affluent segment of Jewish society in Spain has already been discussed.[10] In this chapter we shall touch upon post-Expulsion despair as reflected in Saba's writings. It will include religious problems stemming from the series of blows absorbed by Iberian Jewry in the last decade of the 15th century. Saba's personal reaction to the great upheaval in Jewish history was a renewed sense of faith in the coming Redemption and a strong sense of responsibility towards his brethren in despair. It is around this theme that the other major themes in his writings, such as Redemption, polemics, suffering, and theodicy, revolve.

This study based on Saba's writings attempts to capture the atmosphere and mood prevalent at the turn of the 15th century in North Africa and therefore has its limitations. One man's conception of a problem is not necessarily the correct one. Thus, the issue of despair and its causes and effects in Saba's works might have been more a reflection of his personal feelings as to what the problem was. Moreover, he might have been much more preoccupied with this problem and with particular aspects of it due to his own more recent experience in Portugal, which was fresh in his mind. At the time of Saba's arrival in Fez the Spanish *megorashim* community there seems to have already been well on the road to material and spiritual recovery.[11] Therefore, we cannot arrive at absolute historical conclusions by relying on Saba alone.[12] However, this study certainly gives us a glimpse into the sensitive soul of a dedicated and caring preacher. But even beyond that we might safely assume that the bad news from Portugal had a depressing and gloomy effect on many of the Spanish exiles for whom the tribulations of their coreligionists, some of whom had relatives in North Africa, were but an extension of their own Expulsion in 1492.

2.1. Despair...

In both Reproof Sections (Lev. 26, Deut. 28) Saba goes to great lengths to prove that there is an absolute parallel between the Blessings (consisting of 11 and 14 verses, respectively), and the Curses (29 and 54, respectively), saying:

> So you see with your own eyes that all these Curses are included in the Blessings (and I say this) so that the adversary [*baàl ha-din*] will not be able to claim that because of God's hatred towards us he shortened the Blessings, while dwelling on Curses at length, adding cruel plagues which were not alluded to in the Blessings, because this is false [*ki zeh sheqer*]. All the Curses are included in the Blessings. Moreover, we could say that all the Curses are included in two verses of Blessings and even in one verse...[13]

Saba here refutes those who would claim that God's punishment in Exile does not carry with it the seeds of a better future after the cleansing through suffering, that He punishes out of hatred for the sinful Jewish people; and that He is being cruel to them.[14] The "adversary" is readily identifiable as

Christianity. It is clearly the Christian understanding of post-Christ Jewish history that here served as a catalyst for despair - a theological claim with exegetical support.[15]

This idea is repeated elsewhere:

> As the prophet Isaiah said...:'The Lord says: Where is the bill of divorce of your mother whom I dismissed' (50,1), to hint that although God was saying that He is their redeemer they had despaired of Redemption since they thought they had sinned to God and that He had already handed them over, selling them into their enemy's hands, with no way back. Therefore he came to say that this is false.[16]

Here again, Saba fights the false notion that God's wrath against the Jews for sins they have committed[17] is irrevocable. This belief, that the cruel fate of the Jewish faith was determined and sealed due to the sinful past of the Jews, was a major factor in the reigning despair. However, it was a century earlier that it had penetrated forcefully into Jewish thought. After the forced mass conversions and deaths in 1391 and the massive voluntary conversions in the wake of the disastrous disputation at Tortosa, R. Joseph Albo writes about the individual and collective despair and the hope for the future:

> And Jeremiah the prophet clarified this...discussing the profound troubles that each one of Israel was suffering in Exile...: 'For the Lord will not cast off his servants forever...' (Lam. 3,31), and therefore I do not lose hope [*mityaésh*] of emerging from the troubles...and similarly said David about the collective hope [*ha-tiqvah ha-kelalit*]: '0 Israel, look to the Lord, for in the Lord is mercy...' (Ps. 130,7), namely, do not despair of hoping in God due to your multitude of sins, for you will not be saved through your own merits, which will not suffice, but the Redemption from the depths of trouble will be through Grace.[18]

We find another argument of despair echoed throughout Ẓ.M., namely, that God is not capable of saving the Jews. It does not seem to be a carefully thought-out idea based on theological grounds, but rather the emotional reaction of people who could not understand why they were afflicted with so much suffering. Their lowly and desperate situation led them to question God's omnipotence, saying that even He could not raise up the Jewish nation which is rapidly declining in status and number. It is not that He does not want to save the Jews, as the first argument claimed, but that He was incapable of doing so.[19]

One is impressed with Saba's special efforts to prove God's omnipotence [*yekholet ha-shem*]. It seems to us that this very issue is the link that connects the end of Saba's commentary on the Portion of *Bereshit* to its beginning. Rejecting any mystical interpretations for reasons of esotericism, Saba says that there are two major ideas that can still be derived from the story of Creation: a) that God is omnipotent; and b) that the world was created for Israel.[20] He attempts to demonstrate this in commenting on the six days of Creation and what follows. Then, due to the contents of the following chapters, Saba digresses from these two points for ten long pages. In the last paragraph of the Portion, however, he returns to them, ending with Israel and with God's omnipotence. Using the same verses we have already mentioned, Saba compared the situation prior to the deluge to the present:

> And this is similar to what the prophet (Isaiah) said: 'Where is the bill of divorce of your mother...' (50,1). Since above he said: 'For I will contend with your adversaries and will deliver your children' (49,25), and perhaps Israel will say that they already lost any hope [*noáshu*] in the long Exile [*be-galut yashan*],[21] and have no more hope. Therefore he said that this is false!...and if you repent...And perhaps they think that I am already incapable of rescuing them. This is false (too), for 'with a mere rebuke I dry up the sea' (50,2), and I have the absolute power at all times.[22]

Saba here is countering two arguments: a) the one we encountered before, namely, that God divorced the Jewish people, an argument enhanced by Christian belief concerning the Jews; b) the contention that the reality is so grim that even God could do nothing in order to raise the faltering nation.[23]

However, the specific cause of despair against which Saba struggles most, is the feeling of rapid extinction. Saba had to deal with faithful people who could have stayed in Spain or returned there on terms that would have made their lives much easier. Both before and after the Expulsion, many of their relatives and friends had chosen to live in Spain and practise crypto-Judaism rather than practise Judaism openly elsewhere. Saba is talking to a remnant of a Jewry that had been decimated through voluntary conversions in Spain, death by natural causes during migrations southward or eastward, mass forced conversions in Portugal, and desertion of the remnant by individuals who could no longer bear the difficulties and had left their old religion.[24] Saba seems to be speaking, then, to people who under the pressure of circumstances, still clung to their Faith but were in danger of losing faith in any positive prospects for the future. Such people could end up being lost to Judaism as individuals. Moreover, their choice would serve as a demoralizing factor enhancing the process they were involved in. The clear feeling of "shrinking unto (national) death" was the most severe factor of despair with which Saba tried to contend. This is reflected clearly in Ẓ.M. and renders the above-mentioned arguments secondary, being *effects* of, rather than *causes* for despair.[25]

In his interpretation of Ps. 93, part of his description of the sixth millennium, Saba captures the feelings of the remnant of Spanish Jewry:

> ...And since 'Your testimonies have proven infinitely faithful' (93,5), and all Your words, promises and decrees come to pass and are of steadfast faithfulness as we have seen with our own eyes in the decree of the sea and its masses (i.e., the Fourth Kingdom), that when it was tossing

and sweeping over [*ve-shataf ve-àvar*, i.e., persecutions and forced conversions], it was in an immediate danger of breaking up (Jonah 1,4) '...0, Lord, for the length of days.' For he was complaining about the Exile of Israel and their troubles, that because of their multitude Israel remained very few, and if He would wait to redeem them until the day alluded to by the prophets...'And it will be in the end of days,' and so He promised[26] (concerning the fall of Edom, 'Nevermore shall it be settled [*la-neẓaḥ*],'...and all this would take a long time and it alluded to a long Exile). And therefore said Jeremiah, 'For this our heart is full of sorrow' (Lam. 5,17), on the killing of old and young people, but 'on Mount Zion which is desolate, 0 Lord, You are enthroned forever...' (ibid 5,19), and You will build it whenever You want... But we, who decrease in number every single day, to the extent that there is almost no remnant left, 'Why do You forget us forever [*la-neẓaḥ*]' (ibid, 5,20), referring to that "forever" mentioned by the prophets. And also here (Ps. 93,5)..., but as for Israel, You should not wait for them for such a long time, because there are new troubles every single day so that, when that time arrives, nothing will be left of them.[27]

This particular cause for despair has earlier and later expressions.[28] But those seem to be expressions of individual sensitive souls or part of a convention. The fear, in those cases, is usually expressed in one sentence which does not seem to have been entrenched deeply in reality, and there is no impression of an atmosphere of urgency and emergency. There was, however, a period when such expressions conveyed the same powerful and dramatic message rooted in contemporary historical events - the post 1391 period. Joshua Lorqi writes to Paulus de Sancta Maria analyzing the possible reasons for conversion to Christianity:

Or when you beheld the doom of our homeland, the multitude of the afflictions that have recently befallen us which ruined and destroyed us, the Lord having almost turned His countenance away from us and given us as food to the birds of the sky and to the wild beasts - did it then seem to you that the name of Israel would be remembered no more?[29]

Again, some of those people justify their despair.[30] Their arguments are exegetical and theological, complementing each other. The verse "Why do You forget us forever [*la-neẓaḥ*]" might present a difficulty for the faithful Jew, since it might be understood as implying that God will indeed forget Israel literally forever. Saba, therefore, associates the problematic expression with other uses of it by the prophets where it refers to the distant Redemption in the "end of days." Saba does not say explicitly that this verse was a potential "promoter of despair," but such would seem to be the case because, about another verse implying the same conclusions, Saba says:

And what is written ('The Lord will bring upon you sickness and plague...until you are destroyed [*àd hishamdakh*]" (Deut. 28,61), this will never happen, as it says, 'I will make an end of all the nations...

> but I will not make an end of you' (Jer. 30, 11), and He only tried to scare and frighten them through the extra length of the Curses... so as to cause them to return to God and (then) He would pity them....[31]

Continuing this passage Saba adds: "...and He is good, not cruel," referring to the claim that God does not intend any good in inflicting such severe punishment on Israel or, in other words, that there is no hope for an end of the suffering which will stop only when Israel will cease to exist.[32]

The theological reason for God's lack of forgiveness is expressed elsewhere:

> And perhaps Israel would say that because of the length of the days (of the Exile), and the multitude of troubles and the decrease in correct beliefs and faith [*be-miùt ha-deòt veha-émunah*] Israel will cease to exit...[33]

This is the gloom prevalent in the immediate post-Expulsions' period as sensed by Saba and reflected in his writings.

3. Consolation

The problem discussed above is the background for Saba's exaggerated preoccupation with the subject of Redemption. One can feel the centrality of this theme throughout his writings.[34] It would be incorrect to attribute Saba's interest in it solely to post-Expulsion despair, witness his sermon before the "gathering of scholars in Castile."[35] But his stress on the eternity of Israel, its indestructibility, and related "despair catalysts," is suggestive. Moreover, the form and content of his discussions point in the same direction.

Saba uses several basic methods of consolation and encouragement: a) countering the "despair theology," and refuting the exegetical text proofs of it; b) proving in a positive way the eternity of Israel; c) talking of redemption; d) endowing suffering with meaningful value. Thus, by brightening the present and showing the ray of light at the end of the long tunnel, Saba attempts to break through the thick darkness of despair.[36]

3.1. The Eternity of Israel

In order to disprove the exegetical foundations people might have relied upon, Saba shows, exegetically, by highlighting the Blessings in the Reproof Section that God does not mean to torture Israel unto complete annihilation. This way he could claim that God is not "cruel" but is simply trying to "attract Israel's attention," so that they will repent and He will be able to "lead them to water at bubbling springs" (Isa. 49,10).[37] He also concentrates on proving that the idea of repentance is logically valid and therefore past sins are not necessarily enduring.[38]

In positive terms, Saba tries to show that Israel will not perish, for mystically they are attached to the Name of God itself and therefore He must forgive them. Since God is eternal, it follows logically that so must be the nation that is a part of Him.[39]

3.2. The Certainty of Redemption

Saba tries to find as many allusions to the Four Kingdoms or Four Exiles as he can. He is not so concerned with the first three, but wherever they appear, the fourth one, Edom, is bound to accompany them. For example, Saba dwells on the story of the Hasmoneans, although it is known that Hanukkah was not one of the more popular holidays in the Jewish literature of the Middle Ages. But the patient reader will find out that the importance of that historical event lies in its serving as a milestone on the road to redemption.[40] The fact that the Kingdom of Edom is alluded to, gives Saba the opportunity to cite scriptural allusions to its particular nature and even to specific contemporary persecutions, expulsions and hardships. Once this is established, Saba can proceed to repeat, over and over again, his most popular verses: "Behold I have made you small among the nations, you are greatly despised...Though you exalt yourself as the eagle, and though you set your nest among the stars, thence will I bring you down, said the Lord."[41]

The fulfillment of the bad parts of the prophecies ensures that eventually the good parts will be fulfilled as well.[42] There have been no changes in the master-plan of history. On the contrary, all that has been happening has been foreseen. The present Exile is the longest and harshest[43] and contains more troubles than all the previous exiles put together.[44] Due to the "multiple tortures, suffering, and expulsions (of this Exile), which in previous exiles Israel did not have to endure, it has been said concerning the present Exile, 'How shall Jacob stand for he is (too) small' (Am. 7,2.5), to contain all that was decreed upon him."[45]

The conditions prior to the Redemption were described through the name of Judah, by his mother, who revealed the greatest secrets through her sons' names.[46] Saba chooses to communicate the idea in verse:

> הפעם אודה את ה׳ יותר מבשאר הגלויות שקמתי במהרה / אבל עכשיו שהייתי שכולה
> וגלמודה / שכוחה ועזובה / מאוסה כנדה / וה׳ עזרני / ומעפר הקימני / ראוי לי להודות
> לה׳ על טובות גמלני.[47]

Specific troubles such as the expulsions are alluded to by the Torah, not only in general but through details that enable the careful reader (i.e., Saba) to identify those events positively.[48]

By using the Torah - the blueprint of history - to portray the Exile and, especially, by pointing to specific verses as referring to the events leading up to the present crisis, Saba attempts to restore the reader's faith in the divine guidance of history by a benevolent God who warned Israel beforehand, has punished them as promised, and eventually will keep the second part of the promise - redemption.[49]

3.3. The Nature of Redemption

This leads to another aspect of the problem which Saba would have to handle since for many people this would not be a sufficient consolation. Suffering people seek rest. They are tired of answering the bell for the coming round in an ongoing fight for everlasting rounds. Saba could not change the reality of their lives. He could try, however, to talk of better things to come and predict an approaching Redemption on the horizon.

Without understanding this motivation it is difficult to comprehend why Saba "painstakingly" tries to make certain points while neglecting others or mentioning them only briefly. Herein lies the reason behind the repeated stress upon the tranquil and peaceful character of life to come with the Redemption. This also explains the emphasis that the coming peace will not be marred by a subsequent period of Exile, as happened before in Jewish history, but would be perpetual. By this Saba intended to eliminate insecurity and worries about dangers of war and oppression.[50]

3.4. Messianic Calculations

With regard to the delicate question of predicting the date of the Redemption, Saba acts with extreme caution. One cannot doubt that he knew of the apocalyptic euphoria in some circles and of dates set by impatient enthusiasts or by consolers like Abravanel. It seems to us that he dismissed all contemporary calculations as not authoritative.

In Ẓ.M. he mentions only the last stage to be completed in 5408 (1647-48). This is taken from *Midrash ha-Neèlam*.[51] He does not use the fuller discussion there in order to deduce dates for earlier stages. Saba does refer to it, however, in Ẓ.Ḥ. along with another reference to an "ancient manuscript of the *Zohar*," but it is clear that he does this because of the authority of the *Zohar* and because he had the inner need to discuss it albeit briefly and hesitantly. It seems evident to us that had this not been a passage from the *Zohar*, Saba would not even have mentioned it.

The prediction itself designates four years as four stages of which one had passed and another was about to pass. The years are 256, 260, 266, 272 (1496, 1500, 1506, 1512), and Ẓ.Ḥ. was written in the third quarter of 260. In explaining the fact that nothing had thus far happened in reality, Saba says that "perhaps" redemption must first be performed with the letters of the Name and, only then, will the actual earthly redemption take place.[52] By doing so Saba achieves three things: a) he retains the infallibility of the *Zohar*; b) he remains loyal to his conviction that no man knows the exact date of the Redemption; c) he impresses upon his readers that the process of redemption has already been set in motion and that its earthly manifestations are imminent.[53] Saba maintains that the exact date was not revealed to any man: "...and this secret was never revealed as it says, 'For a day of vengeance is in my heart,' (Isa. 63,4) and only God knows this thing."[54]

And again in the end of the description of the long punishment of Israel:

> And all this is due to our sins in the Fourth Exile in which we are now. And since this is the longest of all exiles, and one might ask: 'How long, 0 Lord,' (Isa. 6,11) or: 'When will be the end of the wonders?' (Dan. 12,6), therefore He answered saying: 'This was not asked out of wisdom, since the eye of no one has seen it' (Job. 28,7), 'and it is laid up in store with me sealed up among my treasures' (Deut. 32,34). I have never revealed it to any man, and only I foresee it. And this is the meaning of, 'To me belongs vengeance' (ibid, 32,25) - and not to anyone else, as the Sages said: 'My heart did not reveal it to my mouth,' and it is a mystery.[55]

This contradicts the position taken by the author of *Sefer ha-Temunah* who bases his Messianic calculation on the very same verses (Deut. 32, 34-35).[56] It is all the more striking if we consider that the apocalyptic visionary, who was in the Lisbon jail together with Saba, used the same verse as a *gematria* that reveals the year 1453 and the fall of Constantinople as an important date in the process of redemption.[57] One can hardly doubt that Saba knew of this calculation.[58]

On the other hand, Saba did believe in the imminence of the Redemption and expresses this belief several times. He sees in the forty-two marches [*masaòt*] in the desert during the forty years an indication of the duration of the Exile. He ends by saying that after counting all the *masaòt* of the Jews in the last 1500 years the conditions for redemption seem to have been fulfilled.[59] Here again Saba does not attach the coming redemption to any definite date.

Saba states it again explicitly: "...and I wrote it here to inform you that immediately after the destruction of Rome our redemption will take place...and we are confident that it will be soon in our days."[60]

And again, using the traditional dual-date of redemption Saba says:

> ...the Messiah Son of David who is mentioned in this book (Ruth) whose time of arrival is very near, very soon in our days and, if we will correct our deeds, he will come even sooner, as He says: 'I, the Lord, will hasten it in its time' (Isa. 60,22).[61]

To sum up then, Saba chose a Messianic golden mean, namely, consoling his people through the dissemination of the belief in the forthcoming Redemption but avoiding a commitment to any specific date.

In this respect he has distinguished himself from many of his contemporaries. He is not indifferent to the Messianic atmosphere and popular needs as R. Joseph Garson apparently was.[62] On the other hand, his works reflect a different, more restrained and responsible attitude to the crucial topic as compared to R. Abraham ben Eliezer Halevi's intense apocalypticism, to *Kaf ha-Qetoret*'s multiple-dates and confusing calculations, to the Messianic hallucinations of the anonymous visionary in Lisbon, to Zacut's astrological messianism, and even to Abravanel's elaborate Messianic system and computations. A generally similar conservative attitude we find in a short poem written by R. Abraham Ibn Baqrat, who arrived from Spain at North Africa with the initial wave of refugees in 1492. Evidently it was written in an historical atmosphere saturated with apocalyptic activity of *ḥishuvei qeẓ*, against which he is warning:

לחשב קץ ולשאול על שנותיו / חדל פן תהרוס לעלות במרי
ואל תשאל אבל חכה ויבא / ומישאל ואלצפן וסתרי.[63]

3.5. Revenge

There is another aspect to consolation within the framework of redemption. It is only natural that a tortured person's will to live would be strengthened by the promise to see the downfall of his torturer. One of the emphasized features of the beginning of the new era is the revenge that God promised to take upon Edom. It will occur at the peak of its success and might,[64] so that the downfall be all the more painful. In fire will they burn while their blood will be spilled like water.[65] Those remaining will be put to shame through enslavement to Israel, and thus the latter will have full satisfaction in the reversal of "duties." Christianity is not to be annihilated completely but, as a punishment must be degraded and despised:

> ...'Thence will I bring you down' (Oba. 1,4), from your greatness. You will not be annihilated completely, but rather you will serve as hewers of woods and drawers of water for the congregation, so that in this you will become greatly despised as it says: 'You are greatly despised' (ibid, 1,2).[66]

This is quite a proper and deserving destiny for a religion which treated the Jews in a similar manner in accordance with the Augustinian doctrine.

The universal element of Redemption as displayed in Jewish tradition from the prophets onward, is being played down to the extent that one feels that it exists in Saba's writings under the coercion of tradition. Thus, even when it is mentioned, the element of revenge does not vanish.

> As it says: 'For then will I return to the people a pure language, that they may all call upon the name of the Lord, to serve Him with one accord' (Zeph. 3,9). And since the Messiah will descent from Perez, it

> says: 'And these are the generations of Perez' (Ruth 4,18), (the Messiah) who is going to break the nations.[67]

This shade of the revenge motif is at odds with what seems to be the main trend within Sefardic tradition since the Islamic period, namely, that Redemption will bring upon the conversion of the nations.[68] However, it seems to be quite common among Qabbalists. Generally speaking, the two contending conceptions could be explained as signifying the split between the two major spiritual trends within Hispano-Jewish society. It was the rationalistic trend, deeply rooted in Spanish consciousness, with its universalistic outer-directed *weltanschaaung*, and ongoing conscious dialogue with non-Jewish culture that emphasized the universalistic aspect of the religious (and humane) Utopia. On the other hand, the Qabbalistic trend with its distinct particularistic nature, rejecting the nations, Christianity in particular, as representing the forces of Impurity in the world, left no common ground for a dialogue with Christian religion and culture in the present stage of history, and it could hardly be conceived that it will share a positive part in the future scheme of *Jewish* Redemption. Christianity is Amaleq, and the war declared in ancient times by the Lord against that arch-enemy was eternal.[69] It was mainly in Qabbalistic circles that the revenge motif, as found in the Midrashic and apocalyptic literature could be adopted, and the Expulsion only intensified it.[70] This view certainly could not be expected to be expressed throughout most of the history of the Jews in Spain in the philosophically oriented *intelligentsia*.

3.6. Other motifs in Saba's Scheme

As to other basic elements of Redemption, Saba's attitude might seem paradoxical at first glance. Being a person who believed that the major theme of the entire Bible is redemption, a man who devoted a considerable amount of attention to this theme, Saba almost does not care to discuss various aspects of it. When Saba studies the subject in depth in order to draw conclusions about the different stages of redemption such as, *Yemot ha-Mashi'aḥ*, *Òlam Habba*, and *Teḥiyyat ha-Metim*, he leaves the reader with the distinct feeling that, after all, it is of secondary importance.[71] He does give us details here and there, and one can attempt to assemble the parts of the puzzle as Saba would have done had he written a separate treatise on the subject.

But, was that picture of any importance to him? Or better, was it important enough for him to communicate it clearly to his readers? The answer is affirmative only insofar as it has any bearing on Israel's life in the present. Consequently, an emphasis is put on Biblical allusions to the present, on the coming of the Redemption, on its enduring nature of quiescence, the downfall of Edom, etc. It was this message of encouragement in the most trying and crucial time of Jewish history - the period of "the pangs of the

Messiah," that Saba attempted to communicate through his works. As a preacher, he naturally assumed the mission of the post-destruction prophet, whose main task was to heal the national spirit through uplifting the morale of the demoralized and despondent.

3.7. National Theodicy

The problem of theodicy is part of our topic and its importance is evidenced in the multiplicity of solutions offered by Saba. The emphasis is put squarely upon collective national suffering.[72]

Saba recognizes the difficulties in convincing people to accept what seems to them unjust. Ultimately, he identifies with such people saying that "even though it might seem to us that God perverts judgment in delaying our redemption etc., this is (in truth) false and only a product of the imagination since there is no fault in Him."[73] Saba also knows that all his answers might not be sufficient to provide complete peace of mind to the people and he says:

> ...and he (Esau) had long peaceful life, and all his people [*ve-khol àmo*], 'their houses are safe from fear, neither is the rod of God upon them' (Job. 21,9), And Jacob from his youth...'was not safe, neither had he rest' (ibid, 3,26) and all his people [*ve-khol àmo*] and sons lived in sorrow and worry... And especially to hint that as a ladder which has stages, likewise 'there is a high one that watches over him that is high' (Ecc. 5,7), 'and these are ancient and profound things, exceeding deep, who can find it out' (ibid., 7,24), and one should not wonder how and why, for He alone knows it.[74]

But this does not prevent Saba from utilizing almost the entire arsenal of answers to be found in Jewish tradition. He does not doubt that the suffering of Israel comes as a punishment for sins,[75] but God is not without mercy. He informs them that they sinned and tries to direct them to the right path. The consistency of the suffering is to be taken as grace, for if the accumulation of sins were not constantly balanced, Israel would suffer much more.[76] Besides, Israel and the nations are like the heart and the body. The former suffers more for its centrality and importance.[77]

Another benefit of Israel's suffering is its continued existence, for the external pressure contributes to it. In this respect, it is not a curse but rather a divine blessing.[78]

Saba does not forget to connect suffering and reward. The excess of the former will yield dividends where it really counts - in the World to Come. Israel is being punished in the present in order to earn the supreme reward.[79] Indeed, the "seating arrangement" will depend on the amount of suffering:

> For then will be there all those who were assigned to life in Jerusalem, each one according to his deserved share in direct proportion to the amount of pain and misery he suffered.[80]

Saba generalizes about this problematic issue: "for what one considers to be bad could be good and no man knows...but God."[81] The faithful should take a deep breath and wait until the waves pass. The present has its religious long-range purpose. Those who pass the tests will come out purified, ready for their just reward.

As in the issue of redemption, one should not look for great ideological innovations. Saba was mainly a preacher, not a profound thinker. By trying to dwell on his view of technical terminology, we would be doing the job of a technician and miss the main point in the process. The uniqueness of Saba's treatment of our subject is in certain nuances, but more so in its degree of intensity. The general definition of the problem and the constructive directions of thought for treating it had been already prescribed by R. Judah Halevi in abbreviated form. Shifting the focus from the individual to the national realm, he says:

> Thus it is with (his own troubles, and also with) general ones. If his mind is disturbed by the length of the exile and the diaspora and degradation of his people, he finds comfort first in 'acknowledging the justice of the decree,' as said before; then in being cleansed from his sins; then in the reward and recompense awaiting him in the world to come, and the attachment to the Divine Influence in this world. If an evil thought make him despair of it, saying: 'Can these bones live?' - our traces being thoroughly destroyed and our history decayed, as it is written: they say: 'our bones are dried' - let him think of the manner of the delivery from Egypt[82]... He will, then, find no difficulty in picturing how we may recover our greatness, though only one of us may have remained.[83]

It is precisely a condensed passage such as this that reveals the prominence and centrality of this theme in Saba's works.

NOTES

[1] This phenomenon can, in part, account for the Jewish tendency to join new movements, explore new avenues of thought on the universal level, and to establish nationalistic movements of a self-redemptive character. Some sources referring explicitly to problems caused by despair during the 14th-16th centuries will be discussed in the following pages.

[2] Baer's volume, *Galut* (New York, 1947) contains, not without reason, only Sefardic theoretical views of the problem (ibid, pp. 48ff, 54). There were other elements, characterizing the general transition of medieval European Jewry to the modern era, that contributed to the changes in Jewish thought; but it seems to me that the "Sefardic factor" has not yet been studied (See J. Elbaum, "Aspects of Hebrew Ethical Literature in 16th Century Poland," *Jewish Thought in the Sixteenth-Century*, Cambridge, Mass., 1984, p. 153. Ben-Sasson examined possible Sefardic influence in Eastern Europe in the areas of philosophy and rationalism only (*Hagut ve-Hanhagah*, p. 15), while one must look for it in all spheres of religious literary creativity. (For some influence of Ẓ.M. see below n. 7 and in the Epilogue below. See also *Matteh Mosheh*, Frankfurt, 1720, nos. 250, 832). On Elbaum's more recent contributions see below p. 178 n. 1.

[3] *Major Trends in Jewish Mysticism*, New York, 1961, p. 247. In a more recent parallel passage Scholem ignores the intervening period completely (*Elements of the Kabbalah and its Symbolism*, Jerusalem, 1976, p. 105).

[4] See e.g., I. Tishbi, "Upheaval in the Research Of Kabbalah," *Ẓion* 54, 1989, pp. 213-18. M. Idel, "What is New is Forbidden," *Ẓion* 54, 1989, pp. 230-35.

[5] About other factors that must be added as causes for the Messianic mood see A. Gross, "The Ten Tribes and the Kingdom of Prester John - Rumors and Investigations before and after the Expulsion from Spain,"*Peàmim* 48, 1991, pp. 5-41.

[6] Perhaps it would be more accurate to make a further distinction between the years immediately after the Expulsion, when the pendulum swung to the extreme of despair as many adopted Christianity (the sources are unanimous on the great extent of conversions to Christianity in the year immediately following the Expulsion. See e.g. Gross, Messianic Commentary, p. 396, fol. 41a.), and subsequent years, when apocalyptic epistles, Messianic predictions and calculations coupled with the resettlement and return to a more routine and normalized life (See e.g. R. Abraham Shamsulo's description of the process of remarrying in *Maámar veha-Ádam Yada*, published by M. Benayahu, *Michael* 7, 1982, p. 203. See also above, p. 12), created a more stable situation. This would vary, of course, with the different absorbing communities, depending largely on socio-economic factors. Generally one might note a conspicuous decline in the literary preoccupation with the Expulsion, its causes and its aftermaths as time goes by. A good example of this process is R. Joseph Yaàveẓ, who wrote his *Ór ha-Ḥayyim* blaming philosophy for the Expulsion, in the first year after it. A year later he wrote *Ḥasdei ha-Shem*, in order to help those who could not fully accept what had happened to them. However, interestingly enough, in later writings the impression of the Expulsion is waning. That great event that seems to have had a profound traumatic effect on Yaàveẓ leaves almost no trace in his commentaries on Psalms and Tractate Avot.

[7] This is so, since the concept of *galut*, in its traditional interpretations, has potential as a driving religious force through the basic recognition that the state of affairs is less than ideal and the Jew must act positively in order to bring about a change in his present national status. For a general classification of despair, see R. Harper, *The Path of Darkness*, Cleveland, 1968, and the bibliography in the footnotes).

[8] *Sefer ha-Ḥayyim*, Jerusalem, 1968, p. 95, and again a little differently: ...ומיד כאשר גבר עלינו חסד השי״ת לתת אותנו לחן לחסד ולרחמים לפני שובינו מיד אנחנו מתנחמים וחושבים עצמינו כנגאלים (ibid., p. 98). Here he complains about a "confusion" between a respite from occasional troubles and the real Redemption. This motif is borrowed from the writings of Sefardic pre- and post-Expulsion moralists. We find it in Alami's *Iggeret Mussar* and later in Sa-

ba (see above pp. 101-2). R. Ḥayyim was deeply influenced by that tradition as published, and also as transmitted orally by his mentor, R. Yiẓḥaq Sefardi, the only one he cares to mention in his introduction to *Iggeret Tiyyul* (Jerusalem, 1957, p. 13) . We intend to devote a separate study to some aspects of this influence. For now suffice it to say that he read Ẓ.M., was influenced by it, and saw in Saba a worthy authority (e.g. *Sefer ha-Ḥayyim*, p. 96). Compare also H.H. Ben-Sasson, "Wealth and Poverty in the Teaching of the Preacher R. Ephrayim of Lenczyca," *Tarbiẓ* 19, 1954, p. 144-163, n. 69.

[9] E.g. *Sefer ha-Ḥayyim*, pp. 110-11. (R. Ḥayyim's long discussion concerning what the prophets knew and believed is a reaction to a certain measure of skepticism caused by despair). See also below n. 25.

[10] See above pp. 101ff.

[11] See above p. 12.

[12] There is only one study that deals with this issue in our period. It is a general overview of the theme (Ben-Sasson, Exile and Redemption). Another article discusses an individual view of the problem but is three generations removed from the focal point of despair (J. Hacker, "Despair of the Redemption in the Writings of R. Solomon le-Beit ha-Levi," *Tarbiẓ* 39, 1970, pp. 195-213). Some of the many similarities to Saba are striking. However, they do not indicate a direct influence. About the lack of extant rabbinic writings from this period in Fez, see below n. 24.

[13] Ẓ.M. Deut. p. 47b (and less explicit in Lev, p. 33b). This question is also raised by *Sefer Ḥasidim*, no. 411 (See also B.T. Bava Batra, p. 88b).

[14] Ẓ.M., p. 48a.

[15] This argument rests on the fact that at the end of the Deuteronomic version there is no consolation. (See *Yosef ha-Meqaneh*, p. 62. The Christian claim seems to have relied on this section. See also A. Lukyn Williams, *Adversus Judaeos*, Cambridge, 1935, pp. 50, 127, 290). As for the Christian claim in connection with despair, see Arama, *Ḥazut Qashah*, chapter 12, p. 31a, and Yaàveẓ, *Ḥasdei ha-Shem*, New York, 1934, p. 15. (The author tells us in his introduction that he wrote it in an attempt to raise the low morale of the Spanish exiles, p. 12).

[16] Ẓ.M. Deut. p. 54b. Isa. 50,1 was used in anti-Christian polemics (See D. Berger, *The Jewish-Christian Debate in the High Middle Ages*, Philadelphia, 1979, pp. 31, 35) and an example of the 15th century, R. Ḥayyim Ibn Mussa, *Magen ve-Romaḥ*, Jerusalem, 1970, p. 105.

[17] Here again Saba uses the expression זה שקר, which is significant since one can often link passages in his writings through the concept of *gezerah shavah*. The passage appears in the context of what seems to have been a sermon for *Shabbat Shuvah* (the Sabbath before the Day of Atonement). Its subject is the logic behind the idea of repentance. The nature of the discussion is such that it is directed to the individual but, as a digression, Saba turns to the issue's national dimension, saying that proper national repentance can bring about the Redemption and that there is no need to despair over previous sins (See also ibid pp. 52a, 53b). Shifting swiftly from the individual to the national level is characteristic of Saba.

[18] *Ìqqarim* 4, 48.

[19] We suppose that, theoretically, it could be maintained along a Qabbalistic line of thought, claiming that Samael is reigning at present and Israel is doomed. But our case is a reflection of human feelings of simple people, some of them survivors by the skin of their teeth, who seek not theology but faith and hope.

[20] להיות ענין מעשה בראשית ענין נשגב מאד כאומרם, ולא במעשה מרכבה בשנים...לכן אין ראוי להאריך ולדבר בו, אלא על דרך כלל נוכל להוציא מכאן שני דברים, האחד יכולת השם וגודלו, והשני מעלת ישראל שכל העולם לא נברא אלא בשבילם (Ẓ.M. Gen. p. 3a)

[21] The theme of despair due to the extraordinary length of the present Exile appears several times, but Saba does not seem to see in it one of the major immediate causes for despair, an approach that can be understood in a decade when contemporary suffering was the foremost concern.

[22] ולי היכולת הגמור בכל הזמנים (Ẓ.M. Gen. p. 22b). For a review of the arguments, see ibid., Ex. 17, 9b-l0b. (About Saba's attempts to connect the end of the Portion to its beginning, see above p. 66?).

[23] Elsewhere Saba explicitly relates doubt in God's omnipotence to despair: "...'I lift my hand to heaven' (Deut. 32,40), since it says above 'See now that I, I am He' (ibid 32,39), which refers to Israel who will be transgressors and sinners and will not recognize God's omnipotence and grace, since they have almost despaired of the Redemption. Therefore He says to them: 'See now [*àtah*],' namely, see and look at that time [*èt*] which is the time of the fullness of time [*be-ìtah*] I will bring to pass"(Isa. 60,22), how I possess the absolute power...and I can put to death and revive, to wound and to heal. (Ẓ.M. Deut. p. 69b, and see also ibid., Gen. p. 75b).

When Gideon asks the angel about the subservience of Israel to Midian, he complains: "Now the Lord has abandoned us," (Jud. 6,13). Saba comments "as if He does not have the power to rescue" (ibid., p. 24a). God's omnipotence is stressed in numerous places (e.g. Ex. p. 27a-b).

[24] This trend was strong right after the Expulsion from Spain, (see above n. 6). It certainly weakened with time, as the exiles settled in new Jewish centers. In 1500, their situation in Fez, for example, only started to improve (D. Corcos, The Jews of Morocco from the Expulsion, p. 269), and there were occasional debates with Christian priests (ibid, p. 272-73). While Jewish sources do not tell us of conversions, we can infer from Inquisitorial records that there were Marranos who returned to Judaism only to change their minds later. (See H. Beinart, "Fez, A Center of Return to Judaism in the XVI Century," *Sefunot* 8, 1964, especially, p. 321, n. 1). I believe that such cases were not that rare, and the study of Inquisitorial archives should substantiate this. (Concerning the beginning of the 17th century, see idem in *S.W. Baron's Jubilee Volume*, Hebrew part, Jerusalem, 1974, pp. 15-39). About the Hebrew sources see, J. Gerber, *Jewish Society in Fez*, p. 50. The author notes the lack of information about returning Marranos and their problems.

[25] In turn, we can assume that most of those returning to Spain did it not out of conviction but for practical considerations. We are not trying to suggest that Saba addresses himself only to people who were on the verge of mental and religious collapse, packing their few belongings in order to return to Spain. He certainly felt the natural obligation to raise the morale of "his people"- as a devoted preacher should feel. But, at times, he must have thought of the results of extreme despair and tried to avoid it. He was aware of the fate of many exiles earlier (Gross, Messianic Commentary, p. 396), and his description of the attraction of the Jews to Egypt and their wish to return there from the desert reflects the parallel to contemporary circumstances and his awareness of the problem: והשם סבב שימררו חייהם בעבודה קשה כדי שיאנקו בני ישראל ויזעקו לצאת משם. כי לולא זה לרוב שמנינות הארץ וטובתה, כגן ה' כארץ מצרים והם אזרחים בה אחר מאתיים שנה לא ירצו לצאת ממנה. והעד נתנה ראש ונשובה מצריימה (Z.M. Ex. p. 12b. We also find descriptions of Spain as paradise. See S. Dapiera's *Diwan* [ed. S. Bernstein], New York, 1942, p. 55, line 17, and T.F. Glick, *Islamic and Christian Spain in the Early Middle Ages*, Princeton, 1979, pp. 53-4. For a 17th-century expression of this idea see Y. Kaplan, *From Christianity to Judaism*, Jerusalem, 1982, p. 273).

There is one more heretical claim: ...בענין שלא יאמר כי משה עשה דבר מדעתו...וכל זה לפי שראה אורך הגלות ואולי בצרותיהם יאמרו דברים לא כן (Ẓ.M. Num. p. 45b. This seems to be the only place where Saba might be referring to people who doubt the divine authenticity of parts of the Torah. Cf. Baḥya's comment on Num. 16,29).

[26] The following lines in parentheses were omitted by censorship.

[27] Ẓ.M. Gen. pp. 6b-7a. (The last sentence was quoted by Ben-Sasson, Exile, p. 218). Later, there follows a passage relating Ps. 124 to the various exiles. A few lines describe the latest one (most of it was censored): אזי עבר על נפשנו המים הזידונים, כנגד מלכות אדום שהיא מלכות זדון כאמרו בו, זדון לבך השיאך, וזהו, המים הזידונים. ואמר ג"כ, אזי עבר על נפשנו, לפי שדעתם ג"כ להעבירנו על דת ולצוד נפשותינו כמו שראינו בעינינו בגירוש פורטוגאל. ברוך שלא נתננו וגו', נפשנו כציפור נמלטה, להורות על רוב הצרות... (The "escape of the bird" does not refer to more than a few).

The same feelings in the form of dry statistics - correct or incorrect - are presented by Abravanel in the introduction to his Wells of Salvation: ...היה מספר בני ישראל בשנה ההיא (רנ"ב)...שלש מאות נפש אדם...ויהי היום לקץ ארבע שנים לגירושו לא נשאר מהם כיום כעשרת אלפים טף ונשים בכל ארצות גרותו ומחוזות גלותו The exaggeration of the loss only stresses the gloomy situation as perceived by the author. This was written even before the Expulsion from Portugal. Abravanel addresses the problem of despair in his commentary on Ps. 115, 116, 118. From his discussion we can distinguish three factors: a) the decrease in numbers; b) the length of the Exile; c) the excess of suffering in its various forms (*Zevaḥ Pesaḥ*, Venice 1545, pp. 57b-59b). Abravanel's explicit reference to the claim that the prophets' consoling predictions are false does not appear in Saba's writings. (See however, above n. 25, and compare Hacker, Despair, p. 198).

28 E.g. R. Baḥya ben Asher in his commentary on Gen. 17,20 and in *Kad ha-Qemaḥ*, in *Kitvei R. Baḥya* [ed. Chavel], Jerusalem, 1970, p. 116 (*Geulah*). MaHaRaL in the end of his introduction to *Neẓaḥ Yisraél*.

29 L. Landau, *Des Apologetische Schreiben des Joshua Lorqi*, Antwerp, 1906, and Baer, History II, p. 143. It is clear that this is a good description of the prevailing mood within the camp of faithful Jews. It was definitely a major, if not the major, cause for voluntary conversions in the years following that catastrophe (and might well have been the root of Lorqi's own conversion some years later). Despair of the same type is attested to after an accelerated pace of voluntary conversions in the wake of the disputation of Tortosa: ...ובעבור זה כל זמן שנראה אות הברית הזה קיים באומה, אף אם נראה תוקף הצרות העוברות עלינו תמיד, לא בעבור זה נתייאש מן הגאולה. כי אנחנו דומים היום לחולה שהוא קרוב למות וכל האנשים אומרים עליו שאין לו כח לחיות, כי כל עוד שנראה בו דבר מן החיות נשאר לא נתייאש מחולי זה. וכן אף אם כל האומות אומרות עלינו שאנחנו באפס תקוה ושאבדה תקותינו נגזרנו לנו, הנה כאשר נראה אות הברית...נדע בודאי שעדיין יש בנו כח לחיות ושע"י הקשר הזה תשוב האומה לקדמותה ולאיתנה ולהדבק בענין האלוהי... (Albo, *Ìqqarim*, 4, 45, and compare *Kad ha-Qemaḥ* in note 28). Albo seems to see the influence of Christian propaganda as an effect of the despair, due to the dark historical reality. (Differently and not so powerfully, we find it expressed by S. Bonafed. See F. Talmage, "The Francesc de Sant Jordi - Solomon Bonafed Letters," in *Studies in Medieval Jewish History and Literature* I [I. Twersky ed.], Cambridge, Mass. 1979, p. 354). A different diagnosis, which could be termed as "numbness," is given by P. Duran, *Qinnah*, in *Maàseh Éfod*, p. 191. (See also F. Talmage, "Trauma at Tortosa: The Testimony of Abraham Rimoch," *Mediaeval Studies* 47, 1985, p. 409.)

30 Saba does not mention explicitly those who were abandoning the ship without any attempt at rationalization, and we assume there were such people. He does mention such a phenomenon while describing the period between the announcement of Haman's edict and the date set for its implementation (see above p. 24?). But here, when he fights those who had arguments to support themselves, there is, of course, no echo of the silent potential deserters.

31 Ẓ.M. Deut., p. 48a. This passage comes at the end of Saba's long effort at equating the Blessings with the Curses (see above p. 219?).

32 The adjective אכזרי should not be taken here as implying that God actually derives pleasure from torturing Israel. It means only that there is no good end to which the suffering is the means, but that the suffering unto death itself is the end.

33 Ẓ.M. Num. p. 13b. One must note that there is no mention here of philosophy as a cause for despair, as one finds alleged by R. Isaac Arama. He sees the tragedy of Exile mainly in its length, that leads to agreement with Christian claims concerning the abandonment of Israel by God. Nonetheless, those who remain Jews outwardly, do so, among other reasons, because they realize that Christianity has even less to offer in terms of truth, and so they are left with heretical philosophy, putting their trust not in God but in the constellations. Their beliefs, in turn, cause the Exile to go into an even lengthier and harsher "overtime," because they dissuade the simple people from repenting. Moreover, they cause religious demoralization by spreading their heresy. The effects are especially felt in the present in the depressing state of Spanish Jewry. (*Ḥazut Qashah*, ch. 12 especially pp. 31a, 33b-34a. Compare also, *Àqedat Yiẓḥaq*, 6, p. 44b). Although the circumstances of post-Expulsion North Africa cannot be equated to those

of pre-Expulsion Spain, one must remember that Saba still refers several times in very vivid fashion to Jewish philosophical antinomianism. (See above p. 85).

34 Saba believed that the theme of redemption is the key to the understanding of the whole Torah and the entire corpus of Prophets: לפי שהיא (פרשת ויחי) מפתח וחותם ומנעול הספר הזה ומפתח וחותם כל התורה כולה ומפתח וחותם כל מה שנתנבאו הנביאים כולם עד לימות המשיח...לפי שבברכת יעקב רמוזות כל הגליות והגאולות עד יבוא מורה צדק... (Ẓ.M. Gen. pp. 119b-120a. See also É.K. Ruth pp. 2a, 4a. Esther p. 1). Compare *Sefer ha-Geúlah* (*Kitvei ha-Ramban*, p. 261).

35 Below App. C.

36 On Israel's place in history as an idea of consolatory value, see above p. 131.

37 Ẓ.M. Deut. p. 48a. Compare Yaàveẓ, *Ḥasdei ha-Shem*, pp. 9ff.

38 מכל זה יראה איך התשובה ראויה לחוטא והשכל יחייב דבר זה כמו שכתבתי (ibid., p. 55a, and see above n. 16).

39 Ibid, p. 74a. There are several things that symbolize this idea (Ẓ.M. Gen. P. 97a, Ex. P. 43a, Num. P. 13b. Gross, Messianic Commentary, p. 396). Using Qabbalistic ideas to counter despair might give us an indication as to the potentially despondent people to whom Saba directed his remarks (possible indirectly through preachers reading the book, see above p. 42). This seems to be another advantage enjoyed by Qabbalah over philosophy, one that enabled the Qabbalists to rise to spiritual leadership where rationalism was doomed to failure. Human logical analysis of tragedy fails to comfort, as has been shown as early as the book of Job. (This, of course, is not to say that Saba did not use logical arguments as evidenced throughout the following pages). As to the idea itself, it has its roots in the *Zohar*, which says that Israel must be eternal since they form some of the letters of the Name (*Zohar*, II, p. 105a). But the particular symbols Saba uses seem to be original. (The change of Jacob's name to Israel, the chains on the High Priest's breast-plate, and the *Menorah* in the Temple).

40 Ẓ.M. Gen. pp. 26b-27a.

41 Oba. 1,2-4. He praises Obadiah for being the harshest of all prophets concerning Edom's destruction: וכן תמצא בעובדיה שלא נמצא בכל הנביאים מי שנתנבא על עקירת אדום כמוהו... (É.K. Ruth p. 6a). Compare this with the interesting remark by R. Ḥayyim ibn Mussa: וזאת הנבואה כבר פחדו ממנה הרבה מהנוצרים עד שאמי הכהן הגדול שבאשביליא שלא היה נביא קטן ורע כנגדן יותר מכל הנביאים כזה (D. Kaufman, "A Letter of R. Ḥayyim Ibn Mussa to His son R. Judah," *Beit Talmud* 2, Vienna, 1882, p. 122 (See also *Zohar* I, p. 171a).

42 The method is not novel. See Nachmanides' Commentery on Deut. 32, 40, and already B.T. Makkot, p. 24b.

43 Ẓ.M. Deut. pp. 63a, 64b.

44 Ibid., p. 69b.

45 Ibid., Lev. p. 35b. The context of the verse cited is God's promise to the prophet that He will not annihilate Israel.

46 וכן יוצא...שיעקב לא שם שמות בניו אלא רחל ולאה לסבה שהיו חכמות ונביאות עד שלפי דעתי ראתה עינם בענייני אלו הבנים ובקריאת השמות כל מה שראה יעקב בברכת בניו...וכל מה שראה משה בברכת השבטים...ולא די בזה אלא שאני סובר שכל הדברים העתידים שיקרו להם עד סוף העולם כלם כלולים בדברי האמהות ומדבריהם הוציא יעקב אבינו ומשה רבינו...כל מה שאמרו בברכתם...ואין בכל התורה למעלה ממנה... (Ibid. Gen. p. 72b. Saba dedicated his interpretation of this section to his sons who were taken away from him in Portugal). Compare *Sefer ha-Émunah veha-Bitaḥon*, in *Kitvei ha-Ramban* vol. 2, p. 439.

47 Ibid, p. 72b.

48 E.g. Ẓ.M. Gen. p. 7a. Lev. p. 35a, Num. p. 46a-b. Deut. pp. 46a-b. Gross, Messianic Commentary, p. 396. Some of the references come toward the end of the Reproof Sections for the obvious reason that they signify the last torments of the long Exile. In the case of Num. p. 46a-b, one must remember the significance of the location, since for Saba the end of that book is considered the end of the Torah (See above p. 126).

49 It would be wrong to think that all this was for public consumption only, because in that case we would have to assume that Saba himself did not believe in his "Midrashic" interpretations. If Saba had invented them strictly for his readers without being convinced of their authenticity (or at least of their probability), he would have looked for more convincing textual proofs in order to substantiate his argument about the

allusions of Scriptures to the present low state of the Jewish people.

The impression that Saba uses the Bible for his purposes indiscriminately and without any discipline or guiding rules, would also be inaccurate. To begin with, we must realize that he follows a Midrashic sort of interpretation. A perfect example of this is the Midrash on Ex. 25, 3-5, which Saba quotes: כמוזכר בזאת הפרשה במדרש השכם...זהב, כנגד מלכות בבל דכתיב, אנת הוא רישיה דדהבא. וכסף, גלות מדי דכתיב ביה, הכסף נתון לך. ונחשת, כנגד יון דכתיב ביה, מעוהי ודרעוהי די נחש (השווה: דניאל ב׳, ל״ב. מדרש תהלים ו׳, ב׳). ותכלת, ...ועורות אילים מאדמים, כנגד מלכות אדום דכתיב ביה, מן האדום האדום הזה (Ẓ.M. Ex. p. 41b-42a. and similarly in Lev. p. 14a). This is the style Saba uses and he, of course, follows specific Midrashic homilies such as the above-mentioned one. When his allegorical interpretation is novel, it follows two limiting rules, either a) the subject matter has been traditionally a source for such interpretations, or; b) the context is one of the following: blessings, dreams, names, poetry, and psalms. (One additional rule is that the phrase or verse can be divided elegantly into four parts). The version of the "Covenant Between the Pieces" refers to the Exile in Egypt, but already the Midrash extends it to the Four Exiles (e.g. *Bereshit Rabbah*, 44, 15 and 17). Saba has a slightly different interpretation which he extends to another verse, as well as to the following chapter which apparently deals with another matter altogether (Ẓ.M. Gen. pp. 36b-37b). The chapters in Genesis which relate Jacob's meeting with Esau served as a model for future encounters between the descendants of those twins [*maàseh ávot simman la-banim*]. Saba follows the tradition again, extending the basic method by applying it to new verses (ibid, pp. 91a-94a. See also above p. 55).

As to the second rule which is concerned mainly with form, it seems sometimes as if Saba carries it almost *ad absurdum*, but his model was the Midrash that interprets even the dreams of Pharoah's chief butler and chief baker as reflecting (on their esoteric level) the future exiles. (See Ginzberg, *Legends* vol. 2, p. 61-2). Saba, of course, does not miss the opportunities inherent in Jacob's and Moses' blessings, the Song on the Sea, the names of the Tribes, numerous psalms, etc.

50 Ẓ.M. Gen. pp. 6a, 72b, 77a-b, 86b. Deut. p. 40b. Saba foresees a domination of Israel over the nations, but the point in all that is: וכל הממשלה תינתן לישראל בענין שלא יהיה עוד גלות כמו שהיה בשאר הימים (ibid, Gen. p. 6b. The enduring character of the third Temple is strongly emphasized in Saba's commentary on Hagai and Zechariah (Gross, Messianic Commentary, pp. 392-401). This is also the idea with which Saba chose to conclude his commentary on *Avot*, fol. 46r. ff).

51 *Zohar* I, 139b.

52 This seems to be connected to the Qabbalistic discussion of the phrase "a king enclosed by his guard" (Cant. 7,6), which is interpreted as referring to *Tiféret* which is "imprisoned" during Israel's Exile. (Ẓ.M. Deut. p. 35a-b). That whole passage is a straight Hebrew translation of the Aramaic in *Tiqqunei Zohar* (6, pp. 21a-23b). Parts of it were censored in the 1567 edition but do appear in the Warsaw edition which is based on an earlier edition.

53 In the end of his comment on the passage from the *Zohar* Saba adds: שוב ראיתי שבשנת רנ״ו היינו בפורטוגאל וכו׳ (Gross, Massianic Commentary, p. 401). Tishbi conjectures that he was referring to King Manuel who, upon ascending the throne, liberated in 1496 all the Jews who had been enslaved in 1493. This sentence is obviously fragmented. Its end "etc." is explained by Tishbi (Messianism, p. 96) as referring to a detailed account in the introduction to Ẓ.Ḥ. which unfortunately is not extant. This is improbable, since Saba added a short bibliographical note concerning the loss of his books in Portugal at the end of Ẓ.Ḥ., contrary to all of his other commentaries, where he recounted it (admitedly in a longer fashion) in the introductions. Thus it is likely that if there were an introduction to Ẓ.Ḥ., it dealt only with the nature of the tractate and the commentary. The relatively short autobiographical note in Ẓ.Ḥ. can be explained by the fact that he had already recounted it at least three times in other commentaries. As to the the liberation of the Jews by Manuel, Saba does not refer to it at all in any of his writings.

54 Ẓ.M. Num. 38a.

55 Ẓ.M. Deut. p. 68a-b.

[56] A.H. Silver, *A History of Messianic Speculations*, Boston, 1927, p. 105. From Saba's description of his great collection of Qabbalistic writings, it seems probable that he read this book. This, of course, is not conclusive evidence, especially since we are told that *Sefer ha-Temunah*, which was prominent in Qabbalistic circles in Byzantium, was not quoted by pre-Expulsion Qabbalists in Spain (M. Idel, "The Spanish Qabbalah after the Expulsion," in *The Sephardi Legacy* [H. Beinart ed.], Jerusalem, 1992, p. 509 n. 20).

[57] Tishbi, Messianism, p. 112.

[58] For a discussion of Saba's visionary jail mate see below App. D.

[59] ויש לנו להבין ולחקור באלו המסעות שלא לחינם נכתבו בתורה...מיום אשר גלינו מארצנו עד היום הזה שהוא קרוב מאלף וחמש מאות שנה, יעלו המסעות לאין מספר כשתוציא אלף וחמש מאות שנה לארבעים ארבעים שנה, ובכל ארבעים שנה ארבעים ושנים מסעות. וכל שכן שאם נמנה המסעות שהלכנו מעת שגלינו מספרד עד היום שהם שמונה שנים תמצא שהם יותר מאלף מסעות בים וביבשה, בענין שראוי שכל אלו המסעות יהיו כתובים בספר זכרון...וישלח לנו שני משיחים... (Ẓ.M. Num. p. 46b). The marches assume this significance partially because they are written at the end of Numbers which is, according to Saba, the real end of the Torah (See above p. 173?).

[60] Ẓ.M. Deut. p. 36b, and also ibid., p. 68b. This hope must be understood against the historical background of the rise of the Turks. Saba seems to have deduced it from the *Tiqqunei Zohar*. (Apparently there was also an ancient Christian tradition that connected the fall of Rome with the eschaton. See T. Mommsen, "Augustine on Progress," in *Medieval and Renaissance Studies* [Ithaca, New York], 1959, pp. 268-69.) Saba might have relied on the Talmudic prediction that עתידה רומי שתיפול ביד פרס (B.T. Yoma, 10a). Persia was for him, as it was for others in this period, Turkey (Ẓ.M. Num. p. 46a, and see Hacker, Israel Among the Nations, p. 87.)

[61] É.K. Ruth p. 41b. This dichotomy is expressed in Saba's stress, on the one hand, upon the Redemption through the merit of the Patriarchs (the religious status of Israel notwithstanding) and, on the other hand in his unrelenting appeal for repentance upon which the coming of the redemption depends.

[62] J. Hacker, "On the intellectual Character etc.," *Sefunot* [n.s.] 2 (17), 1983, pp. 44-5.

[63] Ms. Moscow, Ginzburg 214, fol. 154b. See also, Gross, The Ten Tribes, p. 35.

[64] Below App. C. É.K. Ruth, p. 2a. That kingdom is the mightiest (Ẓ.M. Gen. p. 6b) and has never been subdued (ibid Num. p. 30a. Taken from *Zohar* II, p. 237a), and as it had been prophecied, it has reached high heavens in its wordly success (App. C.). For some reason, the heavy taxes seem to have especially bothered Saba a great deal (Num. p. 91b, p. 32a. Num. 32a Deut. p. 4b. É.K. Esther p. 13, and more). See also above ch. 1 n. 166.

[65] Z.M. Gen. p. 75b, 91b, 127a. Num. p. 32a.

[66] Ibid., Deut. p. 36b. É.K. Ruth p. 23b. Edom is the villain while Ishmael is almost ignored, because Edom is the last Exile and nobody else is going to have domination over Israel although, temporarily, Ishmael does exercise lordship over them (e.g. É.K. Esther p. 66) and occupies the Holy Land (Ẓ.M. Gen. p. 37a). The place of Islam in Saba's scheme of redemption seems to have been described in the following passage where he interprets Ps. 20: "And He also alluded to Edom and the Ishmaelites. 'Some in chariots' - the people of Edom, 'and some with horses' - the people of Ishmael. 'But we will pronounce the Name of the Lord. They will kneel down' - the riders of the chariots, 'and will fall' - the riders of the horses, 'but we will rise...'"(Ẓ.M. Gen. p. 91b-92a). Saba does not clarify, however, the question of whether they will face each other in war or will face Israel. (Compare also Judah Halevi's poem in H. Schirmann, *Hebrew Poetry in Spain and Provence* vol. I, Jerusalem, 1954, p. 479).

[67] לעשות פרץ באומות (É.K. Ruth p. 43b). On the Midrashic origin of this interpretation see L. Ginzberg, *Legends* 5, p. 336, n. 92.

[68] I.J. Yuval, "Vengeance and Damnation, Blood and Defamation: From Jewish Martyrdom to Blood Libel Accusations," *Ẓion* 58, 1993, pp. 45-50.

[69] Cf. Yuval, Vengeance and Damnation, p. 49. The remaining historical question concerns the prevalent view among the masses in Spain. The methodological problem

lies, of course, in the lack of writings of such classes. On the basis of implicit polemics against popular conceptions of Messianism such as that of Maimonides in the end of his *Mishneh Torah* (Yuval, Vengeance and Damnation, p. 47 n. 64), I would venture to suggest that they cannot be represented by the majority of the authors, on whose writings historians rely in their attempt to reconstruct a generalized version of the Hispano-Jewish view. It seems to me that we would find here great affinity to the "Ashkenazic mind". As to the latter, although we do find a definit emphasis on the bloody revenge during the Messianic process, it refers more to those who were involved in the killing of Jews. The "conversion of the Gentiles" motif, found (like all other motifs) already in the Bible, is played down but exists (See sources quoted by Yuval, pp. 42, 44-5). In other words, the revenge, limited in its scope, will bring upon the repentance of the others.

70 This motif is prominent in *Kaf ha-Qetoret*. According to this author the Divinely ordained revenge will include even those who died many years before the Messianic era: כל אויבי ישראל יקומו לתחייה למען יקבלו את ענשם פעם אחת מיד ישראל (p. 43b). On the centrality of this motif in Abravanel's works see Netanyahu, Abravanel, pp. 226-8. As Scholem put it, Abravanel, who was a rationalist thinker, "compromised or gave into the apocalyptic tradition," seemingly under the pressure of the tragic circumstances of his generation (G. Scolem, "Two Medieval Attitudes to Messianism," *Explications and Implications: Writings on Jewish Heritage and Renaissance* vol. 2, Tel Aviv, 1989, p. 237).

71 Only once does Saba devote a lengthy discussion to a "technical" issue, namely, the order of the stages. It consists mainly of a long quotation from R. Joseph Giqqatillia, with whom Saba seems to disagree but not in a definite manner (É.K. Ruth, p. 4b-5b, and compare Manor, p. 149-50). Saba does not care to clarify some obvious contradictions with which Manor tries to wrestle.

72 Only a few times does Saba discuss the suffering of the individual without mentioning the national dimension of the problem (Ẓ.M. Gen. p. 122b, Lev. p. 16b. Num. p. 29a, Deut. p. 18b).

73 É.K. Ruth, p. 4a.

74 לעשות פרץ באומות Ẓ.M. Gen. p. 63a. The same answer is given for the problem on the individual level. (Num. p. 29a).

75 I.e., not observing the commandments. He singles out neglect of the study of the Torah and not honoring it (Ẓ.M. Gen. p. 64a. Ex. p. 57b. É.K. Esther, p. 49. Ẓ.Ḥ. fol. 26r. On the reasons for the expulsions, see Ẓ.M. Lev. p. 32a and our discussion of that passage, above p.140ff). For sources explaining Exile as a punishment, see S. Rosenberg, "Exile and Redemption in Jewish Thought in the Sixteenth Century: Contending Conceptions," *Jewish Thought in the Sixteenth Century,* Cambridge Mass, 1984, p. 404.

76 כלומר, כל שאלתי ובקשתי...ולא ישכח להביא ייסורים על עמו דבר יום ביומו, כי זה חסד גדול...ואם לאו ועזבתים...זמן רב ואח"כ אפרע מהם הכל, ובזה ומצאוהו רעות רבות...לפי שהם חייבים לי מזמן רב (Ẓ.M. Deut. p. 58b. Gen. 61b. Similarly, Yaàvez̧, in *Ḥasdei ha-Shem*, p. 20).

77 Ẓ.M. Ex. p. 34b. Gross, Messianic Commentary, p. 392. (Taken from the *Zohar* III, p. 221a. See also W. Bacher, "Judaeo-Christian Polemics in the Zohar," JQR [o.s.] 3, 1891, pp. 781-2).

78 ורמז להם שהצרות והעינויים מקיימים אותם...בגלותם...אבל כשהם שלוים ושקטים על שמריהם אין זה טוב להם...הייסורים מעמידים אותו בכל הגלויות ויוציאוהו משם ובאלו היסורים היה להם מציאות וקיום (Ẓ.M. Deut. p. 64b. Lev. p. 36a, and ibid, p. 15b, and Gen. p. 126a, citing R. Joseph Qimḥi in his commentary on Isaiah. See also Ben-Sasson, "Expressions of the Uniqueness of Israel in the 12th Century," *Peraqim* 2, 1969-74, p. 206, and also *Zohar* II, p. 47a. III, p. 199a). This idea reminds us of a later explanation for the survival of Israel, namely, that of Spinoza, who attributed it mainly to the external pressure of antisemitism. (Of course, the latter is a secular view while the former incorporates it in the divine plan that ensures the Jews' cleaving to God). See now Y.H. Yerushalmi, "Spinoza on the Existence of the Jewish People," *Proceedings of the Israeli National Academy for the Sciences* 6, Jerusalem, 1983.

In the historical context, Saba virtually reverses the arguement, saying that what was claimed to be a cause for the final destruction of Israel is in fact the element that protects the nation from vanishing and is to be understood as divine grace. He does the same thing with Jewish immoral behavior towards Gentiles (See above p. 96).

79 Ẓ.M. Gen. p. 55b. Ex. p. 32a. Deut. 68b. É.K. Ruth p. 4b. Saba says there: וכן רצו ישראל וקבלו על עצמן הייסורים והמכות והקללות מידו של הקב"ה לכתובה ונדוניה ותוספות (ibid., p. 5a).

80 Ibid, p. 5b.

81 Ibid, p. 3b.

82 Saba, too, associates the redemption from Egypt with the future and final Redemption for the same reason, namely, in order to demonstrate the possibility of the seemingly impossible mission (e.g. Ẓ.M. Ex. p. 20b. All this goes back through Jewish tradition to Mic. 7,15).

83 *Kuzari*, New York, 1964, 3,11, p. 150.

EPILOGUE

Saba, in many ways, represents the bridge between two periods in Jewish history, and at the very least, in that of Sefardic Jewry. His generation suffered the profound experience of being uprooted from Spain, its dear homeland, the tribulations of the fifteenth century notwithstanding. The Expulsion from Spain was the last of the great expulsions, and after the forced conversion in Portugal a long historical process ran its course; almost all Western-Europe had become *Judenrein*. A new map of Jewish demography could be drawn. The East was once again to become a major site of Jewish activity and creativity. The Sefardim revived Jewish centers around the Mediterranean basin, from the Balkans, through the Land of Israel and Egypt, to North-Africa.

While trying to begin rebuilding their lives anew, the emigrés carried with them their traditions, customs and mentality. In most cases of controversies with the local established communities they had the upper hand and eventually "took over," so to speak. This is not the place to discuss the reasons for this socio-religious process. What is of significance for us here is that it lends an additional measure of importance to the study of figures such as Saba and his works, for he was a major carrier of Jewish culture in the Iberian Peninsula. He was not, perhaps, an outstanding thinker. His writings are not directed to a small elitistic circle. But this fact, coupled by his marked conservative views, is what gives Saba such great importance for the historian, because his works, on the one hand, represent trends of intellectual interests and ideas of Castilian scholars in the 15th century and, on the other hand, they reflect the mood and needs of the intended audience - the public, mainly the exiles from Iberia, as a whole.

Three factors converge in his intellectual profile as reflected in his literary output: preaching, exegesis, and Qabbalah. Sefardic tradition played a major role, blazing the way and forming each of these areas of activity in the sixteenth century.

As for Saba's influence, it would suffice here to say that Ẓ.M. was published several times in Italy and once in Poland, all within the first hundred years of his writing, and that it influenced a wide range of authors in North-Africa, Safed, Central and Eastern Europe, be it in exegetical, homiletical, moral, or Qabbalistic ideas.[1] A variety of authors of different tendencies and ideologies used Saba's writings. The Hebraist Conrad Pelikanus found it important enough to translate Ẓ.M. of "Abraham Hispanus" into Latin under the name *Fasciculus Myrrhae* around 50 years after its composition.[2] The 16th century Yemenite author R. Zechariah Al-Dahari recommended Ẓ.M. as a Qabbalistic book and wrote in his *maqqamas* a 25 lines poem in praise of it.[3] Joseph Solomon Delmedigo (YaSHaR of Candia) of the 17th century includes him in a short list of recommended commentaries on the Torah.[4] In the end of that century the anti-semite Johannes Eisenmenger quoted Saba's references to Christianity in his infamous *Entdecktes Judenthum* in order to smear Judaism.[5] The Frankists invoked Saba's authority in order to explain their conversion.[6] An important Hungarian rabbi wrote in the middle of the Second World War, quoting Ẓ.M. and É.K. time and again in his desperate attempt to prove to his Ultra-Orthodox crowd in Budapest that the Zionistic cause is in line with Jewish religion and Biblical promises, and that the only future of the nation is in *Ereẓ Israel*.[7] In recent years Ẓ.M. is enjoying a rejuvenation and was republished several times.

But beside Saba's contributions in areas of intellectual activity, we must not forget Saba the man and his positive influence, written and oral, in the unique historical context of that generation, a fact that cannot be measured exclusively by counting quotations of future generations scholars from his works. In this respect, parts of our study could serve also as a monument to other preachers who did not leave any literary traces for posterity but were instrumental in contributing to the survival of the refugees as Jews by encouraging them during ordeals on the roads and at sea, as well as during the first phases of absorption in their new havens.[8]

Through our study, we have gained an insight into the sensitive soul of a medieval spiritual leader. His perception of the problematics of Jewish life in pre-Expulsion Spain comes through very clearly in his explicit and implicit criticism. Yet, alongside this trait one senses in his works also an attentive ear and a warm heart toward the suffering, wandering, and sometimes confused brethren, who were so sure of themselves even at the twilight of their existence in Iberia. Saba and his likes helped them face the day after.

NOTES

[1] See e.g. J. Elbaum, *Repentance and Self-Flagellation in the Writings of the Sages of Germany and Poland 1348-1648*, Jerusalem, 1993. Elbaum, unlike most of his predecessors, emphasizes in this volume, as well as in other recent works of his on the intellectual history of the Jews in Eastern Europe, the tremendous influence of pre-Expulsion Spanish scholars. (Idem, *Openness and Insularity*, Jerusalem, 1990. Idem, "The Influence of Jewish-Spanish Culture on the Jews of Germany and Poland in the 16th-17th Centuries," *Culture and History, The Ino Sciaky Memorial Volume*, Jerusalem, 1987, p. 104.)

[2] It is extant in the Stiftsbibliothek, Zurich, Car. C24 (L.C. Mohlberg's Catalogue, p. 98). See F. Secret, *Les Zohar chez les Kabbalistes Chrétiens de la Renaissance*, Paris, 1964, p. 20 n. 1.

[3] Z. Al-Dahari, *Sefer ha-Mussar* [Y. Ratzaby ed.], Jerusalem, 1965, pp. 267-69.

[4] "Ílggeret Áhuz," in *Melo Ḥofnayyim* [A. Geiger ed.], Berlin, 1840.

[5] E.g *Entdecktes Judenthum* vol. I, Frankfurt am Main, 1700, pp. 505-6, 572-4, 590, 647, 652.

[6] N. Porges, "Texte de la lettre adressée par la frankistes aux communauté juives de Boheme," *REJ* 29, 1894, p. 285. G. Scholem, *Studies and Texts Concerning the History of Sabbetianism and Its Metamorphoses*, Jerusalem, 1974, p. 63.

[7] Y. S. Teicthal, *Ém ha-Banim Semekḥah*, Jerusalem, 1983. The author was murdered during the Holocaust.

[8] See e.g., Andrés Bernaldes, *Historia de los Reyes Católicos Don Fernando y Dona Isabel* tom. I, Sevilla, 1869, ch. 110, 112, pp. 335, 342.

APPENDIX A

EXTANT MANUSCRIPTS OF SABA'S WORKS

1. Ẓ.M.

Oxford, Bodley 254 (Opp. Add. 4^0 11).
Parma, Palatina 8/5 (3075-6).
J.T.S. L918 (Adler 1214).
J.T.S. L919 (Mic. 953).

2. É.K. Ruth

Frankfurt hebr. 8^0 163/3.
Oxford, Bodley 2349/1 (Opp. Add. 4^0 104).
Cambridge, Trinity 59/2.
J.T.S. L1061.

3. É.K. Esther

Frankfurt hebr. 8^0 163/2.
Cambridge, Trinity 59/1.
Warsaw 89/1.
Oxford, Bodley 2334/3 (Opp. Add. 4^0 406).
J.T.S. Mic. 5572.
Moscow, Ginzburg 935/2.

4. Ẓ.Ḥ. Avot

Frankfurt hebr. 8^0 163/1.

5. Introduction to the Ten Sefirot

Sasoon 919/20.

6. Excerpts from the Commentary on the Prayers

Sasoon 919/39.

7. Excerpts from Saba's Writings

Oxford, Bodley 972.
Budapest, Kaufman A 240.
Sasoon 988.

8. Fasciculus Myrrhae

A Latin of Ẓ.M. by the Hebraist Conrad Pelicanus is extant in the Stiftsbibliothek, Zurich, Car. C24. It was written between 4.10.1552-1.9.1554, and contains 389 folios. See F. Secret, *Le Zohar chez les Kabbalistes Chrétiens de la Renaissance*, Paris, 1964, p. 20 n. 1.

APPENDIX B

TWO EXCERPTS FROM SABA'S COMMENTARY ON TRACTATE AVOT

א. ועוד אני סבור כי הטעם שנקרא זה הפרק קנין תורה הוא להודיענו [24א] מעלת זאת המסכתא שהיא נעקרת מכל ששים מסכתות לפי שיש בה עיקר ושורש הקבלה כמו שקבלוה איש מפי איש כאומרו, משה קבל תורה מסיני, וכלה בכלל שורש המדות והמעשים והמוסרים. ואעפ״י שיש בה ענייני הדינים והדיינים והעדים כאומרו, הוי מרבה לחקור את העדים וכו׳, וכן, אל תעש עצמך כעורכי הדיינין, וכן, חכמיי הזהרו בדבריכם, וכן, החושך עצמו מן הדין, ואל תהי דן יחידי, שכל אלו הם דבריי [...] ומתפרשיי כל אלו הדבריי כשאר מסכתות באורך, אבל בעניני המוסר והמצות והמעשים האריך בזאת המסכתא יותר מבשאר המסכתות. ולכן נקראת מסכת אבות לפי שהיא כמו אבות וכל שאר המסכתות הם כמו תולדות, וזאת המסכתא דומה לתורה שבכתב שכל האזהרות ועונשים ומוסרים ומדות ודרך ארץ לפי שהתורה כלה היא תלויה במעשה דכתיי בה, ועשית ועשית. וכן אמי, לא המדי הוא העיקר אלא המעשה. ולכן עניני הדינים או רובם הם בפי משפטים וכן בשאר כללי התורה [...] ועיקריי נתפרשו באורך בתורה שבע״פ וכל זה להורות על מעלת זאת המסכתא. ולכן תמצא כי כמו שיש בתורה ה״א חומשי תורה כן יש בזאת המסכתי ה׳ פרקיי כנגדם, וכמו שסי אלה הדברים נקרא משנה תורה לפי ששם חזר משה לפרש התורה לבנים וכלל הספור הוא ספור דברי הספרים הראשונים, כן זה הפרק נקרא קנין תורה לפי שאינו פרק בפני עצמו אלא שמפי בו כל עניני המסכתי ממעלת התורה, וכן מפי בו שכר התורה הנאמי בפרקי הראשונים כאומרו, זוכה לדבריי הרבה וכו׳. וכן נקרא קנין תורה לפי שבו מפי דרך כלל ובקצרה כל מה שאמרו בה׳ פרקים הראשונים כמו שעשה משה בסי אלה הדברים, כי כן ראוי לכל מאריך בדבריו שבסוף יפרש ע״ד כללים בקצרה כל דבריו בענין שיבינו דבריו, וכן בכאן בזה הפרק רצו לפרש בקצרה כל מה שדבר בפרקי הראשונים וזהו פיי קנין תורה מה שעלה בידינו וקנינו מזאת המסכתי מענייני התורה והמצוה הכלולים בה וסדר הקבלה שאמי משה קבל תורה מסיני. ולכ״א בזה הפרק ה׳ קנינים קנה הב״ה בעולמו כנגד ה׳ חומשי תורה וכנגד ה׳ פרקים של זאת המסכתי. כנגד ה׳ חומשי תורה ואמי(!), שמים וארץ, קנין אחד כנגד ספר בראשית שמדבר בו בבריאת שמים וארץ...[24ב]...וכן אלו הה׳ קנינים הם כנגד ה׳ פרקים של זאת המסכתא...שמים וארץ קנין א׳ כנגד פרק ב׳ שמדבר בו בענין אדם הראשון שנברא במעשה בראשית כמו שפיי באומרו, אי זו דרך ישרה שיבור לו האדם, ותפארת לו מן האדם הידוע הוא אדם הראשון שרואה הצדיק כשמת...הרי לך ה׳ קנינים [25א] כנגד ה׳ פרקים כסדר שהם כתובים. ואם הייתי רוצה לשנותן שלא כסדרן יתיישבו יפה ואיני רוצה להאריך עתה יותר. העולה מדבריי שזה הפרק נקרא קנין תורה שהוא כמו פירוש לכל הפרקים הקודמים ולכן יש בו ה׳ קנינים כנגד ה׳ פרקים של המסכתי. וכן להורות על מעלת זאת המסכתא יש בה ה׳ פרקים כמנין ה׳ חומשי תורה מכוונים כנגד אלו הה׳ קנינים כמו שפירשתי. וזהו קנין תורה מה שעלה בידינו וקנינו והרוחנו מזאת המסכתא המדברת בענין התורה.

ב. והנה במכתב הראשון הארכתי יותר ואיני זכור כי בעונותי הזקנה והשכחה קפצה בי.
ולכן בני טעם טעם פת במלח / ולחמך על פני המים שלח / ויהיה בעיניך כקטורת ממולח /
ואם שגיתי לעוני סלח / ואם לאו שלי שלי ושלך שלך.

או שיאמר, כך היא דרכה של תורה פת במלח תאכל, לפי שאמ׳ למעלה, והלמד בת״ת הרי זה מתעלה, ושראוי ונהוג כבוד בחכמים וכן אמ׳ שאין כבוד אלא לחכמים ולפי שאולי יאמ׳ אדם אחר שזה כן אין ראוי לאדם לעשות המצות בפועל אלא לעסוק בתורה יומם ולילה ולידע טעמי המצות וייחוד השם ומעלתו כאומרו, השכל וידוע אותי, בענין שבזה לא יטריח את עצמו בעשיית מצות אחר שאין כבוד אלא לחכמים. לזה סמך ואמ׳, כך היא דרכה של תורה, כלומ׳ שקר אתה דובר כי הכל הולך אחר המעשה כאומרו, לא המדרש עיקר אלא המעשה, וכן אמרו שכל מי שמעשיו מרובין מחכמתו חכמתו מתקיימת עד שלזה אמ׳ דוד, כרו לי זדים שיחות אשר לא כתורתך, ומה הם השיחות והרשתות שאומרים לי, כל מצותיך אמונה, כלומ׳ תלויות באמונת הלב ולא במעשים. זה שקר גמור עד שכמעט כלוני בארץ בטענותיהם ועכ״ז אני לא עזבתי מצותיך, לעשותם בפועל. וכל התורה מזה ומזה, ועשית ושמרת ועשית ושמרת ועשית, שזאת היא המשנה והמעשה כאומרם, גדול תלמוד שמביא לידי מעשה, אבל אם לא מביא לידי מעשה אינו גדול לפי שאומ׳ ראו שלמד תורה מה מכוערים מעשיו. ולכן עיקר הכל הוא המעשה לפי שהמעשה נותנת טעם לתורה ונותנת לה ריח וטעם כמו המלח המעמדת הבשר ולכן אמרו שדומה לאילן ששרשיו מרובים שיש לו קיום גדול. וז״ש בכאן, כך היא דרכה של תורה, כלו׳ אעפ״י שאמרתי לך שתעסוק [31א] בתורה לא תחשוב שאני אומ׳ לך שתעסוק בתורה ולא במעשה כי זה שקר, אבל כך היא דרכה של תורה פת במלח תאכל, כלו׳ שפת התורה תמלחהו במעשים כי לחם התורה בלי מלח וטעם המעשים אינה תורה ואין לה קיום כאומרם, וכל שחכמתו מרובה ממעשיו אין חכמתו מתקיימת, ולכן פת התורה במלח המעשים תאכל. וזהו שאמרו, ומלח ממון חסד, לעשות ממנו חסד, ואית דאמרי מלח ממון חסר, באופן שנראה שהמעשים והצדקות נקראו מלח לפי שהמעשים נותנים טעם לתורה וקיום וזהו, פת במלח תאכל. וכן, מים במשורה תשתה, שהם המצות והמדות באופן שתהיה שלם במעלות המדות ובמעלות השכליות אשר בם יבורך כל גבר כאומרו, אשרי איש ירא את ה׳ במצותיו חפץ מאד, וכן אמ׳, את האלהים ירא ואת מצותיו שמור כי זה כל האדם, כלו׳ שכל מין האדם תלוי באלו הב׳ חלקים במדות ובחכמה ולכ״א, ומים במשורה תשתה, ואמ׳ תשתה לרמוז שכשישתה מי התורה וילמדה ילמדה ע״מ לעשות מעשי׳ טובים ולהיות בעל מדות ואז יתקיים הכל בידו כאומרם, הלמד ע״מ לעשות מספקין בידו ללמוד וללמד ולעשות, לפי שהכל הולך אחר המעשה וזהו, ומים במשורה תשתה...

APPENDIX C

AN OUTLINE OF A SERMON ON THE REDEMPTION

לפי הפשט נראה לי שנוכל להוציא מענין תולדות עשו ענין גדול ונורא מאד מי יכיל עניני התורה ועומקה כי אפילו מן הדברים שנראים לנו מיותרים ובלתי צריכים יש להם רמזים גדולים. ולכן כל התורה כולה קשורה בסוד ל״ב נתיבות חכמה מבראשית עד לעיני כל ישראל. ולכן התחילה התורה בבית וסיימה בלמד בענין שיש לשים לב לכל התורה לפי שאין הפרש בין שמע ישראל ובין ותמנע היתה פילגש. ולכן שמתי לבי ועיני לראות מה זה כי בזאת הפרשה בהתחלתה כתיב, עשו הוא אדום, ובסופה כתיב ג״כ עשו הוא אדום. וכן מה זה שמנה בתחלה אלופי עשו ואח״כ מלכי אדום, ואלה המלכים, ואח״כ חזר לכתוב אלופי אדום וחתם הפרשה בעשו הוא אדום. ועלה בידי זהב סגור ומזוקק שבעתיים בהבטחת גאולתינו ובהשפלת עשו שונאינו. ולכן תמצא כי גדולת עשו היתה בלי סיבה כי פתע פתאום עלה למעלת אלופים. כי בתחלה היה איש רגלי וזהו, עשו הוא אדום ומיד עלה לאלופים וכתב, אלה אלופי עשו, ומיד עלה למעלת מלכים כדכתיב, ואלה המלכים וגומר, ואח״כ יגד ממעלתו וממלך ירד למדרגת אלוף וחזר לומר אח״כ, אלה אלופי עשו, ואח״כ ירד ממדרגת אלוף וחזר לאיש רגלי וחתם המאמר ואמר, הוא עשו, הנזכר למעלה שהיה אלוף ומלך ואלוף ועכשיו חזר להיות איש רגלי, וזהו חסרון גדול ולעג וקלס לסביבותיו. ולכן אמר הנביא, הנה קטן נתתיך בגוים בזוי אתה מאד. וכל זה להורות על מפלתו כי כמו שעלה בלי סבה ירד בלי סבה כשיהיה במעלה עליונה ירד עד התחתונה כמאמר הנביא, אם תגביה כנשר ואם בין כוכבים שים קנך משם אורידך נאום ה׳, פתע פתאום כמו שעלית בלי סבה. אבל גאולת ישראל אינה כן, אלא יעלו ממעלה למעלה מקו לקו צו לצו וכמו שאמרו במדרש שיר השירים על פסוק, מי זאת הנשקפה כמו שחר, כך היא גאולתן של ישראל מיד תהיה כמו שחר שמתחלת להאיר ואח״כ יפה כלבנה ואח״כ ברה כחמה ואח״כ איומה כנדגלות שהם דגלי מעלה בסוד ד׳מחנות שכינה המאירים לשמש. והיה זה לפי שישראל הם חלושים מכח הצרות והגליות ולא יוכלו לסבול האור החזק ולכן צריכים לחזקם מעט מעט בענין שיעלו ממעלה למעלה מאור השחר לאור הלבנה ואח״כ לאור החמה. וכן אמרו על פסוק, מגדול ישועות מלכו, במדרש תהלים, בתחלה מגדיל הולך וגדל ואח״כ מגדול זה מלך המשיח שנעשה גדול, כן תהיה גדולתן של ישראל גדולה והולכת ממעלה למעלה. אבל מלכות אדום כמו שעלו שלא כמנהג העולם מעשו הוא אדום לאלופים ומאלופים למלכים וממלכים חזרו לאחור לאלופים וחזרו כמבראשונה לאיש רגלי עשו הוא אדום, כן תהיה מפלתם כאומרו, משם אורידך, מאותה מעלה. וזו נחמה גדולה לישראל שנראה שאע״פ שהמלכות הרשעה עומדת במעלות עד לשמים אנו מובטחים שיפלו ולא יוכלו קום, וירדו ראמים כמאמר ז״ל, אל תקרי ראמים אלא רומיים.

וזה היה כתוב בספר ארוכה, ודרשתי אותו בהיותי בקאשטילייא בקבוץ החכמים ושבחוהו. וחכם אחד מהמקובלים בזוהר היה מגמגם ואומר שנראה לו שהוא מהזוהר. ואמרתי לו שאם ישלחהו אלי עבידנא יומא טבא לרבנן, ולא ראיתיו עד הנה. ופשפשתי בספרי הזוהר ולא מצאתיו (צרור המור, ורשא, תר״מ, בראשית, עמ׳ 98ב-99א).

APPENDIX D

A VISIONARY JAILED IN LISBON

The tragic forced-conversion of the Jews in Portugal (1497) belongs to the sort of events that influenced history profoundly for generations, indeed, for centuries. This is true not only of Jewish and Portuguese history, but also of the course of European and even world history.

Unfortunately, the short descriptions, in Hebrew and Portuguese sources, of the event itself and of the year that preceded and led to it, do not quench the historian's curiosity. This is the reason why we should all the more feel grateful to I. Tishbi, who published a comprehensive study, which clarifies and widens our knowledge of that episode.[1]

The study, that yielded a full volume, took as its starting-point six manuscript folios, partially faded, that are the remains of a tract, written by an anonymous survivor of the above-mentioned event. He did not convert to Christianity, was thrown to jail in Lisbon along with Saba and the group of forty stubborn Jews, and after the release he arrived through North-Africa to Egypt, where he wrote it. The salient character of the tract is messianic. The author is preoccupied with messianic calculations, which he attaches to historical events, that occurred in the fifteenth century to Iberian Jewry. His most unique feature, however lies in his prophetic visions, which he recounts in his tract, testifying that they materialized.

This is not the place for an exhaustive review of the book, which contains novelties in almost every page. We would like, however, to take a new look at the personality of that visionary. It seems to me that Tishbi's description leaves some questions unanswered, and raises some doubts.

We are dealing here with a man who left Spain at the time of the Expulsion (1492), and like so many of his coreligionists crossed the border to Portugal. We do not know anything concrete about his life in Spain.

His Hebrew style is so deficient, that it is difficult to find parallels to it in contemporary Hebrew literature. But while Tishbi recognizes the unusual amount of Hispanisms,[2] he is ready to go only as far as suggesting that this fact, as well as the lack of Jewish sources in his tract, "show that he did not serve in an official religious capacity, rabbinate or *dayyanut*."[3]

There seem to be some more peculiarities in his way of thinking. He uses extensively the method of numerology [*gematria*], to identify years in which certain messianically important events occurred. Biblical words or verses are translated by him to dates. However, it seems like our visionary was walking with a Hebrew Old-Testament in one hand, and a Christian calender in the other, for his calculations correspond to the number of years since Jesus' birth, and not to the creation of the world. We know of only one such a *gematria* by a Jew - Rabbi Abraham Zacut (who, according to Tishbi, was in the same jailed group).

The visionary tells us that he had prophecized the expulsion decree from Portugal two months before it was actually signed, "and I gave it two months before it happened to the (Jewish) scholars in writing." On this Tishbi remarks, "and it would seem that the alarmed scholars approached the author, for he was known to have authentic visions."[4] But how does Tishbi know that it was a "prophecy by reservation"? Why couldn't it be an initiative of the visionary? It seems to me that in Tishbi's evaluation he gets too much credit. Incidently, the above-discussed sentence might teach us that he did not belong to the religious leadership, to whom he claimed to have presented his prediction.

I would like to suggest that our visionary was of a marranic origin. This will explain his strange Hebrew style and syntax, as well as the paradoxical numerology.[5] If this is true, then the author's forgiving attitude to the Marranos can also be explained. Other exegetes in that generation, interpreted the verse "and many evils and troubles shall come upon them" (Deut. 31,17), as referring to the entire Marrano community, who was wavering between Judaism and Christianity. The visionary, however, says that it refers only to the *reconciliados*, namely, to the Marranos that "repented" after being accused by the Inquisition for "Judaizing."[6]

The point that attracts special attention in the visionary's messianic thought is the respectable role he assigns to himself. Redemption started, in his opinion, with the release of the jailed group in Lisbon.[7] How did the release come about? Well, he tells us that he had sent King Manuel prophecies that came true. The most important of them was the one that foretold the miscarriage of the fetus who was to inherit the Spanish crown, and so Manuel got it by virtue of his wife. "In light of the circumstances", says Tishbi, "it would seem that the release was a sort of an amnesty, owing to the realization of Manuel's strong ambition, as an act of gratitude to the Jewish prophet...."[8] Thus, our visionary brought about the opening stage of the redemption, which from then on was destined to roll like a snow-ball.

Moreover, the author informs us explicitly that he, as Tishbi puts it, "sees himself as a partner of the Messias."[9] In a dream he sees the Table of the Lord with only three legs, that symbolize the corners of the world. The missing leg stands for Portugal. "And I was told that I am destined to put that forth leg back to (its proper place in) the table." Tishbi's interpretation, taking the context into consideration, seems plausible; his Messianic vision is to bring the Portuguese Marranos back into the Jewish fold.

The whole thing sounds quite suspicious. The visionary foretells the king good-tidings, and as a reward he attains the release of the remnant of the Jews - mainly scholars. This is almost an exact replica of the famous talmudic story about Rabbi Yohanan ben Zakkai, who told Vespasian of his election for Emperor in Rome, and as an act of gratitude and respect he attains the survival of "Yavneh and its scholars." The Portuguese king "wrote it down in his book of the chronicles" - just like Mordecai's favour which was written in Ahasuerus' book of the chronicles, and this saved the Jews, eventually.

The eccentric and egocentric character of the visionary, which comes across clearly and forcefully out of the six extant folios of his messianic treatise, is doubly accentuated when compared with one of his jail-mates - Saba. The latter, as opposed to the visionary, is mentioned by contemporary historiographers among the important scholars who reached North-Africa. Although he believed, as did most of his contemporary coreligionists, that it was the generation that will see the long awaited redemption, his treatment of this subject is characterized by restraint and by a deep sense of responsibility.[10] This is almost diametrically opposed to the visionary's world of fantasia and hallucination.

Concerning the release from the Lisbon jail, Saba, who undoubtedly knew the visionary, prefers to say that it was due to the merit of the martyr Rabbi Shimon Meme, who died in that jail, "and through his merit the king allowed us (to leave), and they brought us to Arzila."[11] He tells us that the group was given "one broken ship, and R. Abraham Ardutiel adds, "without a navigator or any other man."[12] This is not the way of a king who wants to reward for a prophecy such as that of our visionary. It seems much more plausible to assume, as the scribe of the Parma ms. understood, that after six months, "when the king saw that he has not been successful", in convincing them to convert, he decided to get rid of that group of stubborn Jews. After all, their presence could be a religiously fermenting element that will ill-serve the cause of assimilating the freshly converted Jews.[13]

In general, one must consider also the complete silence of the sources concerning the visionary. He probably told and retold his visions and experiences to everyone who was ready to listen. The "jail colleagues" knew him and his messianic calculations very well. Yet, the fact is that of those, whose writings are extant, including Saba, Zacut and others, no one seems to have been influenced by him, let alone mention him. They did not take him seriously, and for good reasons.

We have here, then, a strange character, to the extent that we feel that one should not take his word for anything, unless we are forced to by other sources or considerations.

However, we should adopt Tishbi's intuitive generalization that, "the author was not unique in his generation, but was one of many."[14] Most of his exceptional characteristics are not unique in the strictest sense of the word, even if we cannot point to another person who "had it all" like him. Certainly he was not the only one, by whom there raged a burning apocalyptic whirlpool that seized every chord of heart and soul.

But the interesting point is that similar phenomena is found mainly in Iberian non-Jewish society (namely, by Old and New-Christian).

One of the technics used by the visionary in order to foresee the future was watching the sky at nights: "Because of this reason I sleep where I can see the sky at night, in order to see the signs that God gives there concerning the kings and the nations...and also concerning Israel."[15] He is not talking about astrological calculations such as those used by Abravanel, Zacut and others, but rather about a kind of observation of an expert who owns spiritual powers making him suitable to identification and deciphering special signs in the sky.[16]

Now this phenomenon is found in this period especially among the Marranos. Recently we have learnt from Inquisitorial documents about the wide extend of the Messianic awakening among them around the year 1500 as well as about the places that where swept by it. One of the conspicuous characteristics of this awakening is the observation of the sky in expectation of signs concerning the coming redemption.[17] In one place they looked for such signs at noon(!)[18]

David Reuveni tells us in his autobiography that the Marranos in Portugal, whose Messianic hopes were raised by his appearance, looked up to the sky for confirmation, and indeed they told that they had seen the shapes of flags, which inspired their imagination and boosted their enthusiasm: "And some of the leaders of the Marranos [*ánusim*] came to me and said they had seen four flags in the sky. And many Christians and priests...and told me and to Solomon Cohen the same thing."[19]

The visionary's self-image as playing a part in the process of redemption also fits in very well with our suggestion, that he was a former Marrano. The phenomenon of messianic awakening accompanied by beliefs in self-participation in the redemptive process, seems to be characteristic of Marranos more than of normative Jews. This is apparent in the messianic movement centered around the Marrano girl Ines de Herrera.[20]

Sometimes we find a Marrano who claims to be the Messiah, as was the case with Luis Dias, the tailor from Setubal, in the middle of the 16th century,[21] and seemingly Solomon Molkho. The immediate significance is, of course, local - the redemption of the Marranos - but a Messiah, even if his claim is done in a remote town in Portugal, is destined to redeem the Jewish people in the four corners of the earth.

In other cases we encounter groups of Marranos who believe that the Messiah will arise from their midst, or that he is going to be born to a certain woman. Thus, toward the middle of the 17th century we read that the Marranos in Mexico expected Juana Enriquez, wife of Simon Vaez Sevilla, to give birth to the Messiah who will be revealed in 1648. Later they believed that the pregnancy of Ines Pereira will bring the awaited Messiah. They dressed the future mother in special clothes and surrounded her with candles. Others yet believed that another pious woman, Blanca Juarez, will bear the Messiah.[22]

This is not the place for an analysis of this phenomenon. Generally, we believe that it is not to be understood on the psychological level alone. Marrano Messianism reflects a strong influence by Iberian religious mentality, both Spanish and Portuguese, where similar phenomena are to be found.[23] What is important for us here is that the belief of our visionary in his own active role in the coming redemption is yet another hint at his origin.

NOTES

1 Tishbi, Messianism.

2 ibid. pp. 13-14.

3 ibid. p. 16, n. 17.

4 ibid. p. 28.

5 One might perhaps add to the list of Christian influences our visionary's interpretation of "Thou art my son, this day have I begotten thee" (Ps.2,7). While Jewish exegesis tried to fight back Christian christology of this verse, the visionary accepts the basic christian interpretation that it refers to the Messiah (p. 120).

Incidently, a suggestion similar to mine is given by M. Idel concerning the author of *Sefer ha-Meshiv*. There too, the Hebrew is "suspicious," and Christian ideas can be traced (See, *Ẓion* 46, 1981, p. 78).

6 Tishbi, Messianism, p. 21-2. His concern for the Marranos welfare can be traced in his prophecy that the king would try to destroy them by the sword, and God will avenge that (ibid. p. 102).

7 ibid. p. 19.

8 ibid. p. 35-6.

9 ibid. p. 72. He means Messiah Son of Joseph and Messiah Son of David.

10 See our detailed discussion above, pp. 161-3.

11 Ẓ.M. Lev. p. 35a.

12 *Hashlamat Sefer ha-Qabbalah*, Jerusalem, 1979, p. 31.

13 I have already noted this elsewhere (Gross, Saba, p. 223 n. 46). This seems to have been the best solution also from a legal point of view, for no Jews were allowed to stay on Portuguese soil.

14 Tishbi, Messianism, p. 58.

15 ibid., pp. 101-2.

16 ibid. p. 57.

17 F. Baer, *Die Juden im Christlichen Spanien* II, Berlin, 1936, no. 423. idem, "The Messianic Movement in Spain at the Time of the Expulsion," *Ẓion* 5, 1933, pp. 68,69.

H. Beinart, "Agudo in La Mancha and Its Marranos," *Tarbiẓ* 50, 1981, p. 427. Idem, "Almaden: The Marranos of a Town in La Mancha," *Ẓion* 47, 1982, p. 31. idem, "The Prophetess Ines and Her Movement in Herrera Her Hometown," *I. Tishbi Jubilee Volume*, Jerusalem, 1986, p. 464. J. Caro Baroja, *Los Judios en la España Moderna y Contemporanea* tom. I, Madrid, 1978, p. 429.

18 H. Beinart, "The Movement of Ines in Puebla de Alkoser and in Talarubias etc." *Tarbiẓ* 51,1982, pp. 638.

It should be pointed out that we find one such a phenomenon in an autobiographical note in *Kaf ha-Qetoret*, an apocalyptic commentary on Psalms: והאמנם בהיות כי אנכי יושב במקום החושך ואשא עיני להביט והנה נפתח לפני עולם אחד גדול כדוגמת הפתח עם אור קטן. עוד אשא עיני להביט...ואדע כי המלך ה׳ צבאות ראו עיני... (*כף הקטורת*, כת״י פריס 845, דף 36א. וכן ראה, שם דף 51א) However, we do not know who the author was and whether he had connections with the Marranos. If he belonged to the circle of *Sefer ha-Meshiv* then there is the possibility that he was in contact with a Qabbalist from a Marranic origin (See above n. 5). The attitude of *Kaf ha-Qetoret* to the Marranos is not as harsh as that of some contemporary rabbis. According to his commentary their redemption is alluded to in Psalms (pp. 149a, 203a).

19 *The Autobiography of David Reuveni* [A.Z. Aescoly ed.], Jerusalem, 1940, p. 79. It is noteworthy that it looked like an inter-faith experience.

20 Y. Baer, "The Messianic Movement," pp. 66ff. H. Beinart, "A Prophecying Movement in Cordova in 1499-1502," *Ẓion* 44, 1979, pp. 192-6.

21 E. Lipiner is preparing a monograph on this self-proclaimed Messiah based on his Inquisitorial file.

22 S. B. Liebman, *New World Jewry 1493-1825: Requiem for the Forgotten*, New-York, 1982, pp. 64-64. Idem, *The Jews in New Spain*, Coral Gables, Florida, 1970, pp. 230, 258. Mathias de Bocanegra, *Jews and the Inquisition of Mexico: The Great Auto de Fé of 1649*, Lawrence, Kansas, 1974, pp. 101-102, 217-218).

23 See my forthcoming article: "Jewish, Christian and Marranic Messianism in Spain and Portugal."

BIBLIOGRAPHY

Primary Sources

Abravanel Isaac, *Commentary on Leviticus*, Jerusalem, 1964.
___, *Zevaḥ Pesaḥ*, Venice, 1545.
Abulafia T, *Óẓar ha-Kavod*, Warsaw, 1879.
Adret Solomon, *Responsa*, Rome edition 1470(?) (reprinted: Jerusalem, 1977).
Africanus Leo, *The History and Description of Africa* [R. Brown ed.], London, 1896.
Alami Solomon, *Íggeret Mussar* (ed. A.M. Haberman), Jerusalem, 1946.
Alashqar Moses, *Responsa*, Jerusalem, 1959.
Albo Joseph, *Sefer ha-Íqqarim*, Jerusaelm, 1964.
Al-Dahari Zekhariah, *Sefer ha-Mussar* [Y. Ratzaby ed.], Jerusalem, 1965, pp. 267-69.
Angelino Joseph, *Livnat ha-Sappir*, Jerusalem, 1913.
Anqawa Abraham, *Kerem Ḥemer* vol. 2, Livorno, 1871, (Reprinted in Jerusalem, 1976).
Arama Isaac, *Àqedat Yiẓḥaq* , Warsaw, 1883.
___, *Ḥazut Qashah*, Warsaw, 1883.
Ardutiel Abraham, *Ávnei Zikkaron* (published by G. Scholem,) *Qiryat Sefer* 7, 1930, pp. 457-65.
___, *Hashlamat Sefer ha-Qabbalah*, in *Two Chronicles from the Generation of the Expulsion from Spain* [A. David ed.], Jerusalem, 1979.
Baḥya ben Asher, *Commentary on the Pentateuch*[ed. Chavel], Jerusalem, 1974.
___, *Kad ha-Qemaḥ, Kitvei R. Baḥya ben Asher* [Chavel ed.], Jerusalem, 1970.
Baqrat Abraham, *Diwan*, Ms. Moscow, Ginzburg 214.
Ben-Ẓvi Institute ms. 2125.
Ben-Ẓvi Institute ms. 2157.
Bernáldes Andrés, *Historia de los Reyes Católicos Don Fernando y Dona Isabel* tom. I, Sevilla, 1869.
Dapiera Solomon, *Diwan* [S. Bernstein ed.], New York, 1942.
Delmedigo Joseph Solomon,"Íggeret Áḥuz," *Melo Ḥofnayyim* [A. Geiger ed.], Berlin, 1840.
Duran Profiat, *Maàseh Éfod*, Vienna, 1865, (Reprinted: Jerusalem, 1970).
___, *Kelimmat ha-Goyim*, in *The Polemical Writings of Profiat Duran* [F.E. Talmage ed.], Jerusalem, 1981.
___, "Qinah ve-Hesped," *Maàseh Éfod*, Vienna, 1865.
Duran Solomon ben Shimon, *Milḥemet Miẓvah*, Jerusalem, 1980.
Eisenmenger Johannes, *Entdecktes Judenthum* vol I, Frankfurt am Main, 1700.
Even Shemuel Y, *Midreshei Geúlah*, Jerusalem and Tel Aviv, 1954.
Gagin H, *Èẓ Ḥayyim* [M. Amar ed.], Ramat Gan, 1987.(H)
Galya Raza [R. Elior ed.], Jerusalem, 1981.
Halevi Abraham ben Eliezer, *Megillat Ámrafel* (published by G. Scholem) *Qiryat Sefer* 7, 1930, pp. 52-55.
___, *Meshare Qitrin*, Jerusalem, 1978.
Ḥayyat Judah, *Minḥat Yehudah*, Mantua, 1558.
Ḥayyim ben Beẓalel, *Sefer ha-Ḥayyim*, Jerusalem, 1968.
_____, *Íggeret Tiyyul*, Jerusalem, 1957.
Ḥayyun Joseph, *Commentary on Esther*, Ms. Moscow, Ginzburg Collection, 168/2.
Hierosolomitanus D, *Sefer ha-Ziqquq*, Ms. Paris, Alliance, 49 (H80A). Ms. Vatican, 273.
Ibn Avi Zimra David, *Meẓudat Ẓiyyon*, Zolkiev, 1862.
___, *Responsa*, Livorno, 1652.
Ibn Migash Abraham, *Kevod Élohim*, Costantinople, 1585, (reprint Jerusalem, 1977).
Ibn Mussa Ḥayyim, *Magen ve-Romaḥ*, Jerusalem, 1969.

___, "A Letter to His Son R. Judah [D. Kaufmann ed.]," *Beit Talmud* 2, Vienna, 1892, pp. 110-25.
Ibn Verga Solomon, *Shevet Yehudah* (ed. A. Shoḥat), Jerusalem, 1947.
Jacob ben Reuven, *Milḥamot ha-Shem* [J. Rosenthal ed.], Jerusalem, 1963.
Joseph ha-Meqaneh [J. Rosenthal ed.], Jerusaelm, 1970.
Judah Halevi, *Kuzari* [trans. Ibn Tibbon], Warsaw, 1880.
Judah he-Ḥasid, *Sefer Ḥasidim* [Wistinetzki ed.] Frankfurt, 1924.
Kaf ha-Qetoret, Ms. Paris, 1845.
Lorqi J, *Des Apologetische Schreiben des Joshua Lorki*, [E. Landau ed.], Antwerp, 1906.
Maimonides Moses, *Epistle to Yemen* [A.S. Halkin ed.] New York, 1952.
Menasseh ben Israel, *Nishmat Ḥayyim*, Leipzig, 1862.
Met Moses, *Matteh Mosheh*, Frankfurt, 1720.
Mizraḥi Elijah, *Mayyim Àmuqqim*, Berlin, 1778.
Moses of Coucy, *Sefer Miẓvot Gadol*, Venice, 1547.
Moses ben Nachman, *Commentary on the Pentateuch* [B. Chavel ed.] 2 volumes, Jerusalem, 1967.
___, *Kitvei ha-Ramban* [B. Chavel ed.] , 2 volumes, Jerusalem, 1963.
Qanpanton Isaac, *Darkei ha-Talmud*, Vienna, 1878.
Qapsali Elijah, *Seder Éliyyahu Zuta* vol. 1, Jerusalem, 1976.
Qaro Joseph, *Ór Ẓaddiqim*, Warsaw, 1902.
Qaro Isaac, *Toldot Yiẓḥaq*, Warsaw, 1877.
Qimḥi J, *Sefer ha-Berit* [F.E. Talmage ed.], Jerusalem, 1974.
Pina Ruy de, *Chronica del Rey Dom João II* [J. Correâ da Serra ed.] in *Collecção de livros inéditos de história portugueza* vol. I, Lisbon, 1790.
Recanati Menaḥem, *Sefer Taàmei Miẓvot*, London, 1963.
Responsa Zera Ánashim, Husiatin, 1902.
Saba Abraham, *Éshkol ha-Kofer on Ruth*, Bartfeld, 1907.
___, *Éshkol ha-Kofer on Esther*, Drohobycz, 1903.
___, *Ẓeror ha-Mor*, Warsaw, 1879.
Saba Isaac, *Qarnei Reémim*, Salonica, 1802.
Sambari Joseph, *Divrei Yosef*, Jerusalem, 1981.
Tam Jacob, *Sefer ha-Yashar*, Berlin, 1898.
Teicthal Y.S, *Ém ha-Banim Semeḥah*, Jerusalem, 1983.
Tiqqunei Zohar, Livorno, 1854.
Toldot Yeshu, [S. Krauss ed.] Berlin, 1902. (*Das Leben Jesu nach Judishen Quellen*).
Trani Joseph, *Responsa*, Tel Aviv, 1959
Usque S, *Consolation for the Tribulation of Israel* [tran. and ed. M. Cohen], Philadelphia 1965.
Yaàveẓ Joseph, *Commentary on Avot*, Warsaw, 1880.
___, *Ḥasdei ha-Shem*, New York, 1936.
___, *Ór ha-Ḥayyim*, Lublin, 1912.
Ẓahalon Yom Tov, *Responsa*, Venice, 1694
Zacut Abraham, *Sefer Yoḥasin* [Philipowsky ed.], London, 1924.
Zohar, 3 volumes, Jerusalem, 1970.
Zohar Ḥadash, Livorno, 1866.

Secondary Material

* (H) = Hebrew

Assis Y., "Crime and Violence Among the Jews of Spain (13th-14th Centuries)," *Ẓion* 50, 1985, pp. 221-40.(H)
Astrain J.C, "Los Conversos Aragoneses segun los Procesos de la Inquisicion," *Sefarad* 18, 1958.
Bacher W, "Judaeo-Christian Polemics in the Zoḥar," *JQR* [o.s.] 3, 1891, pp. 781-84.
Baer Y., *Die Juden im Christlichen Spanien* 2 volumes, Berlin, 1929-36.
___, *A History of the Jews in Christian Spain* 2 volumes, Philadelphia, 1966.

___, *Galut*, New-York, 1947.
___, "Rashi and the Historical Reality of His Time," *Tarbiẓ* 20, 1949, pp. 320-32.(H)
Beinart H., "Fez a Center of Return to Judaism in the 16th Century," *Sefunot*, 8, 1964, pp. 319-35.(H)
___,"The Image of Jewish Courtiers in Christian Spain," *Elites and Leading Groups*, Jerusaelm, 1964, pp. 55-71.(H)
___, *Trujillo*, Jerusalem, 1980.
___, *Conversos on Trial*, Jerusalem (1981)
___, "Moroccan Jews in Spain in the Beginning of the Seventeenth Century," *S.W. Baron's Jubilee Volume*, Hebrew part, Jerusalem, 1974, pp. 15-39.
Beit-Arieh M. and Idel M, "Rabbi Abraham Zacut's Maámar àl ha-Qeẓ veha-Iẓtagninut," *Qiryat Sefer* 54, 1979, pp. 174-94. (H)
Benayahu M., "A New Source concerning the Spanish Refugees in Portugal and their Move to Salonia," *Sefunot* 11, 1971-78, pp. 231-66.(H)
___, "Kabbalah and Halakhah - A Confrontation," *Daàt* 5, 1980, pp. 61-115.(H)
___, "Maàmadot u-Moshavot," *Studies in Memory of the Rishon le-Ẓion Rabbi Y. Nissim* vol. 6, Jerusalem, 1985.(H)
___, "The Sermons of Rabbi Joseph ben Meir Garson etc," *Michael* 7, 1982, p. 42-205.(H)
___, *Copyright Authorization and Imprimatour for Hebrew Books Printed in Venice*, Jerusalem, 1971. (H)
___, *The Relations between Greek and Italian Jewry*, Tel Aviv, 1980.(H)
Ben Sasson H.H., "The Generation of the Spanish Exiles on its Fate," *Ẓion* 26, 1961, pp. 23-64.(H)
___, "Exile and Redemption Through the Eyes of the Spanish Exiles," *Y. Baer Jubilee Volume*, Jerusalem, pp. 216-27.(H)
___, *Trial and Achievement*, Jerusalem, 1974.(H)
___, "A Reply," *Tarbiẓ*, 30, 1961, pp. 69-72.(H)
___, *Hagut ve-Hanhagah*, Jerusalem, 1959.(H)
___, "Expressions of the Uniqueness of Israel in the 12th Century," *Peraqim* 2, 1969-74, p. 145-218.(H)
___, "An Elegy on the Expulsion from Spain," *Tarbiẓ* 31, 1961, p. 59-71.(H)
___, "Wealth and Poverty in the Teaching of the Preacher Rabbi Ephrayim of Lenczyca," *Tarbiẓ* 19, 1954, p. 144-163.
Ben-Sasson J., *The Philosophical System of Rabbi Moses Isserles*, Jerusalem, 1984.(H)
Bentov H., "Methods of Study of Talmud in the Yeshivot of Salonica and Turkey After the Expulsion from Spain," *Sefunot* 13, pp. 5-102.(H)
Baron S.W., *Social and Religious History of the Jews* vol. 11 (2nd ed.), Philadelphia, 1967.
Berger D., *The Jewish-Christian Debate in the High Middle Ages* [a critical ed. of *Niẓẓaḥon Vetus*], Philadelphia, 1979.
Berliner A., *Censur und Confiscation*, Berlin, 1891.
Bettan I., *Studies in Jewish Preaching*, Cincinnati, 1939.
Boyaren D., *The Sefardi Ìyyun*, Jerusalem, 1989.(H)
___, "On the Talmudic Method of the Exiles from Spain," *Peàmim* 2, 1979, pp. 73-82.(H)
Baruchson Z., *Private libraries of Jews in Northern Italy in Late Renaissance*, Ph.D. Dissertation, Bar-Ilan University, Ramat-Gan, 1985.(H)
Brunschvig R., *Deux Récites de Voyage inédits en Afrique du Nord au XV siécl*e, Paris, 1936.
Buber M., *The Way of the Bible: Studies in Biblical Literary Style*, Jerusalem, 1964.(H)
Bultmam R., *History and Eschatology*, Edinburgh, 1957.
Cohn N., *The Pursuit of the Millennium*, London, 1920.
___ ,"The Horns of Moses," *Commentary* 26, 1958, 220-26.
Corcos D., "The Jews in Morocco from the Expulsion until the Middle of the 16th Century," *Sefunot* 10, 1966, pp. 53-112.(H)

Dan .J, *Hebrew Ethical and Homiletical Literature*, Jerusalem, 1975.(H)
___, *The Hebrew Story in the Middle Ages*, Jerusalem, 1974.(H)
David A., "An Unknown Dirge on the Expulsion from Spain," *Peàmim* 49, 1992, pp. 24-31.(H)
Dimitrovsky H.Z., "About the Way of Pilpul," *S.W. Baron Jubilee Volume* [Hebrew Section], Jerusalem, 1975, pp. 111-181.
___, "Rabbi Jacob Berav's Academy," *Sefunot*, 7, 1963, pp. 43-102.(H)
Dunn Ross E., *The Adventures of Ibn Battuta a Muslim Traveler of the 14th Century*, Berkeley, 1986.
Elbaum J., "Aspects of Hebrew Ethical Literature in 16th Century Poland," in *Jewish Thought in the Sixteenth Century* [B.D. Cooperman ed.], Cambridge, Mass, 1983, pp. 146-66.
___, *Repentance and Self-Flagellation in the Writings of the Sages of Germany and Poland 1348-1648*, Jerusalem, 1993.(H)
___, *Openness and Insularity*, Jerusalem, 1990.(H)
___, "The Influence of Jewish-Spanish Culture on the Jews of Germany and Poland in the 16th-17th Centuries," *Culture and History, The Ino Sciaky Memorial Volume*, Jerusalem, 1987.(H)
Fedayah H., "*Pegam* and *Tiqqun* of the Divinity in the Qabbalah of Rabbi Isaac Sagi Nahor," *Jerusalem Studies in Jewish Thought* 6 (3-4), 1987, pp. 157-285.(H)
Freire J.P., *Lisboa do meu tempo e do passado*, Lisboa (1930?).
Friedberg H.D., *The History of Hebrew Typography in Italy, Spain, Portugal etc.* Tel-Aviv, 1956.(H)
Gerber J., *Jewish Society in Fez, 1450-1700*, Leiden, 1980.
Ginzberg L., *The Legends of the Jews*, Philadelphia, 1954.
___, *Genizah Studies* (*Ginzei Schechter*) vol. 1, New york, .
Glick T.F., *Islamic and Christian Spain in the Early Middle*, Princeton, 1979.
Goldman I.M., *The Life and Times of Rabbi David Ibn Avi Zimra*, New York, 1970.
Gottlieb E., *The Qabbalah in the Writings of Bahya ben Asher*, Jerusalem, 1970.(H)
___, *Studies in Kabbalah Literature*, Tel Aviv, 1976.(H)
Graetz H., *History of the Jews* [Hebrew trans. S.P. Rabinowitz] vol. 6, Warsaw, 1898.
Greis Z, "The Ḥasidic Conduct Literature from the Mid-Eighteenth Century to the 1830's," *Ẓion* 46, 1981, pp. 198-236, 278-305.(H)
Gross A., "Rabbi Abraham Saba: 'Expelled in two Expulsions'," *Studies in Memory of the Rishon le-Ẓion R. Yiẓḥak Nissim* vol. 4, Jerusalem, 1985, pp. 205-24.(H)
___, "Rabbi Judah Khalaẓ in Tlemcen: Judeo-Iberian Culture in North Africa," *Exile and Diaspora: Studies in Jewish History Presented to Professor Haim Beinart*, Jerusalem, 1988, pp. 356-73(H)
___, "The Ten Tribes and the Kingdom of Prester John - Rumors and Investigations before and after the Expulsion from Spain," *Peàmim* 48, 1991, p. 5-41.(H)
___, "Rabbinic Academies in Castile in the 15th century," *Peàmim* 31, 1987 , pp. 3-21.(H)
___, "Sefardi Pilpul as Applied to Rashi's Commentary on the Petateuch in the End of the Fifteenth Century," *AJS Review* 18, 1993, 1-20.(H)
___, "The Qabbalistic Commentary on the Prayers Attributed to Rabbi Abraham Saba," *Asufot* 1, 1987, pp. 189-197.(H)
___, "The Reflection of the Expulsions from Spain and Portugal in a Commentary on Esther," *Proceedings of the Ninth World Congress for Jewish Studies*, Section B vol. I, Jerusalem, 1986, p. 153-8.(H)
___, "R. Abraham Saba's Abbreviated Messianic Commentary on Haggai and Zechariah," *Studies in Medieval History and Literature* II, [I. Twersky ed.], Cambridge Mass, 1984, pp. 389-401.
___, "Sefardic Attitudes to Rashi's Commentary on the Torah," *Rashi: Studies in his Works* [A. Steinfeld ed.], Ramat Gan, 1993, pp. 60-90.(H)
___, "The Ashkenazic Syndrome of Jewish Martyrdom in Portugal 1497," *Tarbiẓ*, (Forthcoming).

Haberman A.M., *The History of the Hebrew Book*, Jerusalem, 1968.(H)

___, "A Dirge on the Expulsion from Portugal 1497 by Don David Ibn Yaḥya," *Óẓar Yehudei Sefarad* 5, 1962, pp. 11-16.(H)

Hacker J., "Pride and Depression - Polarity of the Spiritual and Social Experience of the Iberian Exiles in the Ottoman Empire," *Medieval and Society in Medieval Jewry, Studies Dedicated to the Memory of Haim Hillel Ben-Sasson* [M. Ben-Sasson, R. Bonfil, J. Hacker ed.], Jerusalem (1989), pp. 541-86.(H)

___, "'If we have forgotten the Name of our Lord' (Psalms 44:21) : Interpretation in Light of the Realities in Medieval Spain," *Ẓion* 57, 1992, pp. 247-74.(H)

___, "The Intellectual Activity of the Jews in the Ottoman Empire in the 16th-17th Centuries," *Tarbiẓ* 53, 1984, pp. 569-603.(H)

___, Rabbi Jacob b. Solomon Ibn Ḥaviv - An Analysis of Leadership in the Jewish Community of Salonika in the 16th Century," in *Proceedings of the Sixth Congress of Jewish Studies* vol. 2, Jerusalem, 1975, pp. 117-26.(H)

___, "Was Qidush ha-Shem Spiritualized towards the Modern Era?" in *Sanctity of Life and and Martyrdom: Studies in Memory of Amir Yekutiel* [Gafni and Ravitzky ed.], Jerusalem, 1992, pp. 221-32.(H)

___, "Some Letters on the Expulsion of the Jews from Spain and Sicilly," *Studies in the History of Jewish Society in the Middle Ages and in the Modern Period* [E. Etkes, Y. Salmon ed.] Jerusalem, 1980, pp. 64-97.(H)

___, "The Sefardi Sermon in the Sixteenth Century - Between Literature and Historical Source," *Peàmim* 26, 1986, pp. 108-27.(H)

___, "Rabbi Shelomoh le-Beit Halevi's Views of Israel Among the Nations," *Ẓion*, 34, 1969, pp. 43-89.(H)

___, Despair and Redemption in the Writings of Rabbi Solomon le-Beit Halevi," *Tarbiẓ* 39, 1970, pp. 195-213.(H)

Harper R., *The Path of Darkness*, Cleveland, 1958.

Havlin S.Z., "More Concerning the 248 Words of the Shema," *Tarbiẓ* 40, 1970, pp. 107-9.(H)

Heller-Willensky S., *Rabbi Isaac Arama and his Philosophical Thought*, , Jerusalem, 1956.(H)

Herr M.D., "The Hatred of Israel in the Roman Empire in the Light of Ḥazal," *The DeVries Memorial Volume*, Jerusalem, 1969, pp. 149-59.(H)

Heinemann Y., *The Ways of the Aggadah*, Jerusalem, 1954.(H)

Herculano A., *History of the Origin and Establishment of the Inquisition in Portugal*, New York, 1972.

Hirshberg H.Z., *A History of the Jews in North Africa*, Jerusalem, 1965.(H)

Horodetzky S.A., "Rabbi Ḥayyim Vital on Jesus and Moḥamed," *ha-Goren* 10, 1928, pp. 159-60.(H)

Idel M., "The Attitude to Christianity in the Sefer ha-Meshiv," *Ẓion* 46, 1981, pp. 77-91.(H)

___, "The History of the Interdiction against the Study of Kabbalah before the Age of Forty," *AJS Review* 5, 1980 (Hebrew Section), pp. 1-20.

___, "We Have No Kabbalistic Tradition On It," *Rabbi Moses Nachmanides: Explorations in His Religious and Literary Virtuosity* [I. Twersky ed.], Cambridge Mass, 1983, pp. 51-74.

___, "What is New is Forbbiden," *Ẓion* 54, 1989, pp. 223-40.(H)

___, "Introduction," in A.Z. Aescoli's, *The History of Jewish Messianic Movements* 2nd edition, Jerusalem, 1988, pp. 9-28.(H)

___, "The Sefardi Qabbalah after the Expulsion," *The Sephardi Legacy* [H. Beinart ed.], Jerusalem, 1992, p. 503-12.

___, "The Magical and Neoplatonic Interpretation of the Kabbalah in the Renaissance," *Jewish Thought in Sixteenth Century* [B.D. Cooperman ed.], Cambridge, Mass, 1983, pp. 186-242.

___, *Rabbi Abraham Abulafia's Writings and Thought*, Ph.D. Diss. Hebrew University, 1976.(H)

___, "'In the Light of Life' - A Study in Qabbalistic Eschatology," *Sanctity of Life and Martyrdom: Studies in Memory of Amir Yekutiel* [Gafni and Ravitsky ed.], Jerusalem, 1992.(H)

Kaplan J., *From Christianity to Judaism*, Jerusalem 1983.(H)

___, "The Problem of the Anusim and the New Christians in the Historical Research in the Last Generation," in *Studies in Historiography* [M. Zimerman, M. Stern, Y. Salmon ed.], Jerusalem (1988), pp. 177-44.(H)

Kasher M.M, *Torah Shelemah* vol. 7, New York, 1950.(H)

Katz J., *Exclusiveness and Tolerance*, Oxford, 1961.

___, "Halakhic and Homiletical Literature as Historical Sources," *Tarbiẓ* 30, 1961, pp. 62-68.(H)

___, "Halakhah and Kabbalah - First Contacts," *Y. Baer Memorial Volume* (*Ẓion* 44), 1979, pp. 148-72.(H)

___, "Post-Zoharic Relations between Halakhah and Kabbalah," *Daàt* 4, 1980, pp. 57-74.(H)

___, "Halakah and Kabbalah as Competing Subject of Study," *Daàt* 7, 1981, pp. 37-68.(H)

Kayserling M., *Geschichte der Juden in Portugal*, Leipzig, 1867.

___, "Sefardim," *he-Ásif* 6, 1893, pp.1-86.(H)

Keyes G.L., *Christian Faith and the Interpretation of History: A Study of St. Augustine's Philosophy of History*, Lincoln, Nebraska, 1966.

Krauss S., "Fragments Arameens du Toldot Yeschou," *REJ* 62, 1911, pp. 28-37.

Ladero Quesada M.F., "Apuntes para la historia de los Judíos y conversos de Zamora en la edad media (siglos XIII-XV)," *Sefarad* 48, 1988, p. 56.

Lasker D.J., *Jewish Philosophical Polemics against Christianity in the Middle Ages*, New-York, 1977.

Lehman M.R., "Allusions to Jesus and Mohamed in the Commentaries of the Ashkenazic Ḥasidim," *Sinai* 87, 1980, pp. 34-40.(H)

Libowitz N.S., *Abraham Saba and his Books Ẓeror ha-Mor and Éshkol ha-Kofer*, New-York, 1936.(H)

Leibowitz N., *New Studies in the Book of Exodus*, Jerusalem, 1970.(H)

Lipiner E., *Gaspar da Gama; um converso na frota de Cabral*, Rio de Janeiro, 1987.

Lifton R.J., *Death in life: Survivors of Hiroshima*, New-York, Toronto, 1967.

Loewenstamm S.A., "Moses' Death," *Tarbiẓ* 27, 1958, pp. 142-57.(H)

Lowinger S., "Recherches sur l'0euvre Apologétique d'Abraham Farissol," *REJ* 105, 1940, pp. 23-52.

Manor D., *Exile and Redemption in the Thought of R.A. Saba in Light of his Biography and Historical Background*, Unpublished M.A. dissertation, Hebrew University, Jerusalèm, 1974.(H)

___, "Abraham Saba: His Life and Works," *Jerusalem Studies in Jewish Thought* 2, 1982-3, pp. 208-31.

___, A Bibliography of Rabbi Abraham Saba's works," *Sefunot* [n.s.] 3 (18), Jerusalem, 1985, pp. 317-38.

Marx A., "The Expulsion from Spain, Two New Accounts," *JQR* [o.s.] 20, 1908, pp. 24-71.

Mcginn B., *Visions of the End: Apocalyptic Traditions in the Middle Ages*, New York, 1979.

Mckay A., "Popular Movements and Pogroms in 15th Century Castile," *Past and Present* 55, 1977, pp. 33-67.

Mellinkoff R., *The Horned Moses in Medieval Art and Thought*, U. of California Press, 1970.

Mommsen T., "Augustine on Progress," in *Medieval and Renaissance Studies*, Ithaca, New York, 1959, pp. 268-69.

Montgomery J.A., *The Samaritans: Earliest Jewish Sect*, New-York, 1968.

Nahon G., "Les Marranes Espagnols et Porgugaise et les communautés Juives issues du Marranisme dans l'Historiographie Recente (1960-1975)," *REJ* 136, 1977, pp. 297-367.

Netanyahu B., *Don Isaac Abravanel: A Stateman and Philosopher*, Philadelphia, 1972.

___, *The Marranos of Spain in the Fifteenth Century*, New-York, 1966.

___, "On the Historical Meaning of the Hebrew Sources Related to the Marranos," *Hispania Judaica*, 1980, pp. 79-102.

Nigal G., "A Chapter in the thought of the Generation of the Expulsion from Spain," *Sinai* 74, 1974, pp. 67-80.(H)

Oliveira Marques A.H. de, *History of Portugal* (2nd ed.) New York, 1976.

Patrides C.A., *The Grant Design of God: The Literary form of the Christian view of History*, London, 1972.

Pimenta Ferro Tavares M.J., *Os Judeus em Portugal no Século XV* vol. I, Lisboa, 1982.

___, *Os Judeus em Portugal no Século XIV*, Lisboa, 1970

___, *Os Judeus em Portugal no Século XV* vol. 2, Lisboa, 1984.

Porgès N., "Texte de la lettre adressée par la frankistes aux communauté juives de Boheme," *REJ* 29, 1894, pp. 282-8.

___, "Deux Index Expurgatoires de Livres Hèbreux," *REJ* 30, 1895, pp. 261-62.

___, "Der Hebraische Index Expurgatorius," *Abraham Berliner Festschrift* [J. Kaufmann ed.], Frankfurt am Main, 1903, pp. 273-95.

Ravitzky A., "'Waymarks to Zion': The History of an Idea," *The Land of Israel in Medieval Thought* [M. Ḥallamish and A Ravitzky ed.], Jerusalem, 1991, pp. 1-39.(H)

Robinson I., "Moses Cordovero and Kabbalislic Education in the Sixteenth Century," *Judaism* 39, 1990, pp. 155-62.

Rosanes S., *The History of the Jews in Turkey*, Tel-Aviv, 1930.(H)

Rosenberg S., "Exile and Redemption in Jewish Thought in the Sixteenth Century: Contending Conceptions," *Jewish Thought in the Sixteenth Century*, [B.D. Cooperman ed.], Cambridge, Mass, 1983, pp. 399-430.

Roth C. "Religion and Martyrdom among the Marranos," *Holy War and Martyrology*, Jerusalem, 1968, pp. 93-106.(H)

___, *A History of the Marranos*, New York, 1974.

Ruderman D.B., *The World of a Renaissance Jew*, Cincinnati, 1981.

Russel J.B., *Lucifer: The Devil in the Middle Ages*, Ithaca and London, 1984.

Safrai S., "Martyrdom in Tanaitic Thought," *Y. Baer Memorial Volume* (*Ẓion* 44), 1979, pp. 28-42.(H)

Secret F., *Les Zohar chez les Kabbalistes Chrétiens de la Renaissance*, Paris, 1964.

Septimus B., "'Kings Angels or Begars': Tax Law and Spirituality in a Hispano-Jewish Responsum," *Studies in Medieval Jewish History and Literature* 2 [I. Twersky ed.], Cambridge Mass, 1984, pp. 309-35.

Schirmann H., *Hebrew Poetry in Spain and Provence* vol.1, Jerusalem, 1954.(H)

___, "Elegies etc," *Qoveẓ àl Yad* [n.s.] 3, 1939, pp. 69-74.(H)

Scholem G., *Major Trends in Jewish Mysticism*, New-York, 1961.

___, *Elements of the Kabbalah and its Symbolism*, Jerusalem, 1976.(H)

___, "Considerations sur l'Histoire de Débuts de la Kabbale Chrétienne," *Kabbalistes Chrétienes* [ed. A. Faivre and F. Tristan], Paris, 1979, pp. 19-46.

___, *Studies and Texts Concerning the History of Sabbetianism and Its Metamorphoses*, Jerusalem, 1974.(H)

___, *Kabbalah*, Jerusalem, 1974.

Shalem S., *Rabbi Mosheh Alsheikh*, Jerusalem, 1966.(H)

Shatzmiller J., "Towards a Picture of the First Maimonidean Controversy," *Ẓion* 34, 1969, pp. 126-44.(H)

Shoḥat A., "Rabbi Abraham Zacut in Jerusalem," *Ẓion* 13-14, 1948-49, pp. 43-6.(H)

___, "Martyrdom in the Thought of the Spanish Exiles and the Qabbalists of Safed," *Holy War and Martyrology*, Jerusalem, 1968, pp. 131-46.(H)

Silver A.H., *A History of Messianic Speculation in Israel From the First Through the Seventeenth Century*, Boston, 1929.
Stokstad M., *Santiago de Compostela*, U. of Okalahoma Press, 1978.
Suáres Fernándes L., *Documentos acerca de la Expulsión de los Judíos*, Valladolid, 1964.
Talmage F., "The Francesc de Sant Jordi - Solomon Bonafed Letters," *Studies in Medieval Jewish History and Literature* [I. Twersky ed.], Cambridge, Mass. 1979, pp. 337-74.
___, "Trauma of Tortosa: The Testimony of Abraham Rimoch," *Mediaeval Studies* 47, 1985, pp. 379-415.
Ta-Shema Y., "Ashkenazi Ḥasidism in Spain: R. Jonah Gerondi - The Man and His Work," *Exile and Diaspora* (H. Beinart's Festschrift), Jerusalem (1988), pp. 165-94.(H)
Tishbi, I., *Misnat ha-Zohar*, 2 vol, Jerusaelm, 1957-61.(H)
___, "Upheaval in the Research Of Kabbalah," *Ẓion* 54, 1989, pp. 209-22.(H)
___, "The Controversy about the Zohar in the 16th Century in Italy," *Peraqim* I, Jerusalem, 1967-68, pp. 13182.(H)
___, and J. Dan, *Hebrew Ethical Literature*, Jerusalem, Tel Aviv, 1970.(H)
Toledano J.M., "mi-Kitvei Yad," *HUCA* 5, 1928, pp. 403-409.(H)
___, *Ner ha-Maàrav*, Jerusalem, 1911.(H)
Tourneau R. le, *Fez in the Age of the Marinides*, Oklahoma, 1961.
Trachtenberg J., *The Devil and the Jews*, Philadelphia, 1961.
Trompf G.W., *The Idea of Historical Recurrence in Western Thought*, Berkeley, Los Angeles, London, 1979.
Twersky I., "Religion and Law," *Religion in a Religious Age* [S.D. Goitein ed.], Cambridge Mass, 1974, pp. 69-82.
___, *Introduction to the Code of Maimonides*, Yale U. Press, 1980.
Vicens Vives J., "The Economies of Catalonia and Castile," *Spain in the Fifteenth Century 1369-1516* [R. Highfield ed.], New York, Evanston, San Francisco, London, 1972, pp. 248-75.
Walfish B.D., *Esther in Medieval Garb: Jewish Interpretation of the Book of Esther in the Middle Ages*, New York, 1993.
Weinberger Y.L., "A Lost Midrash on Moses' Death," *Tarbiẓ* 38, 1969, pp. 285-93.(H)
Werblowsky R.J.Z., *Rabbi Joseph Caro: A Lawyer and a Mystic*, Oxford, 1962.
Williams A.L., *Adversus Judaeos*, Cambridge, 1935.
Wolff P. "The 1391 Pogrom in Spain Social Crisis or Not?" *Past and Present* 50, 1971, pp. 4-18.
Yerushalmi Y.H., *From Spanish Court to Italian Ghetto*, New-York, London, 1971.
___, *The Lisbon Massacre of 1506 and the Royal Image in Shebet Yehudah*, Cincinnati, 1976.
___, "Clio and the Jews: Reflections on Jewish Historiography in the Sixteenth Century," *PAAJR Jubilee Volume*, Jerusalem, 1980, pp. 607-38.
___, "Spinoza on the Existence of the Jewish People," *Proceedings of the Israeli National Academy for the Sciences* 6, Jerusalem, 1984, pp. 171-213.(H)
Yuval I.J., "Vengeance and Damnation, Blood and Defamation: From Jewish Martyrdom to Blood Libel Accusations," *Ẓion* 58, 1993, pp. 33-90.(H)
Zack B., "RaMaQ and the ARI," *Jerusalem Studies in Jewish Thought* 10, 1992, pp. 311-40.(H)
Zimmels H.J., *Askenazim and Sephardim*, London, 1958.

INDEX

BRILL'S SERIES IN JEWISH STUDIES

The following books have been published in the series:

1. COHEN, R. *Jews in Another Environment.* Surinam in the Second Half of the Eighteenth Century. 1991.
   ISBN 90 04 09373 7
2. PRAWER, S.S. *Israel at Vanity Fair.* Jews and Judaism in the Writings of W.M. Thackery. 1992.
   ISBN 90 04 09403 2
3. PRICE, J.J. *Jerusalem under Siege.* The Collapse of the Jewish State 66-70 C.E. 1992.
   ISBN 90 04 09471 7
4. ZINGUER, I. *L'hébreu au temps de la Renaissance.* 1992.
   ISBN 90 04 09557 8
5. GUTWEIN, D. *The Divided Elite.* Economics, Politics and Anglo-Jewry, 1882-1917. 1992.
   ISBN 90 04 09447 4
6. ERAQI KLORMAN, B.-Z. *The Jews of Yemen in the Nineteenth Century.* A Portrait of a Messianic Community. 1993.
   ISBN 90 04 09684 1
7. BEN-DOV, N. *Agnon's Art of Indirection.* Uncovering Latent Content in the Fiction of S.Y. Agnon. 1993.
   ISBN 90 04 09863 1
8. GERA, D. *Judea and Mediterranean Politics* (219-162 B.C.).
   ISBN 90 04 09441 5. *In preparation*
9. COUDERT, A.P. *The Impact of the Kabbalah in the 17th Century.*
   ISBN 90 04 09844 5. *In preparation*
10. GROSS, A. *Iberian Jewry from Twilight to Dawn.* The World of Rabbi Abraham Saba. 1995.
    ISBN 90 04 10053 9
11. FLESCHER, P.V.M. and D. URMAN. *New Perspectives on Ancient Synagogues.*
    ISBN 90 04 09904 2. *In preparation*
12. AHRONI, R. *The Jews of the British Crown Colony of Aden.* History, Culture, and Ethnic Relations. 1994.
    ISBN 90 04 10110 1